The Life of
LEWIS CARROLL

The Life of
LEWIS CARROLL

(Victoria Through the Looking Glass)

by
FLORENCE
BECKER LENNON

DOVER PUBLICATIONS, INC.
NEW YORK

Published in Canada by General Publishing Company, Ltd., 30 Lesmill Road, Don Mills, Toronto, Ontario.
Published in the United Kingdom by Constable and Company, Ltd., 10 Orange Street, London WC 2.

This Dover edition, first published in 1972, is a corrected republication of the revised and enlarged (1962) edition. The work was originally published in 1945 under the title *Victoria Through the Looking Glass*.
This edition also contains a new Preface by the author and a map that appeared in the first but not in later editions.

International Standard Book Number: 0-486-22838-X
Library of Congress Catalog Card Number: 74-186594

Manufactured in the United States of America
Dover Publications, Inc.
180 Varick Street
New York, N. Y. 10014

DEDICATED TO
VAN WYCK BROOKS,
WHOSE "ORDEAL OF MARK TWAIN"
FOUND THE BITTER ALMOND
AT THE CORE OF
THE MAN WHO LAUGHS

Preface to the Dover Edition

IN CHARLES DODGSON'S LIFETIME, who would have foreseen a Lewis Carroll Society? Dickens, yes, Browning, yes—but Lewis Carroll? To writers of his own time, except perhaps to Henry Kingsley and Christina Rossetti, he was Dodgson the photographer. Oh yes, he wrote children's books and mathematical treatises, but a classic, a world figure, with 160 editions in forty-two languages 100 years after the first *Alice* was written? A part of folksay, of academic and political jargon, a household word? A subject for movies, plays, music, dance, biography, pottery, sculpture, yard goods, metal, chess sets, toys, biscuit tins, soap—part of the consciousness of the English-speaking world?

There can be no doubt that the sale of the manuscript of *Alice's Adventures Underground* in 1928 for an unprecedented sum gave Mr. Dodgson's image a powerful boost. But the American who bought it considered the manuscript worth the price. And Oxford and Columbia Universities considered Dodgson worthy of centenary exhibitions in 1932; Columbia even imported Alice herself, Mrs. Reginald Hargreaves, to celebrate her eightieth birthday and to receive an honorary doctorate for having inspired "this truly noteworthy contribution to English literature." In 1962 and 1965 England held other centenary celebrations of the composition of *Alice Underground* and the publication of *Wonderland,* respectively. In 1972 the Lewis Carroll Society plans activities for the centenary of *Looking-Glass.*

Roger Lancelyn Green, Lewis Carroll's official biographer by fiat of the Dodgson family, editor of the diaries, and faithful Carrollian, has announced in the quarterly organ of the Lewis Carroll Society, "an extravagant Centenary Presentation of *Alice Through the Looking-Glass* at Poulton Hall, Bebington, Cheshire, from June 23-July 1st 1972 at 8:30 P.M. . . ." Chief conspirator is Mr. Lancelyn Green's son, newly graduated from Oxford, who was technical expert to Oxford University Drama Society and was responsible for lighting the Jonathan Miller Shakespeare productions. Ingenious technical effects will be one of the special features of this "Alice" extravaganza, and will include a revolving stand, steam train, pyrotechnics, and back projection.

Places in Britain where Dodgson used to live or visit, or is even rumored to have visited, are now claiming him. In 1961 both the librarian and the town clerk at Llandudno admitted the apocryphal nature of Sir George Richmond's "recollection" that Lewis Carroll visited the Liddells in their new summer home there in 1864, and even composed part of *Wonderland* there. Still, the 1971 edition of the booklet published by the Llandudno Urban District Council, called "Llandudno Through the Looking-Glass," uses the Tenniel picture of Alice stepping through the glass, and ends with a page titled "Reflections on Alice" that repeats Sir George's "reminiscences," as well as quotes Lloyd George's dedication of the hideous White Rabbit statue opposite the Liddell home (now a hotel) with a tribute to Lewis Carroll and another tribute to the bracing Llandudno sea air which supposedly contributed to his inspiration.

Other mythical attributions are less brazen and more tentative. Cranleigh Parish Church, near Guildford, where the Misses Dodgson lived and their brother visited them, puts out an engaging postcard of the stone head of a cat from the north transept. It would be pleasant to imagine this as the original of the Cheshire Cat, except that the Dodgson ladies did not move to Guildford till 1869, and besides that Guildford is in Surrey, not in Cheshire.

Mr. George Arthur Carter, the dedicated librarian of the public library in Warrington (near Dodgson's birthplace in Daresbury), is building up a solid Carroll collection; he took me to see a "real" Cheshire cat on the roof of the old church at Grappenhall, where the Dodgsons did go in Charles' childhood. The cat, while available and authentic, unfortunately looks nothing like Tenniel's.

There are also rival gryphons, one on the lectern of Daresbury Church, where Charles heard his father preach for his first eleven years when they moved to Croft. Again the gryphon bears no resemblance to Tenniel's, though it may have put a gryphon into Charles' mind. Canon T. A. Littleton, the present incumbent of the Parish Church of St. Peter in Croft-on-Tees, where the elder Dodgson preached after leaving Daresbury, has a drawing in his study, made by his daughter, of a gryphon in Richmond Cathedral which is much closer to Tenniel's. Charles certainly saw it as a child, when he attended school at Richmond where his father also preached. Did he send Tenniel to Richmond, or find a picture of the gryphon for him?

The significant fact is that various places in Britain are trying to hitch on to Dodgson's coattails. Guildford, quite legitimately, has a fairly extensive collection of Carrolliana, and The Chestnuts, where the Dodgson ladies lived, has a plaque on the gate. The church in Daresbury has a most attractive stained-glass window of Lewis Carroll telling stories to children, as well as of some of the Wonderland figures. On the other hand, the Darlington Public Library, near Croft, has a less attractive Carroll mural in the children's room.

These oddities are straws in the wind. Lewis Carroll's audience, and its appreciation of him, still grow. He is moving up from the uncomfortable position of secular saint to that of a warm, gifted and vulnerable human being with human difficulties and partial solutions for them. Moreover, as the establishment retreats and the new age emerges, psychoanalytic insights are being recognized as useful tools, as even ten years ago they were not, at least in England. Perhaps Jonathan Miller's movie helped bring down Humpty Dumpty's wall without scrambling him. Certainly the Lewis Carroll Society, with its vigorous young membership, is making a difference. Lewis Carroll's uncanonical biographer is grateful for signs of spring.

Now for the no-longer-to-be-postponed question of the psychedelic Alice. Recently my young neighbors at the University of Colorado have been asking about Lewis Carroll and drugs. What about the hookah? The mushroom? Growing and shrinking as a result of swallowing something? Floating out the door? Even falling down the rabbit hole? Some of these questions may well have originated in the rather psychedelic Disney film, with its mushroom orientation, rather than in Dodgson himself—still . . .

The basic answer has to be "we don't know." But the next most basic answer is, "we think not." Nothing in Carroll's writings or his known history or mythology indicates that he ever took any kind of drugs. The person to consult, of course, is Dr. Phyllis Greenacre, the psychoanalyst who wrote *Swift and Carroll*. Dr. Greenacre generously granted permission to quote her letter:

> I never had any impressions at all that Carroll was a "hop-head" or user of any kind of drugs, though it would have been strange if he had not known of the opium-smoking which was occasional—and may even have been prevalent during some of his period there [at Oxford]. De Quincy who wrote the *Confessions of an Opium-Eater* died in 1859 when Carroll was twenty-seven. I don't know how much stir that book made, but at any rate it is an indication of what was "in the wind" as Carroll was growing up. I suppose it is possible that the mushroom and the hookah, as well as the *eat me* and *drink me* directions, might have references of this kind, but in my estimation this is not enough on which to base any conclusion that he himself was anything of a drug user. Certainly cocaine which probably became known during Carroll's life-time is a drug which produces a mild euphoria in small amounts, depression when used in larger doses and in still larger doses is hallucinogenic, producing bright-colored visions. It too like marijuana and the opium derivatives comes from vegetation, specifically from coca leaves. I believe it began to be used medicinally about 1874. But all those vegetable drugs were known in unscientific ways for years back and were part of the lore of natural magic—witches' brew, etc. So it would not be at all strange if they were known to a man with an inquiring mind, such as Carroll had. He was certainly brought up in an English garden where fox-gloves (digitalis) and deadly night-shade (aconite)

may have been part of garden lore.*

At any rate my own opinion is that he had a very disrupted early childhood, crowded into a big family where births were coming along very rapidly and may have contributed to his mother's early death when he was about nineteen. The question of sexual (or gender) identity was never thoroughly settled in him and he certainly identified with prepuberty little girls.

I doubt whether he had any more of a premonition of things to come than is true of any writer of real genius, granted that that is considerable. The point, to me, is that he had unusual access through imagination to the unconscious feelings and illusions of childhood such as most people lose sight of almost entirely or have them reappear only in daydreams or nightmares.

It is natural for people with special interests to wish to get Lewis Carroll into their acts. Along with Dr. Greenacre, however, I feel the drug culture people have no claim to him. There is no sign of books on drugs in his library.

Another current trend, the occult revival, has more success. Raphael Shaberman, one of the founders of the Lewis Carroll Society, called my attention to the considerable numbers of occult books, including a subscription set of the publications of the Society for Psychical Research, from its inception for eleven years. He also had over thirty books on demon possession, vampires, magic, sorcery, mesmerism, haunted houses, the blessed dead in paradise. As a child he was a talented amateur magician; toward the end of life he spent a good deal of time on eternal punishment, his last writing. It is not surprising, then, that these preoccupations followed him lifelong. His major doodle, *Sylvie and Bruno,* is partly about Esoteric Buddhism, eerie feelings, and such. Whereas the metamorphoses in the earlier books seem perfectly natural,

---

* In one of his letters to a little girl, and according to Isa Bowman, he explained the origin of the name foxglove—"folks' glove" —fairies.

perhaps because they remind us of our own infancy and the magical appearances and disappearances of people and other creatures, the transmogrifications in *Sylvie and Bruno* jolt us much more. The charm turns on and off; the book is not a blend but a mélange of novel, fairy tale, tract and science fiction. The other world that weaves with the "real" world of Victorian fiction is more nightmare than dream.

How much of Carroll's general breakdown was physical? Dr. Selwyn Goodacre of the Lewis Carroll Society, in "The Illnesses of Lewis Carroll,"* has made a thorough and careful study, with an extensive bibliography.

Dr. Goodacre traces Carroll's life-long interest in and study of medicine, as well as his usually accurate diagnoses of his own illnesses, to an observation, when he was twenty-three, of a stranger having an epileptic attack. Carroll caught the man as he was falling, loosened his clothes, and dashed water in his face. "I felt at the moment how helpless ignorance makes one, and I shall make a point of reading some book on the subject of emergencies, a thing that I think everyone should do." He promptly bought such a book, the first of a large number of medical books that he bequeathed to his nephew-biographer.

Attending an operation done under chloroform anesthesia, he astonished himself by finding he "bore it so well" that he might hope to be of use in an emergency. Dr. Goodacre assembles from the Alice books some descriptions of medical syndromes he calls "artistic intuitions, reminiscent of Dickens and Dostoevsky." The Queen of Hearts Dr. Goodacre sees as an example of menopause—she "turned crimson with fury, and . . . screamed 'Off with her head! Off . .' " The Dormouse has narcolepsy, the Mad Hatter's madness is caused by the mercuric compound used to make felt hats, the Duchess and her baby have syphilis.

Carroll's deafness is attributed to "infantile fever," possibly exacerbated by a case of mumps at seventeen. Shortly before

* An expanded version of a prize-winning entry for the first Lewis Carroll Society Essay Competition (1970). To be published in 1972 by a British medical journal called *The Practitioner.*

the mumps he had a bad case of whooping cough, leaving him with bronchiectasis which "continued to trouble him for the rest of his life," probably contributing to the severity of the bronchopneumonia which killed him at sixty-six.

He also had a recurrent "synovitis," first of one knee, then of the other, beginning at age fifty-five, just as he was packing to go to Guildford for Easter. He spent most of the vacation on the sofa, but between attacks he resumed those eighteen mile walks.

Five attacks of migraine are recorded, only one with headache, but all with "moving fortifications." Since the time of the attacks, 1885-91, corresponds roughly to the composition of *Sylvie and Bruno*, Dr. Goodacre thinks the stress under which he squeezed out that dread anomaly may have helped bring on the migraine.

Carroll's most dramatic ailment consisted of two losses of consciousness, in 1886 and 1891. These appear in diary entries not published till 1954, and a further section withheld till after the deaths of the Dodgson ladies in 1969.* They may have been simple fainting fits. Dr. Keith suggests one could have been caused by his high collar pressing on the carotid sinus while he was kneeling in chapel before breakfast. Cohen and Green consulted seven neurologists who seem to feel that epilepsy is unlikely, though two doctors whom Dodgson consulted considered the possibility. The suppression of these entries sheds more light on Lewis Carroll than the episodes themselves, highlighting the constant tension of perfectionism under which he lived. He drove himself relentlessly, went short on food, and on sleep, striving for production and perfection long after the well was dry.

His best book was his first, *Alice's Adventures in Wonderland*. It is pure magic, ripened from the manuscript pre-book, which was not published till twenty-one years after the "real" *Alice*. From there on, beginning with a slight turning to vinegar in *Looking-Glass*, and beginnings of decomposition in *Snark*, his works disintegrate visibly. But since it is not

* "Lewis Carroll's Loss of Consciousness" by Cohen, M., and Green, R. L., *Bulletin of the New York Public Library*, 1969.

vouchsafed us to have a museum tour of the creation of a work of genius, it is, though sadder, almost as instructive to observe its breakdown.

So—is Lewis Carroll for children or adults? Both, of course. After seventy years of swimming in the pool of tears and drying out in the caucus race, may I emphatically say —both!

FLORENCE BECKER LENNON

Boulder, Colorado
October, 1971

Contents

Illustrations

Foreword

How EXHILARATING, after this book had been so long out of print, to learn that it was going into paperback. And what a mountain of revisions loomed! The list of new, or newly accessible, works about Lewis Carroll was not long, but massive —thirteen books, and numerous articles. First in importance and in bulk were the *Diaries,* edited by Roger Lancelyn Green and published in 1954. Another primary source is Helmut Gernsheim's *Lewis Carroll, Photographer,* published in 1949, with sixty-four of Carroll's own photographs and a brilliant history of photography, setting Carroll in his place, that had simply not existed when this biography was being written.

Other vital books were the scholarly biographies by Mr. Green and Mr. Hudson and their monographs, Dr. Taylor's ingenious study of the mathematical games, Dr. Elizabeth Sewell's subtle comparative study of Lear and Carroll, *The Field of Nonsense,* Dr. Phyllis Greenacre's basic *Swift and Carroll,* and Martin Gardner's invaluable *Annotated Alice.* From the first two I must pluck, from the others I cannot resist plucking, many fruits and replanting their seeds in my own basket.

An author who can inspire such penetrating and devoted scholarship on both sides of the ocean—as well as magazine articles, science fiction, films, and dramatic productions—is still very much with us one hundred years after telling his famous story. Everybody with imagination is tempted to pluck a leaf from Alice and replant it, and each leaf proliferates into new and fantastic forms. Logicians, grammarians, statesmen, advertisers, children, and poets all quote the *Alices* and use them as launching pads for their own fantasies.

I have been involved with *Alice* since learning to read— it was my first book, read at least once a year for forty years. This biography first seemed to be "finished" at the time of Lewis Carroll's own centenary in 1932. Now, thirty years and many rewritings later, perhaps it will hold. Most of the writers have expressed their opinions of it since it first

11

appeared in 1945, and they have all been considered with interest and such objectivity as was available.

The British, who so hospitably welcomed and protected Freud in person, allowing him to die in peace and with dignity, have not yet got around to entertaining his already partly obsolete ideas. The sword of Sigmund sits uneasy in the hand of St. George. Yet even England has unconsciously absorbed many of his contributions. Something suspiciously like Freudian concepts is creeping into literary criticism, despite the striving for purity. The protracted dispute in *The Times Literary Supplement* several years ago, much of it about the Freudian aspects of this book, had two sides to it.

For real depth psychology, however, my readers must turn to Dr. Greenacre. And with those words I had intended to evade part of my own responsibility to analytic insights. Some of Dr. Greenacre's findings are unpalatable even to a life-long Freudian like myself (mind you, unpalatable, not incredible), and I had intended to avoid them in this book and leave their discovery to my readers. The overt motive was to spare the elder survivors, who surely have not read Dr. Greenacre, but this will not do.

In fact, this is an example of one of my basic contentions—that the very sweetness and gentleness and charm of the best of the Victorians, which the Dodgsons and the Liddells certainly were and are, not only hid but fostered the fears, the horrors, the cruelties, which modern readers do find in Lewis Carroll. What Dr. Jung called *Die Schattenseite*—the shadow side—must be honestly dealt with, or it piles up more shadows and fears and cruelties. It is because Lewis Carroll sensed the irrationalities, the under side of the carpet, the lions behind the staircase—the beast in man and the indifference of the universe—that he was a great poet. He was able to deal with contradictions and horrors and irrationalities, and to convert them into an art form that gives release to children and adults alike. His books are the art form of which psychoanalysis is the science. So how dare we dodge the gift he brings us?

Psychoanalysis has its place in literary criticism, yet that place is not where we lose sight of the man as a whole human being, in his setting, or of his art. The neurosis is interesting as it gives us insight into the man and his work, but the function of insight is never to take the man apart; nor can the neurosis become the whole story.

Even in America there are prominent critics who have not accepted analytic insights—or had not by 1945, when this book appeared. Orville Prescott in *The New York Times* gave me a going over for using this tool, and thereby got himself, Mr. Dodgson, and me into Stanley Edgar Hyman's lively book, *The Armed Vision*. In the chapter on modern literary criticism, Mr. Hyman says, ". . . as these quotations should make clear, in the course of attacking Miss [sic] Lennon's psychoanalytic study, Prescott gives all the reasons why a psychoanalytic study is very much to the point, and in the course of insisting that Carroll's life was uneventful, fills it full of the most remarkable events. Like many contemporary reviewers, Prescott attacks modern criticism seemingly not so much out of malice as out of simple ignorance. In other cases . . . the picture is clearly of the happily superficial reviewer fighting to preserve his status and investment in what he thinks is criticism against a mob of sans-culottes."

In May, 1932, Edmund Wilson wrote in *The New Republic*, "The only biography of Dodgson is a conventional life by a relative published in 1899 [sic]. No writer, so far as I know, has ever done a serious portrait of him or made a real study of his work." This article was reprinted in *The Shores of Light*, with a supplement in which he called the present book (though not without strictures, some of them correct) "the best thing that has yet been written about Lewis Carroll."

With Edmund Wilson for ally, all was not lost. But then there was another problem. Several serious Carrollians assured me that the diaries were dull—that Collingwood had skimmed the cream and what was left was of little importance. Fortunately nobody sold that bill of goods to Helmut Gernsheim, who had persuaded the Misses Dodgson to allow him to use all the photographic entries for his book, which was of such great interest that Oxford Press decided to go ahead with the full (or almost full) diaries. Mr. Green did extensive and painstaking research to identify persons mentioned and amplify entries; Mr. Hudson followed soon with a biography, also supplemented by letters and articles of great value.

Still it was supposed the diaries were "dull," and the publisher remaindered them. They were written in a telegraphic style; they appear to be brief objective notations of events, with an occasional lapse into subjectivity. It is necessary to be able to read this kind of writing. There were no great new revelations, no cataclysmic changes in the picture I had formed of Mr. Dodgson. In many cases it was possible to exchange speculation for firsthand information, and throughout the roughly forty years covered (with some lacunae) by the *Diaries*, his image fleshed out, moved more freely, became less ethereal and more substantial. It is a matter of knowing what questions to ask. And it is a satisfaction to find so few errata, and those so relatively unimportant. Errata of *fact*, that is. Interpretation remains a legitimate field for disagreement; one sees a dinosaur's footprint on solid rock and deduces that a dinosaur has been there.

Those who saw the dinosaur are fewer every year. Mrs. Hargreaves and Mrs. Skene (Alice and Lorina), whom I saw in 1930 and 1932, respectively, were already gone when this book appeared. Their younger sister, Miss Rhoda Liddell, was also gone, as were Mrs. Skene's daughters, Miss Skene and Lady Schuster. I had made no effort to find Alice's son, Wing Commander Caryl Hargreaves, having been prematurely told he was dead. He wrote four generous and valuable letters after my book appeared. He actually died in 1955. The faithful and learned bibliographers, Mr. Madan, whom I met at Oxford, and Mr. Williams, with whom I corresponded, are gone too. I was fortunate enough to meet the three surviving Misses Dodgson last summer: Miss F. Menella, Miss Violet, and Miss Frances.

Both the Liddell families and the Dodgson families have a lovely candor and gentleness, even today, that makes it possible to believe six impossible things before breakfast. The Misses Dodgson never liked some aspects of the book, but they never questioned my right to say what I believed, and spent many hours searching through material and sending me information, as Mrs. Skene did in her last year.

The only case of obstruction was that of the late Mr. Morris L. Parrish of Philadelphia, owner of the greatest Carroll collection in the world, which is now at Princeton. He permitted me to study and copy his material, sent me photostats, and then asked to see my manuscript, which I sent him in an unfinished condition about 1943. He was indignant at some interpretations, and, since he could not persuade me to accede to his bowdlerizations, forbade any reference to his collection. It was too late to stop me from using the material, and besides, there was more at the Huntington Library and elsewhere. A prohibition or a promise is usually considered to run out after the death of one party, so let me now take this opportunity to thank the Parrish Collection for the use of its valuable material.

A recent loss of which many Carrollians are unaware is that of Professor Robert Hamilton Dundas, Student and Tutor of Christ Church (1884-1960). Mr. Dundas lived for many years in Lewis Carroll's rooms in Christ Church, and was generous about showing them to visitors with legitimate business, but he asked particularly to remain anonymous. After this book appeared he wrote how glad he was about the stipulation, because with his name to guide them, all the American soldiers visiting Oxford would have streamed through his rooms.

The landmarks are going, too. Oxford has industrial suburbs. A London correspondent writes that the Wool and Water Shop at Oxford is doomed. And the pleasant myth of Llandudno is certainly challenged, perhaps destroyed. The *Diaries* have lacunae for the very period when Llandudno claims Lewis Carroll, but the positive evidence falls apart on inspection. There is the large White Rabbit, made of some perishable material, between the former home of the Liddells, now a hotel, and the beach. It surmounts a plaque bearing an enthusiastic and erroneous dedication attested to by no less a Carrollian than Lloyd George. There are letters and newspaper articles, and quotations from Mrs. Hargreaves in her old age, and from Sir William Richmond, who indubitably painted the Liddell sisters sitting by the shore—except that he painted them indoors and dubbed in the landscape.

If you go to Llandudno, as I did last summer, and question the town clerk and the librarian, they will admit they have no real proof that Lewis Carroll was ever there, let alone wrote anything there. But Llandudno is a heavenly spot, and you can sleep where Alice slept, and dream of white rabbits.

The neoplasms that proliferate from people's imaginations whenever a bit of *Alice* plasm is planted lend themselves to study and so cast light on their originals, and such have been reported in this book. Genius is an infinite onion—peel it as you will, you will never find a core, and it will never yield up its last leaf. The *Alice* books are so: we study them, "explain" them, analyze them—and their creator—but they remain triumphantly THERE to savor, to muse and chuckle over, to tell to our children and grandchildren while the English language endures.

It was a May afternoon in 1932. The guests in the rotunda of the university library waited almost in silence for an unprecedented moment. Queen Alice was to be decorated, shortly after the celebration of her eightieth birthday, with which the university had terminated the centenary celebration of the man who had made her a world figure.

The wide aisle from the door to the carved wooden throne on the inner circle was tied off with white ribbons. The rotunda was a garden of live flowers. To welcome Queen Alice with ninety times nine, all the characters were present, not in costume, to be sure, but not too heavily incognito. Oxford is not the only university from whose rostra Tweedledee and Tweedledum, the Walrus, the Carpenter, the Mad Hatter, the March Hare, and especially the Professor and the Other Professor, hold forth.

The hush deepened. The procession was assembling outside the door. At last Alice would be led to her flower-banked throne. The orchestra struck up, and more professors entered, escorting Mrs. Hargreaves in her cap and gown. She was carrying a cane, but not leaning on it. The president of the university entered too, and through some mischance sat on the throne. It must have been Rule Forty-two, for nobody said anything, and only one or two seemed astonished.

The escort tried to persuade the lovely old lady to sit down. She would not sit and would not lean on her cane. She swayed a little, but she stood throughout the ceremony. The quality that looks out of her child photographs endured past her eightieth birthday.

The pompous old gentleman on the throne said: "Alice Pleasance Hargreaves, descendant of John of Gaunt, time-honored Lancaster, daughter of that distinguished Oxford scholar whose fame will last until English-speaking men cease to study the Greek language and its immortal literature; awakening with her girlhood's charm the ingenious fancy of a mathematician . . . you as the moving cause—Aristotle's 'final cause'—of this truly noteworthy contribution to English literature; I gladly admit you to the degree of Doctor of Letters in this University."

Alice Pleasance Liddell Hargreaves, still standing, bowed her head for the hood. In a small but clear voice she said, "I feel that Mr. Dodgson knows and rejoices with me in the honor you are doing him."

If indeed Mr. Dodgson was present, he must have noted that not everything about human nature, and especially not everything about universities, had changed since the day he told his dean's ten-year-old daughter the story that was to bring them both immortal fame.

Time-Table of
Charles Lutwidge Dodgson's Life

Born at Daresbury, Cheshire	Jan. 27, 1832
Moves to Croft	1843
School at Richmond	1844-6
Starts first "home magazine"—	
Useful and Instructive Poetry	1845
School at Rugby	Feb., 1846-9
Matriculates at Oxford	May 23, 1850
Formally comes into residence at Christ Church,	
Oxford (rooms in Peckwater Quad)	Jan. 24, 1851
Death of his mother	Jan., 1851
Visits Great Exhibition	Long Vacation, 1851
Receives Boulter Scholarship	Nov. 1, 1851
Made Student of Christ Church on Dr. Pusey's	
recommendation	Dec. 24, 1852
"Moderations": Second Class honors in	
classical studies	1852
Father made a canon of Ripon Cathedral	1853
Comic Times prints his verse	1853-6
Third Class in "Greats"	1854
Long Vacation at Whitby, studying with	
Bartholomew Price	1854
Whitby Gazette publishes his rhymes	1854
First Class in Final Mathematical School,	
head of list	Oct., 1854
Bachelor of Arts	Dec. 18, 1854
Made "Master of the House" in honor of	
new Dean, Dr. Liddell	Feb. 15, 1855
Made sub-librarian	Oct. 15, 1855
Begins teaching 3½ hours a day	1855
Bostock Scholarship received	May 14, 1855
Made member of regular teaching staff,	
lecturing 7 hours a day	1856
Editors of *The Comic Times* found *The Train*	1856
Pseudonym "Lewis Carroll" first appears in	
The Train	March, 1856

His verse appears in *The Train*   1856-7
Edits *College Rhymes,* which prints his
   "A Sea Dirge"   1856
Long Vacation in the Lakes District;
   climbs Great Gable   1856
Master of Arts   1857
Meets Tennyson, Ruskin, Thackeray   1857
Visits Tennyson at Farringford   April 13, 1859
Lectures before Ashmolean Society on
   "Where Does the Day Begin?"   Nov., 1860
Ordained deacon by Samuel Wilberforce,
   Bishop of Oxford   Dec. 22, 1861
Trip up the Isis in rowboat with three daughters
   of Dr. Liddell. Tells story of *Alice*   July 4, 1862
   Starts to write it   July 5, 1862
Alice Liddell receives MS of
   Alice's Adventures Underground   Nov. 26, 1863
Final arrangements for publication made with
   Tenniel and Macmillan   April 5, 1864
Chooses title, *Alice's Adventures
   in Wonderland*   June 18, 1864
Alice Liddell receives first presentation copy   July 4, 1865
Tour on Continent with
   Dr. Liddon   July 12-Sept. 14, 1867
Aunt Judy's Magazine publishes
   "Bruno's Revenge"—first "bit" of
   Sylvie and Bruno   Dec., 1867
An Elementary Treatise on Determinants   1867
Death of his father   June 21, 1868
Edition of *The Fifth Book of Euclid*   1868
Moves into rooms in Tom Quad for rest of life   Nov., 1868
Phantasmagoria   1869
*Through the Looking-Glass and What Alice
   Found There* (usually listed as 1872), with
   acrostic to Alice   Dec., 1871
Sees man having epileptic fit. Buys bones and
   anatomical books   1872
Tells second "bit" of *Sylvie and Bruno* to
   children of Marquess of Salisbury   Dec. 31, 1872

Tells same children story of Uggug, 3rd "bit"   end of 1874
Vacation at Sandown (Gertrude)   1875
The Hunting of the Snark, with acrostic
  to Gertrude   Mar. 29, 1876
First dramatic presentation of *Alice* tableaux
  at the Polytechnic   1876
Meets E. Gertrude Thomson   Summer, 1878
Euclid and His Modern Rivals   1879
Vacation at Eastbourne—probably every year
  thereafter   1880
Proposes ⅓ cut in his own salary   Feb., 1880
Acting version of *Alice* published   1880
Proposes resignation of mathematical lectureship
  to give full time to writing and mathematical
  studies   Oct. 18, 1881
Euclid, Books I and II   1882
Made Curator of Common Room   Dec. 8, 1882
Rhyme? and Reason?   1883
A Tangled Tale   1885
Production of *Alice* Operetta   1886
Facsimile of *Alice's Adventures Underground*   1886
The Game of Logic   Feb., 1887
*Curiosa Mathematica, Part I. A New Theory
  of Parallels*   1888
Alice Operetta revived: Isa plays Alice (Isa) 1888
Sylvie and Bruno, with acrostic to Isa Bowman 1889
The Nursery "Alice" (Enid)   1890
Dr. Liddell resigns as Dean of
  Christ Church   Christmas, 1891
Resigns as Curator of Common Room   August, 1892
Curator pamphlets privately printed   1892
Sylvie and Bruno Concluded, with acrostic to Enid 1893
Curiosa Mathematica, Part III. Pillow Problems 1893
Symbolic Logic   1896
Death at sisters' home in Guildford   Jan. 14, 1898
Three Sunsets posthumously published   1898

This map by Gwen Meux of Boulder, Colorado, shows places
where Lewis Carroll lived and visited and the characters from
his books that came to life in those places.

The Life of Lewis Carroll

Chapter 1

The Genie in the Box

> *"I know what you're thinking about," said Tweedledum; "but it isn't so, nohow."*
>
> *"Contrariwise," continued Tweedledee, "if it was so, it might be; and if it were so, it would be; but as it isn't, it ain't. That's logic."*

How DID IT HAPPEN that the Reverend Charles Dodgson, thirty years of age, lecturer on geometry at Christ Church, Oxford, hitherto remarkable chiefly for his precision, on a single July afternoon, while rowing up the Isis with a brother don and three little girls, parthenogenetically gave birth to one of the most famous stories of all time?

There is no complete answer. Calling Dodgson a genius merely side-steps the inexplicable part. Seeing that he was a blocked genius gives a clue, and suggests great compression in his product. It should be possible to show how his early life converged, as in a burning-glass, on that summer day, and how the rays parted once more, occasionally converging in minor nodes, but never again with the same fusion.

Neither summer nor the out-of-doors, however, conveys the fullest flavor of Victorian England. Will you be seated in Alice's drawingroom, on the winter afternoon when the looking-glass melted for the first time? The furniture is upholstered and so are the people. The room is hot near the fireplace and cold in the corners; perhaps more than at any time and place in history there is a waxen-surfaced illusion of safety, of permanence, of progress in an unbroken curve. It is still possible to smother dissenting voices with upholstery, with tea cakes, with manners. England has been civilized and safe for many years, and Victoria has exorcised all recollection of the bad old days of the four Georges. Feelings, like behavior, are supposed to fall into accepted stereotypes. It is not, and has not been for decades, a comfortable setting for a little boy, a ravenous, pugnacious little animal with a

God-given right to be dirty and disreputable. In fact there is something vaguely "not nice" about being a little boy. It is much nicer to be a little girl. Even worse than being a little boy is to be a man, with heaven knows what dreadful impulses. The symbol of the time is a complex of the corset, the flounce, and the hoop skirt, conspiring to attest that women are angels, with positively nothing below their necks, and above—a pair of heaven-turned eyes. Gaiety and charm abound, but of a thoroughly domesticated and feminized sort.

Now into a similar setting, four decades before Alice passed through the looking-glass, drop a genius who also has the misfortune to be a little boy, doomed to grow into that horrid creature, a man; a boy whose thoughts, feelings, and imagination are keen and eager, who accepts with difficulty anything that has not gone through his own mill; a little Bruno, bursting to cut loose and turn somersaults and tease animals and stick out his tongue at his imposing elders. The little boy is to be envied for his ingenious mind, and pitied for living when all the answers are at the back of the book, and somebody is always reading them aloud.

Charles Lutwidge Dodgson was born in Daresbury, Cheshire, on January 27, 1832, with great gifts, but into surroundings that hobbled him from his first step. His father, the charming Rector of Daresbury (later a canon and still later an archdeacon), was stern under his charm, and virtually infallible. His mother, a gentle, shadowy person, seems to have favored Charles, as the eldest son, though he was the third of eleven children.* Active, bubbling with ideas, clever and gifted as he was, Charles was sensitive to praise or blame, and if he was left-handed, this might help explain his feeling that something about him was "not right." Here is a setting for a work of art or a neurosis. Now that the sciences of man teach that the environment too sometimes needs ad-

---

* This is the sequence of the Dodgson children, from Miss Menella Dodgson: Frances, Elizabeth, Charles Lutwidge, Caroline, Mary (married the Rev. Chas. Collingwood), Skeffington Hume (married Isabel M. Cooper), Wilfred Longley (married Alice Jane Donkin), Louisa (who lived till 1930), Margaret, Henrietta, and Edwin Heron (took holy orders, went to Tristan da Cunha in 1880).

justment, it seems truer to call the *Alice* books art, and the
entire Victorian age neurosis.

The verdict of three generations finds Alice perfectly sensible throughout the jungles of nonsense she roams in those
twin works of genius, *Wonderland* and *Through the Looking-
Glass*. Yet those jungles of nonsense were merely the daily
life of an English lady or gentleman of culture in the now
legendary reign of Victoria. As the Red Queen said, "*I've*
heard nonsense, compared with which that would be as sensible as a dictionary!" For around this elegant, rather stilted
life of ladies and gentlemen, flowed the muddy stream of
crude poverty. The Industrial Revolution had rolled over England in a blast of smoke and steam, grinding men, women,
and children for cruel hours at miserable pay. But the French
Revolution—*liberté, égalité, fraternité*—was slower to cross
the Channel. Meanwhile the chasm between those who have
and those who make, deepened and darkened rapidly.

Charles Dodgson, born a romantic and a rationalist, would
have fitted more easily into the world of Voltaire and Goethe
than into the one that received him. His romance, however,
was grounded in logic and mathematics. The elder Dodgson
answered the eight-year-old boy's questions about logarithms
by saying he was too young to understand. Charles countered
respectfully, "But, please, explain." Later, though not believing that the circle could be squared, at the death of De
Morgan he inherited an immense correspondence with those
who did. Perhaps he assumed this burden because of a similar
preoccupation of his own—the hope of making logic square
with common sense, of finding some coherent relation between the ideal Platonic chair, the non-existent Berkeleyan
chair, and the upholstered armchair on which he barked his
shins.

The Lucifer of his lost Paradise—magnificent, maligned,
unmentionable—was no other than the god of the French
Revolution, of which the late reverberations rocked Dover
beach in the 1820's and 1830's with factory acts, parliamentary reform, Chartism, and the Oxford Movement. 1832,
the very year of Charles's birth, was the year of one of the
most famous compromises with which Britain staved off the
actual revolution that threatened her: the Parliamentary Re-

form Bill, itself a compromise with a compromise, but "for the first time in the History of Parliament the voice of the people had obtained articulate utterance, and its accents were a stern condemnation and rejection of those who had resisted reform." [1]* In the church likewise, a middle party attracted virtually all the energy of the right and left whirlpools, subsiding into a thin and rather glassy surface over a continuing heave and swell. This heave and swell corresponded with something in Charles himself. The piety of his upbringing, and his own mildness, docility, and eagerness to believe, collided with a stubborn integrity of mind and produced a lifelong conflict. The Alice who "pretended to be two persons" spoke for her author, a Church of England Rousseau, whose "noble savage" was—the child; and whose pastoral symphony welled out under the great beeches and chestnuts of the Dean's garden in Oxford.

In the limitless air of 1789 Charles could have answered his own questions, but that air reached England filtered through the scandals and stupidities of the four Georges, not to speak of the monstrosities of Boney and the anxieties of the Europe of 1830; so that by the time the waves broke on the ears of young Dodgson in the thirties and forties, the tune was twisted; and the Anglo-German girl whom the scion of Saxe-Goburg-Gotha remodeled into a German *Hausfrau*, was welcomed as a respite from the Hanoverian libertines. The nine children of William IV, all dull and all illegitimate, had to make way for the impeccably born nine of Victoria and Albert, each birth personally attested by the Archbishop of Canterbury.[2] During the reigns of the four Georges with their scandals and of William with his bastards, the Dodgsons were potential Victorians, and when Victoria reached the throne they were ready for her.

In the year when the Reform Bill passed the Houses of Parliament, then, Charles Dodgson was born. He passed his childhood in country parsonages, far from luxury and even farther from want or squalor. It is not recorded that he ever played with the village children—in fact, at Sunday School, he said, "It made me indignant to be put into the class with the village children, as well as alarmed lest, by some mistake

* Numbered notes within chapters appear at end of book.—Ed.

of mine, I should be put below them." [3] Whenever he was confronted by an unpleasant situation, he met it with avoidance; thus, when in later life he saw the original of Dotheboys Hall, he said only, "Next to a prison or a lunatic asylum, preserve me from living at Bowes!" [4] These are not the reactions of a social reformer, and such indeed Charles never became. But as a man of his time, he had to take cognizance of the misery around him, and of the "two nations" into which England was split.

Charles Lutwidge Dodgson's life in space-time colored his liberated life of the imagination, but his share of space-time was bounded by the reign of the estimable queen, whose hoop skirt, in those distant days when a baby was not respectable until it was born, concealed the imminence of her numerous offspring. The dear queen who, as a young girl, ascended the throne with the simple "I will be good," held it through life with the majestic utterance, "We are not amused." Whether the queen caused the period, or the period created the queen, she represents her time perfectly. A single shaft of white light, passed through a prism, becomes the rainbow. Imagine Victoria and her age as the shaft of white light, and the Reverend Charles L. Dodgson as the prism; then the rainbow is his multicolored fairy tale. Alice might be the gentle little Victoria who came to the throne; and the Red Queen, White Queen, and Queen of Hearts, aspects of the imposing lady who was "not amused"—the social equivalent of "Off with his head." The social satire in the *Alice* books is unconscious, perhaps, but it is there.

Charles, trapped in the cave of his period, was the laughing philosopher who could show others the way out. He spoke the language and played the rôle of Ariel—the mantle of Prospero ill became him, though he fancied it. His proper medium was the looking-glass, in which he caught a sunbeam and flashed it in the eyes of a solemnity, or held a child's laughing face, or cast weird shadows from his cave upon the world outside. The Mad Hatter and the Duchess, the Mock Turtle and the Jabberwock, are as real and as enduring as Punch or Falstaff. Charles tried to carve heavier figures too, but they fell with a dull thud and are heard no more.

Moving to an unseen pattern of wish and will, of fear and

courage, he grew in creative power. He outgrew the tiny rectangular box he spent his life trying to re-enter, and the chess board where Alice saw the game of life being played was too simple to compass his thinking. It is true that no one finds room for complete expansion and expression, but here was a particularly big person who spent his life fitting himself, with infinite art and patience, and even, as if it were one of his own puzzle games, with a certain amusement, into a particularly small and exactly delimited box. It is like the genie trying to climb back into the bottle or like the human brain making more and more convolutions to squeeze itself into that tiny box, the skull. The brain could almost symbolize Charles—almost. But the affectionate soul also demands its due, and likewise the animal soul, though the families of Christian clergymen in Charles's youth (overtly) rejected the tenth talent, while welcoming the eleventh child. The subsidiary souls, excluded from the drawing-room, weep outside, like the Mock Turtle, the Walrus, and all the other sad animals whose whimsical, melancholy expression greatly resembles that of Charles Dodgson.

The freshness and newness of his symbols, their applicability to his own era, or to any era when people stupidly interfere with one another and lay down needless rules, gave his best writings their indubitable vitality. "Vitality" is a suitably perverse word to associate with the old-maidish don he became, with his professorial habits and accuracies, his uncertain gait, his deafness, his stammering, his air of Don Quixote rather than of Don Juan. But the man had a mind, and the mind had almost an independent life of its own, so that when he tired of the game of chess that was his daily life, he could summon a gryphon and fly away to Wonderland.

So one summer afternoon, when he was rowing on the Isis with Canon Duckworth (the Duck in the Caucus-race) and the three entrancing daughters of Dean Liddell, he began putting his escapes into an art form. Some nine years later he deliberately tapped the same vein that had opened spontaneously before, and found his other world again, in that always exciting moment when Alice, who has been hankering to see beyond that tantalizing glimpse into the passage, suddenly finds herself on the mantelshelf with the glass melting, and jumps down into Looking-Glass House.

Later he just as deliberately abandoned that form because of the hordes of imitators, and tried to devise new ways out of the intolerable cramping of his box. The queer animals of the empire, of the university, and of his own inner life, continued to plague him, like Adam in the garden, with demands for names and classifications. In return, he expected the creatures to serve as symbols and carry him on flights.

Perhaps because he was squeezed so tight, and because he was really a genius, he wrung out of himself a complete bible of folklore, poetry, mythology, and humor. Theology was his weak point and must be discounted. He was religious in the sense that he cared truly for the growth of the spirit, but, since he never found Ariadne's thread and would not use an ax, his religion belongs under "Box" rather than "Escape." Wherever he let himself go, however, he helped to smash the box for his contemporaries, and for their children and ours.

Chapter 2

The Fabulous Monster

> *"What's this!" he said, blinking lazily at Alice. . . .*
>
> *"Ah, what is it, now?" the Unicorn cried eagerly. "You'll never guess! I couldn't."*
>
> *The Lion looked at Alice wearily. "Are you animal—or vegetable—or mineral?" he said, yawning at every other word.*
>
> *"It's a fabulous monster!" the Unicorn cried out, before Alice could reply.*

THIS WAS LEWIS CARROLL'S way of saying how children looked to the adults of his time. And yet his home was full of love. Dark gods hovered over England—gods of original sin, of infant damnation, of eternal punishment; but the Dodgson family worshiped the God of Love, who showed his stern face only in the presence of evil. Then what had Charles to escape from into a garden? Merely a certain tightness, a certain finishedness, the state of having all the answers ready. Human life under any conditions is too tight for a genius, and the Victorian era was too tight for anybody. Cramped by his own charts, on a stream itself restricted, his genius directed him to the bottomless ocean of his books, and impelled him to dive under the graciously sparkling surface into the dark swirl of the icy depths. He bobbed up with both treasure and flotsam—but our task is first to study the surface, to observe the flood of white light, and then to hold up our genius, our prismatic Charles, and analyze the light rays as they stream through him.

The queen fulfilled her Albert's ideal—a little girl, of innocence and purity unbelievable, of kindness and gentleness to all. Like Albert, Charles created a Galatea, but she remained a dream—Alice Liddell remained herself and never tried to be the *Wonderland* Alice. The immaturity of the three queens in the *Alice* books in no way slandered England's Queen.

Even in her old age she never progressed in ethics or states-manship beyond the notion of personal virtue her governess had taught her in childhood. The little girl and the governess ruled the manners of the age; whatever was not fit for their consideration was suppressed, carried on in murmurs behind closed doors, blacked out.

In the days of Victoria, left-handedness was not yet respect-able, though the medieval curse had faded. The odds were against even the most enterprising boy discovering such a trait in himself, since, from the nursery, he would automatic-ally be corrected (righted!) in attempts to eat or write left-handed. Nevertheless, there is some evidence that Carroll had this disability. It seems to have given him some trouble, but it supplied the Victorian age with a peerless looking-glass in which to study its imbecilities, and with an escape for the oppressed in spirit into looking-glass land and the enchanted garden, where a fresh perspective beckoned. To children it offered escape from the inevitable dulling and unreason of their elders.

As a painter corrects his drawing by holding a picture to a mirror, so lefthanded persons correct the exaggerations of the righteous by gie'ing them the giftie. "It's my own inven-tion," the White Knight said. Wonderland and Looking-Glass land are totally new territories, whose gold brightened the drabness and poverty of Victorian England. But millions of left-handed persons have lived and died without contributing any more amusement to their neighbors than their enchant-ing manner of blundering into furniture, or their inability to carve a simple joint.

It is astonishing what a storm has blown up over the sug-gestion that Charles Dodgson may have been left-handed. It can only be a hypothesis, never to be proved or disproved. In 1930 Miss F. Menella Dodgson asked her aunt Miss Louisa, the mathematical sister, then in the last year of her life. Miss Louisa said it was quite possible her brother had been left-handed, since she was.

Mr. Roger Lancelyn Green, editor of the *Diaries* and of the new edition of the *Handbook,* and author of a book, a monograph, and numerous articles about Lewis Carroll, does not accept the hypothesis. To which Dr. Greenacre replies,

"Certainly, however, he was preoccupied with left and right, as with right and wrong, and was an accomplished mirror-writer . . . a talent which is frequently associated with left-handedness or ambidexterity." [1]

All we have is evidence, for and against, which we can only interpret. The left-handed hypothesis is a key that opens many doors, and until somebody brings cogent evidence against it, it will be used in this book, with the recognition that it is still a hypothesis.

The intensity and manifold symbolism of the *Alice* books increased with the elaborate compression the Victorian censors exercised on Charles's natural impulses, possibly even on his impulse to work left-handed. Reversing a left-handed child may affect his speech, and the timidity and uncertainty of not knowing right hand from left might explain the peculiar gait mentioned by several of his contemporaries, his awkwardness in carving, and even his stammering (although most of his siblings stammered too). The White Knight is the apotheosis of a left-handed man in a right-handed world.

> *And now, if e'er by chance I put*
> *My fingers into glue*
> *Or madly squeeze a right-hand foot*
> *Into a left-hand shoe—*

If Charles was reversed, he took his revenge by doing a little reversing himself. A characteristic indication of what bothered him is the following passage between the two children in his last story, *Sylvie and Bruno*. Sylvie is all innocence and purity; her life work is to eradicate her little brother Bruno's elfin mischief and outcroppings of the old Adam, for the alleged wickedness of the natural man poisoned the lives of children in those days. Carroll found an unexceptionable way of criticizing the fundamental assumptions under which he floundered:

"Sylvie was arranging some letters on a board—E-V-I-L. 'Now, Bruno,' she said, 'what does *that* spell?'

"Bruno looked at it in solemn silence for a minute.

" 'I knows what it doesn't spell!'—he said at last.

" 'That's no good,' said Sylvie. 'What *does* it spell?'

"Bruno took another look at the mysterious letters. 'Why, it's "LIVE," backwards!' he exclaimed. (I thought it was indeed.)

" 'How *did* you manage to see that?' said Sylvie.

" 'I just twiddled my eyes,' said Bruno, 'and then I saw it directly. Now may I sing the Kingfisher Song?' "

Here, with the pathos of the little boy whose impulses are forever colliding with prohibitions, often needless and unmeaning, Dodgson holds up the glass to the age in which Evil was the same as Live. The function of the left-handed person is thus to hold the mirror, and though such a nature may develop either stubbornness or perversity as its keynote, Charles leaned to the perverse rather than to the stubborn adaptation. He suffered from a sort of obsession—a persistent little messenger, always trying to get its message accepted. Rich deposits of perversity crop up in his humor—and his sudden attacks of virtue or sentimentality midway through his own or other persons' jests hint that his imp has just suggested to him something particularly funny and unpardonable.

Yet there was no harshness in his home—his fears were those, not of a child who has been threatened, but of one whose standards are unchildlike. The merits and defects of the period permeate the Dodgson household; the Carrollian *opera* need use little caricature or distortion. To the solidity of the English genteel tradition add a special familial solidity —the Dodgsons were not only ultra-Victorian but ultra-conservative. The pattern fitted some family need—only Charles questioned it, and he only with the greatest subtlety and tact.

The Dodgsons lived in the north of England, more especially in Yorkshire, and several of them were high up in the church. Bishop Dodgson was doubly the great-grandfather of Charles, whose father and mother were cousins. The Bishop's daughter, Elizabeth Anne, married Charles Lutwidge. Her brother, Charles Dodgson, became a captain of dragoons, and was killed in an Irish rebellion. His elder son, Charles, born in 1800, married, in 1830, his cousin, Frances Jane Lutwidge, (daughter of Elizabeth Anne Dodgson Lutwidge), and presented his country with eleven children, the third of whom was Charles Lutwidge Dodgson.

The parsonage where he was born was isolated on a farm a mile and a half from the small village of Daresbury, in Cheshire, home of the Cheshire cats. The family lived there until Charles was eleven, when Sir Robert Peel presented Mr. Dodgson with a crown living at Croft, in Yorkshire.

On February 13, 1829, Greville made the following entry in his now famous diary: "I read a curious thing in the newspapers today. In the Common Council a sum is asked for the maintenance of floating chapels on the Thames. Somebody asks why the sailors don't go to some of the churches on shore. The reply was that nothing will induce them to go there, and that they will attend divine service on their own element or not at all." The bargees of the canal that flowed through Daresbury must have been of a like mind, for the elder Dodgson told the local landholder, Lord Francis Egerton, "If I only had £100, I would turn one of those barges into a chapel." Lord Francis listened to the plan and said nothing, but a few weeks later Mr. Dodgson had his barge, where he thenceforth conducted Sunday evening service.

This was probably the major incident of the years at Croft, comparable only to a three-day journey to Beaumaris, Wales, Mrs. Dodgson's visit to her sick father at Hull, and the flowering of the night-blooming cereus, on which occasion all the neighbors were invited to the greenhouse. Playmates, outside of their own growing family, were few. But the Reverend Thomas Vere Bayne, headmaster of Warrington Grammar School, used to traverse the seven miles between Warrington and Daresbury to assist Mr. Dodgson in his clerical duties, and often brought his son, also named Thomas Vere. This boy, three years older than Charles, became a lifelong friend. He matriculated at Christ Church in 1848, and after Charles "went up," in 1851, their youthful friendship never lapsed again.

With their arduous programs of study and devotions, it is hard to see how children of well regulated families found time to play. But play the Dodgsons did, and Charles's ready inventiveness kept the whole brood occupied. The unusually fine garden was large enough for a train with "stations" constructed by the children, at which they stopped regularly for refreshments. Charles made the train out of a wheelbarrow, a truck, and a barrel, and he was also the ticket agent. Mrs. Livingston's *Catalogue of the Amory Collection* prints a fac- simile of the "Railway Rules" in Charles's writing. Rule 3 follows: "Station master must mind his station and supply refreshments: he can put anyone who behaves badly to prison, while a train goes round the garden: he must ring for the passengers to take their seats, then count 20 slowly, then ring again for the train to start. The L one shall be a surgeon, the wounded must be brought there gratis by the next train going that way and cured gratis. There shall be a place at the L station for lost luggage. If there is anyone to go, a flag is to be hoisted."

The budding cleric showed only in his occupation of peel- ing rushes to give the pith to "the poor," without specifying what "the poor" were to do with it. His usual interests were more dramatic than pious. A favorite pastime was to dress up in nightshirt and brown wig, and, as an "astrologer," to baffle the audience with sleight-of-hand tricks. One winter he traced a maze on the snow-covered lawn—the earliest of his mathematical puzzle-games.

Charles was eleven when the family moved to Croft. His room was near the nursery. According to family tradition, there was a loose board in the nursery floor. Reverend D. Edward Charlesworth, rector and incumbent of Croft Rectory in 1950, showed Mr. Hudson some childish treasures dis- covered under the nursery floor in the course of repairs. There was a hair-slide (?), the lid of a doll's tea set and other china, a child's embroidered handkerchief, a piece of clay pipe, a small penknife, a scrap of paper in Mrs. Dodgson's handwriting, a bit of parchment, a crab shell, a crochet hook, a letter from a child's alphabet, a child's white glove and left shoe, and a small thimble.

Further, there were three small pieces of wood inscribed in pencil, two with the same date: June 18, 1843. One says further, "This floor was laid by Mr. Martin and Mr. Sutton." The third, in Charles Dodgson's handwriting, says,

> *And we'll wander through*
> *the wide world*
> *and chase the buffalo*

which has been identified as a slight misquotation from a contemporary song.[2]

But what a treasure trove—the White Rabbit's glove, the Dodo's thimble, the Aged, Aged Man's left-hand shoe, the ever-recurring buffalo in Charles Dodgson's poems. His roots were long and deep and often buried beyond probability of uncovering, and as in any complex work of art, every symbol must be expected to have multiple determinants. Little is known directly about those early years, so every fragment is hoarded.

Stuart Dodgson Collingwood, Charles's nephew, published a biography shortly after his uncle's death. He speaks of Charles's fondness for scrambling among the marlpits, square pits that dot the landscape, whence the Cheshire soil, of clay, sand, and limestone, is dug to spread over the fields for fertilizer. Besides the mere climbing, these pits fascinate children with the round balls of granite, sea shells, and occasional fossils found in them. The marlers, found only in Cheshire, had a peculiar ceremony which Charles must have witnessed annually. They elected a Lord of the Pit, who levied a toll on passing landowners. The men formed a ring, joined hands, and inclined their heads to the center shouting, "*Oyez, oyez,* Mr.— has been with us today and given my lord and his men part of £ 100" (or "part of £ 1000," if more than sixpence).[3] The money was spent at the ale-house Saturday night, as indeed too much Cheshire money was spent. Charles had an opportunity to compare uses and abuses of drink in the notoriously bibulous county.

His early love of the theater, like his friendship with Vere Bayne, lasted throughout his life. Canon Dodgson, while indulgent toward home theatricals, never relaxed his principled objections to the stage, and none of his daughters ever attended a commercial theater. Charles, however, was not discouraged from building, with the help of the village carpenter, a marionette theater, in 1932 still in Creswell Brigham's Museum for Children in Darlington. By rectory standards at least, Charles was an excellent puppeteer, besides making the marionettes and writing the plays himself; the most popular production was *The Tragedy of King John.*

Finally, he wrote and illustrated numerous magazines for his home circle. *Mischmasch* and *The Rectory Umbrella* are in the Amory Collection, and the others too survive. *The Rectory Umbrella* contained the essay, "Difficulties." Postulating a world with one language and one government, Charles seeks the logical basis for division of days. For this question he never found an answer, though he lectured on it at Oxford years later, then naming the subject, "Where Does the Day Begin?"

His long white fingers were as skillful as they looked, and a good deal stronger. At fourteen he made his sister Elizabeth a box, two by one and one-eighth inches, containing eight miniature tools, also probably made by himself—mallet, plane, gimlet, saw, two braces, screw-driver, and chisel.

He liked to climb trees and scramble in the marlpits, but his principal diversions carried the creative principle even into adult life: photography; mending music-boxes; endless, never successful attempts to draw; infinite games and puzzles. His life, not integrated in the sense of guiding disjunct streams into a single outlet, was at least a well organized chessboard, where the squares balanced one another.

So much of the academic training of children then consisted in mere passive memorizing that it fatigued the most active minds. A few lesson books were used all over England—Mangnall's *Questions*, Joyce's *Scientific Dialogues*, Pinnock's *Catechism*, and Marcle's *Natural Philosophy*. The best of these was the *Scientific Dialogues*, in Socratic form, wherein precise and learned children, Charles and Emma, catechize a father more omniscient than Socrates. This was the last overflow of the Age of Reason—the book actually suggested experiments and offered logical explanations, but, alas, it was the first of these texts to be retired from general use. It seems likely that the Dodgson family might have owned a copy, for Charles's orderly and logical mind must have received some encouragement in childhood.

Mangnall's *Questions*, subtitled *Historical and Miscellaneous Questions for the Use of Young People with a Selection of British and General Biography*, eschews the scientific attitude and endows the author's opinions—backed, perhaps, by the Church of England—with the same importance as known facts. The cumulative effect is overpowering, but an extract must suffice:

"Who was Henry the Sixth's wife? Margaret of Anjou; a woman of keen penetration, undaunted spirit, and exquisite beauty; she fought twelve pitched battles in her husband's cause, but ambition, not affection, guided her actions; and wanting principle, she may engage our pity, but has no title to our esteem and reverence."

G. G. Bradley, Dean of Westminster, writing of his childhood and schooldays in the thirties, recalls that boys who were destined to rule a vast empire were kept in ignorance of current events, except for what they might overhear in the form of gossip. Boys from six to eleven used memory only, except for the mental work and writing required in Latin and arithmetic. History, general information, astronomy, biography, Mangnall's *Questions*—all were memorized. "Lists of kings, of metals, of planets, were repeated without interest and without discrimination . . . I learned by heart the chief countries of Europe, and provided I said them in a sense correctly, was allowed to simplify matters by saying the columns separately or in pairs, Spain, Portugal, Madrid, Lisbon, was quite sufficient. I remember an elder brother's amusement on returning home on my insisting that Portugal was the capital of Spain, Lisbon of Madrid. 'Why not?' I said. 'I always say it so in school.' " [4] Or, as Alice said, "London is the capital of Paris, and Paris is the capital of Rome, and Rome—no, *that's* all wrong . . ."

Sylvie and Bruno oozes with pathetic passages where Bruno says, in one form or another "I wiss oo would say 'oo *may* do oor lessons,' " because Sylvie had told the elf-child: "You *will* do your lessons." No wonder he rebelled. In those days lessons were severe, and he was only five.

Girls fared even worse than boys, since their learning was more passive, less accurate, and often confined to mere memory work and "accomplishments," both taught by governesses themselves ill-trained. The choice was "between well-born, well-bred ladies, driven by circumstances to a profession for which they were imperfectly qualified, and underbred, but clever women, who really know what they profess to

Drawing from *Mischmasch*.

teach." [5] This author proposed as a solution that the "clergy should train their daughters to be prizes in the governess lottery." Actually something like this was done—a school for clergymen's daughters was founded to teach them to teach others. The Reverend Patrick Brontë sent his daughters to a murderous half-charity school, where Maria and Elizabeth contracted the tuberculosis that killed them; the surviving sisters all became governesses.

In the family of Thomas Arnold's grandchildren, where the best in education might be expected, the Mary Arnold who became Mrs. Humphry Ward has nothing good to say about her education from 1858-67. "As far as intellectual training was concerned, my nine years from seven to sixteen were practically wasted. I learnt nothing thoroughly or accurately . . . [nor] that firm hold on the structure and literary history of any language, which my brother William, only fifteen months my junior, got from his six years at Rugby, and his training there in Latin and Greek. What I learned during those years was from personalities." [6]

Girls lacked the boys' chance of escaping into schools where masters might be found who could teach them something—and where boys were, at last, supposed to be boys. But the Dodgson girls were more fortunate than most, for they learned Latin and mathematics at home, probably with their father's aid. Charles's letters to his sisters, especially to Louisa, the mathematical one, are written as to equals, exchanging ideas, and even asking advice on literary questions.

Charles never lost interest in children, or in alleviating their sufferings by any device common or uncommon sense could contrive. Professor Harry Morgan Ayres, in his *Carroll's Alice*, suggests that the *Alice* books are a satire on education and its distortion of the natural child. This extract from *The Game of Logic*, published when Dodgson was fifty-five years old, shows his keen recollection of childhood sorrows:

". . . spoken by a fond mother, in answer to a friend's cautious suggestion that she is perhaps a *little* overdoing it in the way of lessons:

" 'Well, they've got their own way to make in the world. *We* can't leave them a fortune apiece, you know . . . they must work if they want to live. . . . A child will learn more in an hour than a grown man in five. . . . Of course that doesn't do unless children are *healthy:* I quite allow that . . . only just look at my darlings! Why, their cheeks bloom like peonies! Well, now, they tell me that, to keep children in health, you should never give them more than six hours altogether at lessons in the day, and at least two half-holidays in the week. And that's exactly our plan, I can assure you! We never go beyond six hours, and every Wednesday and Saturday as ever is, not one syllable of lessons do they do after one o'clock dinner!' "

The Sabbath was no better. In *Sylvie and Bruno,* published when Dodgson was fifty-seven, Arthur says, of a child:

"It was really touching to hear the melancholy tone in which she said, 'On Sunday I musn't play with my doll! On Sunday I mustn't run on the sands! On Sunday I musn't dig in the garden!' Poor child! She had indeed abundant cause for hating Sunday!"

Lady Muriel then quotes from a letter:

"When, as a child, I first opened my eyes on a Sunday-morning, a feeling of dismal anticipation, which began at least on the Friday, culminated. I knew what was before me, and my wish, if not my word, was 'Would God it were evening!' It was no day of rest, but a day of tests, of catechisms (Watts'), of tracts about converted swearers, godly char-women, and edifying deaths of sinners saved.

"Up with the lark, hymns and portions of Scriptures had to be learned by heart till 8 o'clock, when there were family-prayers, then breakfast. . . .

"At 9 came Sunday-School; and it made me indignant to be put into the class with the village-children, as well as alarmed lest, by some mistake of mine, I should be put below them.

" 'I wandered in [the Church-Service], pitching the taber-nacle of my thoughts on the lining of the square family-pew, the fidgets of my small brothers, and the horror of knowing that, on the Monday, I should have to write out, from memory, jottings of the rambling disconnected extempore sermon, which might have had any text but its own. . . .

". . . cold dinner at 1 (servants to have *no* work), Sunday-School again from 2 to 4, and Evening-Service at 6. The intervals were perhaps the greatest trial of all, from the efforts I had to make, to be less than usually sinful, by reading books and sermons as barren as the Dead Sea. There was but one rosy spot, in the distance, all that day, and that was 'bed-time,' which never could come too early!"

The keen memory of his own miseries made him sympathetic with children whose sufferings, like his, were of the mind. But it is hard to see why he never took the next step of sympathy, never reached out to the much larger class of children whose sufferings were quite as real—that is, physical. He told the story of *Alice* to three little girls who, like his own sisters, had known only loving parents and sunny gardens, shadowed only by lessons and a somewhat exigent religion. In the same year Parliament appointed a commission to inquire into the "Employment of Children and Young Persons in Trade and Manufacturing not already Regulated by Law." The commission found young children working from early morning till late at night in potteries, in match factories, in fourteen occupations. Little girls sat all day making lace, in a room hot and stuffy in summer, cold and stuffy in winter. Eight or ten children shared one candle. Two-year-olds pulled threads. Instead of saying, like Alice, that "London is the capital of Paris," these children told the commissioners that London was a county, that a violet was a bird, that a primrose was a red rose, that a lilac was a bird. They had no idea what a robin or an eagle might be, where fish lived, or where snow came from, and many of them had never heard of Charles Dodgson's God.

Perhaps this was too horrible for him to contemplate—against these evils, and others he saw no cure for, he wrapped himself in nonsense. Nonsense is a cloak, or a thin fine blade. He used it well in both forms, but we need not forget, when he fences with a gnat, that a camel is also present.

So far the tightness and concealed grimness of Victorian England have obscured the charm. But the Dodgson family and the Liddell family, linked forever in our minds through Alice Liddell, carried the same tradition of charm. In her last year Lorina Liddell Skene—Imperious Prima—lived in a sunny apartment full of flowers. Sir William Richmond's portrait of the three sisters on the sands of Llandudno in

1864, like the old lady herself carried the daisy chain back to an earlier day. In 1930, with no introduction other than a desire to write a life of her famous friend, a stranger was received, with indescribable Victorian Oxford charm, in Mrs. Skene's home. Present besides Mrs. Skene were two of her daughters, who contributed their recollections of Mr. Dodgson, and whose relationship with their mother carried that same subtle perfume of a lifetime of frankness and gentleness. Mrs. Skene spoke of her great age—she was then eighty-one—and of her wish to live to see a *Life* of Mr. Dodgson published; she spoke with complete simplicity, and without the tension which overcomes many moderns when they contemplate their own death.

Judging from the records of the Dodgson family back to the seventeenth century, and from the members of the family living in Guildford in 1930, their tradition too was consistently one of gentleness and graciousness. The younger Dodgsons, whose photographs appear in Langford Reed's book, still carry on with charm and good looks.

A letter from Bishop Dodgson, Charles's great-grandfather, in a new living in a cold and uncomfortable parsonage, describes the inconveniences with the greatest good humor and whimsicality. Charles's father, the Archdeacon, was noted for the same qualities. His granddaughters mentioned a letter he wrote when, on his travels, a member of the family asked him to bring back a file. The letter, like some of Charles's to little girls on nothing in particular, was made up of elaborate and charming nonsense about files.

The Dodgsons and their relatives visited back and forth a good deal. The parsonage at Croft had not enough guest rooms, and one of Charles's letters home asks whether a visitor is still sleeping "in the ballroom." He is asked about by his relatives, and writes of visits to London, to Tunbridge Wells, to Putney, and especially to Hastings, where his mother's sisters, the Misses Lutwidge, lived. The favorite uncle seems to have been his mother's bachelor brother, "Uncle Skeffington," who often entertained Charles and always had something of interest to show him.

What of Charles's mother? She ". . . was one of the sweetest and gentlest women that ever lived, whom to know was to love . . . she seemed to live always in the conscious presence of God . . . her children . . . never remember to have heard an impatient or harsh word from her lips." [7]

"It is easy to trace in Lewis Carroll's works," writes Collingwood, "the influence of that most gentle of mothers . . . an old friend of his . . . said to me, 'Tell me about his mother.' . . . When I had finished my account she said, 'Ah, I knew it must have been so; I felt sure he must have had a good mother.' "

The only other traces she left are some letters. One she wrote to Charles when she visited her sick father at Hull:

"My dearest Charlie,

"I have used you rather ill in not having written to you sooner, but I know you will forgive me, as your Grandpapa has liked to have me with him so much, and I could not write and talk to him comfortably. All your notes have delighted me, my precious child, and show me you have not quite forgotten me. I am always thinking of you, and longing to have you all round me again more than words can tell. God grant that we may find you all well and happy on Friday evening. I am happy to say that your dearest Papa is quite well—his cough is rather *tickling,* but is of no consequence. It delights me, my darling Charlie, to hear that you are getting on so well with your Latin, and that you make so few mistakes in your Exercises. You will be happy to hear that your dearest Grandpapa is going on nicely—indeed I hope he will soon be quite well again. He talks a great deal and most kindly about you all. I hope my sweetest Will says 'Mama' sometimes, and that precious Tish has not forgotten. Give them and all my other treasures, including yourself, 1,000,000,000 kisses from me, with my most affectionate love. I am sending you a shabby note, but I cannot help it. Give my kindest love to Aunt Dar, and believe me, my own dearest Charlie, to be your sincerely affectionate

"Mama." [7]

Through all the other messages, it might be possible to suspect a special preference for her own dearest Charlie, who is acknowledged head of the family in his parents' absence.

Love and responsibility twined the magic thread with which she held him to her beliefs, when his stretching mind would have snapped anything weaker than that powerful cobweb.

A close relative told Mr. Reed, "the singular reticence displayed [in Collingwood's book] may also be traced to the fact that, on account of his extraordinary solicitude for them, as well as for his literary gifts, his sisters regarded him with almost reverential affection, so that it would have been impossible, while any of them lived, for any of the younger generation to even suggest that he *might* have had human failings." [8] That he retained a certain formal distance even with his own sisters is indicated by the signature to a letter, written to Louisa in 1896—"Ever yrs. afftely., C. L. Dodgson." [9]

All the stories about the elder Dodgson emphasize his charm, merely implying the iron hand in the velvet glove. The most the Misses Dodgson would say about their grandfather was that he was a man of strong personality, with definite ambitions for developing his children's characters. Three of his four sons took holy orders, and of the eleven children only one daughter and two sons married. The daughter married a clergyman, and one of her sons took orders. None of the Dodgsons married till both parents were dead. . . . Edwin Dodgson, Charles's brother, voluntarily spent eight years on the island of Tristan da Cunha, a dot in the South Atlantic Ocean, teaching school and serving as clergyman to some ninety polyglot and polychrome Christians.

The elder Dodgson stood up for his ideas when Dr. Goode, Dean of Ripon Cathedral, charged him before his bishop with "publishing and preaching false doctrines." Canon Dodgson answered by "printing his sermons, and his defense of them, in a pamphlet which made a considerable sensation at the time." His orthodoxy was vindicated, for he succeeded eventually to the post of Archdeacon of that same Ripon Cathedral.

At Christ Church, Dodgson *père* took a "double first." The British Museum Catalogue gives a column to his published works, none of which casts any light on his son; for Dr. Pusey's exhaustive Library of the Fathers he translated Ter-

tullian, and then, as Charles did later, he deserted the classics
for mathematical studies.

During his undergraduate days the Tractarian Movement
was raging; on the question of baptismal regeneration he
sided with the Tractarians, but he showed no such leanings
toward the Roman Church as many Tractarians did. In fact
the Tractarian Movement grew into the Oxford Movement,
that high church group of whom many, following John Henry
Newman, eventually went over to Rome. The elder Dodgson
was "a man of deep piety and of a somewhat reserved and
grave disposition," says Collingwood. "In moments of relaxa-
tion his wit and humour were the delight of his clerical
friends, for he had the rare power of telling anecdotes effectively. His reverence for sacred things was so great that he
was never known to relate a story which included a jest upon
words from the Bible." [7]

This picture fits Charles almost as well, save that he went
no further in the Church than his Studentship at Christ
Church required him to. He was ordained deacon, and no
more, and that reluctantly. While less grave and more humorous than his father, he was equally pious, equally a good
student, *raconteur,* and mathematician (though not of the
very highest order), and equally unable to stomach a biblical
jest. At Christ Church he was noted for walking out of
Common Room, like Alice from the Mad Tea Party, at the
least indelicacy or irreverence.

For this sort of fabulous monster the boys' school of the
1840's provided poor stabling indeed. Study was no hardship to Charles—in fact he mastered his lessons with ease
and pleasure; but he was critical enough to know how much
of his time was being wasted by inefficient educational practice, and he often hankered for the leisure and spontaneous
companionship of the rectory garden full of eager followers,
happy to carry out his delightful inventions.

Chapter 3

Reeling, Writing, and Fainting in Coils

> . . . *said the Mock Turtle with a sigh, "I only took the regular course."*
> *"What was that?" enquired Alice.*
> *"Reeling and Writhing, of course, to begin with . . . then Drawling—the Drawling-master was an old conger-eel . . . he taught us Drawling, Stretching, and Fainting in Coils."*

IT IS IMPOSSIBLE to trace Charles's education in full detail. Four volumes of his diaries, extant when his nephew wrote the *Life,* have vanished now, and few letters survive from his early youth. Richmond School, to which his father sent him at the age of twelve, is hardly recorded in history. It has been necessary, therefore, to reconstruct the three usual stages of an English boy's education from other sources.

Young boys were taught at home or in dame's schools; next came the "private" schools, such as Richmond; then the college preparatory or "public" schools. About Rugby there is plenty of material, especially from Arnold's regime; one illuminating article about his own schooldays is by G. G. Bradley, Dean of Westminster. An unfailing source is the immortal *Tom Brown's Schooldays.* About Westminster School under Liddell, Captain Markham's reminiscences are useful. In fact, it is possible to restore the background rather fully, and if Charles Dodgson *in propria persona* moves against it too seldom, that is due to the scantiness of the records.

Richmond, nine miles from Croft, was a clean old town. In the 1840's it retained a somewhat medieval air. The houses in the market place had heavily carved gable ends, and their great bow windows with leaded panes overhung the hilly streets that slope to the river Swale, one of those turbulent Yorkshire rivers that suddenly and violently overflow their banks.

46

Nine miles was a gentle remove, and Charles wrote later, "I loved my kind old schoolmaster," [1] who was only in his forties. His name was Mr. Tate; his first name has not come down to us. Perhaps he was shadowed by the relative fame of his father, Dr. James Tate, one of the best known heads of Richmond School. Mr. Tate took over the headship from his father, who had held it since 1796.

The school was founded in Elizabeth's time by several burgesses who willed their closes to found a free grammar school. After 1688 the mayor and aldermen chose the master, and it was provided that all children of "burgesses and other persons inhabiting in the said borough and exercising any trade, mystery, or manual occupation therein, shall be admitted and entitled to be taught free in the same school." [2] British custom, however, permitted children of the nobility and the gentry also to attend those schools before they were ready for the great public schools. A Yorkshire historian says: "This school is conducted upon a large and liberal plan, and has long been considered as a seminary of sound learning and religious education, nor will it lose its credit in the hands of its present and very worthy principal." [2] This was the elder Tate, who, himself a graduate of the school, was a classical scholar, something of an innovator in education, and a friend and correspondent of the Headmaster of Shrewsbury. This latter was Dr. Butler, grandfather of Samuel, between whom and Charles Dodgson there are interesting parallels. Their origins had so many similarities and so many divergences, and their flowering, in each case on a bent bush, was so different.

The Butlers lacked the Dodgsons' golden key, fused of love and charm. Samuel developed, not a dual personality, but an emotional dualism—he loved where he hated and hated where he loved. This is the basic difference between him and Charles, and the explanation for what must be termed his relative failure, since even today his full stature is not accorded him. With an almost Goethean grasp of half a dozen fields, Butler failed, in his lifetime, in every enterprise except *Erewhon*, though his books have risen from the dead, as he must have known they would. Samuel's fatal disorientation from his fellow man led him into all his blunders, whereas Charles was schooled from the first in that good taste and good feeling Samuel so greatly coveted. But how those two would have detested each other!

One of the few surviving documents of Charles's schooldays is a letter, probably his first, to his sisters from Richmond. While it is no doubt humorous in intent, to our taste it is decidedly pathetic.

"My dear Fanny and Memy:

"I hope you are all getting on well, as also the sweet twins, the boys I think that I like the best, are Harry Austin, and all the Tates of which there are 7 besides a little girl who came down to dinner the first day, but not since. . . . The boys have played two tricks upon me which were these— they first proposed to play at 'King of the Cobblers' and asked if I would be king, to which I agreed. Then they made me sit down and sat (on the ground) in a circle round me, and told me to say 'Go to work' which I said, and they immediately began kicking and knocking me on all sides. The next game they proposed was 'Peter, the red lion," and they made a mark on a tombstone (for we were playing in the churchyard) and one of the boys walked with his eyes shut, holding out his finger, trying to touch the mark; then a little boy came forward to lead the rest and led a good many very near the mark; at last it was my turn; they told me to shut my eyes well, and the next moment I had my finger in the mouth of one of the boys, who had stood (I believe) near the tombstone with his mouth open. For 2 nights I slept alone, and for the rest of the time with Ned Swire. The boys play me no tricks now. The only fault (tell Mama) that there has been was coming in one day to dinner just after grace. . . . Papa wished me to tell him all the texts I had heard preached upon, please to tell him that I could not hear it in the morning nor hardly one sentence of the sermon, but the one in the evening was I Cor. 1.23. . . . I have had 3 misfortunes in my clothes, etc. 1st I cannot find my tooth-brush, so that I have not brushed my teeth for 3 or 4 days, 2nd I cannot find my blotting paper, and 3rd I have no shoe-horn. The chief games are, football, wrestling, leap frog, and fighting. Excuse bad writing.

Yr affect brother Charles." [1]

The result of the hazing in his case was to make him a champion of the weak, feared by bullies: "Long after he left school his name was remembered as that of a boy who knew well how to use his fists in defense of a righteous cause." [1] There must have been plenty of these righteous causes, and in his three years at Rugby Charles must have been glad he could defend himself.

Education was still primarily linguistic, and the languages were classic. "If we are to understand at all what we read, then some knowledge of our language must be acquired. The question is—how. The favorite answer is by learning Latin." [3] The author deplores the time wasted in his youth: "hours upon hours spent by many boys in the moiling evolution of one or two wintry and wooden elegiacs, consisting of halting hexameters and hypermetric pentameters; boys whose inability might have been predicted at thirteen, kept at the same galley-work up to eighteen or nineteen, as unprogressive as the seamen who plied the oar upon the land." [3]

This type of education was no hardship to boys who, like Charles, had a natural facility for thinking in words, and handled language easily. Mr. Tate wrote of him: "He possesses, along with other excellent and natural endowments, a very uncommon share of genius. Gentle and cheerful in his intercourse with others, playful and ready in conversation, he is capable of acquirements and knowledge far beyond his years, while his reason is so clear and so jealous of error, that he will not rest satisfied without a most exact solution of whatever appears to him obscure. . . . You may fairly anticipate for him a bright career." [1] Mr. Tate was a judicious man.

After Richmond, however, came the ordeal of Rugby. The seven great public schools—so called because they were supported by foundations controlled by trustees, who hired and could fire the headmaster—were on a comparable level. They were Eton, Harrow, Rugby, Westminster, Winchester, Charterhouse, and Shrewsbury.* While tacitly theocratic, they were conducted as boys' republics, and public opinion, on the boy level, combined with medieval tradition to form a dreadful tyranny. A boy like Charles, moreover, softened by a kind mother and a houseful of sisters, would have been in great danger at a public school without the preliminary toughening at Richmond.

From grammar school he might have been sent to any of the seven schools. Perhaps the afterglow of Arnold's prestige caused Canon Dodgson to send his son to Rugby rather than to his own school of Westminster, where the Head from 1846 to 1855 was Dr. Liddell, whose daughter Alice was to play a part in Charles's life. During his school days Charles already had indirect contact with Dr. Liddell—a letter to his sister Elizabeth from Rugby says: "There are some books I should like to have leave to get: these are . . . Liddell & Scott's Large Greek-English Lexicon Mr. Price quite despises the little one and says it is only fit for my younger brothers. It is hardly any use in Demosthenes." [4] But if Charles had met Dr. Liddell this early, he might have seen the great scholar's darker side. A former pupil tells with how scornfully nasal a tone the Head addressed two not very brilliant students: "You and Markham row in the same boat, and if you wish to be watermen, you had better go and be apprenticed." [5] A cut in the class pride was worse than a flogging. James Anthony Froude, describing the mental and physical cruelty endured by a youth at Westminster School and at home, finds that incomparably his worst experience was his father's threat to apprentice him to a tradesman.

For the chasm between "gentlemen" and those "below" was wider than the rift between royalty and gentry. Two generations earlier, George III, asked how he wished his son educated, replied, "Like the sons of any English gentleman. If they deserve it, let them be flogged. Do as you used to do at Westminster!" [5] And how was that? As at Rugby, boys were tossed in blankets, and flogged for errors in Latin grammar or behavior. There was "handing"—five or six cuts on the back of the hand with a birch rod—and flogging "on

* Some lists include Merchant Taylors'.

the person"—also five or six strokes, used only for very serious offenses, such as smoking, "cheek," and false quantities. A century earlier, Richard Steele said: "It is wholly to this dreadful practice that we may attribute a certain hardness and ferocity which some men, though liberally educated, carry about them in all their behavior. To be bred like gentlemen, and punished like a malefactor, must, as we see it does, produce that illiberal sauciness which we see sometimes in men of letters." [6] Charles never developed that "illiberal sauciness." It seems unlikely that he was ever flogged, though it is highly improbable that he totally escaped "handing."

Toward the end of Charles's stay at Rugby, his mother wrote her sister, Lucy Lutwidge, on November 11 (no year given, but 1849 or 1850 is probable), "With regard to dearest Charlie I had *hoped* to have heard from him again today, but I have not. In his letter received on Tuesday he says that the mumps had gone but that they had left him much more deaf than usual—this we trust is quite to be accounted for from the nature of the complaint and may probably last longer than the *visible* swelling of the glands. Charles has however written to Dr. Tait telling him of Charlie's former deafness & its source (Infantile fever) & requesting him to take the best medical opinion within his reach & to report it immediately to us. . . ." [7]

Apparently the acute deafness subsided, but Charles continued deaf in one ear all his life. Hudson says the right, Dodgson's later child friend Ethel Rowell says the left, and is very specific about it because she, too, was deaf in one ear, and on walks she and Dodgson jockeyed for position, each trying to present the good ear to the other. [8]

On June 18, 1856, there is a diary entry, "called on Mr. Toynbee, the aurist." Whatever Mrs. Dodgson's diagnosis, we have a possible piece of evidence from Charles himself. In one of the magazines he wrote and illustrated for his brothers and sisters, *The Rectory Umbrella,* there is a drawing, "The First Ear Ring," showing a boy being dragged by his right ear by a very determined man, perhaps a teacher, holding a switch in one hand. The boy's face shows agony—the whole is, perhaps, a comic picture. But the abominable practice of hitting children on the ear, or dragging them by the ear, must have caused many a case of deafness almost to our own times.

Tom Brown's Schooldays gives a marvelous picture of the life and of the boys, but the physical setting is hardly described; knowledge on the part of the readers is perhaps assumed. A picture of Eton in the thirties to fifties will give a hint about Rugby.

At Eton in 1838 a deputation waited on the authorities, asking them to install a hot water system similar to that which piped heat to the rooms in Westminster. The answer was, "You will be wanting gas and turkey carpets next!" [9] (How true!) A few years earlier, at the suggestion of adding potatoes to the school diet, the authorities had countered, "Who is to peel the potatoes?" Even as late as 1858 scandalous conditions existed. A musty smell was noted in the hall all winter. In the summer holidays the floors were removed, and "two large cart loads of bones, chiefly of necks of mutton, were removed from between the floor and the ceiling of the room below . . . the 6th form boys took their supper there, and rats came out to eat the bones . . . when the rats became too numerous, a fag went around while they were feeding and dropped open stockings over the holes. They were trapped in the stockings and banged to death against the beds." The narrator was asked, "And you went to school in the same stockings next morning, sir?" "Of course, of course,—we could not get clean stockings when we pleased." [10]

In 1848 the heating system and water supply were installed, and tea and breakfast provided. Sick rooms and lavatories were built, and servants engaged to do the necessary work— it was the lack of servants that had deprived the boys of potatoes.

At Rugby, Arnold gradually took the boarding houses from the jurisdiction of village women and placed them, one by one, under his masters. There was a direct correlation between poverty—or rather parsimony, for the schools were wealthy— and fagging. Arnold said: "If you do not provide servants to clean the boys' boots, or to wait on them at their meals, undoubtedly the more powerful will get these things done for

them by the weaker." [11] (Clean shoes were more regarded
than clean stockings!)

Fagging—the system of subjecting the younger boys to the
older for service and punishment—had another side. Arnold
further claimed: "Fagging is necessary for a number of boys
when living together: the boys for nearly nine months of the
year, live with one another in a distinct society, and for this
habitual living they require a government. It is idle to say
the masters form, or can form, this government; it is impossible to have a sufficient number of masters for this purpose."
Modern education rests on *enough* teachers.

Corporal punishment was also retained, though the amount
of it was reduced by Arnold's method of trusting the boys
and treating them like gentlemen until they violated his trust.
He said: "The fault of the old system of flogging at Winchester was not its cruelty but its inefficiency. . . . If a boy
above fifteen is of such a nature as to require flogging, the
essentially trifling nature of school correction is inadequate to
the offense."

Salomon Reinach says in his *Orpheus, a History of Re-
ligions,* "A prohibition, which belongs to the class of *taboos
of majesty,* forbade a child to approach its father armed; the
result was that the boys were brought up in strange families
or by the Druids, a curious custom which persisted for a long
time in Ireland; the English and French institution of boarding schools may be a survival of this practice." It has further
been suggested that behind the Spartan discomforts, brutality,
and infantile tyranny, there was a purpose, as definite, if as
uninscribed, as the British Constitution—a philosophy of
training for the upper classes, consisting of elimination of the
unfit (mentally) by letting them drop out, and of the unfit
(morally) by bullying. Developing contempt for discomfort
in the schools helped make Empire builders, and while only
certain boys attained scholarship, there were giants among
them. Stanley says of Arnold: "He governed the school precisely on the same principles as he would have governed a
great empire." [12] The universal moral toughness of the English—for better, for worse—may have some relation to public
school education, and its emulation by the "lower" classes.

There can be no doubt that Arnold elevated the tone and

improved the teaching of the public schools. Whether his total influence was for good or for ill, no one denies the immensity of that influence. He respected the boys' immortal souls while tanning their hides, but he was in a dreadful hurry to get them tuned in with immortality. He introduced the brief Sunday sermon, lasting no more than twenty minutes, on subjects aimed at the boys' interests. He felt that "their age did not prevent their faults from being sins, or their excellences from being noble and Christian virtues." Within the limits of his sympathies, he was a great and inspiring teacher. He divided the boys into three age groups—with the youngest he was playful, with the middle group he was stern, and with the older ones he unbent again, drawing closer to them and expecting them to share the burdens and problems of keeping the school in order.

His first aim was to develop Christian men—then gentlemen—then scholars. Christian boys he considered an impossible anomaly. The sooner boy-nature was transcended, or exorcised, the better he was pleased. Born scholar-prigs like Arthur Penrhyn Stanley, future Dean of Westminster, did very well. John Bull Englishmen like Thomas Hughes, future author of *Tom Brown's Schooldays,* were refined and elevated by contact with Arnold's virile Christianity. Intelligent but not too robust boys who needed rounding out, cherishing, and encouragement simply went to pieces; as, for instance, Arthur Hugh Clough, the child prodigy who came down like a stick. Clough attributed his untimely collapse to idealistic overstrain in his schooldays. He was an intimate of Matthew Arnold, who himself escaped virtually unscathed. Perhaps Matthew was a chip of the old block; then too, he studied only one year at his eminent father's school.

Education both in public school and university was primarily concerned with Greek and Latin. Among Arnold's modifications were the improvement of the language teaching itself and the addition to the curriculum of other subjects, particularly French, which was taught by English masters, and as if it were a dead language. When foreign masters were employed, the boys were not taught to respect them; hence, understandably, Arnold was afraid to entrust the boys' discipline to them. The Dean of Westminster excuses teaching of modern languages by English masters: "How were boys reared in insular and midland ignorance of the great world that lay beyond the 'silver streak,' to submit to teachers who, when a sparrow was designedly let loose in school, called it a 'chicken,' or a cockchafer a 'chafer-bird'?" [13] Under the circumstances, Arnold hoped no more than that the boys would learn to read French—he considered it improbable that they could learn to speak it well in any case. Somewhere, somehow, Dodgson learned to communicate adequately in German and French. On his Russian tour he managed with these languages, saying, "The English I hear is not much worse than the German I speak." He picked up a little Russian too.

Arnold brought life into the teaching of the classics by having the boys translate whole passages rather than construe phrases piecemeal. As a literary man himself, he had a feeling for the form and meaning of what he read, and hence gave more interesting subjects for original compositions than his predecessors had given. Instead of the well-worn *Carpe diem* and *Virtus est bona res,* he assigned subjects from geographic discoveries, travel, letters, and other live springboards for composition.

He taught geography as part of history, and he encouraged mathematics, geology, and general science—not to an extent that would impress a modern schoolboy, but still enough to open the doors for those who might wish to go further. His interests were catholic. Arthur Stanley, who rode on a coach with him one holiday, reported that the great man spoke of "Coleridge, chivalry, geology, and phrenology, of Queen Caroline, mobs, and Niebuhr, Thucydides, triremes, genealogy, and races, and then fell asleep." [14]

He fell asleep in the school too, to the extent that he did not—perhaps could not—correct all abuses of teaching methods or discipline. Even in his successor's time, Charles Dodgson wrote: "I spent an incalculable time writing out impositions" (lines of Greek or Latin assigned as penalties). "During my stay I made I suppose some progress in learning of various kinds, but none of it was done *con amore.*" [1] Other sources tell us the "vulgus" was retained—a short exercise in Greek or Latin verse, on a given subject, the mini-

mum of lines being fixed for each form. It was dull work, so
the usual plan was to have a "vulgus," or a number of them,
handed down from previous victims, from which the day's
lesson was prepared *au pot pourri*. It seems unlikely that
Charles would ever have cheated, or needed to cheat, but he
certainly wasted a great deal of time and acquired the habit
of mental doodling that went through life with him.

Charles's stay at Rugby might have been happier under
Arnold, but Arnold was dead and Dr. Archibald Campbell
Tait had succeeded him in 1842. No man of comparable
stature would have tried to fill those boots. Tait did his best,
but as a schoolmaster he was inconsequential, as a scholar
mediocre, as a personality nothing much. He was not particularly interested in boys, and had no profound grasp of the
peculiar ethics of the public school. His seven years at Rugby
constituted a marking time for him and a slow downward
slide for the school. Attempting to carry on in Arnold's spirit,
he made no great mistakes—and no great contributions. The
angelic Stanley had urged him to take the position, though his
"sermons would probably be dull and Latin prose weak." [17]
So he did, and so they were.

Matthew Arnold, who was assistant headmaster at Rugby
in 1851, after Charles was at Oxford, gives an indirect picture of Dr. Tait: "I do not give satisfaction at the Masters'
Meetings," Arnold writes to Clough. "For the other day when
Tait had well observed that strict Calvinism devoted thousands of mankind to be eternally '——,' and paused—I, with I
trust the true Xtian simplicity suggested '——.' " [15]

In her own pleasant little house, with the fresh grass of the
close for her children to romp on, Mrs. Tait played hostess
to the boys of the school, asking the younger ones to tea and
the older ones to dinner, and dutifully making conversation
with all. She visited sick boys and kept the school accounts;
managed the servants, instructed the maids in religion, and
taught a class of little girls at the village school "almost daily."
Every day began with a visit to the parish church, followed
by family prayers; on Sundays "there were bright stirring
services in the school chapel, and when she appeared, the
boys loved to look upon her face." [16]

Her baby boy was a great favorite with the schoolboys,

who put a football cap on him and enjoyed seeing him run
with it. In 1856 the five little Tait sisters died, within five
days, of scarlet fever, and the little boy lived to be graduated
from Oxford, become a doctor of divinity, and break what
was left of his parents' hearts by dying at twenty-nine. Dr.
Tait himself contracted rheumatic fever in his last year at
Oxford and nearly died. With permanently injured health, he
yet lived to become Archbishop of Canterbury.

The Taits' only pleasure seems to have been riding horse-
back through the green lanes of Rugby, for the dinner parties
with the Sixth Form boys and the social gatherings with the
families of the masters must have been more penitential than
pleasant. "Those who knew what Rugby was when Arnold
left it, will understand that every interesting question of
politics and the latest speculation on theology and philosophy
were flying in the somewhat excited society of the masters." [17]
Dr. Tait had his own way of relaxing the strain. "The over-
heated temper of Rugby was probably none the worse for
the liberal cold douches he occasionally applied." But that he
allowed any unbending of the tight bow of morals is specifically controverted by his students, his masters, and what is
known of himself. He said: "The earliest recollection I have
of a deep religious impression made on my mind has often
recurred to me with the vividness of having heard a voice
from above. I suppose I must have been some ten or twelve
years old. I distinctly remember in the middle of the night
awakening with a deep impression in my mind of the reality
and nearness of the world unseen, such as through God's
mercy has never left me. That it was made by God and the
Holy Ghost working on my soul I have no doubt." [17]

Tait's years at Rugby were admittedly the least successful
of his life. While he overdid the inculcation of moral responsibility, his limitations kept him from doing as much harm
(or good) as Arnold. When he left, Rugby was again more
like an ordinary public school—but the other schools had
raised themselves to meet Arnold's challenge.

Between fagging and corporal punishment, boys were apt
to have all the sensibility toughened, or all the manhood
softened, out of them. But of a batch of unregenerate little

rascals, let the bully catch the hindmost; what was left was refined into Christian gentlemen. It is hard to see why Charles's spirit was not broken after the three years which "no power on earth would induce [him] to go through again." Perhaps he was of tougher fiber than his later development suggested—his record at Richmond indicates this—or perhaps he slid by as Arthur Stanley did under Arnold. Stanley was studious and prematurely adult—really never anything so vulgar as a boy—and he took all six possible prizes. Instead of being tormented, he escaped fagging after six months because the boys admired his prowess and called his study the "poet's corner." Without such conspicuous distinction, Charles maintained his personal dignity, and no doubt his quick wit and ready humor saved him. At any rate, he was never called into the tower for misbehavior, it is not recorded that he was ever flogged, and Tait of Rugby, like the other Tate of Richmond, wrote his father an enthusiastic letter:

"My dear Sir—
  "I must not allow your son to leave school without expressing to you the very high opinion I entertain of him. I fully coincide in Mr. Cotton's estimate both of his abilities and upright conduct. His mathematical knowledge is great for his age, and I doubt not he will do himself credit in classics. As I believe I mentioned to you before, his examination for the Divinity prize was one of the most creditable exhibitions I have ever seen.
  "During the whole time of his being in my house, his conduct has been excellent.
                    Believe me to be, my dear Sir,
                        Yours very faithfully,
                            A. C. Tait." [1]

  In a letter to his sister Elizabeth, discussing two prizes he received—apparently one in mathematics and one in divinity —Charles says:
  "The report is certainly a delightful one: *I* cannot account for it; I hope there is no mistake. As to the difference between Walker and myself (papa seems satisfied about Harri-

son) it must be remembered that he is in the 6th and has hitherto been considered the best mathematician in the school. Indeed no one but me got anything *out* of the 6th (I hope you understand this last sentence." [4]

In his first year he seems to have suffered nothing worse than the routine robbery of small boys' blankets to cover the big boys' beds. Compared with Tom Brown's roasting before the fire and tossing in a blanket, this seems trivial. But years later, when he visited Radley school, noting that the boys there slept in cubicles instead of dormitories, he wrote: "I can say that if I had been thus secure from annoyance at night the hardships of the daily life would have been comparative trifles to bear." [1]

The overtones of that remark imply a good deal of misery. As at home, his emotional development continued to be too tightly channeled. With parents and masters of such perfection, against what can the adolescent revolt? Fortunately, parents and teachers often fall short of their own ideals; most young people have ample excuse for their necessary revolt, since so few adults—now, at least—reach the dread perfection some of the Victorian giants seem to have achieved.

A child must strive to surpass his parents—if this seems hopeless he may give up, and twist himself into perverse patterns to escape becoming a mere carbon copy. Charles, with his natural love of excellence fostered too far for mortal flesh to bear, suffered from every manifestation of the old Adam, and his ingenious mind never rested from the problem of finding a way out without damaging the beloved box.

He kept no diary at school—all we have is this note of 1855: "During my stay I made I suppose some progress in learning of various kinds, but none of it was done *con amore,* and I spent an incalculable time writing out impositions—this last I consider one of the chief faults of Rugby School. I made some friends there . . . but I cannot say that I look back upon life at a Public School with any sensations of pleasure, or that any earthly considerations would induce me to go through my three years again." [1]

"The Palace of Humbug," a poem also dated 1855, contains the lines:

> *And one, a dotard grim and gray.*
> *Who wasteth childhood's happy day*
> *In work more profitless than play*
>
> *Whose icy breast no pity warms*
> *Whose little victims sit in swarms*
> *And slowly sob on lower forms.*

Perhaps Charles found a way of living, or perhaps he did not choose to write of his misery at the time. A letter in the Huntington collection, dated 1849, follows:

School House
May 4

"Dearest Elizabeth,

"I can not promise you that this will be as long a letter as the sheet admits of, but I will do my best that way. First, to explain the enclosed picture. Brinklord is a village about 6 miles from Rugby, rendered famous by the presence of a Roman camp, or rather the remains of one, which I suppose will have existed about 1800 years. I went there in Ap. one day accompanied by two others, having got leave from Dr. Tait to 'skip' both callings-over, thus having about 3½ hours clear. We got there in about 1½ hours, remained in the camp about ½ an hour and returned. The rough sketch, from which the enclosed is taken was made from the largest of the mounds (of course not included in the picture) as it afforded the best view. You must suppose it exactly in front of the picture, filling up the space between the two side mounds, and thus completing the circuit of the camp: a bridle road runs through the middle, and on the right is Brinklord church and Brinklord itself. You may remark that it is divided into two camps, thus affording them a safe place to retreat into, if they were beaten out of the 1st. The great mound is so steep on all sides, that I shd think it must have been nearly impregnable. It most likely contains the bodies of the slain, as another mound similar to it, about a mile off, was found full of bones, urns, &c when excavated. There are several single mounds of the same sort about Rugby, one of them in the playground itself, & as it is full of trees, it is used for gymnastics, swinging, &c. This morning we had 2nd lesson at ½ before 10; over about ½ past, so I determined, as I had 3 clear hours before dinner, to visit Brinklord again. I took my rough sketch with me & made a few alterations which I have introduced into the copy I send you. We did not get back until about ½ to 2 but Dr. Tait was satisfied with the reason, & seemed surprised that we had done the whole distance without running.

"Thanks for the two letters received yesterday, also for the promise of the box, about which I wish to offer one more hint & that is, please do *not* send me one of Mrs. Pattinson's seed loaf cakes, they are so light that they are gone directly & are worth neither the carriage nor the money. I never heard the 'Erl King': what is it about? & why should the child die in the other piece of music?

"I have neither written to, nor heard from Featherston for a long time: we seem to have mutually forgotten one another. Do you happen to know how long he has been home from America how long is Miss Greenside going to remain in Edinborough?

"The day before yesterday I went up to Mr. Vicars' house, to ask Henry Vicars for some Greek verses we had to copy out. He was not at home, & I found Mr. Vicars alone, who very kindly asked me to remain for tea. Mrs. Vicars and the daughters are gone to the seaside, leaving Mr. Vicars and his two sons at Rugby. He asked after Uncle Skeffington: by the bye, I never heard how his wound in the head got on: is he well again by this time?

"Yesterday evening I was walking out with a friend of mine who attends as mathematical pupil Mr. Smythies, the second mathematical master, we went up to Mr. Smythies' house, as he wanted to speak to him, and he asked us to stop and have a glass of wine and some figs. He seems as devoted to his duty as Mr. Major, & asked me with a smile of delight, 'Well, Dodgson, I suppose you're getting well on with your mathematics?' He is very clever at them though not equal to Mr. Major, as indeed very few men are, Papa excepted. For fear I should forget it I will here mention that I intend sending in this letter the words of 'Jeanette and

Jeanot,' which I learned by hearing them sung here: see if Fanny can get them to fit to the music. You never told me if she succeeded with 'long long ago.' There is a comic song came out 'The Sea Serpent.'

"I have read the first number of Dickens' new tale *Davy Copperfield*. It purports to be his life & begins with his birth & childhood: it seems a poor plot, but some of the characters and scenes are very good. One of the persons that amused me, was a Mrs. Gummidge, a wretched melancholy person, who is always crying, happen what will: & whenever the fire smokes or other trifling accident occurs, makes the remark with great bitterness and many tears, that she is a 'lone lorn creetur, & everythink goes contrairy with her.'

"I have not yet been able to get the 2nd vol: Macaulay's *England* to read: I have seen it however & one passage struck me when 7 bishops signed the invitation to the pretender, & King James sent for Bishop Compton (who was one of the 7) & asked him 'whether he or any of his ecclesiastical brethren had had anything to do with it?' He replied after a moment's thought, 'I am fully persuaded, your majesty, that there is not one of my brethren who is not as innocent as myself.' This was certainly no actual lie, but certainly as Macaulay says, it was very little different from one. On the next day the king called a meeting of all the bishops, when Compton was present, but the other 6 absented themselves. He then for form's sake put the question to each of them 'whether they had had anything to do with it?' Here was a new difficulty, which Compton got over by saying, when it came to his turn, 'I gave your lordship *my* answer yesterday.' It certainly showed talent, though exerted in the wrong direction, have you ever met with the passage in other histories?

"I have got a new hat, which I suppose Papa will not object to, as my old one was getting very shabby which I have had ever since the beginning of last holidays. I have also got a pair of gloves, as I found I had not *one* pair of summer gloves, as I thought I had.

"Will you answer my questions about the clocks, when you next write? How do you get on with the poetry book with Willy and Long? Shall I send you or bring you any more numbers of it? & have you seen the *Vast Army?* There is a 3rd part of *Laneton Parsonage* come out, have you seen it? How do you like the *Diversions of Hollycott?* Will my room be ready for me when I come home? & has it got any more 'visitors'? Have you been many walks with Aunt and Cousin Smedley? & how long are they going to stay with you? Are my two pictures of cricketing framed yet? When is Papa going to the Ordination? & when to the Durham examination? Has Fanny yet finished Alison's *Europe?* Have you finished your *Hutchinson?* Are the mats finished? is Skeffington's ship finished? Have you left off fires yet? Have you begun the evening walks in the garden? does Skeffington ride Henderson's donkey much now? has Fanny found any new flowers? have you got any babies to nurse? Mary any new pictures to paint? Has Mr. Stamper given up the ball room yet? Will you tell me whose and when the birthdays in next month are? Will you condense all these questions into one or answer each separately? Lastly, do you believe that I subscribe myself your afette Brther sincerely or not? Is this letter long enough?" [4]

Indeed it was, and, as a letter from a brother to sisters, singularly unpatronizing. The same tone continues in his letters to his sisters to his last year—he always showed interest in their activities and even in their ideas. But not a word about his troubles at school.

After the impression he made on Dr. Tait, and with his record at Rugby, Oxford was inevitable. Christ Church, his father's college, was chosen. With our perspective, we can see that he would have been happier at Balliol, with Jowett for mentor, and literary and mathematical prodigies as his fellow students; but the elder Dodgson may not have realized that Christ Church was upper-class socially rather than intellectually. Thus, while Oxford gave Charles freedom to be his somewhat eccentric self, he found little real companionship on his own mental level.

Collingwood failed to note—perhaps because he knew the reason and saw no problem—that there is no documentation for Charles's doings between the end of 1848 or the beginning of 1849, and his entrance into residence at Oxford in January, 1851. It is just for these years that some diaries are lost. Miss Dodgson attempted to check the records at Rugby, at Christ Church, and in the newspaper cuttings of the centenary year, but found nothing more definite than "a list of prizes he brought back from Rugby, and the last ones mentioned were brought home Xmas '48, which points to that being his last term, making his stay at Rugby exactly three years." This fits his own remark about the three years that he would not voluntarily live through again.

Since he was producing his home magazines in these very years, it is to be presumed that he was living at Croft. But why? He matriculated at Oxford in May, 1850. Perhaps he needed time to prepare, but this seems improbable for such an excellent student. Neither could lack of family funds explain his long vacation, for, as Miss Dodgson says, "Mrs. Dodgson's family was well off and she had a most generous brother—a bachelor [Uncle Skeffington?]—Also, if money had not been forthcoming I don't think the Archdeacon would have within a few years of sending Lewis Carroll to Oxford, sent also my father (Wilfred), and Skeffington, the brother just older."

In his notes to Dodgson's *Diaries,* Mr. Green explored this question. He says "Three years" at Rugby is "certainly inaccurate," and believes four or five more likely. The last school report from Rugby is dated December 18, 1849. "It seems probable that Charles spent most of the year 1850 at Croft, working alone (and probably with the aid of his father), in preparation for Oxford. He matriculated at Christ Church May 23, although he does not appear to have gone into residence until the following January."

Perhaps it was in these years of partial idleness that he acquired the habits of literary and artistic creativity padded with doodling. And perhaps the added years at home intensified the lifelong mood of nostalgia that permeates his writings: nostalgia for childhood—even for infancy, for a mother's care, for innocence, for gentleness, for all the aura of his early home, so rudely disturbed at school. He caught the mayfly of childhood in the amber of his art, and throughout life he was able to recreate the mood of loved children playing gaily in an English garden. That is one source of his charm, but the price exacted for the child heart was an old-maidish exterior: the fact that he adventured more and more deeply into the earlier layers of himself and his familial relationships kept him from any external adventures whatsoever.

There is some evidence of two turning points in his life, the one documented and dated, the other only surmised. In both cases he was defeated by the enemy without and turned back to the inner world over which he had easy mastery. The second turning was final—for the Snark *was* a Boojum, you see.

Chapter 4

"Thou Tea-Chest"

Here's to the Freshman of bash-
ful eighteen!
Here's to the Senior of twenty!
Here's to the youth whose mous-
tache can't be seen!
And here's to the man who has
plenty!
Let the men Pass!
Out of the mass
I'll warrant we'll find you some
fit for a Class!

CHARLES DODGSON "went up" to Oxford in 1851 and stayed there the rest of his life—forty-seven years. In the external sense, hardly anything ever happened to him; but a few days after he entered college one of those rare occasions befell. His mother died suddenly, and he was called home for the funeral. His nephew, as usual, draws the veil, merely quoting Dr. Pusey's letter of condolence to the bereaved husband, which casts no light on the son's feelings. But Charles's "Easter Greeting to Every Child who Loves Alice," written twenty-five years later, describes, rather too touchingly, a child waking on a summer morning, "And is it not a Mother's gentle hand that undraws your curtains and a Mother's sweet voice that summons you to rise?" Thirteen years later still, in the poem he considers his masterpiece, he portrays love in three forms only—mother love, brotherly love, and divine love; and Sylvie, the heroine, resembles his mother even to her "gentle voice."

Charles's father outlived his mother by many years, during the last fifteen of which he was Archdeacon of Ripon. Collingwood gives excerpts from two letters, one written thirty years after the event, in which Charles called his father's death "the greatest blow that has ever fallen on my life."

Apart from the loss of his parents, his life moved smoothly and is quickly told. He took a B.A., an M.A., a Boulter scholarship,* a Bostock scholarship,† first class honors in mathematics, second in "Classical Moderations," third (but still honors) in Litterae Humaniores; he was made Student of Christ Church, sub-librarian, lecturer, full member of the teaching staff, deacon of the Church of England, and—climax Curator of the Common room—a sort of club steward.—‡ In January, 1862, he moved to new quarters in Tom Quad; in November, 1868, he moved again, still within Tom Quad, where he remained.

He traveled once to the continent, including Russia, with Canon Liddon, later Canon of St. Paul's; he took numerous vacation trips to his sisters' home in Guildford and to his aunts' home in Hastings; to Eastbourne, the Isle of Wright, the Lake country, and Wales. He also rowed five miles up the Isis with the Liddell girls, told them the story of *Alice,* and published his books. There is his tangible life.

Virtually all his Dodgson life was academic. He was a student always, and a teacher for twenty-seven of his middle years. He was firmly imbedded in Oxford, sharing its prestige or disgrace. When in 1872 architectural changes in Tom Quad paused, leaving a hideous square box for campanile, Dodgson came out with a comical pamphlet entitled *The New Belfry,* calling the monstrosity every name from "Greek Lexicon" to "meatsafe." The last paragraph deflates tower and university with one arrowy pun: "What traveller is there, to whose lips, when first he enters that great educational es-

---

* Named for Hugh Boulter, rector of St. Olave's, Southwark, archdeacon of Surrey, in the suite of George I. (*Oxford Handbook,* 1858.)

† Named for Joan Bostock of Windsor, who bequeathed in 1630 certain tenements there, the rents to be given to four poor scholars, with preference to her kindred. (*Liber Scholasticus,* London, 1829.)

‡ "The Curator would correspond to the chairman of the House Committee in an American club." (*Catalogue of the Lewis Carroll Centenary Exhibition,* Columbia University.)

tablishment and gazes on its newest decoration, the words do not rise unbidden,—'Thou tea-chest?' "

Except for vacations or trips to London to see a play, he stayed at Oxford, so the simple university routine was all his outer life. Though his family did not move to Yorkshire till he was eleven, he is, like the Brontës, in the Yorkshire tradition; a microscope will yield more of his texture than a telescope.

Charles's forty-seven years at Christ Church started a little before, and ended a little after, the thirty-six years' tenure of Dean Liddell, Alice's father; they corresponded to the period of Oxford's quick crawl from a medieval to a modern university. Charles himself, though modern thought tempted him, was emotionally more in tune with Oxford's medieval aspects.

The physical beauty of the place, especially in spring and summer, wrings nostalgia from many pens. Mrs. Humphry Ward writes: "The chestnuts were all out, one splendour from top to toe: (during 'eights' races) the laburnums, the lilacs, the hawthornes red and white, the new-mown grass, spreading its smooth and silky carpet round the college walls, a May sky overhead, and through the trees glimpses of towers and spires, silver grey, in the sparkling summer air." [1]

Oxford lies "on the spit of gravel between the Isis and the Cherwell, the two branches of the Thames." [2] Boat races were confined to the Isis; the Cherwell was pre-empted by the flat punts then called "water lilies" by the students, as well as by the actual flowers. The ground is low, and sometimes flooded. In a wet year it has been possible to skate or boat on Christ Church meadows.

The university looks even more medieval than it is. "Many of the seemingly aged buildings are merely Stuart." [2] Among the oldest are the School of Divinity and St. Mary's Church, where Mr. Dodgson preached in his last year. Tom Tower, designed by Christopher Wren, holds Great Tom, the bell that tolls 101 strokes—one for each student on the original foundation—at five minutes past nine every night. It had, up to the second war, missed only one night since the anniversary of the Restoration, May 29, 1864, when the students, restrained from attending the ball at Blenheim given for the Duke of Marlborough, cut the ropes in protest. The smaller bells, taken from Osney Abbey in the reign of Henry VIII, are named Hautclerc, Douce, Clément, Austin, Marie, Gabriel, and John. Great Tom, which rings a cracked B flat, weighed 17,000 lbs. originally, and was inscribed *"In Thomae laude resono Bim Bom sine fraude."* Recast, it now reads *"Magnus Thomas Clusius Oxoniensis Renatus Ap. 8, 1680."* [3] Tom Tower belongs to Christ Church, but the great bell calls curfew for the whole university.

"Each college is a little polity in itself," says Goldwin Smith. "Oxford is a federation of colleges." [2] Each college is set apart from the others by special physical features and traditions: Magdalen Bridge, the great Tudor kitchen at Christ Church, the still older kitchen and buttery at Worcester; and each college has its own library and chapel, save that Christ Church, as the bishop's seat, uses the cathedral for its college chapel.

Ruskin, who was at Oxford less than a decade ahead of Charles, writes: "On the whole, of important places and services for the Christian souls of England, the choir of Christ Church was at that epoch of English history virtually the navel and seat of life. There remained in it the traditions of Saxon, Norman, Elizabethan, religion unbroken—the memory of loyalty, the reality of learning, and, in nominal obedience at least, and in the heart of them with true docility, stood every morning, to be animated for the highest duties owed to their country, the noblest of England's youth. The greater part of the peers of England, and, as a rule, the best of her squirealty, passed through Christ Church.

"The cathedral itself was the epitome of English history. Every stone, every pane of glass, every panel of history, was true, and of its time—not an accursed sham of architect's job. . . . The Norman vaults above were true English Norman. . . . The roof was true Tudor—grotesque, inventive, delicately carved; it, with the roof of the hall staircase, summing the builder's skill of the fifteenth century . . . the plain final woodwork of the stalls represented the last art of living England in the form of honest and comfortable carpentry.

"In this choir, written so closely and consecutively with indisputable British history, met every morning a congregation representing the best of what Britain had become—orderly as the crew of a man-of-war, in the goodly ship of their temple. Every man in his place, according to his age, rank, and learning; every man of sense or heart there recognizing that he was either fulfilling, or being prepared to fulfill, the gravest duties required of Englishmen." [4]

But this beautiful building was falling into disrepair. One of Dean Liddell's first acts was to remove the screens that obstructed the students' view of the preacher; then, using the old wood already in the building, he restored the interior to its pristine beauty. Next he remedied the abuses and slovenly conduct of the services. He removed the beer the verger had stored under the pews, near the part of the cathedral reserved for ladies of the deanery. The ancient verger lost another prerogative too—the heavy dog whip with which he had formerly chased the dogs that followed the students to chapel.

Mrs. Humphry Ward had impressive memories of St. Mary's Church in the sixties: "I seem to be looking out from those dark seats under the undergraduate's gallery—where sat the wives of Masters of Arts—at the crowded church, as it waited for the preacher. First, came the stir of the processions; the long line of Heads of Houses, in their scarlet robes as Doctors of Divinity, all but the two heretics, Pattison and Jowett, who walked in their plain black, and warmed my heart always thereby! And then, the Vice-Chancellor, with the 'pokers,' and the preacher [Canon Liddon]. All eyes were fixed on that slender willowy figure, and the dark head touched with silver. The bow to the Vice-Chancellor, as they parted at the foot of the pulpit stairs, the mounting of the pulpit, the quiet look out over the church, the Bidding Prayer, the voice—it was all part of an incomparable performance." [1]

If both Ruskin and Mrs. Ward, who eventually lost their orthodoxy and a good part of their faith, were so profoundly moved by this "incomparable performance," how must it have stamped young Dodgson, who, even at the age of thirty-five, was moved to tears by the beauty of Cologne Cathedral? The dice were loaded against him; as Samuel Butler says in his *Apology for the Devil:* "It must be remembered we have only heard one side of the case. God has written all the books."

And the same could be said for architecture, music, and painting.

In the Middle Ages Oxford sometimes had 13,000 students at one time—nearly all poor. The Town and Gown street battles, marked by ringing of bells on one side, and by blowing of horns on the other, were earnest, bloody, often fatal affrays. Even into the nineteenth century serious battles took place, as recorded in *Tom Brown at Oxford* and *Mr. Verdant Green.*

Gowns originated in the need for something to cover the poor student, and from a philanthropic gift became a compulsion. The undergraduate has a short gown; gorgeousness increases up through the scarlets and crimsons of the doctors' gowns and hoods. But "tufts" are seen no more—the gold tassels worn by noblemen undergraduates on their caps, accompanied by velvet-sleeved gowns and white tabs. Gone are the "servitor's" gown, and his cap without a tassel. Gone, too, are the servitors and gentlemen-commoners, by the Act of 1854. The servitors were the poor young men who worked their way through college by tutoring others for pay—in no sense to be confused with college tutors, permanently on the teaching staff and including the best teachers. In their day the noblemen and gentlemen-commoners paid double fees, had easier examinations, and sat at table with, or even "above," their instructors. In abolishing these distinctions, the university gave back a belated echo to the world without.

As the Victorian hoop skirt muffled a woman, Victorian smugness covered doubt, revolt, potential chaos. Charles was born in 1832, the year in which the Parliamentary Reform Bill passed, and in which Dr. Arnold said: "The English Church as it now is no power can save." [5]

What threatened the English Church? Was it saved—and if so, by what agency? The Industrial Revolution changed the economic base of society, and the French Revolution changed its social base, while British statesmen and clerics were trying to arrange that *plus ça change, plus c'est la même chose.* The waves of scepticism that followed the French Revolution scared the more enlightened of the English clergy, who tried three types of solution besides that of welcome: first, the Tractarian movement, which led to the Oxford Movement, which, in turn, led to desertions to the Church of Rome; second, the Christian Socialist Movement, which dabbled with Chartism and social reform, but essentially tried to change without changing; and finally, internal reform, based on compromise with social reformers, with High Church ritualists, and eventually with the Darwinians and the neo-Malthusians.

Oxford attracted representatives of all schools, and many of the historic duels of ideas occurred there. No Oxford man could escape lively discussions. By the time Charles arrived, however, the great shock had passed, and the Church still stood. Newman had crossed the Rubicon to Rome, taking younger men with him, and building a Roman road that still stands. Pusey, canon of Christ Church, an intimate of Newman's, had been "playing around the precipice, but when he saw his friend plunge over, he drew back in horror." [6] Newman's personal charm and integrity, however, held most of his friends for this life at least, however much they may have doubted his hereafter. Even Charles, staunch Anglican that he was, rejoiced to hear that Newman was delighted with his "Easter Greeting" of 1876.

Canon Pusey was one of the most elaborate forms of a doomed species. His personal life helped to explain him and his influence. His father was fifty-two and his mother thirty-six when they married. Their home was "built on military exactness and religious punctiliousness." [6] His mother, a conscientiously cultured lady, used to sit upright in a hard chair, reading a "good book" with a watch beside her. The boy was delicate, docile, careful, and industrious—but was flogged at school for cutting a pencil at both ends. The fears engendered in some children by the Napoleonic wars made his childhood hideous; he felt the wars established "awe and the Divine presence." His father disapproved of his traveling abroad, and of his engagement, which lasted eight years. Thwarted and deprived on all sides, he developed a remarkable adaptation—he said, "I love my grief better than any hollow joy." [6]

"National apostasy" and other chimeras buried him in

gloom and a sense of sin. He asserted that sin after baptism
was irreparable, and he was one of the moving spirits in a
"declaration of faith" sent out jointly by the High Church
and Evangelicals to every clergyman in England in 1864. This
document affirmed belief in the "verbal inspiration of the
Scriptures and the hopeless torments of future punishment,"
and the clergyman were asked to sign "for the love of
God." [5] Frederick Denison Maurice, leader of the Christian
Socialists, publicly protested against the declaration. Pusey
said that he and Maurice worshiped different gods. Maurice
said that, tremendous as this statement was, it was true.

The Christian Socialists undertook to "build Jerusalem in
England's green and pleasant land," but their task was not a
green and pleasant one. Kingsley's *Alton Locke,* while ex-
posing conditions of the working class, introduced a Christian Socialist leader who blocked the workers just as they were
about to seize control. Kingsley, like the author of *Tom
Brown's Schooldays,* was a disciple of Maurice, and of that
"muscular Christianity," an offshoot of the Christian Socialist
movement, which, in the form of Y.M.C.A.'s, survives into
our time.

The third tendency—the "center"—is at present the official Church of England. Whether it would have skated over
those rough times without the burden of the Christian Socialists in the left hand and the Tractarian-Oxford movement in
the right, is dubious. The Church liberalized itself gradually,
"muddling through" in English style, and Oxford too abolished—gradually—the religious tests and the requirement of
celibacy and ordination for students, and outgrew Bishop
Wilberforce's attitude towards Darwin, divorce, and the workingman. The Bishop was the Holy Terror of his time; he
shows up on the wrong side of every dispute, and Dodgson's
photograph of him betrays the fighting parson. Jowett wrote
Stanley: "Samuel of Oxford is not unpleasing if you will
resign yourself to be semi-humbugged by a semi-humbug." [7]

Men like the sardonic Pattison, who had to wait ten years
to become Rector of Lincoln, like Jowett, who waited fifteen
years for his appointment as Master of Balliol (those were
Mrs. Humphry Ward's "two heretics"), like Liddell, who

spent much of his energy rationalizing Oxford and, eventually, the attitude of Christian gentlemen toward their own times, —such men saved the University and saved the Church from splitting violently between right and left and letting the sceptics grab the pieces. Jowett was religious almost to mysticism, but anti-clerical and unorthodox. He, like Liddell, Pattison, and most of the middle-men, had a sense of humor. "While [Samuel] Johnson's oddities were elephantine, Jowett's were cherubic." [8] He himself said, "In 1856 I had resolved to read the Fathers, and if I found Puseyism I was to become a Puseyite." Instead, among the Tractarians, who inclined to celibacy, "I found that Ward was going to be married! After this the Tractarian impulse subsided, and while some of us took to German philosophy others turned to lobster suppers and champagne. They called it being unworldly." [8] Jowett himself apparently considered marriage at one time, but his romance was blighted.

Charles, unfortunately, came under the ægis neither of the bland and cherubic Jowett nor of the incisive and "pagan" Pattison, and Liddell reached Christ Church too late to save him. He was fated for nomination to the Studentship by the terrible Dr. Pusey. A contemporary recalls the old Canon: "The habit of acting towards others as a confessor seems to have generated a scientific pleasure in religious vivisection. He made an idol of celibacy. His obscurantist dread of worldly influence begot the feeling that no young woman was safe except in a nunnery, no man except in orders. He would urge young men to be ordained at the earliest possible period [the lower age limit was twenty-three], controversial knowledge, systematic reading, theological erudition, might come afterwards, if only the youth were pious, earnest, docile, the great thing was to fix, to secure, to *capture* him. His wife, whom he had loved at eighteen, married at twenty-eight, lost at thirty-nine . . . overwhelming impression of personal saintliness." [9] This is the man who nominated poor Charles Dodgson for a Studentship, thereby "capturing" him—for life, as it happened.

The momentous nomination to the Studentship, once accepted, committed Charles to taking orders and remaining unmarried during his incumbency. His father wrote:

"My dearest Charles:

The feelings of thankfulness and delight with which I have read your letter just received, I must leave to *your conception;* for they are, I assure you, beyond *my expression;* and your affectionate heart will derive no small amount of joy from thinking of the joy which you have occasioned to me, and to all the circle of your home." He adds that he had asked Dr. Pusey to show no special consideration to his son, that Dr. Pusey had then thanked him, and had recently written: "I have great pleasure in telling you that I have been enabled to recommend your son for a Studentship this Christmas. It must be so much more satisfactory to you that he should be nominated thus, in consequence of the recommendation of the College. One of the Censors brought me today five names; but in their minds it was plain that they thought your son on the whole the most eligible for the College. It has been very satisfactory to hear of your son's uniform, steady, and good conduct." [10]

Canon Dodgson's own letter resumes the thread:

"The last clause is a parallel to your own report, and I am glad that you should have had so soon an evidence of what I have often inculcated, that it is the 'steady, painstaking, likely-to-do-good' man, who in the long run wins the race against those who now and again give a brilliant flash, and, as Shakespeare says, 'straight are cold again.' "

It was no small honor Charles had won, and the examinations he passed so well were strenuous disciplines. As soon as a man entered Oxford, he decided whether to work for "honors," or to be a "pass-man." That procedure was different, and even fourth-class "honors" placed a man in a different category than the pass-men, who covered about the ground of an American fresh-water college. In 1858 "responsions" covered Euclid, Books I and III, or algebra to simple equations inclusive, arithmetic principles and practice, including vulgar fractions, decimal fractions, Rule of Three and their applications. The Honors School of 1901 gave a considerably fuller course. In logic there was a choice of three books of Euclid or algebra, first part. But candidates for honors in *Disciplina Mathematica* were examined in pure mathematics. Dodgson took all there was, and came out at the head of the list. When he taught, which was almost at once, the subjects were algebra, Euclid, and arithmetic.

In classical moderations he took a second class. The Honors Schools in Greek and Latin, established in 1852, gave a preliminary examination in the poets and orators, and a final one ("greats") in the historians and philosophers. Philology, ancient literature, and logic, with composition and sight translations in both languages, made up the rest of the examination. The four compulsory books were Homer, Virgil, Demosthenes, and Cicero's *Orations;* then a choice of three books from four optional groups. It was no doubt this part of the examination Charles referred to when he wrote Elizabeth he had to cover "the Acts of the Apostles, 2 Greek plays, & the Satires of Horace." This was when he felt "almost totally unable to read at all: I am beginning to suffer from the reaction of reading for Moderations." For that examination covered, besides two-way translations and grammar, the contents, style, literary history, criticism, and antiquities of these books. Greek prose and Greek and Latin verse were optional.[11] It was supposed to take a year and a half of college work to prepare for "greats," * but Charles, after taking a second class in moderations (1852), gave up classics. What he had learned stayed with him, however. In Russia, in 1867, he followed the part of the service that was in Greek, and he used his Greek Testament in the nineties to make a point about eternal punishment.

In philosophy and history he took third-class honors—but still honors, quite different qualitatively from merely passing. Students in all schools, of course, were examined in religion: "A passage in the Greek Testament is given him to construe, and he is tried by questions arising out of it, whether he has a proper view of the Christian scheme, and of the outline of sacred history. He is expected to give some account of the evidences of Christianity, and to show by his answers that he is acquainted with the Thirty-nine Articles, and has read attentively some commentary on them." [13] For one whose divinity examination had impressed the future archbishop of Canterbury, this was no stumbling-block.

* Originally "greats" applied to any final examinations. Later it referred chiefly to finals in classics.

By no means indifferent to his success, Charles wrote home, giving the order in which mathematical honors had been apportioned: "Enclosed you will find a list which I expect you to rejoice over considerably; it will take me more than a day to believe it, I expect—I feel at present very like a child with a new toy, but I dare say I shall be tired of it soon and wish to be Pope of Rome next . . . : Dodgson, Bosanquet, Cookson, Fowler, Ranken." [10]

Not all men rejoiced in examinations. In 1872 an Oxford paper, *The Light Green,* published a parody on "The Walrus and the Carpenter," called " 'The Vulture and the Husbandman,' by Louisa Caroline." it contained these lines:

> *O Undergraduates, come up,*
> *The Vulture did beseech,*
> *And let us see if you can learn*
> *As well as we can teach;*
> *We can not do with more than two*
> *To have a word with each.*
>
> *Two more came up, and then two more;*
> *And more, and more, and more:*
> *And some looked upward at the roof,*
> *Some down upon the floor,*
> *But none were any wiser than*
> *The pair that went before.*

The nineteenth century brought rapid changes to Oxford. In 1825 changes in the Examination Statutes caused omission of the oath excluding Henry Simeonis, "which ever since the thirteenth century had been a solemn part of the ritual for degrees. In the year before Mr. Gladstone entered Oxford the sins of that forgotten sinner found acquittal, and the venerable vow which proscribed him was silently permitted to expire." [7] In 1859 the first Prince of Wales since Henry VI matriculated at Oxford, and in the same year the traditional sermons commemorating the "martyrdom" of King Charles and the Gunpowder Plot were abandoned. Barely three years later, morning service in English was introduced into Christ Church.

As the University struggled out of its medieval chrysalis, the arts and sciences, as in any renaissance, burgeoned—at first tentatively, then boldly. The school of social criticism in art came in with Ruskin. Carlyle, writing *Sartor Resartus* in 1831, before Karl Marx had reached London and discovered the British Museum, already knew that England was divided into the Dandies and the Drudges. He was a peasant who had broken through the earth's crust and stood, like a tree or a philosopher, his feet on the ground, his head in the clouds, knowing that man must eat and man must read. He had complex branches—through his correspondence with Goethe and Emerson, he set up communications between England, Germany and the United States; between Concord on the one hand, and Heidelberg and Weimar on the other; and between Concord, Massachusetts, and Alcott House in England.

The British literati continued to revolve about the Lake District and the Grand Tour as before, but Carlyle was not without honor at home. The Siamese-twin condition of his social and artistic conscience, while a sport, became a dominant characteristic, and was by him transmitted to Ruskin ("We stand in a minority of two," the older man said), by Ruskin to Morris, and by Morris to Bernard Shaw, who did not indicate his successor. Ruskin, through his friendship with Liddell and Dr. Acland, became an influence. He was called into consultation about the architecture of the Science Museum. The Regius Professor of Medicine had "neither books, drawings, apparatus, nor apartments" [7] for his teaching. In 1847 Dr. Acland said: "In truth there are no proper lecture-rooms or laboratories for students, and it is quite certain that, till provisions are made by which they can work practically themselves without inconvenience, no real progress will be made." [7] By 1855 Lord Derby had laid the foundation stone of the Science Museum.

Of architecture, strictly speaking, Ruskin knew little more than that a building was a box to hold up sculpture, and about the goodness or badness of the box he cared little, as long as it was Thirteenth Century Gothic or Venetian Gothic. The latter style Henry Acland managed to wangle for the Science Museum; but somehow, with all the care for the creativity and enjoyment of labor of the Irish stonecutters, with all the window-work and stone lilies, the building was a horrid fizzle. But it stands, and it housed the first university science teaching in England.

The entomological and other huge collections, stored hitherto in boxes, could at last be exposed for study. Lecture rooms, laboratories, a library, and a glass-enclosed central court were built, and the stage was set for the famous controversy between the apes and the angels. In 1860 Huxley ("Darwin's bull-dog") told Bishop Wilberforce (also known as Soapy Sam): "I should be sorry to demolish so eminent a prelate, but I would rather be descended from an ape than from a divine who employs authority to stifle truth." This helped to turn the tide—in ten years Huxley's attitude prevailed.

Dodgson's diaries have two entries that give us a hint how he reconciled the apes with the angels. At least he was able to be courteous to Charles Darwin. On December 26, 1872, speaking of "unseen correspondents," he says, ". . . thirdly, Mr. Charles Darwin, whose book on *The Expression of the Emotions in Man and Animals* I am now reading, and to whom I have given a print of 'No Lessons Today.'" Mr. Green notes, "This book was illustrated with photographs by O. G. Rejlander" (who photographed Dodgson with his lens).

The other entry on evolution is dated November 1, 1874: ". . . read the whole of Mivart's *Genesis of Species,* a most interesting and satisfactory book, showing, as it does, the insufficiency of 'Natural Selection' *alone* to account for the universe, and its perfect compatibility with the creative and guiding power of God. The theory of 'Correspondence to Environment' is also brought into harmony with the Christian's belief."

Mivart may have solved a headache for Dodgson, but he created one for the Catholic Church, which excommunicated him for this book, later adopting the very position. But in the march of progress pioneers know they are expendable.

Dr. Acland's lectures on anatomy began (not in the Science Museum) in 1845. The students sat at tables 'furnished with little railroads on which ran microscopes charged with illustrations of the lecture, alternately with trays of coffee." [9] Dodgson used this idea in *Sylvie and Bruno:* the Professor, describing his life on another planet, mentions "moving pictures" that run on tracks and pause before the diners at a banquet, supplying them with fresh conversational topics!

One extra-curricular activity always encouraged at Oxford was debating and oratory. In 1857 the Oxford Union building was being constructed under the guidance of Benjamin Woodward. Rossetti, who was visiting him during the Long Vacation, was inspired by the blank spaces on the gallery walls to propose a set of murals. He said: "Its beauty and simple character seemed to make it a delightful receptacle for wall paintings. With the exception of Arthur Hughes and myself, those engaged upon it have made there almost their debut as painters—Jones [Burne-Jones], Morris, Prinsep, and others." Presently the damp walls began to look like "the margin of an illuminated manuscript." [7] Within two years, however, they were fading. If the Pre-Raphaelites had asked Ruskin about the method of applying frescoes, their gorgeous paintings might be there still, but Ruskin had advised them *ad nauseam* on How to Paint and How to Draw, till they could not stomach asking him what he really knew, and what they never dreamed they knew not. In 1870 Rossetti said: "The only remedy now is whitewash, and I shall be happy to hear of its application." [7] In 1875, however, Morris put in a ceiling, from a cartoon drawn in one day—the ceiling still remains. But Morris always was the practical one—it was he who found out the right way of painting glass: on the back; it was he who established the firm of Morris and Company, which practically as well as verbally revolutionized industrial design and public taste. But the undecorated Oxford Union became the proving-ground for prelates and politicians—undecorated, that is, save for a carving, over the door, of the Round Table with Arthur and his Knights, from a design of the omnipresent Ruskin.

Oxford's music movement was temporarily backward. The Holywell Music Room, built in 1748, was the oldest in Europe built expressly for music. Handel gave five performances at Oxford in 1733, and in 1791 Haydn was made Doctor of Music there, at which time the town boasted the best concerts of any place outside London. By the 1820's and 1830's, however, the eclipse was almost total, lasting till 1856, when John Stainer, Frederick Ouseley, Walter Parratt, and Hubert Parry joined to raise the standards once more, and were all knighted for their pains. Thereafter musical organizations cropped up, and by 1892 music teachers' training was introduced.

In the early nineteenth century, music was considered no occupation for an English gentleman. Few amateur pianists and no chamber music groups existed. Heads of Houses gave parties at which young ladies might inoffensively tinkle Haydn, Handel, or Mozart. A man who played piano was considered effeminate, and, except during Lent, music was an impertinent intrusion on the incessant card games. As in mathematics, England was far behind the continent in music. Even in Germany, Bach emerged from his eighty-year eclipse in 1829, when Mendelssohn conducted the *St. Matthew Passion* in Leipzig and demonstrated that the "great Bach" was not the "London Bach," but his father. It took *St. Matthew* thirty-three years to cross the Channel and get a performance in London, and another twenty-one years to be performed at Oxford, in March, 1875, by the joint choirs of Christ Church, Magdalen College, and the Chapel Royal, Windsor. Liddell's influence probably shortened the normal cultural lag from Leipzig to London to Oxford, for by Christmas of that same year Bach's *Christmas Oratorio* was given in Christ Church Cathedral. By that time Arthur Sullivan and George Grove, still innocent of knighthood, had stretched British taste to include Schubert and even the hitherto "barbaric" Schumann.

Bach's renaissance owed nothing to Dodgson. On March 20, 1873, he writes in his diary, "Bach's 'Passion-music' performed in the Cathedral to about 1200 people. I did not go. I think it a pity churches should be so used." Mr. Green adds, "This is the day on which Piscator and Venator visit Christ Church in *The Vision of the Three T's,* and the concert is the 'music' to which the characters with whom they converse are all hastening. Hence also the adapted quotation on the title-page, 'Call you this baching of your friends?' and the description of the final parody as a 'Bachanalian Ode,' which has puzzled commentators."

Dean Liddell helped choose the architect for the new Art Museum, and, as Curator, was responsible for restoring and arranging the treasures, including drawings by Leonardo and Raphael and etchings by Rembrandt. Here again he called in Ruskin as consultant. Though they were only three years apart, the younger man looked up to Ruskin, and finally even secured his appointment as Slade Professor of Art in 1869. Ruskin held this post, with some interruptions, until his mind began to weaken. He also taught in the School of Drawing, and one of his pupils was Alice Liddell.

In the sixties, and long after, the drama remained under a cloud. As late as 1879, Canon Liddon, Dodgson's companion on the Russian tour, write: "I have never been inside a theatre since I took orders in 1852, and I do not mean to go into one, please God, while I live." [14] Studentships were still granted primarily to men who were willing to take orders, which implied no theater-going. Even amateur theatricals were rare, and it required courage to defy orthodox opinion. Our Mr. Dodgson had this courage, though his own father was one who disapproved of the theater. When Mrs. Hatch asked for a prologue for two plays she was putting on at Clevedon House on November 1 and 2, 1871, Charles complied with a not very distinguished prologue which may be found along with another written the following year for the Hatch children, in Williams' & Madan's *Handbook*. But Dodgson had his reservations. Years later he wrote that he was "interested in reading about Oberammergau. I thoroughly believe in the deep religious feeling with which the actors go through with it; but I would not like to see it myself. I should fear that for the rest of one's life the Gospel History and the accessories of a theatre would be associated in the most uncomfortable way. I am very fond of the theatre, but I had rather keep my ideas and recollections of it *quite* distinct from those about the Gospels." [15]

Nevertheless he contributed to the growth of theatricals at Oxford. Jowett too gave a hand, fostering the construction of a theater and the amateur dramatic groups which in the eighties became a genuine dramatic society. Jowett set the condition that the O.U.D.S. should "neither put men into women's parts nor import professional actresses." [16] This seems odd in so thorough a Grecian, but Jowett had his reservations too—even about ancient Greece. Euripides he abominated: "he is immoral when he is irreligious, and when he is religious he is more immoral still." [17]

The sports situation at Oxford was not much better than that of the arts. "At that time there were no football and no sports, only one cricket field, comparatively few men boated. . . . Rich men hunted. . . . At two o'clock, in pairs and threes, the whole University turned out for an eight or ten miles, heel and toe on the Iffley, Headington, Woodstock Roads, returning to five o'clock dinner." [9] So they *did* walk. And Charles Dodgson outwalked them, too. Eighteen or twenty miles was not an unusual daily stint for him. He liked to go to bed tired, but rarely succeeded. Insomnia was his shadow, though he retired late—anywhere from 11:00 P.M. to 3:00 A.M., according to how much work he felt in the mood for. In any case, however, he arose at 6:15, breakfasted at 7:00, and attended eight o'clock chapel.

Afternoon tea seems not to have come into being simultaneously all through England. Accounts of its antiquity vary from family to family. In 1874 Dodgson wrote: " 'Five o'clock tea' is a phrase that our 'rude forefathers' even of the last generation, would hardly have understood, so completely is it a thing of today; and yet, so rapid is the March of Mind, it has already risen into a national institution, and rivals, in its universal application to all ranks and ages, and as a specific for 'all the ills that flesh is heir to,' the glorious Magna Charta." [10] Tea and coffee seem first to have been passed around after the evening meal, and in 1845 Dr. Liddell mentioned taking tea "if any," at nine P.M., before retiring. As long as dinner remained at five, tea could hardly become an institution, but as the dinner hour was pushed back, perhaps because of improved artificial lighting, tea gradually took its place. For children, tea was originally a special treat for rainy days, but it slowly became common.

Five o'clock dinner was disproportionately important at the University. The food was badly prepared and untidily served on pewter plates, the joint being passed around for the students to cut off what they liked. The importance of the meal lay in the fact that attendance at dinner was the test of residence (three years' residence being necessary for graduation), and, regardless of a young man's attendance at lectures, absence from dinner without reasonable excuse caused him to be marked absent. These indifferent, compulsory meals were also scandalously expensive. It was several years after Charles's graduation that the students took the situation in hand, discharged the cook and butler, and appointed a steward to supervise the new kitchen staff and watch expenses.

Every student was entitled to "commons"—an allowance of bread, buttermilk, and ale or beer—supplied at breakfast time from the "buttery" in each college. When the students visited each others' rooms, they sent their "scouts" to carry the commons wherever the breakfast was to be held. The scouts were menservants who took care of one or more students on a given staircase. There were no bells, so the scouts were shouted for through the back windows over the courtyards where they gathered with the "bedmakers," the old charwomen who emptied slops, gossiped, and pounced on leavings. The day of the really poor student was past—even a "servitor" had a scout and bedmaker. The poor student of the early nineteenth century was a "gentleman"—perhaps the son of a clergyman—who could hardly make beds or work with his hands.

Charles seems never to have had any real financial worries. There was enough to take care of the eldest son, and soon he was able to help care for the others. In 1857 he wrote of the year: "I began it a poor bachelor student, with no definite plans or expectations; I end it a master and tutor in Christ Church with an income of more than £300 a year, and the course of mathematical tuition marked out by God's providence for at least some years to come." His brothers Skeffington and Wilfred followed him at Christ Church, and eventually Edwin too, who, like Charles and Skeffington, was ordained.

Charles's Studentship corresponded to a teaching fellowship—"it was not meant to tie him down to lectures and examinations." [10] He tutored men who were working for honors in mathematics, but he was not considered a tutor because he was not responsible for their prowess in other subjects. At that time undergraduates were still treated rather like schoolboys, but "no statute precisely defined what work was expected of them, that question being largely left to their own discretion." [10] There was not much social contact between the students and their instructors, not because of any rules, but because, as Charles said later, "we are rather shy of each other, and I fancy the undergrads as a rule don't care for our society." As a matter of fact, he tended to study by himself, and rarely hurdled the age barrier except when, as in the case of George Baden-Powell, the student was especially congenial to him. After Mr. Dodgson resigned his lectureship, the presence or absence of undergraduates became even more indifferent to him. As Thomas Banks Strong, then Bishop of Oxford, said, "Oxford is almost without event except arrival and departure of students. . . . To those who, like Mr. Dodgson in his later years, pursue their studies in their own way, the presence or absence of the undergraduates is a mere detail. When they are in residence, dinner is in hall, and a gown is necessary; when they are away, dinner is in common room and gowns are not worn." [18]

Every type of student, tutor, and professor wore a different type of gown, and during term was not supposed to be seen without it on the college side of Magdalen Bridge—especially at dinner. A further complication arose from the noblemen's privilege of sitting at the "High Table," above some of their instructors. The noblemen's conversation was not always in keeping with their privileges, and it must have been hard to snub them when they needed it.

In every college there were essentially three "sets"—the "boating set," the "fast set," and the "reading set." ("Reading" is the British word for study—"reading for greats" means "studying for finals.") Men of all sets, however, and their lady-friends, turned out for the boat races that were part of the festivities at the end of term before the Long Vacation. For the full facilities of the college were in use no more than half the year in three terms of eight weeks each. Late in June the sisters and cousins and aunts swept down on the little city —a welcome invasion of the usually monastic atmosphere. They overflowed the High Street and St. Aldate's, fluttered about the colleges, climbed the towers to see the views, bubbled into the libraries, and brought with them a round of "balls, teas, and the grand finale—the evening before Commemoration Sunday, when they promenaded up and down the Long Walk on the arms of brothers, cousins, swains in full fig," [19] until curfew at 9:10. Full fig for gentlemen in 1850 included Wellington boots; dove-colored trousers with two fluted stripes down the sides, buttoned under the foot with broad straps of the same; and "a coat so high in the collar that the hat (real or imitation beaver) rested on it." There was a crescent of thick cloth on the back of the brim, to prevent the beaver from rubbing on the coat collar. Or "a folding *chapeau bras* was carried under the arm—only an apothecary or solicitor would leave his hat in the hall while calling or dining." [20] The hair was worn longer then; it fell over the collar. In fact, in the eighties Dodgson was asking Harry Furniss not to cut the men's hair too short in his illustrations—"that is a fashion that will pass"—and he wore his own hair rather long to the end. "Whiskers drooped or bostrakized. Unless a man was an officer in the cavalry he never wore a beard or moustache—the Duke of Newcastle was the first to wear a beard. Bishops wore episcopal wigs." [20] Bishop Blomfield, who died in 1857, was the last to do so.

During the few days at the end of term, ladies were permitted in the cloistered halls, cubicles, and elegant suites—they hung their cloaks and bonnets on brass hooks usually reserved for the academic cap and gown, rearranged furniture, poured tea, and broke hearts. Those were the days of the boat races, when the eight-oar boats strove for first place, and ladies sat on gilded barges or twittered up and down the river banks, watching the various colleges "bump" one another's boats. The Deans might or might not approve—sometimes there was grumbling and quoting of St. Paul, but the doom of medievalism was the slow encroachment of physical prowess, care for health, and "training." Dodgson, while never to be considered other than in the "reading set," was a tolerably good oar, though it is unlikely he ever rowed in a race. His only reference to athletics is the remark about cricket, that his one attempt to bowl nearly ended in a "wide." [10]

Commemoration Day itself was as medieval as a tournament. Spectators crowded the Sheldonian Theatre to watch the granting of degrees. Doctors in scarlet gowns and the Vice-Chancellor in full regalia, preceded by three beadles (or "bedels") carrying gold and silver "pokers," would be enough to awe the candidates, but besides, the young men must kneel to the Vice-Chancellor in the attitude of medieval homage and receive their degrees in the ecclesiastical Latin of the Middle Ages. Meanwhile, the undergraduates in the galleries were using their annual license to jest aloud and purge the year's accumulation of piety and solemnity. If a candidate had too many debts, the tradesmen were allowed to pluck at the proctor's gown—hence the word "plucking" where an American student says "flunking." This custom was falling into disuse, but Charles witnessed it at least once.

Harvard University has a letter Dodgson wrote to Elizabeth on June 24, 1852, giving his bird's-eye view of Commemoration:

"The Commemoration was a grand sight. I took a long time in getting in, which had to be done by stages like some unpleasant process of cookery: the heat and pressure were tremendous—I spent ¼ of an hour wedged up in a passage, another quarter struggling violently up a narrow winding staircase, sometimes with a man on my head, sometimes getting an arm wrenched [?] round a post, and sometimes crushed away into a corner and hopeless—To make matters worse those above were continually trying to come down, and being told they couldn't they in return told us we couldn't get up, but neither party believed the other. Lastly I spent another ½ with the heels of the boots hitched in among the railings on the other side, through which I got a view of the theatre: resting partly on the hands and partly on a pro-proctor under me, as the feet afforded rather a painful support than otherwise.—In the course of time however I reached the gallery—The gallery for undergraduates and bachelors run round at the top: under that the ladies' gallery, and at the bottom the Dons' & strangers' with more ladies, & in the middle space masters & strangers—the Bp of Oxford and the Bp of Exeter were there; both got loudly cheered: all kinds of subjects were given, some for cheers, some for hisses, but always when they could think of nothing else, they hissed the Junior Proctor.

" 'The Ladies' were cheered under every possible denomination: 'the ladies in pink,' 'the ladies in blue,' 'the ladies in white,' 'the ladies with bouquets,' 'the ladies without bouquets,' &c, &c. The English Verse recitation was loudly cheered: I liked some of it very much, the subject was 'The Feast of Belshazzar.' There were honorary degrees conferred on various people, one an Italian prince, another, I believe, the Bp of New York, &c—" [12]

The day after Commemoration Sunday "everybody" left town—undergraduates, visitors, and many dons and lecturers. This was the ideal time for serious students to stay and do a little quiet work—for actually only half the year was "term time." Dodgson hastened off to Eastbourne or some other vacation resort, or lingered and caught up with his literary or mathematical work. In 1852 he wrote: "Before I left Oxford, I had a conversation with Mr. Gordon, and one with Mr. Tempest on the work of the Long Vacation: I believe 25 hours' *hard* work a day *may* get me through all I have to do, but I am not certain." [12]

He spent the Long Vacation of 1854 at 5 East Terrace, Whitby, reading for the Mathematical Schools with Professor Bartholomew Price, later Master of Pembroke College. After Dodgson's death, Dr. Price wrote of their forty-year friendship. In 1848 Professor Price had published *A Treatise on the Differential Calculus.* His *Treatise on Infinitesimal Calculus* came out in four volumes between 1852-1860. It is hard to see why, with a tutor who by 1858 was doing most of the mathematical teaching in the university, Charles did not work himself into the main stream of mathematics, rather than eddy around in little pools by the shore.

During this particular summer he contributed a not very good poem and story to the *Whitby Gazette,* both signed B.B. Years later, on his Russian tour, he mentioned that the grand staircase of the Schloss in Berlin reminded him of the narrow, irregular streets of the ancient seaport, the White Town of the Danes. Promenading on the long pier, watching the fish auctions, visiting the museum stocked with fossils, observing the jet carvers, Charles and Dr. Price had plenty of opportunity to vary their occupations. But there must have been hard work too, if not quite 25 hours a day, for Charles came out at the head of the examination list.

In the summer of 1856 he spent some time in the English

Lake District, ascending Gable in an icy gale which gave him an attack of facial neuralgia. Once, in his later years, he visited the Isle of Jersey. But he usually spent the Long Vacation either at Eastbourne or on the Isle of Wight. On one of his earliest trips there, in 1859, he visited Tennyson, whom he had met two years previously at Oxford.

In 1857, the same year in which he first met Tennyson, he also made the acquaintance of Ruskin, whom he was to photograph and with whom he was to carry on a long correspondence about art. In May, 1857, he also "breakfasted . . . with Fowler of Lincoln to meet Thackeray (the author), who delivered his lecture on Geo. III in Oxford last night. I was much pleased with what I saw of him; his manner is simple and unaffected; he shows no anxiety to shine in conversation, though full of fun and anecdote when drawn out. He seemed delighted with the reception he had met with last night: the undergraduates seem to have behaved with most unusual moderation." [10]

Thackeray's first visit to Oxford, to judge from a possibly apocryphal story, was not so fortunate. His biographer gives, without being willing to authenticate, an account of the Vice-Chancellor who questioned the novelist before granting a license for the lecture, and who asked if *Vanity Fair* had "anything to do with John Bunyan's book?" The same Vice-Chancellor had never heard of *Pendennis* either, and asked if *Punch* were not a ribald publication. The biographer deduces that the Oxford official was not greatly interested in modern literature.[21]

Among Dodgson's vacation trips, there were at least two visits to Tennyson's home at Farringford, 1½ miles west of Freshwater Gate, Isle of Wight. The poet had taken a house there in 1853; Sidney Dobell said: "The country people are much amazed at his bad hat and unusual ways, and devoutly believe that he writes his poetry while mowing his lawn." In 1859 Dodgson wrote his cousin a long letter about one of the visits to Tennyson. Excerpts follow:

"W. must have basely misinterpreted me if he said that I followed the laureate down to his retreat, as I went, not knowing he was there, to stay with an old friend at Freshwater.

. . . There was a man painting the garden railing when I walked up to the house, of whom I asked if Mr. Tennyson were at home. . . . He said 'He's there, sir,' and pointed him out, and behold! he was not many yards off, mowing his lawn in a wide-awake and spectacles. I had to introduce myself, as he is too short-sighted to recognize people, and when he had finished the bit of mowing he was at, he took me into the house to see Mrs. Tennyson . . . Her husband . . . begged that I would drop in for tea that evening, and dine with them next day. He took me over the house to see the pictures, etc., (among which my photographs of the family were hung 'on the line'), framed in those enamel—what do you call them, cartons? . . . his little smoking-room at the top of the house, where of course he offered me a pipe; also the nursery, where we found the beautiful little Hallam (his son), who remembered me more readily than his father had done . . . up in the little smoking-room, to which we had adjourned after tea, and where we had about two hours' very interesting talk. The proof-sheets of *The King's Idylls* were lying about, but he would not let me look at them. I looked with some curiosity to see what sort of books occupied the lowest of the swinging book-shelves, most handy to his writing-table; they were all, without exception, Greek or Latin . . . He walked through the garden with me when I left, and pointed out an effect of the moon shining through thin, white, cloud, which I had never noticed before—a sort of golden ring, not close round its edge like a halo, but some distance off. . . .

"The next day I went to dinner . . . Tennyson told me that often on going to bed after being engaged on composition he had dreamed long passages of poetry ('You, I suppose,' turning to me, 'dream photographs'). . . . Up in the smoking-room the conversation turned upon murders, and Tennyson told us several horrible stories from his own experience —he seems rather to revel in such descriptions—one would not guess it from his poetry. . . . And so ended one of the most delightful evenings I have spent for many a long day . . . next day . . . showed the photographs to Mrs. T. and the children. . . . The children insisted on reading out the poetry opposite to the pictures, and when they came to their father's portrait (which has for a motto, 'The Poet in a golden clime was born, etc.') Lionel puzzled over it for a moment, and then began boldly, 'The Pope!' on which Mrs. Tennyson began laughing, and Tennyson growled out from the other end of the table, 'Hollo! What's this about the Pope?' but no one ventured to explain the allusion. . . .

No more at present, from
Your faithful cousin,
Charles L. Dodgson

"P.S. Five minutes to 3 A.M.! This comes of beginning letter-writing at night!" [22]

Back at Oxford, the routine began again. Apart from informal "wines" at which the students entertained one another, sociability seems to have been confined largely to dinner and the evening hours. The hall where dinner was served, was, like the cathedral, architecturally glorious. Ruskin again: ". . . Had it only been used . . . for festivity and magnificence—for the refectory daily, the reception of guests, the delivery of speeches on state occasions . . . the hall, like the cathedral, would have had an entirely salutary and beneficently solemnizing effect on me . . . but . . . allowed our Hall to be used for 'collections' . . . the college examination at the end of every term. . . . Scornful at once, and vindictive, thunderous always . . . the majestic torture chamber—vast as the great council hall of Venice, but degraded now by the mean terrors . . . of doleful creatures who had no counsel in them, except how to hide their crib in time . . . a hall about as big as Canterbury Cathedral, with its extremity lost in mist, its roof in darkness, and its company, an innumerable, immeasurable vision in vanishing perspective." [4]

This was the true setting of the Mad Tea Party, where it was always five o'clock, and the meal dragged on with ineluctable, unchangeable associates, eventually producing the sort of phenomena we expect to find in jail, on shipboard, or wherever the same few people are thrown together daily regardless of preferences. The tradition of "Common Room wit" was no doubt greatly exaggerated too.

Charles Stuart Calverley, who left Oxford for Cambridge (and what a pity that his college was Balliol, or that Dodgson's was Christ Church!) had an ear for what went on around him:

"Notes taken at College meetings . . .
"Remarked by the master—that no people give you so much trouble, if you try to collect money from them, as solicitors.
"By the Junior Dean—Except, perhaps, parsons.
"By the Senior Dean—The latter probably because they have not got the money.
"By Mr. A. That a ton weight is a good deal of books.
"By Mr. B. That it is just one o'clock.
"By Mr. C. That that is likely, and that in an hour it will be just two." [23]

In addition to compulsory dinner, there was compulsory chapel. Non-attendance was penalized by writing "lines." "The eight students at the bottom of the list—that is to say, the eight who had been nominated last—had to mark, by pricking on weekly papers called 'the Bills,' the attendance at morning and evening chapel. They were allowed to arrange this duty among themselves, and, if it was neglected, they were all punished . . . an entry in Lewis Carroll's diary for October 15, 1853: 'Found I had got the prickbills two hundred lines apiece, by not pricking in in the morning.' " [10]

Until recently, when overcrowding prevented actual residence in the college buildings, the students were still required to dine in Hall, and remained subject to the police regulations of the Proctor. "They must be in licensed lodgings, as well as in the college, by eight o'clock at night, or they are fined. . . . If a student makes a practice of staying out late, he gets into trouble with the head of his college . . . must not smoke after ten P.M. They rise at eight and invite each other to breakfast; lights are out by midnight. There are walls and watchmen, but freedom of speech is allowed." [24] This was written in 1902, but when Charles came to Oxford, fifty years before, the rules, especially the unwritten ones, were even stricter. Mr. Tuckwell spent a number of pages trying to show that Charles was the sour note in the "joyous cameraderie" of the Oxford set. *What* joyous cameraderie? In the absence of science, art, music, and even sports, on what ground did "society" meet? Halfway between the two *Alice* books, when the arts and sciences were beginning to burgeon, the Heads of Houses, professors, and their families, constituted "a rigid, courtly little group—it was hard, if not impossible, for an 'outsider' to get any footing in Oxford society at all." [25] There was a dearth of women and children, for celibacy was the rule; only the true academic spirit, which was indeed present, gave "society" any vitality. In fact the inhabitants seem to have been as hard up for amusements as transatlantic passengers in the palmy days of this century.

For instance: In 1857 Dr. Liddell and Dr. Acland visited Madeira. On the return trip the sailors caught a large tunny, which was brought back to Oxford, stuffed, and mounted in the Anatomy School. In 1860 it was set in a handsome case in the new museum with an elaborate inscription on *Thunnus quem vides.* "Soon appeared a sham Congregation notice, announcing a statute for the abrogation of the label, and substituting another, *Thunnus quem rides,* a line-upon-line travesty of the first. . . . It was believed to have been roughhewn by Lewis Carroll, handed around the Common Room, retouched by . . . others." [9]

So he could co-operate on a joke, even a rather inflated one. Nor was he wholly unappreciated in his own lifetime and his own milieu, to judge by the popularity of his books at Oxford. A younger contemporary, writing in *The Academy* shortly after his death, said: ". . . His books . . . formed the storehouse for undergraduate nicknames. In my own day it even became the fashion to set them in foolish paradox by the side of Shakespeare. . . . *The Hunting of the Snark* was popularly supposed to contain all the metaphysics in the world."

Mr. Strong remarked on his "unfailing courtesy to those with whom he was brought in contact." [18] But Mr. Tuckwell remained unimpressed. Despite that gentleman's judgment, however, it seems that Dodgson was less solitary than he wished to be, rather than more. One limitation he imposed on himself: by refusing to rise higher in the church than to a diaconate, he was prevented from preaching in the cathedral, which he probably did not care to do, since he rarely availed himself of his existing opportunities for preaching. The real pity is that he lacked both literary and mathematical stimulus among his fellows at Christ Church. Calverley would have been a boon—and how much more Henry John Stephen Smith, also a Balliol man and a really superior mathematician. In 1849 Smith took a Double First at Balliol, where he remained, later becoming Savilian Professor of Geometry. He loved "every form of social enjoyment—from croquet parties and picnics to dinners." [26] His friends compared him to Pascal. What a friend he might have been to Charles, whose artificial isolation fostered whatever oddities he may have started with—an intensification, perhaps, of the oddities around him. His love of logic and cultivated perversity caused him to carry beliefs and customs to their logical conclusions, which was eccentric of him to be sure, and put him to the same sort of embarrassment as Alice met in Wonderland and Looking-Glass land. He was the only reasonable man in the world, recalling the old lady who, watching her son in a parade, exclaimed, "Faith, they're all out of step but Johnny!" Johnny, while he alone may be right (or left), is not likely to be popular in the regiment.

In his later years Dodgson lived more and more unto himself. There were certainly many persons in Oxford who did not know him by sight, and more who did not venture to speak to him. Popular in the free-and-easy way he could never have been, but loved he was, and most of all by those whose love he most treasured—little girls. That very fact worked against him, no doubt, with his celibate colleagues, who were unaccustomed to children.

Physically he lived in comfort. The suite of rooms he occupied from 1868 was the best in the college, and his student-ship never worked him too hard. From the time when his excellent behavior and mathematical pre-eminence won him Dr. Pusey's nomination, he had no financial problems—as long as he accepted ordination and refrained from matrimony.

A letter from his father, written in 1855, follows:

"I will just sketch for you a supposed case, applicable to your own circumstances, of a young man of twenty-three, making up his mind to work for ten years, and living to do it,

on an Income enabling him to save £150 a year—supposing
him to appropriate it thus:—

	£	S	D
Invested at 4 per cent	100	0	0
Life Insurance of £1,500	29	15	0
Books, besides those bought			
in ordinary course	20	5	0
	£150	0	0

"Suppose him at the end of ten years to get a Living enabling
him to settle, what will be the result of his savings:—

"1. A nest egg of £1,220 ready money, for furnishing
and other expenses.

"2. A sum of £1,500 secured at his death on payment of
a *very much* smaller annual Premium than if he had then
begun to insure it.

"3. A useful Library, worth more than £200, besides the
books bought out of his current Income during the
period . . ." [10]

Between the lines his father delicately indicates that Charles
is not expected to remain an eternal celibate. The hints about
furnishings and life insurance point to a possible home and
family, but perhaps the inertia rising from a settled income
fostered his bachelorhood.

Charles's attitude toward money was that of a professing
Christian. For instance, "In February, 1880, Mr. Dodgson
proposed to the Christ Church 'Staff-salaries Board,' that as
his tutorial work was lighter he should have £200 instead of
£300 a year. It is not often that a man proposes to cut *his
own salary.*" [10] At first his eagerness for independence made
him rejoice at each addition to his salary, for instance the
appointment as sub-librarian. He undoubtedly helped his
family, to judge from this entry in his diary, of July 14, 1881:

"Came to a more definite decision than I have ever yet
done—that it is about time to resign the Mathematical Lectureship. My chief motive for holding on has been to provide

money for others (for myself, I have been many years able to retire), but even the £300 I shall thus lose [then they did not cut his salary?] I may fairly hope to make by the additional time I shall have for bookwriting." [10]

In addition to books, he wrote numerous topical pamphlets, which were no source of income, and in which he did not hesitate to take a fling at figures as well-known as himself. Though he had the good sense to publish some of the Oxford pamphlets anonymously, there must have been many who guessed their authorship. Nor did he mind correcting his colleagues where he found them dry, diffuse, or undignified. The famous scene in Wonderland, where the strange creatures have all fallen into the pool, and the Dodo offers them the driest passage he knows, is a quotation from a contemporary historian. The passage:

"William the Conqueror, whose cause was favored by the pope, was soon submitted to by the English, who wanted leaders, and had been of late much accustomed to usurpation and conquest. Edwin and Morcar, the Earls of Mercia and Northumbria—" The author, Havilland Chepmell [2] must have become an enemy.

Dodgson probably made an enemy of the great Benjamin Jowett, translator of Plato, mentor of Calverley, Matthew Arnold, Francis Palgrave, and other literary men, and of the great mathematician, H. J. S. Smith. The outrageously Carrollian pamphlet, *The New Method of Evaluation as Applied to Pi*, broke a lance both *for* and *on* Professor Jowett. "Pi" stood for the Professor's salary. Under Henry VIII, five Regius Professorships were established, at both Oxford and Cambridge, at the then adequate salary of £40 a year. Jowett, as Oxford's Regius Professor of Greek, was still receiving the same £40. After three hundred years, it was beginning to be time to do something about it, and in fact something was about to be done. In 1867, in *The Deserted Parks*, Carroll had written,

In peaceful converse with his brother Don
Here oft the calm Professor wandered on;
Strange words he used—men drank with wondering ears
The languages called "dead," the tongues of other years.

A man he was to undergraduates dear,
And passing rich with forty pounds a year.
And so, I ween, he would have been till now,
Had not his friends ('twere long to tell you how)
Prevailed on him, Jack-Horner-like, to try
Some method to evaluate his pie,
And win from those dark depths, with skillful thumb
Five times a hundredweight of luscious plum—
Yet for no thirst of wealth, no love of praise,
In learned labour he consumed his days.

Jowett was a poor man, and as a youth could not have
taken advantage of the scholarship he won, had not the
Mercers' company raised the small additional sum needed to
keep him in the University. He spent forty years on the translation of Plato which, in spite of recent scholarly improvements, is still the most readable version. Carroll was on the
right side in tilting for him against the whiskered Fafnir that
guarded the treasury. But our hero, like St. Margaret, had
a private imp. And when the pamphlet was published (anonymously) in 1865, the imp had its innings: "Let U equal the
University, G equal Greek, and P equal Professor. Then GP
equals Greek Professor; let this be reduced to its lowest
terms, and call the result J." Lest there be any doubt that
Carroll is calling Jowett the lowest kind of Greek Professor:
"It had long been perceived that the chief obstacle to the
evaluation of pi was the presence of J, and in an earlier age
of mathematics J would have been referred to rectangular
axes, and divided into two unequal parts—a process of arbi-
trary elimination which is now considered not strictly legitimate." Off with his head? The reference is to the fact that
Jowett's position, because of his imperfect orthodoxy, was
never as secure as he deserved. This pamphlet may not have
added to Carroll's popularity. . . .

But after the imp had its way, Carroll's sense of justice
prevailed, and he once more proposed that Pi—the salary—
be raised from £40 per annum to £500, which was done, at
Liddell's and Stanley's insistence. Even Pusey, though he was
opposed to Jowett's religious ideas, had accepted the decision
of the Chancellor's Court that a professor's theological teach-

ing could not be impugned unless it was given in his professorial lectures, and in 1864 he voted for the endowment of the chair; this failing, he helped find the money for the raised salary.

Another Oxford pamphlet of 1876 was the one opposing the removal of Max Müller and the substitution of a Deputy Professor in Comparative Philology at a reduced salary. Müller almost alone was creating the science of etymology on the foundation laid by Leibniz. It was he who placed Sanskrit as the oldest of the co-ordinate Aryan languages—not, as previously supposed, itself the ancestor of the others. Certainly, no assistant could have replaced him. This is the second instance of Carroll upholding another man's salary—only his own seems to have been too high!

But at the same time Dodgson opposed giving Müller an assistant, on the ground that the proposed salary was too low. Something provoked Müller, who retaliated in his essay on Liddell, referring indirectly to Dodgson, Dr. Taylor thinks.[28] Speaking of the dean, Müller wrote, "Even in the university there were those who could not bear him towering high above them as he did, not in stature only, but in character and position. Nasty things were said and written, but everybody knew from what forge those arrows came." It is true that Dodgson usually found himself on the opposite side of almost every reform proposed by Liddell, so that the Dean's supporters were not necessarily his friends.

Other pamphlets, published or republished in 1874, as *Notes by an Oxford Chiel,* still anonymous, were milder than the one on Jowett. One, called *Dynamics of a Parti-cle,* reviewed the election which defeated Gladstone after his eighteen years representing the University in the House of Commons. Another, *Facts, Figures, and Fancies,* dealt with Oxford trivia, but included a good parody of Goldsmith's *The Deserted Village,* and attacked a proposal to make the Parks, or open space near the museum, into a cricket ground.

The funniest of his pamphlets is the one on the *New Belfry,* which structure did not long survive the attack. Dean Liddell had called in an architect named Bodley, whose scheme included a campanile of wood and copper to house the bells taken from the cathedral when the tower was opened up inside to the base of the spire. But meanwhile Mr. Bodley erected a temporary campanile, square and wooden. Carroll christened it the Tea-Chest, adding: "Credible witnesses assert that, when the bells are rung, the Belfry must come down. In that case considerable damage (the process technically described as 'pulverization') must ensue to the beautiful pillar and roof which adorn the Hall staircase." Indeed, the pillar and roof constitute one of the loveliest fan vaultings in the world, and Mr. Dodgson's portrait by Sir Hubert Herkomer hangs in Hall.

The pamphlet presents this etymological lesson; "The word 'Belfry' is derived from the French *bel,* 'beautiful, becoming, meet,' and from the German *frei,* 'free, unfettered, secure, safe.' Thus the word is strictly equivalent to 'meatsafe,' to which the new Belfry bears a resemblance so perfect as almost to amount to coincidence.

"The style is that which is usually known as 'Early Debased': very early, and remarkably debased."

The Vision of the Three T's again attacked Mr. Bodley's art work. Finally, *The Blank Cheque, a Fable,* inquired whether Oxford really proposed to "sign a blank cheque for the expenses of building New Schools [examination rooms] before any estimate has been made of these expenses." His jealousy for Oxford's good fame and good management in no way compensated for his piercing pen.

Too little is known about Dodgson's intimates. Of his elders, the chief seem to have been Dr. Price and Uncle Skeffington. The latter shared—in fact encouraged—Charles's passion for gadgets. A letter of 1852 says:

"He [Uncle Skeffington] has as usual got a great number of new oddities, including a lathe, telescope stand, crest stamp (see the top of this note-sheet) a beautiful little pocket instrument for measuring distances on a map, refrigerator, &c &c. We had an observation of the moon and Jupiter last night, and afterwards live animalcules in his large microscope: this is a most interesting sight, as the creatures are most conveniently transparent, you see all kinds of organs jumping about like a complicated piece of machinery, & even the circulation of the blood. Everything goes on at railway speed, so I suppose they must be some of those insects that only live a day or two, and try to make the most of it." [12] Charles seems to have had a great deal in common with Uncle Skeffington and to have enjoyed his occasional visits. In his letters he inquires for him.

And when it came time to try something new, something that became of major importance in Dodgson's life, he turned to his uncle for help. In the diary for January 22, 1856, he enters: "Wrote to Uncle Skeffington to get me a photographic apparatus, as I want some other occupation here, than mere reading and writing."

The old neighbor and playfellow from Croft, Thomas Vere Bayne (1819-1908), crops up again. By now he is the Reverend T. Vere Bayne, who matriculated at Christ Church in June, 1848; took his B.A. in 1852, with a Second Class in litteræ humaniores and his M.A. in 1855; and became Proctor in 1867. From 1852-72 he was Tutor at Christ Church; from 1863-77, he was Senior Censor; and in 1885 he became Keeper of the Archives. He appears in no encyclopædia, in no biographical dictionary, and in no Who's Who, except the British Clergy List. The Times published a brief obituary, and the Oxford Magazine said: "He was not a scholar in the modern sense, though he made some modest contributions to Jelf's Greek Grammar, a Christ Church book. But he had never annotated a classic, nor invented a new hypothesis, nor broken a lance with Carp of Brasenose. . . . Nor was he a preacher nor an orator. Few had ever seen him in the pulpit; still fewer on the platform. Devout and regular in all the observances of the Church, he yet shrank from publicity of any kind. . . . Stiff as he was where honour or conscience or the social amenities were involved, he was one of the kindest, most courteous, most companionable of men; very simple, very modest, very affectionate, very human. He was fond of a good story either to tell or to hear, but there was no gall in his pleasant chat. An occasional touch of gruffness was the utmost sign of disapproval that his sweet temper allowed him to express." [29] A blurred outline of Bayne emerges, like the

Baker in the *Snark*. Mildness, vagueness, an undifferentiated sort of goodness.

He had a sense of humor, too. Alice's son, Wing Commander Caryl Hargreaves, wrote in a letter: "I remember T. V. Bayne well and used to go to luncheon with him in his rooms and often saw him with the Skenes. He was a delightful companion full of anecdotes and humor, and one of the kindest people that ever stepped."

Bayne was always one of the first to receive an inscribed copy of Carroll's books, but the inscriptions illuminate nothing except the continuity of the friendship. They range from "Thomas Vere Bayne, with the author's sincere regards," to "To T.V.B., from C.L.D." Some inscriptions include the "Rev.," and the most effusive is the last, in the copy of *Sylvie and Bruno Concluded*—"T. Vere Bayne, from his old friend the Author, Dec. 27, 1893." What can we expect from a man who signed himself "C. L. Dodgson" to his sisters?

Like a true friend, Bayne did not hesitate to call Dodgson's attention to what he considered remiss. At the time of a dispute about some rebuilding at Oxford in which Dodgson took sides, he notes in his diary for November 4, 1874: "Received a letter of remonstrance from Bayne: he thinks me disloyal in protesting against the decision of a majority. This I had not done: my 'protest' being only against cloisters, which are not yet decided on."

Evidently Bayne's mother lived in London. Numerous entries in the diary record visits to her. On July 10, 1878, he says "Dined with Mrs. Bayne, and went with her and T. V.B. to the Haymarket to see Southern [sic] in *The Hornet's Nest*, a feeble production." The reference is doubtless to the American actor, E. A. Sothern.

Bayne showed his regard by collecting scrapbooks of rare and ephemeral Carrolliana, which he willed to the Christ Church Library. No more is known about him except that he was Commissary for the Bishop of Gibraltar from 1894-1904, a post that seems not to have taken him out of England. Dr. Strong writes: "Commissary means a deputy, sort of vice-bishop if I may coin a phrase. He acts in the Bishop's absence." [30] Finally, Bayne was instrumental in raising a statue to Dean

Liddell in Christ Church, and assisted in the writing of the Dean's biography.

Another friend of Dodgson's was Charles Kingsley's brother, Henry, a roving, irresponsible, charming novelist, whose books had a contemporary vogue. And of course there was Dr. Bartholomew Price, whose letter to Collingwood mentions "forty-four years of unbroken friendship."

The principal juxtaposition the microscope discloses is that between Carroll and the Liddell family. Charles was often in conflict with Dr. Liddell, the father of his three fates, and the two men's lives were criss-crossed. Liddell became Dean of Christ Church in 1855, less than a year after Charles took his B.A., and before he began teaching. In honor of the new Dean, Charles was made "Master of the House." This meant "A man has all the privileges of a Master of Arts of the University," [10] though, not having eaten enough dinners in Common Room, he was not yet eligible for the title.

Also in 1855 Charles became sub-librarian, thus gaining access to the litle room looking down on the Dean's garden. Perhaps as he sat there, wishing for the key to childhood that would admit him to the garden, the germ of *Alice* sprouted. He told the story extempore in one afternoon—how long it must have been germinating! Miss Ethel Arnold, granddaughter of Thomas, niece of Matthew, and sister of Mary Arnold Ward, says: "In the summer term, and particularly the early part of it, Oxford is a city of dreams; effort of any sort is more or less difficult, and one lives on from day to day in a sort of trance, full of vague aspirations, and feeling very far removed from the actualities of life. Library . . . cricket . . . grass . . . bells . . . moon . . . fragrant air." [25]

Many elements of this excerpt appear in *Alice*—dreams, grass, bells, fragrant air. The library is present, but masked— it was from the library window that Dodgson had been wistfully gazing down on the Dean's garden where the little girls played demurely under the trees, as he worked in the little room that opened into the Great Hall of the library, the image of the Hall of Tears.

"Nobody expected anything of this shy young man," [31] wrote Alice Liddell's son, Captain Hargreaves, in *The New York Times*. This shy young man, rather tall, so straight he leaned over backwards, with one shoulder higher than the other; thin and pale, with dark wavy hair that "wanted cutting"; rather good-looking, despite incongruities of form and movement—the young man with the "two profiles," * the crooked smile, the trembling upper lip, the housemaid's knee and jerky gait, the stammer, the high-pitched voice, the slow, precise speech, the one deaf ear, but also with the deep blue eyes that held yours, and that changed from a warm, kindly glance to a suppressed twinkle, while the large hands gripped yours with unexpected strength—was to surprise a good many persons, including himself. His grandfather's literary style was admirable and his father's writings fill a column of the British Museum Catalogue—the fluidity of his ink was taken for granted, and no more was expected of him than the docility which enabled Dr. Pusey to capture him, and the intelligence that enabled him to capture a lifelong sinecure.

Dean Liddell was an innovator in education. Despite numerous handicaps, he acquitted himself remarkably well as Head of Westminster School—a post he took to earn enough money to marry Lorina Reeve in 1845. Ten years later he was recalled to Oxford as Dean of Christ Church. He had never relinquished certain Oxford posts, nor had he ceased to agitate for reforms on many fronts—educational, artistic, architectural, financial, social. When he returned to Oxford his several positions gave him the chance to ripen most of his projects before his retirement in 1891, after thirty-six years of deanship.

The Dean was a man of unusual vigor and consistency. The Greek Lexicon he started as an undergraduate never left him till the last edition appeared in his eighty-seventh year. Originally based on a German-Greek lexicon by Passow, this monument of love and learning after three editions outgrew its source and became the sole work of Liddell and Scott. After Scott's death Dr. Liddell carried on alone, keeping the Lexicon open on his standing desk, and working at it between lectures and at odd times. His infinite committee meetings dragged on endlessly, unless he was chairman. His device against total annihilation was—doodling. On the pile of pink blotters that were part of every meeting, the Dean would

* See Appendix A.

doodle trees, figures, architectural designs—and more trees. Some that survive indicate that Ruskin was right in lamenting the Dean's abandonment of art. "You kept dictionary-making instead of drawing trees at Madeira in colour," [7] he said. Sir William Richmond also thought Liddell might have made a career in art.

Awe-inspiring he was, especially in his later years. "I have heard that boys used to say they could not tell Liddell a lie and look him in the face; and I have heard him say 'I can call no man a gentleman if he can act a lie, even if he does not tell it.' "[32] Max Müller said that whenever Liddell was chairman of committees, the tone was noticeably raised. No gossip, no backbiting, no good academic fun, not even permissible parliamentary tricks for railroading through his own measures. But when real fun was at hand he was no wet blanket. His children's vacations were never complete without him, and he could take a joke on himself. His standard joke was, when someone found an error in the Lexicon, to call it Dr. Scott's. A boy at Westminster School made hay in a verse contest with this:

> Two men wrote a Lexicon, Liddell and Scott;
> Some parts were clever, but some parts were not.
> Hear, all ye learned, and read me this riddle,
> How the wrong parts wrote Scott,
>   and the right parts wrote Liddell.[33]

The victim was delighted and gave the versifier a prize. It is hard to imagine Dr. Arnold enjoying such a joke; in fact, he was said to be humorless, and his only recorded jest was, concerning the Oxford movement, "If I had two necks, I should have a good chance of being hanged by both sides." [34]

Awe-inspiring himself, Dr. Liddell was not awed by the great. When his portrait, by Watts, was presented to him with speeches in 1876, he wrote: "I had to sit under a shower-bath of praise from Mr. Gladstone." [35] But the Dean was accustomed to high society. He had been chaplain to Prince Albert in 1846, and young Edward was put in his charge at Oxford. The prince frequently dined at the Liddells' home, dislocating their dinner hour to the fashionable one of seven-thirty.

It was under Liddell that the new block of buildings was erected. When the chapter house and cloisters were restored, Dodgson expressed himself in *The Three T's*. Two of the eight canonries were suppressed in the interest of modernization, and the powers of the dean and the chapter, including the power to nominate students, were curtailed. A few years later, the Studentship Charles received from Dr. Pusey would have been won competitively.

Although Charles and Dr. Liddell were twenty-one years apart—the former was a child when the first edition of the Lexicon appeared—the two men went downhill at the same speed. The Dean resigned in 1891 because of failing strength, and in the following year, perhaps also for reasons of health, Charles resigned his one office, the Curatorship of the Common Room. Finally, the two men died four days apart.

They lived diagonally across Tom Quad from each other from 1862-8. Dodgson's earlier rooms overlooked the Board Walk. The Deanery, built by Cardinal Wolsey, on one side overlooked Tom Quad, and on the other, the garden under the Library windows, whence Dodgson, then sub-librarian, could watch the sisters playing croquet. Nothing noisier was permitted them in the college precincts, and their friend tried to introduce variety by inventing "castle croquet," to be played with ten balls, ten arches or wickets, five flags or stakes, etc.

The odd thing about this friendship is that it began with a little boy, an animal Dodgson later had little use for. In his diary for March 6, 1856, he notes: "Made friends with little Harry Liddell (whom I first spoke to down at the boats last week), he is certainly the handsomest boy I ever saw." Not long after, he met Lorina—Alice came later.

He spent a good deal of time with them, being perhaps lonely for feminine company, especially young company. He was accustomed, we must remember, to a home with seven sisters. A recent Oxford historian remarks: "Before the seventies you might almost have counted the University ladies on your fingers, though Mrs. A. L. Smith's story of the four whom some dignified lady still spoke of regretfully, as late as 1879, as having formed a delightful circle, must, I think, be apocryphal."

Oxford exhales a strange blend of stuffiness and Arcadia, in the very temper of *Iolanthe*. The undergraduates, drawn at this time from the "upper classes" rather than from any cultural level, had not the highest intellectual standards. Flatly, till Liddell, Huxley, Jowett, Pattison, Ruskin, and others set bits of yeast working on them, they were rather a Philistine lot. For more reasons than one, Dodgson found his best companionship in these young ladies. Cut off from older women, and from the friends he might have made, say, at Balliol, he gradually withdrew into himself, emerging freely only when he felt—quite literally—at home!

Among the factors favorable to the burgeoning of "Lewis Carroll" and a whole new literary style, was the influence of the Liddell girls, especially Alice, a singularly beautiful child with a keen imagination and sense of humor—the perfect constellation to release Dodgson's genius. Mighty man though Dr. Liddell was, Alice did not spring full-panoplied from his brain. In the Liddells' home, as in the Dodgsons', love and charm prevailed, and circumstances favored the flowering of lovely children. The gracious and literate daughters of the Dean gave the young sub-librarian an appreciative audience, and he repaid them many times over. Outer circumstances and inner forces gradually molded him, however, into a bizarre yet fruitful form.

Chapter 5

Pillow Problems

I engage with the Snark—
every night after dark—
In a dreamy, delirious fight:

TESTIMONY TO DODGSON'S INSOMNIA includes the title of his book, *Pillow Problems*, and the various devices he used when sleep denied itself to him. He invented several night-writing aids; the best was the Typhlograph, which he later rechristened the Nyctograph. This was a series of cardboard squares; in a blind alphabet of his own invention he wrote on the edges and corners of the squares.

Since his dream self was exiled to the nursery, it gradually split from his acceptable public self. This is the Dodgson-Carroll split, but it must finally appear that he did not always present the same two segments. Once having learned the technique of separation, since he was, like Kipling's solitary mariner, a man of infinite-resource-and-sagacity, he could, within the limits of his patterns, split where he would. In those long nights of insomnia, the interaction betweeen conscious choices and unconscious desires gradually perfected his poetic instrument.

A rich source of Carrollian anecdote, Isa Bowman's little book gives clear instances of his dualism. Isa, who played *Alice* on the stage and was one of the most favored child friends, had the actress temperament. While this hardly insures literal accuracy, it enables her, as a woman who from childhood was close to Carroll and responded to his play, to light up facets that escaped his nephew.

Isa relates how Charles Dodgson overtook Lewis Carroll on a walk. One afternoon, when he had been strolling with her in Christ Church meadows, holding her hand and explaining how rivers flow downhill to the sea, another don came upon them suddenly. Lewis Carroll vanished and the embarrassed Mr. Dodgson emerged. For the rest of the walk,

107

she says, he "became difficult to understand and talked in a nervous and preoccupied manner." [1] The shyness and stammering that left him in his hours of ease with girl-children, returned abruptly when he was jolted back into the adult world.

In 1888 the strain took a new form. Collingwood claimed that overtaxing his brain caused optical delusions of "seeing moving fortifications," [2] now called scintillant scotoma. Apart from his eighteen-mile strolls, he did spend most of his time reading or writing, but this was natural use of his natural powers. Something else caused the strain.

In the introduction to *Pillow Problems* he gives his own bedtime solutions, disclaiming any unusual mathematical abilities. "I intend my little book . . . rather for the . . . class of *ordinary* mathematicians." He describes his inability to clear his mind of worries on retiring. His problem is not to put himself to sleep—mathematical games will not do that; but if the brain is too wakeful, the games keep it from mischief and worry.

He took those long walks daily, and tried to retire physically fatigued. He also had a fair amount of mental work to do, but his short hours of sleep seem to have produced no ill effects. His letters sometimes mention that it is three o'clock, and it is not certain he fell asleep promptly even then. He surely had a constitution that required little sleep, but in addition he had some chronic recurrent problem—a pillow problem indeed.

"It is not possible . . . to carry out the resolution, 'I will *not* think of so-and-so.' (Witness the common trick, played on a child, of saying 'I'll give you a penny, if you'll stand in that corner for five minutes, and *not once* think of strawberry jam!' No human child ever yet won the tempting wager!) But it is possible . . . to carry out the resolution 'I *will* think of so-and-so' . . . the worrying subject is practically annulled. It may recur, from time to time—just looking in at the door, so to speak. . . . There are sceptical thoughts, which seem for the moment to uproot the firmest faith: there are blasphemous thoughts, which dart unbidden into the most reverent souls; there are unholy thoughts, which torture, with their hateful presence, the fancy that would fain be pure.

Against all these some real mental work is a most helpful ally."

His readers misunderstood him, he thought, for in the preface to the Second Edition he says:

"In the title of the book, the words 'sleepless nights' have been replaced by 'wakeful hours' . . . in order to allay the anxiety of kind friends, who have written to me to express their sympathy in my broken-down state of health. . . . I have never suffered from 'insomnia': and the over-wakeful hours, that I have had to spend at night, have often been the result of the over-sleepy hours I have spent during the previous evening!"

But actually he was a hard, even an over-conscientious worker, "always disliking to break off from the pursuit of any subject which interested him; apt to forget his meals, and toil on for the best part of the night, rather than stop short of the object which he had in view. . . . Though this passion for violent labor was irregular, he never seemed idle; his mind was original and perpetually busy, and the general average of his working time was high." [3]

In fact he worked even in bed, with his Nyctograph and other night-writing gadgets. The dream quality of his writings arose undoubtedly from his skill in catching flashes that came in the borderland state, as well as from his ability to induce dreamy states in the daytime. A former child friend says: "He found that his most absurd ideas came to him on the borderland of dreams."

His devices for resting from emotional tensions included all sorts of games—halma, chess, backgammon, logic, and mathematics; puzzles and games of his own contriving (he invented the "ladder" puzzle, which he called "doublets"); the repeating of "memory gems"; and finally the escape through the looking-glass and the enchanted garden.

The introduction to *Sylvie and Bruno* dwells on memory gems. Among the books he hoped to edit were: a children's Bible and a book of selections from the Bible—". . . not single texts, but passages of from 10 to 20 verses each—to be committed to memory. . . . Thirdly, a collection of passages, both prose and verse, from books other than the Bible. . . . These two books . . . will help to keep at bay many anxious thoughts, worrying thoughts, uncharitable thoughts, unholy thoughts." He then quotes from a contemporary theologian: "Let these [selections] be to him the sword, turning everywhere to keep the way of the Garden of Life from the intrusion of profaner footsteps."

This solemn thought brings us to the threshold of the vestry, and introduces the principal character in Dodgson's life—his God. Who was the God of the Dodgsons and the Liddells, and especially of Charles Dodgson? Was this a male or female deity—Jahweh or Isis, Jesus or Mary?

Charles had one of his portmanteau answers. The female aspect, Mother Isis, looks a good deal like Mother Sylvie. Carroll thought his greatest poem was the theme song of *Sylvie and Bruno*—one of his last works, and to his own notion, the best:

A SONG OF LOVE

Say, what is the spell, when her fledgelings are cheeping,
That lures the bird home to her nest?
Or wakes the tired mother, whose infant is weeping,
To cuddle and croon it to rest?
What's the magic that charms the glad babe in her arms,
Till it coos with the voice of the dove?
'Tis a secret, and so let us whisper it low—
And the name of the secret is Love!
    For I think it is Love
    For I feel it is Love
    For I'm sure it is nothing but Love!

Say, whence is the voice that, when anger is burning,
Bids the whirl of the tempest to cease?
That stirs the vexed soul with an aching—a yearning
For the brotherly hand-grip of peace?
Whence the music that fills all our being—that thrills
Around us, beneath, and above? . .
'Tis a secret: none knows how it comes, how it goes:
But the name of the secret is Love!
    For I think it is Love
    For I feel it is Love
    For I'm sure it is nothing but Love!

Say, whose is the skill that paints valley and hill,
Like a picture so fair to the sight?
That flecks the green meadow with sunshine and shadow,
Till the little lambs leap with delight?
'Tis a secret untold to hearts cruel and cold,
Though 'tis sung by the angels above,
In notes that ring clear for the ears that can hear—
And the name of the secret is Love!
> *For I think it is Love*
> *For I feel it is Love*
> *For I'm sure it is nothing but Love!*

The author of *Jabberwocky, Father William, The Walrus and the Carpenter,* and countless other memory gems called *this* his greatest poem. . . .

Carroll's idea of love, God, and heaven was bound up with his idea of mother, as his *Easter Greeting,* originally written for an edition of *Through the Looking-Glass,* shows. The cumulative effect is overwhelming—the Greeting should be quoted entire—but it is too long:

AN EASTER GREETING

TO

EVERY CHILD WHO LOVES

"ALICE"

"Dear Child,

Please to fancy, if you can, that you are reading a real letter, from a real friend whom you have seen, and whose voice you can seem to yourself to hear wishing you, as I do now with all my heart, a happy Easter.

Do you know that delicious dreamy feeling when one first wakes on a summer morning . . .? It is a pleasure very near to sadness, bringing tears to one's eyes like a beautiful picture or poem. And is it not a Mother's gentle hand that undraws your curtains, and a Mother's sweet voice that summons you to rise? To rise and forget, in the bright sunlight, the ugly dreams that frightened you so when all was dark?

Some perhaps may blame me for thus mixing together

things grave and gay; others may smile and think it odd that anyone should speak of solemn things at all, except in church and on a Sunday. . . .

I do not believe that God means us thus to divide life into two halves—to wear a grave face on Sunday, and to think it out-of-place to so much as mention him on a week-day. . . . Surely their innocent laughter is as sweet in his ears as the grandest anthem that ever rolled . . . surely your gladness need not be the less for the thought that you will one day see a brighter dawn than this—when lovelier sights will meet your eyes than any waving trees or rippling waters—when angel-hands shall undraw your curtains, and sweeter tones than ever loving Mother breathed shall wake you to a new and glorious day—and when all the sadness, and the sin, and the darkened life on this little earth, shall be forgotten like the dream of a night that is past!

Your affectionate friend,
Lewis Carroll"

Easter, 1876

Besides showing how memories of his mother evoked thoughts of heaven, poignant passages in this letter high-light the religion of his time. First, the long apology for thinking of God and of laughter together, reminiscent of Nietzsche, and of Shaw's disgusted remark that "the church that was founded with a jest becomes the church in which you must not laugh." Shaw also speaks of the "rank diabolism" that excluded beauty and gaiety from the English Church.

Dodgson seems never to have feared death. He knew he was doing his best, and it would be a relief to escape from the constant conviction of sin into eternal blessedness. How little sin one can find, either in his life or in his heart—how unkind of his God to punish the best of his children with this awful burden, from which death is a release! Even the death of children seemed natural enough—it was certainly common enough in those peaceful days. What nightmares would a good man have, and expect even children to have, so that they dread the night? The man who denies or stifles an essential part of his own nature is more in danger of nightmare than the one who consciously restrains unsuitable impulses—

such as the common urge to "take a bite out of" a nice fat
baby. One who, through fear of his own nature, or through
fear of upsetting preconceived notions of how he "ought to
be" and therefore "is"—will deny having had such notions.
The example of actually biting the baby clarifies the idea.
Most of us will admit to having impulses we prefer to restrain. But Carroll never heard of these impulses except
through the Snark, Father William, and his other underworld
messengers, and would not ask himself whether, in cannibal
isles, he too might not be a cannibal.

Dr. Greenacre[4] gives a hair-raising description of the
"primary-process" world of early childhood, before speech
is developed, which she believes to be the secret of
Dodgson's charm for the rest of us, bought at great expense to himself. It is the world in which "animals, humans,
and flowers have similar characteristics and similarity in appearance or other attributes is enough to furnish the presumption of identity; inanimate objects become animate;
there are constant allusions to creatures eating each other up;
behavior is constantly controlled by threats of extinction,
and morals do not exist except as the sing-song maxims of
the little girl observer. All that is about as close a portrayal
as can be accomplished in language of that realm in childhood's development when the child is emerging from its
primitive state of unreason, to the dawning conception of
consequence, order and reason. It belongs to that time, generally between fifteen and thirty months, when the language of
body activity and response is being supplanted by verbal language. Then utter dependence on the adult's omnipotent
power is giving way to awareness of the increased autonomy
of walking and talking; then conceptual thought and memory
are developing, and past and future gradually become separate from now.

"In the language of the psycho-analyst this is the period
of transition from primary-process to secondary-process of
the psychic life. . . . Charles Dodgson the ultra-rationalist
has, as Lewis Carroll, so far reproduced this period of
'feeling-thought' in *Wonderland* (with perhaps a little less
success in *Looking-Glass*), with such gentle ease that it
awakens in the reader a feeling of fantastic familiarity with

an extravaganza of outlandish nonsense. Such an extraordinary gift . . . can come only from some special exigencies in Dodgson's own life from this early period, such that it remained unusually active till it came forth and demanded expression in his stories for little girls.

"Stories for children that ignore children's fears lack substance. A man who could write 'I engage with the Snark/ every night after dark/ In a dreamy, delirious fight,' had something to say to children."

The father aspect of Charles's God is less like the awful Jahweh than like the just but kindly Archdeacon Dodgson. Nearly the last work Carroll wrote was a paper on "Eternal Punishment," which was to have been part of a book on religious essays.

Here is the problem he states, with a wealth of detail that shows he has been working on it for years:

"I believe that God is perfectly good. Yet I seem compelled to believe that He will inflict Eternal Punishment on certain human beings, in circumstances which would make it, according to the voice of my conscience, unjust, and therefore wrong.

"This difficulty, when stated in logical form, will be found to arise from the existence of *three* incompatible Propositions, each of which has, apparently, a strong claim for our assent. They are as follows:—

"I. God is perfectly good.

"II. To inflict Eternal Punishment on certain human beings, and in certain circumstances, would be wrong.

"III. God is capable of acting thus."

After ten pages of close reasoning, definition, and examination of possibilities, he suggests:

"We are now supposed to have taken up the following position: 'I do not believe that the Bible tells us that God has declared He will inflict Eternal Punishment on human beings, who are either incapable of sinning, or who, being capable of sinning, have ceased to sin.' "

He says this side-steps the difficulty which would have led to the abandonment either of Christianity or of faith in one's own conscience; that the biblical passage used as authority for the doctrine of eternal punishment depends on the translation of the word *aion* (or æon).* If this means not "everlasting," but merely "a very long time," then the Bible does not say that infinite punishment will be visited on finite sin. (His Greek Testament came in handy!) He states the four logically possible propositions—(1) that endless punishment would be unjust—therefore God is capable of sinning. (2) That God is perfectly good—therefore he would be right even if conscience says, "No." (3) That God is good—such punishment is wrong—but the Bible says he could act thus. Hence the Bible is unreliable. (4) That God is perfectly good—such punishment is wrong—God would not act thus —the Bible (in English) *seems* to say he acts thus—therefore the translation is wrong, and the Bible, my conscience, and my God are all trustworthy.

"Anyone of these four views may be held without violating the laws of logical reasoning.

"Here ends my present task; since my object has been, throughout, *not* to indicate one course rather than another, but to help the Reader to see clearly *what* the possible courses are and *what* he is virtually accepting, or denying, in choosing any one of them." [5]

Carroll is not playing fair here. Actually, he *is* telling the reader what to think. In *Bibliotheca Sacra,* in 1878, an American pastor, Cephas Kent, uses the identical device to produce the opposite conclusion, that the Bible *does* say "eternal punishment." [6] Checking the given references and other articles, as well as Liddell and Scott, and Thayer's *Greek-English Lexicon of the New Testament,* we find that Dodgson was guilty of sophistry. Whether he liked it or not, and whatever conclusions may be implied, the promise of eternal life in the Bible is identical with the promise of eternal punishment. His structure has no logical flaws, however, other than a basic false premise, and he never learned that neither logic nor mathematics yields truth as cows yield milk. For himself he could never have been troubled: first of all, his behavior was blameless, and second, in *Sylvie and Bruno,* he shows an intimation of the tedium of any sort of eternal life. His worry was purely for the honor of his God and the safety of his erring brethren.

* αιων.

The controversy on eternal punishment had been going on openly since Frederick Denison Maurice had first challenged the orthodox interpretation in 1853, and had lost his teaching position at King's College for his pains. Maurice considered the doctrine of eternal punishment "a human tradition, resting on no adequate scriptural authority," [7] and selected a passage from St. John (xvii, 2, 3) to explain "eternal life" as he chose to understand it. His case differs little from Dodgson's; though less sophistical, it is equally impossible to "prove."

Maurice and Ruskin may have collaborated, since they were colleagues at the Working Men's College. In a speech before a working class audience in 1867, Ruskin used a form closer to Dodgson's, again presenting four possible theories about the Bible and, supposedly, giving the audience free choice. Though by 1867 Ruskin was coming a little loose from orthodoxy, all four men were forced by their preconceptions to play with loaded dice.

The Misses Dodgson spoke of the subtle way their uncle had of challenging the most elevated ideas without giving anyone a handle by which to pin him down. Consciously, he accepted the fourth proposition, but he must have entertained the others, which he brings to mind as he does the latent horrors in his dream books, laying them to rest for the moment, but leaving them in the offing. Of course he is at a disadvantage compared with the other three men who treated the same subject—since he came later, he was closer to the awakening from the dream of a revealed scripture. Despite his orthodox background, the contemporary of Bishop Colenso, Nietzsche, Darwin, Karl Marx, Samuel Butler, and Ibsen, could not wholly shut out the spirit of the age. His thinking mind viewed all possibilities. His habits, reinforced by love, brought him back to the old pattern: instead of slaying the Jabberwock, he was eaten by the Snark; but he must have been a prickly mouthful after catching goose flesh from nineteenth century winds of doctrine.

At the end of every year he reviews it, always charging himself with negligence, indolence, and things undone. During the year he also gave himself an occasional prod. On September 1, 1857, he records: "I am now settled into

a tolerably regular habit of three or four hours' work every
morning, Divinity and Mathematics alternately. One good
result, at least, springs out of my former habits of indolence,
and that is a continual spurring to work, as a retribution for
lost time."

On the last day of that year he makes a resolution: "There
is little to record of the Vacation hitherto—I have worked
a little at Mathematics. . . . The Old Year comes to an end.
. . . I have begun a scheme which occurred to me the other
day, by which I hope to save a great deal of waste time, especially the six days which are inevitably consumed every year
in travelling to and from Oxford.

"A list of things to be learned by heart and kept up at such
times as Railway travelling, etc., e.g.:

Poetry
Elements of Mathematical Subjects
Proofs of Formulae of Mathematical Subjects
Formulae themselves
Chronology by Memoria Technica
Geometrical Problems."

This may well have been the germ of *Pillow Problems,* as
well as of *Memoria Technica* and other pamphlets.

Dr. Thomas Banks Strong, Dodgson's Bishop of Oxford
and later Dean of Christ Church, remarked his extreme
precision in terminology and logical form, "but," he says, "his
skill lay rather in tracing consequences than in criticizing
fundamental assumptions; and he was apt at times to exag-
gerate the importance of side-issues." [8]

Did his inability to criticize fundamental assumptions
spring from having given his mind in love-bondage to his
parents? Dr. Freud says: "So long as a man's early years are
influenced by the religious thought prohibition, and by the
loyal one derived from it, as well as by the sexual one, we
cannot say what he is really like." [8] We know what Dodgson
was "actually" like, but "really," perhaps, he was quite different. Behind every man stands his Platonic shadow, usually
much larger than himself, and it is tempting to speculate what
keeps him from filling that outline.

Save for the loyal prohibtion, Dodgson's logical bent would
have carried him through the revaluation of all values. His

argument on eternal punishment was logically fool-proof, and even his rare sermons were logical. Instead of writing them out, he used his *Pillow Problems* technique. He saw, in the mind's eye, a diagram of what was to be proved, and proved it, point by point, with earnestness and conviction.

The feelings that—presumably—kept him awake by trying to burst through into consciousness were not unique with him. Other Englishmen were tempted to question and criticize their God. Not only Dr. Pusey suffered from feelings of guilt and sin. Good men, whether writers, churchmen, or whatever, were all oppressed by feelings of guilt and sorrow. Was the God who was so angry, and especially angry with good men, the God of the French Revolution—of *liberté, égalité, fraternité?*

Many of the good men themselves had such adumbrations. We think of poor stammering Charles Kingsley at a workingmen's meeting, saying, "I am a Ch-ch-church of England parson and a Ch-ch-chartist." We think of the Ancient Mariner—for Coleridge, with Southey, planned an ideal community on the banks of the Susquehanna—we think of Oxford men saying, like Matthew Arnold, "Our inequality materializes our upper class, vulgarizes our middle class, brutalizes our lower class," or, like James Anthony Froude, "The endurance of the inequalities of life by the poor is the marvel of human society." Victoria's own Laureate asked:

> *Is it well that while we range with Science, glorying in the time,*
> *City children soak and blacken soul and sense in city slime?* [9]

And Oxford's Slade Professor of Art, John Ruskin, answered: "I feel the force of mechanism and the fury of avaricious commerce to be at present so irresistible, that I have seceded from the study not only of architecture, but nearly of all art; and have given myself, as I would in a besieged city, to seek the best modes of getting bread and water for the multitudes."

This undercurrent of guilt and sorrow that pulses through the lives of the best men of the time is not sufficiently accounted for by their anachronistic education, or even by the great incubus of other-worldly religion that hung over them; there was a real guilt and a real sorrow, such as our time knows even more poignantly—the crucifixion of their fellow man. But the tender Ariel-soul of Charles Dodgson could not meet this problem head-on. He could make a logical game of eternal damnation, or tell moral tales, or preach sermons to children and college servants, though not the kind of sermon Charles Kingsley could preach to workingmen. Dodgson felt the absurdity of inequality, but his surface showed little disturbance from that source.

Though he sometimes read the lesson in the Cathedral, he was not high enough in the church to preach there. At Christ Church, Eastbourne, he preached a sermon for children that contained a story called "Victor and Arnion," and another sermon with a story about Margaret. A third sermon was on the Good Shepherd, and when he finally preached at St. Mary's, Oxford, in his last year of life, his subject was the need for reverence.

His creed for adults, beginning with himself, was less cheerful than the one for children, and he seems to have believed in the Devil. He wrote: "Yet how often one hears in society the ready laughter with which any sly allusion to the Devil is received—ay, even by clergymen themselves, who, if their whole life be not one continuous lie, do believe that such a being exists, and that his existence is one of the saddest facts of life." [5] Another time he said: "I believe that when you and I come to lie down for the last time, if only we can keep firm hold of the great truths Christ taught us—our own utter worthlessness, and His infinite worth; and that He has brought us back to our one Father, and made us his brethren, and so brethren to one another—we shall have all we need to guide us through the shadows." Although a Puseyite feeling of his own worthlessness often oppressed him, fortunately he neither acted nor seems to have felt as if other persons were worthless, either to him or to his God.

His idea of heaven, excerpted from *Sylvie and Bruno,* is related to the future on this earth adumbrated in Shaw's *Back to Methuselah:*

"*Eternity*—involving, as it seems to do, the necessary *exhaustion* of all subjects of human interest . . . *Pure Mathematics,* for instance . . . take the subject of circles and ellipses —what we call 'curves of the second degree.' In a future Life, it would only be a question of so many years (or *hundreds* of years, if you like) for a man to work out *all* their properties. Then he *might* go on to curves of the third degree. Say *that* took ten times as long . . . I can hardly imagine his *interest* in the subject holding out even for those. . . . And so of all other branches of Science . . . through some thousands or millions of years . . . I ask myself 'What then?' . . . I have sometimes thought one *might,* in that event, say 'It is better not to be,' and pray for personal *annihilation*—the Nirvana of the Buddhists."

Then Lady Muriel staves off the evil moment by suggesting the blessed thought of working for others, but the Earl counters by reminding her that in infinity there will be no others needing help. The young Doctor then speaks: "Now let me tell you how I have put it to myself. I have imagined a little child, playing with toys on his nursery-floor, and yet able to *reason,* and to look on, thirty years ahead. Might he not say to himself, 'By that time I shall have had enough of bricks and ninepins. How weary Life will be!' " But he is to be a great statesman, with joys no child could have anticipated— "so perhaps all those descriptions of Heaven, with its music, and its feasts, and its streets of gold, may be only attempts to describe, in *our* words, things for which we *really* have no words at all."

Poor genie, thrashing around in his box and trying so hard to be kind and considerate and not smash it. His tongue in his cheek, he hints at endless æons of heaven, reminiscent of Shaw's insight into the keen tortures of bliss unduly prolonged, as well as of the truly Shavian concept that man is still infantile ("the world is governed by babies of sixty, interested in golf and cigars"). By merely moving the locale of his drama from heaven to Brompton Road, Dodgson would have had a Shavian treatise.

But in the best sense he was honestly and deeply religious. He believed that God was in man, and that man was destined to approach nearer and nearer to God. So far, except for terminology, who could quarrel with him? He was a good world citizen in that he demanded from his God justice to all, and all decent men can accept his code. It nourishes the desire to rise on the evolutionary ladder—man cannot live by bread alone. An evolutionary philosophy, such as that worked out in the nineteenth century by Nietzsche and Samuel Butler, and later elaborated by Shaw, treating God as the end-product rather than the cause of man, is perhaps the modern form of religion. Nothing in Dodgson's beliefs restrained him from such a communion, and this religio-philosophy, which must have encroached on his ear at times, should have pleased him, for his reverence for truth was basic, and his attempts to bolster up the tottering theology of his father showed that he felt the structure was collapsing. True, he believed it was his mission to buttress the crumbling cathedral, and to "lose his faith" would have been hideous, unless he had won through to the "revaluation of all values." He was forced to attack this religion as atheism, and perhaps *it* was the "devil" that caused him insomnia, "just looking in at the door," as he said of the unholy thoughts that plagued him.

Lack of an outlet for one's sex nature, especially in an affectionate person, causes a good deal of torment, but it is not a constant and remorseless problem. Charles lived a blameless life, but something chased and bothered him and kept him awake. The nature of his religious writing, or his stern withdrawals from any company where the least irreverence was tolerated, and his own constant playings around the border, indicate that the sin to which he was constantly tempted, and against which he constantly drugged himself with games and uplifting quotations, was the sin of thinking for himself about religion. For a man of intelligence to live from 1832 to 1898, studying, caring for the life of the mind and spirit, and to finish with almost the same body of doctrine he had started with, was a *tour de force*. He prided himself on wriggling out of eternal punishment—but how many camels he did swallow! His humorous, yet wryly wistful, poems about ghosts hint that ghostly visitants bothered him. Too sensible to mistake them for objective facts, and knowing he threw their shadows on the wall, he could not, within the rules of his game, take their messages literally: he had to distort and symbolize them. These split-off parts of himself, not acceptable in his personal league of notions, gave minority reports in foreign languages, which he faithfully reported and which his readers must translate. One message was that the box was too tight, that he deserved more freedom of thought, and especially of religious thought.

His essay, "The Stage and the Spirit of Reverence," appeared in *The Theatre* in June, 1888. "And may not the word *good*, also, have a broader meaning? . . . May it not fairly include all that is brave, and manly, and true in human nature? Surely a man may honour those qualities, even though he own to no *religious* belief whatever? . . . by 'reverence' . . . I mean . . . simply a belief in some good and unseen being, above and outside human life as we see it, to whom we feel ourselves responsible . . . 'reverence' is due, even to the most degraded type of religion, as embodying in a concrete form a principle which even the most absolute atheist professes to revere in the abstract."

He had two codes—the tight one for himself, the more elastic one for the rest of humanity. His letter to Miss Edith Rix in 1886 says: ". . . what a person *is* is of more importance in God's sight than merely what propositions he affirms or denies. *You,* at any rate, can do more good . . . by showing them what a Christian *is,* than by telling what a Christian *believes.* . . ." [2]

"I have a deep dread of argument on religious topics: it has many risks, and little chance of doing good." Yes, there *was* a risk—of his conversion to a less corseted and hoopskirted belief, which would have felt loose and abandoned at first. He often hinted at such fears; yet he maintained a delicate balance that allowed others to think as they pleased. Just those with doubts and difficulties of their own become fanatical reformers of others; Dodgson's essential delicacy showed in his elegant poise on a tight-rope wide enough for himself alone, in his beautiful tolerance and reverence for other people's rights to their own poise, and in the avoidance of any attempt to grab at the herd in order to stabilize himself. His letter to Ellen Terry suggests that from Shylock's punishment there should be deleted the phrase:

> . . . *that for this favour*
> *He presently become a Christian.*

"It is a sentiment that is entirely horrible and revolting to the feelings of all who believe in the Gospel of Love . . . the may be, is . . . simply horrible." [5] Again, in a letter to Miss Manners in 1889: "I was much interested in your letter, telling me that you belong to the Society of Friends. Please do not think of me as one to whom a difference in creed is a bar to friendship. My sense of brotherhood and sisterhood is at least broad enough to include *Christians* of all denominations; in fact, I have one valued friend . . . who is a Unitarian." This was more broad-minded than it seems; the movement admitting other than Church of England men to Parliament started shortly before Charles's birth, extended the right gradually, and culminated in the Affirmation Bill of 1888, which admitted the atheist, Charles Bradlaugh. As to Oxford, when Gladstone was an undergraduate he remarked of another, "I fear he is a Unitarian." Mansfield College, for dissenting clergymen, was not founded till the nineties.

Another letter to Edith in 1885 gives his ideas of resurrection:

"One subject you touch on—'the resurrection of the Body' —is very interesting to me. . . . *My* conclusion was to give up the *literal* meaning of the *material* body altogether . . . the actual *material* usable for *physical* bodies has been used over and over again, so that each atom would have several owners. The mere solitary fact of the existence of *cannibalism* is to my mind a sufficient *reductio ad absurdum* of the theory that the particular set of atoms I shall happen to own at death . . . will be mine in the next life . . . all . . . difficulties . . . are swept away at once if we accept St. Paul's 'spiritual body,' and his simile of the grain of corn." [2]

A letter to his biographer's brother, outlining his projected book on religious difficulties, says:

"But I had better add that I do not want to deal with any such difficulties, *unless* they tend to affect *life.* . . . These axioms are:

1. Human nature is capable of being *right,* and of being *wrong.*
2. I possess Free Will, and am able to choose between right and wrong.
3. I have in some cases chosen wrong.
4. I am responsible for choosing wrong.
5. I am responsible to a person.

6. This person is perfectly good.

"I call them axioms, because I have no *proofs* to offer for them. There will probably be others, but these are all I can think of just now." [2]

This "perfectly good" person, a little like Archdeacon Dodgson, seems, like the Archdeacon, to have had a lighter side. From a letter to Miss Dora Abdy, dated 1896:

". . . While the laughter of *joy* is in full harmony with our deeper life, the laughter of amusement should be kept apart from it. The danger is too great of thus learning to look at solemn things in a spirit of *mockery,* and to seek in them opportunities for exercising *wit.* That is the spirit which has spoiled, for me, the beauty of some of the Bible. Surely there is a deep meaning in our prayer, 'Give us an heart to love and *dread* Thee.' We do not mean *terror:* but a dread that will harmonize with love; 'respect' we should call it as towards a human being, 'reverence' as towards God and all religious things." [2]

Whether he himself ever experienced the "laughter of joy" is doubtful. Miss Ethel Rowell, who knew him in his last years, says: "I don't think he ever laughed, though his own particular crooked smile, so whimsical, so tender, so ironic, was in and out all the time." She also mentions "his long upper lip which had a trick of quivering as he spoke, a movement I think connected with a slight stammer that he sometimes had." [10]

All his brothers and sisters had some speech difficulty, says Mr. Reed, who attributes this to the consanguinity of their parents.[11] Miss Dodgson, in a letter to the author, said "all but two sisters." The stammer nearly prevented his ordination, for he felt it unseemly in a clergyman. His diary for March 27, 1881, reads:

"Went to S. Mary's . . . and, as Ffoulkes was alone, I mustered up courage to help him. I read the exhortation, and was pleased to find I did not once hesitate. I think I must try preaching again soon, as he has often begged me to do." [2]

On February 1, 1894, he wrote: "*Dies notandus.* As Ragg was reading prayers, and Bayne and I were the only M.A.'s in the stalls, I tried the experiment of going to the lectern and reading the lesson. I did not hesitate much, but feel it too great a strain on me to be tried often." [2] When he was an undergraduate, his fellow students maneuvered him into reading the chapter where Saul changes his name to Paul, because poor Charles stammered so badly on P.[12]

Whenever he heard of a teacher who worked with stammerers, Dodgson tried again, sometimes bringing his siblings en masse. Here are a few entries from the diaries:

"June 5, 1872. A day whose consequence may be of the greatest importance to me. I went to Nottingham, by the advice of my friend Hine, and heard Dr. Lewin lecture on his system for the cure of stammering. . . . The lecture lasted until after midnight, having begun about 9."

"June 6. Tried Dr. Lewin's system by reading to Hine and Mrs. Hine and was well pleased with the result."

"September 18, 1873. Interview with Mr. Rivers."

'October 14. Interview with Rees, a stammerer, and recommended him to go to Mr. Rivers."

"April 2, 1874. I went to London with Elizabeth and Caroline, and we had an hour with Mr. Rivers (I have arranged for all the sisters who like to go to him)." Roger Lancelyn Green's note on this entry is: "It has never been suggested that *all* Dodgson's sisters stammered, though this entry suggests that most of them suffered from some sort of speech-defect—due, as in Dodgson's own case, to nervous and not physical causes. Besides Dodgson himself, only Elizabeth, Caroline, and Edwin stammered at all seriously."

In spite of his hesitation he made a reputation for himself as a preacher in Oxford, Guildford, and Eastbourne, but preaching never ceased to be a task.

One other possible barrier to ordination was his love of the theater. Since his childhood he had written plays, beginning with his marionette theater at home. Playgoing was still under suspicion in godly circles, especially for the ministry. For himself, Charles sensibly decided that if playgoing was not evil, it was not wrong for ministers. But. Dr. Wilberforce, Bishop of Oxford—he of the apes and the angels—had affirmed that the "resolution to attend theatres or operas was an absolute disqualification for Holy Orders." Charles was in a dilemma until it was decided that this pronouncement referred only to the parochial clergy. Dr. Pusey was consulted, and likewise Dr. Liddon, Carroll's companion on the continental tour. Liddon thought "a deacon might lawfully, if he felt himself unfit for the work, abstain from direct ministerial duty." [2] So, still fretting about his unworthiness—and perhaps his unwillingness—Charles prepared for ordination.

On December 22, 1861, "Holy Terror" Wilberforce ordained him deacon. This in no way resolved his difficulties—it merely set them in a frame of reference. On October 21, he wrote: "Called on the Dean to ask him if I was in any way obliged to take Priest's Orders—(I consider mine as a Lay Studentship). His opinion was that by being ordained Deacon I became a Clerical Student, and so subject to the same conditions as if I had taken a Clerical Studentship, viz: that I must take Priest's Orders within four years from my time for being M.A., and that as this was clearly impossible in my case, I have probably already lost the Studentship, and am at least bound to take Priest's Orders as soon as possible. I differed from this view, and he talked of laying the matter before the electors."

October 22 he wrote: "The Dean has decided on not consulting the electors, and says he shall do nothing more about it, so that I consider myself free as to being ordained Priest."

As to the theater, he was quite capable of drawing fine lines himself as to what—how—where. A letter to Mrs. Daniel, 1895:

"As to your wish that I should give my approval of a dramatized *Alice* for the benefit of the S. Thomas Schools, well, you certainly put me into rather a 'fix' there, as the Americans would say. . . . Long ago I made up my mind that I do not approve of that method of getting money for charitable objects, and I have again and again declined to let it be said that 'it is done with the sanction of Mr. L. C.' . . . I don't in the least want to prevent your doing as you think right . . . *all* I ask is, that it shall not be announced as done with my approval." [13]

He would attend only unexceptionable plays, never music halls, and he wished to expurgate Shakespeare, especially in his projected edition for young girls; but he considered the drama both relaxing and uplifting, and stuck to his rusty musket.

The diary recorded many impressions of plays. In 1855 he mentioned "the great play *Henry VIII*, the greatest theatrical treat I ever had or ever expect to have . . . I never enjoyed anything so much in my life before." [2] On June 18, 1856, he noted a new sun that was to mellow his life and many others. The Mamillius in *A Winter's Tale* was an eight-year-old girl named Ellen Terry, who later wrote in her memoirs: "I can't remember when I didn't know him." [14] By this we might surmise he went back stage even then.

He was always full of schemes, practical and otherwise, to improve the standards of acting and the theater. In 1882 he wrote a letter to the theatrical profession, recommending a prospectus of a scheme of play-acting, perhaps by founding a school of dramatic art.

For his marionette theater at Croft, he wrote *The Tragedy of King John* and other plays. On his continental tour he saw many plays and recorded the events in his diary. Actors and actresses, especially the latter, and especially child actresses, were among his most valued friends and photographic subjects, and he had definite notions about all aspects of the stage. Most serious of all, rather than renounce the theater, he nearly refused ordination. His love of Thespis must have been powerful, to compete with his love of his official God. Before his spirit uneasily protests any incompatibility between the two, here are some of his own words from that rather dull essay, *The Stage and the Spirit of Reverence,* giving a broad philosophical basis for distinguishing between good and evil, regardless of creed. Reverence for the good he found greater on the stage than elsewhere, even among the clergy; Shakespeare's mirrors of nature, however, needed washing and draping.

"But the lowest depths of conscious and deliberate irreverence that my memory recalls, have been, I am sorry to say, the utterances of *reverend* jesters. I have heard, from the lips of clergymen, anecdotes whose horrid blasphemy outdid anything that would be even *possible* on the stage." [5]

He further quotes examples of elevation of morals and feelings through reverence, on the stage, for sacred or sentimental subjects. Reading his own article might have helped even his insomnia. He gives W. S. Gilbert a good hard slap for making fun of the clergy, and asks for serious treatment of the devil, hell, and so on, leading up to another stricture on Gilbert for the "damme's" in *Pinafore*, especially the chorus where "a bevy of sweet innocent-looking little girls sing, with bright, happy looks, the chorus, 'He said "Damn me!" He said "Damn me!" ' " Even Sir Arthur earns a harsh word for having "prostituted his noble art to set to music such vile trash." [4] (Dodgson had tried, in March, 1877, to get Sullivan to write music for the projected dramatization of *Alice*. Sullivan had begged off, presumably because of the difficult rhythms.) [15]

He loved the stage in his own way, with reservations. Beatrice Hatch said: "He was able many a time to induce stage managers to correct, or omit, anything that might jar sensitive ears. Of course, the plays he cared to go to were limited in number." [16]

Excerpts from three pamphlets circulated among friends, underline his feelings about the drama:

"May I ask for your kind coöperation in a project of mine for editing the Plays of Shakespeare for the use of girls? . . . *what* plays are suitable . . . my wish is to collect opinions from ladies. . . .

"My hope is to produce a book which any English mother may, without any scruple, put into the hands of her daughters. No edition, that I have yet seen, appears to me to meet this want. . . ."

The second pamphlet:

"The stage is . . . an engine of incalculable power for influencing society; and every effort to purify and ennoble its aims seems to me to deserve all the countenance that the great, and all the material help that the wealthy can give it, while even those who are neither great nor wealthy may yet do their part, and help to

> *"Ring out the darkness of the land*
> *Ring in the Christ that is to be."*

The aspect of the stage that lured Charles, perhaps, was the careless bohemianism of backstage life, always within the limits of strict Victorian morality and propriety. Miss Arnold wonders about that too: "Side by side with this narrowness of outlook in one direction, was a certain strain of what can only be called Bohemianism, manifested in his love for the theatre, his enjoyment and pride in the friendship of distinguished theatrical artists such as the Terry sisters, and more particularly his love for child actresses." She says his favorites were Kate and Ellen Terry, Richard Mansfield, Frederick Robson—"the greatest actor our age has yet produced," and the Vanbrugh sisters. "Although he himself never went to a music-hall, he believed in temperance, not prohibition, of them. He liked comic operas and old-fashioned pantomimes. The pantomimes that were coming into vogue in his middle years, on the contrary, he detested." [17] Judge Parry, speaking of Dodgson's contributions to the *Comic Times,* also wondered if bohemian life attracted him. Clearly it did, but there is no proof that his association with the bohemian contributors to the *Comic Times* was other than on paper. The nearest to a scandal was caused by the stage doorman who had "seen so much of parsons backstage" that he tried to stop Dodgson from visiting the same Irene Vanbrugh with whom he strolled on Eastbourne Front discussing the Thirty-nine Articles.[14]

As in any art, of course, the techniques interested him. Ellen Terry quotes Dodgson's letter suggesting that the minor actors should have a chance to watch the stars from the wings, because the stars' "acting is to a great extent *lost* if they have not good acting in the minor parts to support them." Another naïve solution to a real evil. She also mentions his love of "dressing up" photographic subjects, and his great pleasure in the stage production of *Alice.*

He wrote a long letter to Isa Bowman, directing her how to speak her part. Isa's copy of the *Alice* operetta is marked to correspond with these instructions; the words to be emphasized are underlined. Precise as he was in all things, he was even more so in his speech. Mr. Madan claims he used his stuttering to time a climax effectively! His own difficulty may have focused his attention on the art of speech.

His use of italics is consistent throughout his works; in fact a forgery could be detected by reading aloud and listening for the Carrollian cadences. His ear for the utterable sentence was exceptional; not an awkward or cumbersome construction is to be found even in his dullest works, and they

are all so closely woven they defy condensation. His cadences
have found their way into our daily speech, often anonymously. Involved as his reasoning is, he presents it step by
step and phrase by phrase until it insinuates itself into the
mind. With that gift, he should have collaborated with some
master of plot to produce drama—but who could have collaborated with him? It is too bad his project for working
with Calverley never developed. Collingwood mentions a plan
he had to write a play with a part for a pantomime actor,
Percy Roselle. He wrote Tom Taylor about it in 1866, giving
a synopsis of the play.[2] We are told no more.

Dodgson's interest in speech forms, and even his very stammering, hint he might have wished to act. Miss Menella
Dodgson thought it unlikely, but her cousin Mr. Collingwood
mentioned a "clairvoyant's" saying that he would make an
actor, and Bert Coote, one of the few boys Dodgson ever
showed an interest in, spoke of his "exceptional sense of the
theatre." The reverse side of a stammerer, we see from
Demosthenes, is an orator, and the reverse side of a shy and
shrinking man may be one who likes to strut his little hour
and spread himself in varied rôles.

Partly, perhaps, to compensate for his own frustrated dramatic ambitions, Dodgson made himself useful to (female)
stage children, paying for their lessons, coaching them himself, introducing them to Miss Terry, who remarked his great
kindness to them. Collingwood affirmed his uncle's wish to
write for the stage, adding that he "had not the necessary
constructive powers." It is touching to hear Lewis Carroll
refer to the dramatization as "Mr. Savile Clarke's play, *Alice
in Wonderland*." [2]

Isa says that to improve his stammer he read a scene of
Shakespeare aloud daily for years. The reading was pleasurable in itself too—stammerers take an added pleasure in
speech, and tend toward loquaciousness rather than taci-
turnity.

The problem of poverty was a camel that strained even
Dodgson's faith. In *Sylvie and Bruno* he discusses the Socialist
solution, but since he presents all the standard misconceptions
as original discoveries, his reading could not have covered
even the Christian Socialist material. Again he tries to clear

the name of the Lord from suspicion of carelessness or in-difference: "The simplest form of the problem [of 'idle mouths'] is a community without *money*, who buy and sell by *barter* only; and it makes it simpler to suppose the food and other things to be capable of keeping many years with-out spoiling.'" The hero, Arthur, goes on to outline the argu-ment for a man being allowed to leave money to his children, assuming that if he were a superior worker he would already have performed enough services to entitle them to idleness! The narrator takes up the thread: "'. . . There is something wrong *somewhere* if these four people are well able to do useful work, and if that work is actually needed in the com-munity, and they elect to sit idle . . . It seems to me to arise from a law of God—that everyone shall do as much as he can to help others, and not from any *rights*, on the part of the community, to exact labour as an equivalent for food that has been fairly earned.'"

The British Constitution takes precedence over the Sermon on the Mount. Charles once told a friend that he was "first an Englishman, and then a Conservative." Was he first an Englishman, and then a Christian? Arthur goes on to say: "I should like to *force* them (the Socialists) to see that the money, which those 'haristocrats' are spending, represents so much labour *already* done for the community, and whose equivalent, in material wealth, is *due* from the community."

"'Might not the Socialists reply "Much of this money does not represent *honest* labour *at all? . . .*"'"

"'No doubt, no doubt,' Arthur replied, 'but . . . if we once begin to go back beyond the fact that the *present* owner of certain property came by it honestly, and to ask whether any previous owner, in past ages, got it by fraud, would *any* property be secure?'" Q.E.D.

Among the prophets Dodgson seems not to have heard of, was Proudhon, and if he had heard of Marx it was at second hand. This is all original thinking in the sense that he did it for himself, but the quality is such that he might as well have got it ready-made. It is a characteristic of British thinking, on the whole, that each man thinks for himself, yet all reach the same conclusions, so that a Carrollian invention might have been a National Thinker.

The Warden of Merton College, Oxford—seat of the oldest public library in England, and in 1264 already training teachers—writes: "The college system founded by Walter de Merton was destined to survive the temporary decay of the University and continues to exercise a profound influence on the whole spirit of our higher education. Instead of being divided into different faculties, or left to group themselves into clubs by social or professional distinctions, English students of various ranks and pursuits have been united into families by college life. A common stock of culture, sentiments, tastes, mould the character of the British nation." [18] People other than British constantly wonder at the unanimity of the British cultured classes, and the seepage of that culture down to the relatively unlettered. Dodgson, himself, especially in his letters, shows a strong sense of class, though the *Alice* books soar far above such limitations. His letters to Gertrude Thomson repeatedly ask her to draw the children's ankles thinner and make them more aristocratic. Such phrases constantly recur: "Are his wrists and ankles capable of change? They're terribly thick! Why should these fairies be so *very* plebeian?" Or: "The elder girl's ankles look rather thick! The younger is, apparently, of gentler birth." [19]

His cultural class feeling shows in another letter to Miss Thomson: "I have just promised to give the little girl, of the porter who always carries my luggage, a book: and had intended it to be *The Nursery 'Alice,'* as the child is 10, and I consider children of the lower orders to be 2 or 3 years behind the upper orders. But a lady, whom I consulted, advised me to give the real *Alice,* as probably more interesting, even now, to the child (they certainly do get very well taught now-a-days), and certainly of more permanent interest." [19] What would this ten-year-old have thought, if the author had presented her with a book of which the preface states it is for "children from Nought to Five?"

Helmut Gernsheim[20] feels Dodgson was both a snob and a lion hunter, especially in his insistence on photographing royalty and eminent men. It is true he tried hard to photograph the Prince of Wales and had finally to content himself with an autograph. It is true he seemed pleased to learn from Lady Stanley that she had shown some of his photographs to the Queen, who said, "They are such as the Prince would have appreciated very highly and taken great pleasure in." Two months later however he registered the sad fact that the Queen had apparently not kept any of the photos.

But when he passed her carriage in the park, she gave him a bow and smile all to himself. This naturally he recorded. And he hoaxed the little Drury girls with a letter which he pretended to have received, and which was written by himself in a disguised hand:

"Dear Mr. Dodgson,
I hope you will be able to come to our garden party this afternoon.
Yours truly,
Victoria R." [21]

Perhaps he consoled himself a little with the fact that the Queen's youngest son, Prince Leopold, did accept the invitation to be photographed when he came up to Oxford, and asked Mr. Dodgson to lunch besides. Poor Prince Leopold died young, but not before malice had claimed Mrs. Liddell wanted him to marry Rhoda.

Lewis Carroll's value for his age, and perhaps "for all time," lies not in his mimeographs of what "everybody" is thinking, but in the periods when he lets loose his gryphons to hold, as 'twere, the mirror up to the nation.

The discussion about "idle mouths" in *Sylvie and Bruno* takes up ten pages, and ends: "That strength and skill do *not* belong to the community, to be paid to *them* as a *debt:* they do *not* belong to the man *himself,* to be used for his *own* enjoyment: they *do* belong to be used according to *His* will; and we are not left in doubt as to what this will is. '*Do good, and lend, hoping for nothing again!* ' "

The Christian emerges triumphant, but we smell the blood of an Englishman. Where else could we find, after nineteen centuries, such trust that the will of God would be done? Dodgson, looking in his own heart and finding it pure of intention, supposed this was the rule. If only, like Samuel Butler's Ernest, he had had a chance to spend six months in jail! He might have written a *Pilgrim's Progress*—not that it could have been better than the *Alice* books, but some such experience would have prevented his maturity from sagging into the morass of *Sylvie and Bruno*. A vital shock would have saved (or destroyed) him. He could no longer fit into the box except by softening his tissues. His salvation as an artist would have been to break the box, but this he was committed not to do.

His heart was in the right place, and with a little more daring he might have dreamed of abolishing poverty, just as he groped toward liberation in other ways. Suppose the philosopher in the cave, about to find his way out, is stopped by the angel with the flaming sword? Dodgson's work is shadowed from being written inside the cave, and the brightest light is the flaming sword reflected in the mirror. Only in his dream life did he find the enchanted garden, only in his dreams could he pass through the wall of the cave that was only a looking-glass after all.

Chapter 6

Escape into the Garden

*Poor Alice! It was as much as she could do,
lying on one side, to look through into the
garden with one eye; but to get through was
more hopeless than ever: she sat down and
began to cry again.*

WHEN CHARLES DODGSON became sub-librarian of Christ
Church in 1855, he was privileged to use the little room off the
upper library, overlooking the deanery garden. On the smooth
grass, under the majestic old trees, first Lorina and Alice, then
baby Edith, and gradually more and more children, chuckled
and tumbled and learned not to make too much noise. The
lonely young man upstairs, looking out of the window, must
have remembered his childhood days in the garden at Croft,
with many little sisters and brothers—especially sisters; and
gradually the light of the Never-Never land illuminated the
Oxford garden and the Dean's daughters. And the more Mr.
Dodgson was captured by Dr. Pusey, the more ravishing the
garden and the little girls must have looked.

A few months after his installation in the library, Dodgson
took his new camera to the Deanery, and a new phase of his
life began. The entry for April 25, 1856, reads: "Went over
with Southey in the afternoon to the Deanery, to try and
take a photograph of the Cathedral: both attempts proved
failures. The three little girls were in the garden most of the
time, and we became excellent friends: we tried to group
them in the foreground of the picture, but they were not
patient sitters. I mark this day with a white stone."

That was Dodgson's symbol for a memorable day. Green
thinks this was his first meeting with Alice, then about four
years old, though he had made friends with her older brother
Harry and sister Lorina.

On June 3 he says, "Spent the morning at the Deanery,
photographing the children." Green says this was the first

135

record of his photographing children, and quotes Gernsheim's claim that he was "the best photographer of children in the nineteenth century."

When the three eldest girls were ten, eight, and six years old respectively, the story sessions started. Lorina Charlotte had brown hair and clean-cut features; Alice's hair was cut across her forehead in a fringe—"bangs," we say in America —that emphasized her wistful eyes and dainty three-cornered face; Edith had fluffy bright auburn hair. They commonly wore white cotton frocks, white open-work stockings, and black strap slippers, all alike. The girls would cross Tom Quad with Miss Prickett, the less-than-omniscient governess whose boners are represented in *Alice in Wonderland*. In Mr. Dodgson's rooms, they would pull him down on his large sofa and beg for stories. Seizing the nearest piece of paper, he would start, illustrating as he went along. If one of the girls asked a good question, the story, not perhaps a new one at first, would branch off into some new direction.[1]

Unlike the later child-friends, the Liddell sisters never took tea at his lodgings. In fact, tea for children was still an innovation and a special treat, but on the river trips they took along a big basket with cakes and a teakettle to boil beside a haymow. Four or five times in each summer he took the three on a picnic for either a whole or a half day. Miss Prickett was left behind, but chaperonage was supplied by Canon Robinson Duckworth or one of the brothers Dodgson (for Skeffington and Wilfred had matriculated in 1855), and, on one occasion, by two Dodgson sisters. This was the least successful picnic, for the young ladies, still in their twenties, seemed old and gloomy to the children. (To Ethel Arnold, as a child, they seemed "austere and evangelical.") Songs and stories were omitted; the visitors were plump, and lowered the boat alarmingly. Finally it rained; the boat was abandoned and the return trip made by carriage, with time out in a farm house to dry the bedraggled hoop skirts.[2]

The path to the Isis from Tom Quad passed the smelly Trill Mill stream. Dean Liddell had a new and more appetizing path dug; meanwhile, stepping gingerly, the girls in their big shade hats clung to the hands of the two young men who were simultaneously juggling the luncheon basket. Ar-

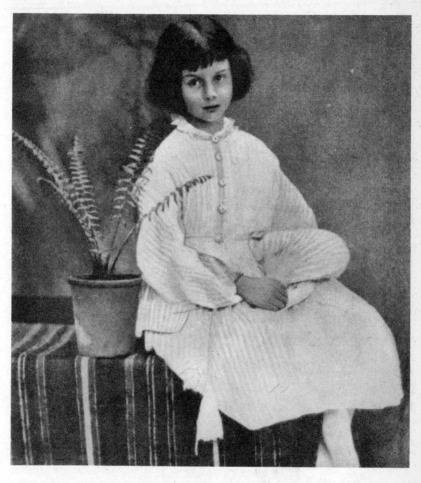

Inspiration for Lewis Carroll's *Alice in Wonderland*, photographed by Carroll in 1862, Courtesy of the New York Public Library Picture Collection.

of her own little sister. So the boat wound
slowly along, beneath the bright summer-day,
with its merry crew and its music of voices
and laughter, till it passed round one of the
many turnings of the stream, and she saw it no more.

Then she thought, (in a dream within
the dream, as it were,) how this same little Alice
would, in the after-time, be herself a grown
woman : and how she would keep, through her
riper years, the simple and loving heart of
her childhood : and how she would gather around
her other little children, and make _their_ eyes
bright and eager with many a wonderful tale,
perhaps even with these very adventures of
the little Alice of long-ago : and how she
would feel with all their simple sorrows, and
find a pleasure in all their simple joys,
remembering her own child-life, and the
happy summer days.

The MS of last page of _Alice's Adventures Underground_

rived at the river, young Mr. Dodgson would select the safest, roomiest, and most comfortable boat, stock it with cushions, and bestow his guests and the luncheon baskets with accurate balance. He rowed stroke and Mr. Duckworth rowed bow; an extra pair of oars was added for the girls' rowing lessons. One of them might hold the tiller rope, and if the boat wove a crooked course, it was all in the name of education.[1]

Dodgson celebrated by doffing his new clericals, and appearing in white flannel trousers and a hard straw hat, with black shoes, of course, since tennis shoes had not been invented. These were the most festive times of his life—he was only thirty on July 4, 1862, when all the rays converge. His life was before him and his powers were at their height. Drifting on the slow Isis that becomes the Thames, in his pleasant, slow voice with its "curious stutter," he wove a dream story for three lovely young ladies and a don. Duckworth asked if it was purely extemporaneous, and he truthfully answered. "Yes."[3] Germination acts that way—one moment there is a brown bud; next moment it is cracked, and a green shoot pushes out. The preparation has been going on in the dark.

They rowed up to Godstow, had tea beside a haymow, and rowed back again, returning by about eight-thirty. Stories had been told and songs had been sung, and at the Deanery door ten-year-old Alice said, "Oh, Mr. Dodgson, I wish you would write out Alice's adventures for me." If she had not sensed something special in that story, perhaps he might not have thought to write it down. Years later he attributed his beginning as a writer to her "infant patronage." How and when he wrote out the story has been told variously by Duckworth and by Alice, in her old age, to her son. But now that we have Dodgson's diaries there is no need to speculate. On the day when he finished the drawings for the manuscript, September 13, 1864, he wrote the data in the diary under July 4, 1862. On a blank page in Volume 9 of the *Diaries* he wrote the following:

"It was first told July 4 (F.) 1862.
Headings written out (on my way to London) July 5, 1862.
M. S. copy begun Nov. 13 (Th.) 1862.

Text (of *Alice's Adventures Underground*) finished before Feb. 10, 1863.
Pictures in M. S. finished Sept. 13 (Tu.), 1864.
M. S. finally sent to Alice, Nov. 26, 1864."

On July 5 he met the Liddells at the station. They were all on their way to London by the same train. It seems likely he did not sit with them, because he noted writing out the "heads" of the story on the train. It was nearly two and a half years before Alice received the weirdly illustrated little green book, with the story beautifully written out in Dodgson's best library script.

The Liddell children read and reread it, and kept it on the deanery table for their guests to enjoy. When Mrs. MacDonald read it aloud to her children, Greville, then aged six, said, "There ought to be sixty thousand volumes of it."[4] And Henry Kingsley wrote the author that it should be published.

Dodgson hesitated to risk a loss on the hunch of a child and the praise of one fellow-writer. Duckworth suggested that the book would surely succeed if Tenniel would illustrate it. Eventually the actor Tom Taylor introduced the two men, and on April 5, 1864, arrangements were completed with Macmillan and with Tenniel.

The arrangements with Macmillan are the first of Dodgson's peculiar special methods of doing business. His books, says Charles Morgan, "were, by his own wish, published 'on commission'—that is to say at his own and not the publisher's risk. . . . What Lewis Carroll understood . . . is that in persuading a great house to publish for him on commission he was rarely fortunate." [5]

Tenniel, who had started as a child prodigy, nearly ended as one. When a boy, fencing with his father, he lost the sight of one eye. But the remaining eye saw more than most. At sixteen he exhibited—and sold—an oil painting; not caring for art school, he studied by himself and at the British Museum, with the help of the trustees and free access to all collections. He spent a good deal of time on the Elgin marbles, also known as the Parthenon frieze and pediments, and on the collections of armor and costume. He also liked to visit the Zoölogical Gardens, but without a sketch book. His memory was phenomenal, and the only model he used was an oc- casional photograph—with one exception, to be noted later.

His first book illustrations were for a volume of Aesop, published in 1848. When the second cartoonist of *Punch* re- signed over a religious difference, Mark Lemon remembered the illustrator of Aesop and engaged him. At first the new man had little chance to show what he could do, apart from title page, decorated initial, and so on, for the first cartoonist was John Leech. Tenniel's earliest cartoons appeared in 1851, without especial success, but by the following year they had improved. He made his name with the drawing for the death of Wellington and the creation of the British Lion. By 1862 he was doing at least one cartoon a week, and, when Leech died in 1864, Tenniel became cartoonist for *Punch,* where he remained for fifty years, retiring at eighty, and living to with- in three days of his ninety-fourth birthday.

Tenniel was a mild and gentle man who knew his own mind. In illustrating, he put himself in the author's place and used all his imagination and artistry to recreate the latter's ideas. He was, like Dodgson himself, incorruptible and origi- nal. These two incompatibles in double harness won the race —and cut the traces. "With *Through the Looking-Glass,"* said Tenniel tactfully, "the faculty of making book-illustra- tions departed from me."

By 1864 he was in a position to ask £148 for illustra- ting *Alice.* Dodgson paid this himself, as well as the Dal- ziel brothers' engraving bill, which for both books came to £203/16. Further, he paid for the plates of the 1865 edition, the rare true first edition, which he called in because the repro- duction of the plates left Tenniel dissatisfied. Before photo- engraving, the artist drew directly on the wood block—then re- sponsibility passed to the engravers. Fortunately, the Dalziels were at the top of their profession, though Dante Gabriel Rossetti blessed them with: "These engravers! What ministers of wrath! Your drawing comes to them, like Agag, delicately, and is hewn in pieces before the Lord Harry. . . . As yet, I fare best with W. J. Linton. He keeps stomach-aches for you, but Dalziel deals in fevers and agues." [6] Tenniel, however, worked well with the Dalziels, and also with Joseph Swain, who handled Dodgson's later illustrators' work. The subtleties that this method of engraving could produce required full understanding between engraver and illustrator, and plenty of time and patience —perhaps Rossetti's short suit. Dodgson was never too busy for a conference, never hurried his co-workers, and expected— perfection.

He would have liked illustrating the books himself, till he found that a special technique was required. He is said never to have been satisfied with Tenniel, though everybody else was. Dodgson and Tenniel, like Gilbert and Sullivan, complemented each other artistically, but not without friction. Perhaps Dodgson was a little jealous, and his exacting methods may have gotten on Tenniel's nerves. He proposed a model—Tenniel said he no more needed one than Dodgson needed the multiplication table!

Dodgson's own drawings always expressed two principal aspects of his nature—the humorously horrible and the sweet. The latter gradually encroached on the former, but without quite replacing it. Tenniel's work, of course, was infinitely more vigorous, without much of either the sweet or the horrible, so that Carroll told Harry Furniss he had not liked any of Tenniel's drawings except Humpty Dumpty! But by that time Tenniel was telling Furniss, "Dodgson is impossible! You will never put up with that conceited old Don for more than a week!" [7] How far Harry Furniss' own jealousy colored —or invented—this gossip no one knows. He too drew for *Punch,* but he had to sit in the gallery of Parliament, catching expressions red hot, while Tenniel, working at home, immortalized his subjects often without having seen more than a photograph.

Mr. Madan asks, "Where did Quentyn Matsys, or Leonardo, see the Ugly Duchess who lived 150 years before their time?" [8] And where did Tenniel see their portraits of poor Margarethe Maultasch? The drawing, attributed—rather doubtfully—to Leonardo, is in the Windsor Castle Library, where Tenniel may have seen it. Once would be enough for that elephantine memory. But it is more likely that he saw the Matsys portrait, for he uses the detail of costume in that painting, which in 1856 belonged to Alfred Seymour. [8]

Mr. Madan himself solved the question of Tenniel's Alice. Dodgson's drawings of her are sweet and gentle, but not

Miss Mary Hilton Badcock, Tenniel's Alice, from *Handbook of the Literature of C. L. Dodgson.*

otherwise good likenesses of Alice Liddell. Tenniel's Alice, however, is distinctly someone else, and that someone else was Miss Mary Hilton Badcock, later Mrs. Probert. For once in his life, Tenniel was persuaded to use a model. [9]

First he and Dodgson held numerous conferences to determine whether Alice should have a fringe, or "bangs," like Alice Liddell. Since Dodgson deleted the lovely photograph of Alice from the facsimile of the manuscript published in 1886, it was doubtless his idea to have the illustrations in no way resemble her. When he saw a photograph of Mary at a Mr. Gray's, of Sharon, everything was solved. He had only to obtain Canon Badcock's permission for his daughter to sit, and Tenniel's consent to break the habits of a lifetime. Nevertheless Dodgson prevailed, and the artist made several trips to Ripon to sketch the Canon's daughter, who had bright gold hair and was quite a different type from the dark, dreamy Alice Liddell. Dodgson profited by his new friendship to photograph, not only Mary, but also Lucy, Clara, and Emily, her sisters.

Tenniel got a bit of his own back when he was illustrating *Through the Looking-Glass*. There were thirteen chapters, of which Dodgson decided to delete one. The artist suggested sacrificing the one that required him to draw a wasp in a wig. He wrote: "Don't think me brutal, but the wasp chapter doesn't interest me in the least." [5] Whatever Dodgson thought of the brutality, he took the advice.

Canon Duckworth was rewarded for his share in the book. Whenever a batch of Tenniel's engravings arrived, the Canon was invited to dinner, and spent an exciting evening with Dodgson over the pictures, in spite of Harry Furniss' rather spiteful gossip about author and artist.

For the *Alice* books this collaboration was ideal. In their first form, the books are as finished as the Parthenon was before the Turks thought of storing gunpowder in it. The futile attempts to make new illustrations to the *Alice* books resemble the further finishing of the Parthenon when the gunpowder exploded. An explosion that harmed neither Dodgson nor Tenniel, however, is Marguerite Mespoulet's book, *Creators of Wonderland*. With text and illustration she shows that Tenniel, at least, and Dodgson very probably, was influenced by

the work of J. J. Grandville. In the picture of the two foot-
men in *Wonderland* Tenniel definitely used a frog footman of
Grandville's. The Paris *Charivari,* founded in 1832, that
used Grandville's pictures, circulated quite freely in England.
Punch, of course, is the London *Charivari,* and Thackeray,
one of its founders, shuttled back and forth between Paris
and London, and knew Grandville's work well, as indeed
many art lovers in England did.

Miss Mespoulet nowhere claims that Dodgson was necessarily influenced by Grandville, though it seems quite likely he had
absorbed Grandville's work, as he had certainly absorbed
Lear's *Nonsense Book,* which appeared when he was fourteen. She prefers to call Tenniel the link between the two.
Grandville's *autre monde* has much in common with *Wonderland,* but whatever Dodgson took, and wherever he found it,
he made it his own.*

Angus Davidson finds no mention of Lewis Carroll in
Lear's diaries or letters,[10] and Mr. Madan found *"no trace* of
Lear"[8] in Dodgson's library at Oxford, yet the two moved in
some of the same circles and could hardly have avoided
meeting. But, as John Livingston Lowes says in *The Road to
Xanadu:* "origins prove nothing. . . . William James bluntly
declared . . . All they do is to afford a welcome answer to the
question: *What has creative Genius framed from its inert
stuff?"*[11]

This holds for Tenniel too, who simply lifted his Frog
Footman and Fish Footman from Grandville. And yet—
simply? He split up Grandville's Frog Footman into two persons, giving the Fish costume to the Frog. And besides, as
Alice said, "She was she, and I was I, and oh dear—" Tenniel
too made his own whatever he touched. His personal style,
unmodified by Grandville, would have been too harsh and
uncompromising for the dream books. His taste told him
what to use, as in the case of the Ugly Duchess, whom he
handled much more mercifully than her original Creator did.

Strained relations or no, Dodgson was not one to forget a
collaborator. In 1886 he gave Tenniel an autographed copy
of *The Hunting of the Snark,* and in the same year Canon
Duckworth received a copy of the facsimile of *Alice Under-*

* See Appendix B.

ground, inscribed: "The Duck from the Dodo, June, 1886."

Canon Duckworth, to be sure, was the Duck in the Caucus-race, and Dodgson was the Dodo. It is hard to see any reason other than a linguistic one for the Dodgson-Dodo constellation. Since 1507, when Portuguese navigators discovered the island later called Mauritius, the dodo (from *doúdo,* Portuguese for *simpleton*) was known to Europeans by hearsay. Dutch sailors called them *Walckvogel,* or *Walgvögel*—disgusting birds—because, after knocking the poor simpletons down with clubs, they found the meat almost inedible. Conservationists know whether the sailors then stopped knocking them dead. . . .

Between 1610 and 1620 several live specimens were brought to Europe, where they lived a short time. One of the last skeletons to be set up was in the Ashmolean Museum in the seventeenth century. About eighty years later nothing remained but the skull and right foot, which were still there recently. There was also a large painting of the bird, which Dodgson and Tenniel may have seen. The last records of a living dodo date from 1681, so the expression "dead as a dodo" was no doubt current in the last century. The name, *Didus ineptus,* connotes stupidity. Today—though not in 1862—Dodo and Dodgson are juxtaposed in the *Encyclopædia Britannica.* Why, except for phonetic reasons, should Dodgson have associated himself with this unfortunate bird, lacking wits enough to hide its single egg or to run from its enemies? Can we reconstruct our Dodo from a single boner?

Dodgson's recent biographers, starting with Green, who claims to have been a stammerer himself, feel that "Dodo" may also have referred to Dodgson's way of saying his own name: "Do-Do-Dodgson." It may indeed, though the only documentation we have so far (in a letter from Mrs. Skene) refers to his stammering on the "P" sound.

As to Canon Duckworth—in the manuscript the Duck has a speech later transferred to the Eaglet (Edith). After the Dodo has said:

"In that case, I move that the meeting adjourn, for the immediate adoption of more energetic remedies—" in the manuscript it is the Duck and not the Eaglet who answers:

" 'Speak English! I don't know the meaning of all those

long words, and what's more, I don't believe you do either!'
And the Duck quacked a comfortable laugh to itself. Some of
the other animals tittered audibly."

Dodgson made a practice of weaving members of the party
and topical events into his story. Dinah, for instance, was a
real cat. The Liddell children had two tabby kittens, which
they named "Villikens and his Dinah," after a popular song.[1]
Villikens was short-lived, but Dinah lived to be chased out of
Christ Church library many times, and to be consoled and
bathed and loved by Alice, though technically she belonged
to Lorina.

Topical allusions appear in the Dormouse's story too. The
three sisters in that tale were Elsie, Lacie, and Tillie—L. C.
for Lorina Charlotte; Lacie, an anagram for Alice; and Tillie,
for Matilda—the sisters' pet name for Edith.[1] Elsewhere the
play on names produces variants—Lory for Lorina, and
Eaglet for Edith. The first version, reminiscent of the day
when the Misses Dodgson were caught in the rain, takes the
party into a little cottage to dry their clothing. Some of the
stories told on earlier river excursions extended *Alice's Adventures Underground* into *Alice's Adventures in Wonderland*, but the manuscript corresponded to the story told on
July fourth.

There is no Caucus-race in the manuscript, but there is a
picture by Grandville, showing the animals seated in a circle,
much like Tenniel's. In the manuscript, this takes the place
of the caucus:

" 'I only meant to say,' said the Duck in a rather offended
tone, 'that I knew of a house near here, where we could get
the young lady and the rest of the party dried, and then we
could listen comfortably to the story which I think you were
good enough to promise to tell us,' bowing gravely to the
mouse.

"The mouse made no objection to this, and the whole party
moved along the river bank (for the pool had by this time
begun to flow out of the hall, and the edge of it was fringed
with rushes and forget-me-nots) in a slow procession, the
Dodo leading the way. After a time the Dodo became impatient, and, leaving the Duck to bring up the rest of the
party, moved on at a quicker pace with Alice, the Lory, and

the Eaglet, and soon brought them to a little cottage, and there they sat snugly by the fire, wrapped up in blankets, until the rest of the party had arrived, and they were all dry again."

Then after the mouse's tale, and its departure in a huff, "she sat for a while sorrowful and silent, but it was not long before she recovered her spirits, and began talking to herself, as usual: 'I do wish some of them had stayed a little longer, I was getting to be such friends with them—really the Lory and I were almost like sisters! And so was that dear little Eaglet! And then the Duck and the Dodo! How nicely the Duck sang to us as we came along through the water: and if the Dodo hadn't known the way to that nice little cottage, I don't know when we should have got dry again—' and there is no knowing how long she might have prattled on in this way, if she had not suddenly caught the sound of pattering feet." Well enough for a manuscript destined for an intimate circle, but he had enough of a public mind to realize that these paragraphs did not belong in a printed book.

His public mind and his private one were now on their way to taking up separate residence. For he decided to sign *Alice* by the pseudonym he had been trying out in *The Train*, Edmund Yates's paper. Collingwood tells how Dodgson submitted several names for the five poems and one story that appeared in *The Train* in 1856-7, but he gives the wrong name and date for the first poem, which was actually "Solitude," in March, 1856. Yates rejected "Dares," from Daresbury, and two anagrams, "Edgar Cuthwellis" and "Edgar U. C. Westhall," as well as "Louis Carroll," in favor of the now famous version. Dodgson evolved it by the simple process of latinizing, reversing, and reanglicizing his given names: Carolus Ludovicus, Ludovicus Carolus, Lewis Carroll.[5]

A pseudonym, once started for whatever reason, may activate a split, but of course in this case the split had already begun. There is, however, a tendency to assign certain moods or behavior to the pseudonym, which gradually acquires autonomy as a snowball acquires snow.

From *Wonderland* to *Looking-Glass* the man, and therefore his work, changed in other ways. The refinement, sharpening, and concentration of the next seven years produce a different emotional tone—the creatures in *Through the Looking-Glass* are less sad, and more pedantic and querulous; for instance, compare the weeping Mock Turtle with the belligerent, snivelling, contrary twins, the Tweedles. His weeping self was less sad and more complaining by that time. In a sense Carroll distinctly slid downhill from *Wonderland. Through the Looking-Glass* is more mature, and *Sylvie and Bruno* more elfin—*too* elfin— as well as more bothered with ethical and other problems arising from the anomaly of a benevolent deity who is also omnipotent. . . . Carroll's power of pure play was duller at sixty than at thirty, and his power of thought was scarcely sharpened.

In *Wonderland* he transports the dream characters to a dream country, where the traveler is sane and the natives mad—like an Englishman abroad. In *A Tangled Tale,* however, Mad Mathesis runs wild in the heart of London, making the citizens stare. It is almost trite to say that Carroll remained a child to whom the world looked even madder than it does to most of us. He was too polite, or too cautious, to say so, and perfected a technique for getting around freely without any worse tag than "eccentric," but one of his logical dilemmas was "They are sane. I am not like them. I am insane." Or vice versa. Do cats eat bats? Or do bats eat cats?

The appearing and disappearing Cheshire Cat is a sort of guardian imp and liaison officer between the two worlds; an undercurrent of *Wonderland* is Alice's longing for Dinah, so perhaps the cat with the disappearing head (the Cheshire Cat, from Charles's birthplace) is Dinah's dream-self, who, by the laws of dreamland, instead of frightening the creatures away, only keeps them pleasantly on edge. It is significant that the Cheshire Cat remarks, "We're all mad here." Dinah is the one link to the daily world, the one person (?) Alice misses; she says, "They will put their heads down and say 'Come up again, dear!'"—is the Cheshire Cat Dinah's head recalling her to the world across the border?

Dinah is not the only double exposure. There are: the Rabbit and the March Hare; the furious little Mouse in the pool and the Dormouse; and finally, the Queen of Hearts and the Duchess, who in the manuscript were one person—Queen of Hearts and Marchioness (not Duchess) of Mock Turtle.

The whole Mad Tea Party sounds like four aspects of Mr. Dodgson sitting about a table, calling one another names, like those arrangements of mirrors in "amusement" parks where you can photograph yourself from several angles at once. Or perhaps Alice stood for Mr. Dodgson, who was so easily offended, and who walked out of Common Room at the drop of a bad word. The peculiar creatures who spoke something that was "certainly English," yet made no sense, may have been the other members of Common Room. Speculation about the Hatter makes him an Oxford character— Mr. Collingwood thinks a classmate of his uncle's; Mr. Madan suggests Theophilus Carter, a furniture dealer of the High Street.

"It is really dreadful the way the creatures order one about here." Is that Oxford, the British Empire, or the whole world? In his childhood home " 'twas Love that made the world go round." The King and Queen of hearts had ten children, which might mean the ten numbered cards in a suit, or the ten Dodgson children besides Charles—making him the Knave! "She's all my fancy painted him" was his first form of the White Rabbit's testimony against the Knave. To the Duchess' remark about Love making the world go round, Alice replied, "Somebody said that it's done by everybody minding their own business!" At sixty-one Alice's creator sank into the morass, gurgling

> For I think it is Love,
> For I feel it is Love,
> For I'm sure it is nothing but Love!

" 'Once,' said the Mock Turtle at last, with a deep sigh, 'I was a real Turtle.' " "Once," said Charles Dodgson, "I was a real boy." Until he was five, perhaps—for Bruno, his only endurable boy character, is five years old. Alice, in *Wonderland,* is seven; in *Through the Looking-Glass,* "seven and a half exactually." The face of the Mock Turtle, both in Carroll's drawings and in Tenniel's, has the sad, yearning expression of Charles himself in all his pictures, yearning, perhaps, for his crucified manhood and liberty of thought. . . . No wonder, after another seven years of a don's life, the Mock

Turtle's sadness became the valetudinarianism of the Tweedle brothers. Brother against brother. Instead of the mildly antagonistic Gryphon versus the lachrymose Mock Turtle, we have the furious identical twins. As if, after parting one's hair on the side, one had decided to part it in the middle and get two even but less symmetrical divisions, the not-so-heavenly twins.

The mathematical mind of the author gave pungency to his dream-books, though as a mathematician *per se* he never rose above mediocrity. He enjoyed logical exercises, and pure thinking, and he especially enjoyed mystifying people by keeping his Alice-self sacred and secret—a ventriloquist's dummy in a cupboard. It may be this desire to protect his excursions into a four-dimensional world, rather than his so-called "modesty," that explains his dislike of being known at Oxford or in unselected adult society as the author of the *Alice* books. He even hated to sit for his photograph, much as he liked to photograph others, and while, unsolicited, he autographed his books for all his friends, he dreaded autograph hunters to the point of tricking them with a typewriter, or having a friend forge his name to letters.[5] Caricatures went only one way, too. Once, when she was small, Isa Bowman drew a caricature of him. He went flaming red, snatched it away, and burned it. Then when she apologized, he embraced and forgave her.[12] It is doubtful that he could have seen Harry Furniss' caricatures of him and forgiven them. However he looked to others, he was the White Rabbit to himself, though he would have preferred to be the worse-tempered but more dignified March Hare.

Taylor found some ingenious mathematical cryptograms in *Alice*. Of the procedure where she starts counting, "Four times five is twelve," and so forth, concluding, "I'll never get to twenty at that rate," he says it could bring her only to 19, never to twenty, because it is based on scales of notation.[13] He also asks why the Mad Hatter's watch is two days wrong. "What time is it at the center of the earth, at no longitude? By the sun it is all times or no time. It tells the day of the month. Hatter's watch goes by the moon." It is the fourth, two days wrong—there are two days between the lunar and the calendar month. And the fourth is Alice's birthday.

Another gem comes from Robert Graves's article in the *Atlantic Monthly* for August, 1957, *"Mushrooms, Food of the Gods"*: ". . . the scarlet-capped fly amanite, which . . . mycophobes regard as the most poisonous of all, though no one is ever recorded to have died from eating it! Oddly enough, its earliest appearance in English Literature is a charming one: Lewis Carroll's account of how Alice ate the mushroom on which the Caterpillar sat smoking his hookah, and could thus become shorter or taller at will. ('Curioser and curioser,' said Alice.) This hallucination, produced by the fly amanite, was described in a text-book, M. C. Cooke's Plain and Easy Account of British Fungi, published on October 4, 1862, just before Alice in Wonderland was put on paper."

There is little material on the Pig-and-Pepper episode. The famous lullaby is a triple satire on parental feelings, on Carroll's ideas about boy-nature, and on a bad poem, "Speak softly to a little child." The cook's silence is sinister. She speaks three words. The King says, "Give your evidence." She answers, "Shan't." He asks, "What are tarts made of?"; she says, "Pepper, mostly," and vanishes. She is a grotesque yet sibylline figure, naming the condiment Charles felt himself lacking in.

Lastly, Alice tries to carry the baby who becomes a pig. This is how a bachelor holds a baby, finally tying it into a knot and holding one leg and one ear, gazing at it in dismay until it becomes a pig and "trots off quietly into the wood." But what about Uggug, in *Sylvie and Bruno*—the horrid boy produced by straining off all the pleasant qualities of boy-nature for Bruno? Uggug turns into a porcupine, or prickly pig, because he is "loveless, loveless." Is the pig that runs away the boy-self that left a purified Alice? She feels relieved, because "it would have made a dreadfully ugly child [to one who did not like little boys]: but it makes rather a handsome pig, I think."

The card game is as basic to *Alice's Adventures in Wonderland* as chess is to *Looking-Glass*. An interesting attempt to explain the card game is made by Muriel Bruce Hasbrouck in her *Pursuit of Destiny*. She claims the Tarot cards are a device of learned Muslims to keep the ancient learning alive against the Christian relegation of the arts and sciences to the devil. She finds a rationalized astrology, based not on "influences" of planetary conjunctions, but on early knowledge of regular fluctuations in solar energy and the earth's field.

"Call the celestial sphere *the field* . . . maybe the four-dimensional space-time continuum. The formula is based on a mathematical relationship between the four major divisions of the ancient universe . . . called elements, and a series of 36 ten-degree cycles of the year. . . ." She quotes Pythagoras and Dr. Jung as dividing humanity into four types—the four basic blood types—and so forth, leading up to Alice's cry, "You're nothing but a pack of cards!"

No matter how many editions of this book may be called for, it is safe to guess that each one will have to list new interpretations of the *Alice* books, which is as it should be. It is the first dream book, made up of simple everyday materials freshly seen, and a classic plot.

Many persons who have read *Wonderland* at least once a year since they could read, fail to notice the plot. The story revolves about the golden key to the enchanted garden and Alice's endless frustrations and wanderings in bypaths until she enters at last, to find the flowers really beautiful, though some of them need painting—but the place is populated by disagreeable persons attempting to play croquet under trying circumstances. Then comes a Last Judgment with the entire cast—and an anti-climax.

The garden is an equally rich symbol if we call it adult life viewed by a child, or vice versa. The protean Alice with her formulas for growing and shrinking and cutting back and forth across the borders of childhood and maturity, yet remaining always a wise child, is of course Dodgson himself —or herself. It is hard, studying some of his portraits and reading some of his works, to realize that he was a man indeed. It is still harder to find any evidence that he himself realized it. He seems increasingly like a maiden aunt with the heart of a girl, even with all the satires on his fellow dons and the refined cruelties of his verse. All these traits are present in a maiden aunt, of the type that in the United States writes faintly sardonic articles for the highbrow magazines and finds an outlet for affectionate impulses in her nieces and nephews.

Dodgson was a lonely soul—no matter how much love and admiration he evoked, his reticences and rigidities and shyness kept him from reaching out to adults. For the really free interchange of gaiety and comradeship he was limited to children—and to girl children at that. Later he could not mention that afternoon on the river without an access of lyricism:

"I distinctly remember . . . how in a desperate attempt to strike out some new line of fairy-lore, I had sent my heroine straight down a rabbit hole, to begin with, without the least idea what was to happen afterwards.

"Stand forth, then, Alice, the child of my dreams. . . . What wert thou, dream-Alice, in thy foster-father's eyes? How shall he picture thee? Loving, first, loving and gentle: loving as a dog (forgive the prosaic simile, but I know no earthly love so pure and perfect), and gentle as a fawn: then courteous—courteous to *all,* high or low, grand or grotesque, King or Caterpillar, even as though she were herself a King's daughter, and her clothing of wrought gold; then trustful, ready to accept the wildest possibilities with all that utter trust that only dreamers know; and, lastly, curious—wildly curious, and with the eager enjoyment of Life that comes only in the happy hours of childhood, when all is new and fair, and when sin and sorrow are but names—empty words signifying nothing!

"And the White Rabbit, what of *him?* . . . For *her* 'youth,' 'audacity,' 'vigour,' 'swift directness of purpose,' read 'elderly,' 'timid,' 'feeble,' and 'nervously shilly-shallying,' and you will get *something* of what I meant him to be. . . .

"Let me cull from the two books a Royal Trio—the Queen of Hearts, the Red Queen, and the White Queen. . . . Each had to preserve, through all her eccentricities, a certain queenly dignity. . . . I pictured to myself the Queen of Hearts as a sort of embodiment of ungovernable passion, a blind and aimless Fury. The Red Queen I pictured as a Fury, but of another type; *her* passion must be cold and calm; she must be formal and strict, yet not unkindly; pedantic to the tenth degree, the concentrated essence of all governesses! Lastly, the White Queen seemed, to my dreaming fancy, gentle, stupid, fat, and pale; helpless as an infant . . . just suggesting imbecility but never quite passing into it. . . . There is a character strangely like her in Wilkie Collins' novel, *No Name:* by two converging paths we have somehow reached the same ideal, and Mrs. Wragge and the White Queen might have been twin sisters." [3]

Such a richly variegated personality need not go outside himself for portraits. If Alice is his seeking self, his best-beloved ego to which he assigns all the desirable traits, then the White Rabbit is his timid, donnish self, struck inarticulate for half-an-hour when a brother don catches him walking with a little girl; the man with the little black bag, the gloves (my paws and whiskers, the gloves!), the pocketbook with the many compartments—the man with the peculiar gait, the stammer, the inability to carve a joint, who softly and suddenly vanished away if anyone mentioned his books.

The penultimate paragraphs of *Alice's Adventures Underground* follow: "But her sister sat there some while longer, watching the setting sun, and thinking of little Alice and her adventures, till she too began dreaming after a fashion, and this was her dream.

"She saw an ancient city, and a quiet river widening near it along the plain, and up the stream went slowly gliding a boat with a merry party of children on board—she could hear the voices and laughter like music over the water—and among them was another little Alice, who sat listening with bright eager eyes, to a tale that was being told, and she listened for the words of the tale, and lo, it was the dream of her own little sister. So the boat wound slowly along, beneath the bright summer-day, with its merry crew and its voices of music and laughter, till it passed round one of the many turnings of the stream, and she saw it no more."

To so accomplished an acrobat, a dream within a dream is a small matter. It is indeed the blend of logical with dream material that gives Carroll's works their distinct and inimitable flavor. The fall down the Rabbit hole, for instance, is a birth dream indeed—and what a symbol—the Rabbit for fertility! The motif is always cropping out; when Alice is in the long hall, later the Hall of Tears, she finds the key to the little door, that "led into a small passage, not much larger than a rat-hole: she knelt down and looked along the passage . . . but she could not even get her head through the doorway." Later she slips into the pool of tears and swims about easily. Then, in the Rabbit's house, she starts to grow uncomfortably large and threatens to burst the house. When Bill the Lizard comes down the chimney after her, she makes a final effort and succeeds in retracting one leg far enough to kick him back up.

Birth dreams are universal, but since we are born without language, they use visual and muscular imagery; whatever reminds us of birth retains a mysterious fascination, unaccountable till this great discovery of Dr. Rank's. *Wonderland* contains all the elements—the comfortable swimming about in the water, the doubt of being able to get her head through the narrow passage, the constriction of the small room, increasing threateningly as she grows; the attempt to kick out in a narrow space. To name and classify a dream element is merely to recognize the unconscious. But these birth images must have had a meaning to their inventor; a spiritual rebirth, perhaps—for Dodgson was just over the hill from one of his major crises. He had looked down into the Deanery garden from the library window for years, he was thirty years old, and he had taken holy orders six months before. And perhaps that was it.

Acceptance of ordination after so many doubts and such a long postponement—he had been eligible for six years— must have required a new synthesis. The scene in the Hall of Tears, where Alice gives herself good advice, the one where "Once she remembered trying to box her own ears for having cheated herself in a game of croquet, for this curious child was very fond of pretending to be two people," and other hints, suggest Dodgson may have had fleeting doubts of his own identity, no doubt intensified since his ordination. For it was not Alice Liddell who pretended to be two people, or who needed rebirth.

As Lowes says again: "Great art is more often than not

the product of tendencies which are art's undoing when uncontrolled . . . there enter into imaginative creation three factors which reciprocally interplay: the Well, and the Vision, and the Will . . . the long, slow storing of the Well . . . the flash of amazing vision through a fortuitous suggestion . . . the exciting task of translating the vision into reality." [11] All these factors were present, and he resigned himself—on the surface—to being the Reverend Charles Dodgson; but, as the outer bonds gripped tighter, the inner self soared more and more. For such a nature, actually, stone walls do not a prison make, since the space inside a spirit of genius is infinite.

The *Alice* books are frankly dream stories; both have an elaborate and rather orgiastic nightmarish awakening, though only in the first one does the dreamer direct the dream. Both use the materials of the universal dream or folk tale; their prime value lies in this articulation of the inarticulate impressions of childhood and in their multiple use on several planes simultaneously, which make them interesting to all ages and cultural levels.

Here may be, for instance, a memory of school, of Oxford, of the ordination. It takes place in the Rabbit's house, after Alice has grown too large for comfort: " 'It was much pleasanter at home,' thought poor Alice, 'when one wasn't always growing larger and smaller, and being ordered about by mice and rabbits. I almost wish I hadn't come down that rabbit-hole—and yet—and yet—it's rather curious, you know, this sort of life!' " There is the humorous resignation of a young man who finds himself, against his wishes, growing up and forced to take on the attributes of Father William. That poem is not the expression of secure manhood, and Carroll's own illustrations show the youth's surprise, intensified almost to agony, at his father's smug competence. In one picture the youth is distinctly what Gilbert took the liberty of calling a *je ne sais quoi* young man.

The next challenge Alice meets is even more serious. " 'Who are *you?*' said the Caterpillar." When Alice courteously tries to answer him, he makes himself more disagreeable.

" 'I—I hardly know, Sir, just at present—at least I know

who I *was* when I got up this morning, but I think I must
have been changed several times since then.'

" 'What do you mean by that?' said the Caterpillar, sternly.
'Explain yourself!'

" 'I can't explain *myself*, I'm afraid, Sir,' said Alice, 'because I'm not myself, you see.'

" 'I don't see,' said the Caterpillar.

" 'I'm afraid I can't put it more clearly,' Alice replied very
politely, 'for I can't understand it myself, to begin with; and
being so many different sizes in a day is very confusing.'

" 'It isn't,' said the Caterpillar."

Another distressing scene, when Alice's neck has grown so
long it winds over the tree-tops, and a Pigeon challenges her:

" 'But I'm *not* a serpent, I tell you!' said Alice. 'I'm a—I'm
a—'

" 'Well! *What* are you?' said the Pigeon. 'I can see you're
trying to invent something.'

" 'I—I'm a little girl,' said Alice, rather doubtfully, as she
remembered the number of changes she had gone through,
that day.

" 'A likely story indeed!' said the Pigeon, in a tone of the
deepest contempt. 'I've seen a good many little girls in my
time, but never *one* with such a neck as that! No, no! You're
a serpent; and there's no use denying it.' "

Some biographers thought Dodgson lived a calm and placid
life under the spreading oaks of Oxford. But is the following,
for instance, pure fun? " 'In *that* direction,' the Cat said,
waving its right paw round, 'lives a Hatter: and in *that* direction,' waving the other paw, 'lives a March Hare. Visit either
you like: they're both mad.'

" 'But I don't want to go among mad people,' Alice remarked.

" 'Oh, you can't help that,' said the Cat: 'we're all mad
here. I'm mad. You're mad.'

" 'How do you know I'm mad?' said Alice.

" 'You must be,' said the Cat, 'or you wouldn't have come
here.' "

This gives some idea of what Charles felt about the world
around him and his part in it. But in some way the very
sacrifice it cost him to take orders seems to have fired him

to the highest point of his career. *Alice in Wonderland* is the choice flower of his genius. *Through the Looking-Glass* is witty, inventive, quaint, what you will; but the shadow of the Red Queen of Logic and the mysterious threat of the Red King hang over it; the dreamer who may own not only the dream but even the characters in it, keeps it from being an unclouded childish story. The little girl who said she liked both stories, but thought *Through the Looking-Glass* was "stupider" than *Wonderland*, conveys the same idea. Nothing in *Wonderland* parallels the complete severance of the Reds and Whites in *Through the Looking-Glass*. In *Sylvie and Bruno*, author and story have begun to disintegrate. The archness and sweetness of parts, the utter cruelty and loathsomeness of others, predict literal decomposition into his elements.

Wonderland has none of that. In it Carroll wields a nimble shuttle, weaving disparate threads into a unified and perfect textile, of the pattern of the search for the golden fleece, or the golden apples, or the fountain of youth, or the pot of gold at the rainbow's end; the search for the universal treasure, that mankind recognizes with a joyful stirring. It is the plot of our life here on earth, and any honest story that conforms to it, adds to it, finds new forms and characters for it, even for the thousandth telling, will move us. It is not even a special result of civilization that finding the treasure does not bring happiness—what of the fisherman whose wife would be pope, or the one whose wife won three wishes and had to use the third to get the sausage off her husband's nose? The wish can be fulfilled only in a dream, and the happy ending is—to awaken and find one is still oneself, and can trace some of the dream elements, as Alice did, to familiar sights and sounds. As Carroll's fellow-mathematician and Yankee contemporary, Willard Gibbs, remarked, "The whole is simpler than its parts." [14]

Here sits Mr. Dodgson, then, in the tightest kind of box— Christ Church Don by his own exertions, Student by the grace of Dr. Pusey, Deacon of the Church of England by the hand of Bishop Wilberforce; with his thoughts and actions prescribed by medieval tradition, by the prejudices of Prince Albert, by the Dean of Christ Church, by his father the Arch-

deacon and his old schoolmaster the Archbishop of Canterbury, by the whole hierarchy through Oliver Cromwell clear
up to God, not to mention the Reverend Charles Dodgson
himself, one of the strictest of the lot. Tighter and tighter,
oh Lord! The only escape is down the rabbit hole and into
the beautiful garden.

And like Carl Sandburg's *Gimme the Ax,* "when he gets to
the moon he will find everything the same as it always was."

Chapter 7

The Lion and the Unicorn

"I should win easy," said the Lion.
"I'm not so sure of that," said the Unicorn.

IN HIS EARLY YEARS Charles Dodgson was in little danger of
being lionized. Later he was somewhat troubled that way,
but by nature he was more unicorn than lion, and sometimes,
like a minor character in a play, he appeared merely in the
chaste anonymity of "a clergyman." In August, 1864, William
Blake Richmond was painting a portrait of the Liddell sisters
at Llandudno, on the coast of Wales, where their father had
built a summer home. At the same time Matthew Arnold,
also in Llandudno for the Eisteddfod or Bardic Contest,
wrote his mother: "There are one or two people here: the
Liddells, with whom we dined; the Scudamore Stanhopes,
him I knew slightly at Oxford; the Dean of Chichester; a
clergyman or two, who have called." [1] Among the clergymen,
whether or not he called, may have been a unicorn who was
to become more of a lion than Arnold himself.

The Dean's house, "Penmorfa," now a hotel, stands near
the shore at the southwest corner of Great Orme's Head. Says
Richmond: "Behind it rose the wild headland, before it lay
an expanse of shallow sea, so that when the tide was out and
the sun set over the island, wondrous colors were thrown
upon the rugged hills and reflected in glittering lights and
tints upon the wet sands." [2] Matthew Arnold too thought the
sunsets the finest in the British Isles.

The first summer the Liddells spent in this heavenly spot
was in 1862, right after the expedition to Godstow, although
the house had been built the year before. As at Oxford, they
entertained largely, and besides entertaining their house guests,
they were visited almost daily by the Aclands and the Caven-
dishes, who stayed at Penmaenmawr. During the Summer of
1864 they were also visited frequently by Arnold and by
Gladstone.[3] Richmond claimed Dodgson stayed at the Lid-

The Liddell sisters, painted by Sir William Blake Richmond;
left to right: Edith, Lorina, Alice.

dells' during at least part of the painting of the picture, which took six or seven weeks.

The Liddells' house guests were taken on long drives or picnics, sometimes in the brilliant sun, sometimes at full moon through a "silver, shining, mysterious land." It appears that Richmond painted the girls indoors, and put in the background of sand dunes later. He found the sisters eager and patient subjects, sitting for him eight or ten hours at a stretch, without complaint. In the next room the Dean was working away at the Lexicon; regularly every day at twelve o'clock he sneezed. *"Why*—no one knew, but it was a fact about which the children often teased him." [2] The twelve o'clock sneeze signaled one hour more of work till dinner time. The afternoons were devoted partly to painting again, otherwise to walks on the sand dunes or sketching parties.

The painter, then a young man and unknown, found his subjects not only patient but delightful to paint. He says: "It was a household of quite exceptional physical beauty. The Dean was as handsome a specimen of aristocratic manhood as could be seen in a lifetime. Mrs. Liddell was remarkably beautiful, of a Spanish type, although I am not aware if she had Spanish blood. . . . It would be difficult to choose between the beauty of the daughters. I painted them all upon various occasions—Lorna [sic], Alice, Edith, and Rhoda. Their mother dressed them most picturesquely, leaving nothing for me to design in the way of garments." [2]

It is hard to imagine how cloistered these university families were even into the present century. Only Captain Hargreaves' authority makes this story plausible: "Some time" before 1928, he was visiting a home where the guests were playing guessing games. The question arose whether the Alice of *Alice in Wonderland* was a real girl. Captain Hargreaves heard it said she was a myth. [4] This incident determined him to induce his mother to tell, since she would not write, her reminiscences. From these notes he published two articles in 1932. And of Mrs. Liddell still less is known than of her daughters. In the early years of her marriage, when her husband was Head of Westminster School, the boys named a boat for her; she helped them with the costumes for their Latin play and coached those who had female rôles in the gait and manner suitable for their parts. She was a notable hostess, she dressed elegantly, behaved graciously, and was an excellent wife and mother.

One family scene that Richmond gives shows the Dean's tenderer side. During this same August, *Enoch Arden* was published, and the Dean read aloud from it in the evenings while the girls sewed and the painter drew. ". . . When Enoch comes back, looks in at the window and sees the new husband and wife of his youth among their children, he fairly broke down; the strong, stern man was moved beyond his power of restraint . . . a tenderer, more affectionate man did not exist than Henry George Liddell."

With the painting of "The Sisters," or "The Three Graces," as it is sometimes called, Ruskin was delighted, but he had a characteristic objection: "My dear Willie, you have made one great mistake. The rest of your picture being supremely beautiful, why the devil did you paint the damsel's shoes instead of her feet? Perugino would never have made such a mistake." [2]

In 1907 Sir William revisited Llandudno and pointed out the corner room on the first floor where the picture had been painted, and gave an interview to the County Court Registrar about hearing the readings from *Alice*.[3]

Sir William Richmond's reminscences were written down long after his stay at Llandudno, and so were Mrs. Hargreaves's. It seems, from Mr. Green's researches, that either or both of these stories may have grown from a memory of a visit Dodgson did make to the Liddells at another summer home in Charlton Kings in 1863.[5] By the time the White Rabbit in front of the Liddells' old home has finished disintegrating, there will be nobody left to insist that Lewis Carroll slept—and, more important, dreamed—there.

On August 6, 1862, Dodgson and the Liddells were still at Oxford. He writes: "In the afternoon Harcourt and I took the three Liddells up to Godstow, where we had tea; we tried the game of 'Ural Mountains,' on the way, but it did not prove very successful, and I had to go on with my interminable fairy-tale of *Alice's Adventures*. We got back soon after eight, and had supper in my rooms, the children coming over for a short while. A very enjoyable expedition—the last,

I should think, to which Ina is likely to be allowed to come—her fourteenth time."

The shadow was falling—the child friends were starting to grow up—so soon after the apogee came the decline.

Besides the White Rabbit, the Dormouse also has a candidate for the original, which according to Ford Madox Brown (quoted by William Rossetti), was Dante Gabriel's wombat. Dodgson knew all the Rossettis, but William seems to have known him only as unicorn. He said: "I saw him only once or twice. He was a skillful amateur photographer, and he took some few photographs of D.R., and of other members of the family. He continued keeping up some little acquaintance with Christina till the close of her life, sending her his successive publications. My reminiscence of Mr. Dodgson is so slight and indeterminate that it would be vain to attempt any exactness of description. Suffice it to say that he impressed me mainly as belonging to the type of 'the University Man': a certain externalism of polite propriety, verging towards the conventional. I do not think in my presence he said anything 'funny' or quaint." [6]

But William would have been the least attractive member of the family to Carroll. Dante Gabriel was the classic bohemian artist. *Il ne se laisse pas borner; il se permet tout.* Even more than other occurrences, each of his pictures poised on a Humpty Dumpty wall of probabilities—to be or not to be? Each one finished was an individual miracle. The tough, thin spider silk of Elizabeth Siddal's beauty drew him from one luminous painting to the next. After her death the Blessed Damozel leaned down from heaven and coaxed him still to paint her (alternating, to be sure, with Fanny Cornforth and Janey Morris), till he like Keats, was done to death by a review.

In 1870 one pseudonymous "Thomas Maitland" scurrilously reviewed his book as "The Fleshly School of Poetry," and this penny trumpet sounded the doom of Gabriel, whose insomnia intensified till he began overdosing himself with a fatal cocktail of chloral and alcohol; the review still ate at his fiber till he heard voices conspiring against him. In 1871 his "dear glorious Browning's" *Fifine at the Fair* seemed a slander in code, and by 1876 poor Lewis Carroll's *Hunting of the Snark* appeared a long and elaborate pasquinade against him.[7]

If Dodgson knew this, he knew how to take it, for early in 1883 he went to London especially to see the exhibition of Rossetti's paintings in the Burlington Gallery. Naturally, he preferred the worst of them, because it was the most literary: "Found," which Gabriel had been tinkering with from 1854 till 1882, and had left incomplete at the end, so that Burne-Jones washed in a sky over the graveyard Rossetti had sketched. Of this period piece Dodgson says: "A picture of a man finding, in the streets of London, a girl he had loved years before in the days of her innocence. She is huddled up against the wall, dressed in gaudy colors, and trying to turn away her agonized face, while he, holding her wrists, is looking down with an expression of pain and pity, condemnation and love, which is one of the most marvelous things I have ever seen done in painting." [8] Carroll, like the subject of the painting, also had to turn away his face a little, for the model was Fanny Cornforth, Gabriel's one *pied à terre* in an unreliable universe, but nobody for a clergyman to gaze upon.

William says that Dodgson had been a frequent visitor at the Cheyne Walk house to which Gabriel moved after his wife's death early in 1862. Christina says of "Tudor House": "There were various creatures, quaint or beautiful, about the house and grounds, some of them at liberty. I particularly recall Bobby, a little owl with a very large face and a beak of a sort of eggshell green; a woodchuck, a deer, and a wombat. . . . With such inhabitants, Tudor House and its grounds became a sort of Wonderland; and once the author of *Wonderland* photographed us in the garden. It was our aim to appear in the full family group of five; but whilst various others succeeded, that particular negative was spoilt by a shower, and I possess a solitary print taken from it in which we appear as if splashed by ink." [9]

Between Charles Dodgson and that still insufficiently regarded poet Christina Rossetti the sympathy and correspondence was so great as to suggest infinite mutual mirroring. From this distance it is hard to see how those two escaped falling in love with each other. Christina's two beloved but rejected suitors were more footling and infinitely less talented than Charles, and it would seem that the two might have inspired each other to heights of literature and Anglicanism and ended up in the same heaven. But it was not to be.

Edmund Gosse quotes Swinburne as calling Christina Rossetti "the Jael who led their [pre-Raphaelite] hosts to victory," and he, Swinburne, undoubtedly used and elaborated her rhythms. She seems to have been a natural and underivative poet, whose earliest poems, her biographer Mary Sandars points out, were as perfect as her last. Unlike her sister Maria, she seems not to have been a born *réligieuse,* however, and she suffered at the necessity of rejecting first James Collinson, who at the showdown found the Catholic Church more necessary to him than Christina, and second Charles Bagot Cayley, an honest agnostic like her good brother William Michael on whose generosity a marriage with Cayley would moreover have depended, the suitor being penniless to boot. Christina Rossetti's way of handling emotion differed greatly from Dodgson's; her numerous love poems are those of honest frustration and sorrow, and her "Convent Threshold" is renunciation of that which it is pain to renounce. Her attitude toward the so-called "fleshly" poetry of her brother Gabriel, and toward his quite fleshly life, as well as toward the poetry of Swinburne, is compounded of poetic good taste and religious prudery—a combination to delight our Mr. Dodgson. With Gabriel she was never offended, though doubtless she passed over phases of his life in silence; of Swinburne's poetry she read by no means all; *Atalanta* she rejoiced in, but she pasted bits of paper over certain lines, which any reader with Victorian blood in his or her veins can easily discover.

She was quick to give from her little funds, and like Charles, "not [to] *lend,* but [to] *give.*" Her spirituality was superlative—Holman Hunt found her eyes the only ones he could use for the Christ in his famous "Light of the World." Then too there are her love of animals, which indeed was a Rossetti trait, and in her case extended even to the cold and slimy—the frogs, snails, and caterpillars of Carroll's lifelong interest, and the crocodile, which he also loved—and her perfect diction, her pleasant little talent for drawing, her habit of sketching her own illustrations—there is no end to the interests and abilities they had in common, or even to the compulsions and taboos.

Their first meeting was caused by Dodgson's camera, and Christina's last mention of him is when she wrote to William that her *Speaking Likenesses* was "merely a Christmas trifle, would-be in the *Alice* style." [10] But that Charles Dodgson dined at Gabriel's home in Cheyne Walk when Christina was present is certain, and this was also the period of the first and most favored wombat, which used to sleep on the flower-filled épergne on the table. The Mad Tea Party does not appear in *Alice Underground,* so there was time for the wombat to be converted into a dormouse.

Several entries in Dodgson's diaries note his going to call on Christina, but never without a child friend coming along. On June 12, 1886, he records: "Met Beatrice at the station in London. We called on the Cootes; then on Miss Rossetti (whose mother died about two months ago)."

Christina gave of her time to the inmates of the Mary Magdalene Home, and to an invalid who wrote a great deal of mediocre poetry which she sent Christina for criticism—both true Christian charities after Dodgson's heart. She has been called the poet of tractarianism, and like his own sisters, she was self-exiled from the theater.[11]

Her *Goblin Market* was printed in 1862, and her second volume of poems in 1866. The illustrations to the latter volume were "undertaken by Hughes and Houghton with Wigaud and Knestub as his subordinates, while Dodgson (the Oxford man and photographer), celebrated as the author of *Alice in Wonderland,* asked if Rivington, a friend of his, might illustrate one or both volumes of her poems. He would do it very cheaply, and Dodgson sent a design of his idea for 'Passing Away,' which William says: 'Though not advanced in execution, is finely felt, and a good deal like what Christina herself might do, if she knew enough to draw.' " [12] But that is a Rossetti judgment—it seems, from some reproductions that have survived, that her work was not only similar to but as good as his.

In 1864, we gather from the context, Christina wrote: "My dear Mr. Dodgson

"We are not at all uneasy about the Clergy Trading Act,

but sincerely grateful for your kind trouble-taking agency. I hope my list will prove intelligible. We want, please [list of eleven photographs, mostly of their family and of Gabriel's pictures].

"Delightful it would be, that possible visit to Oxford. We contemplate it in a spirit of vague approbation. Stirred up by the kind offer of such a Showman, and by a wish to see the sights of Oxford in general, and Gabriel's handiwork in particular; weighed down by family immobility;—we tremble in the balance, though I fear the leaden element preponderates. It is characteristic of us to miss opportunities. A year or two ago I had a chance of seeing Cambridge, and of course missed it." [13]

But Gabriel and his wife had been to Oxford, to put Lizzie, or "Guggum," under Dr. Acland's care. Violet Hunt claims "Lewis Carroll sketched Gabriel for her [Christina] when he came down [to Oxford] and made her and the chimney sweeps laugh and the undergraduates thaw, but she was too old for *him*." [14] Actually Christina was only two years older than Charles, which explains nothing. To Gabriel, however, he was still "a clergyman"—Gabriel's letter to his mother, July 1855, says: "I went to Oxford some weeks ago when Guggum was there, and met some nice people, Dr. Acland and his family, who, as well as many others, were most kind to her there—too kind, for they bothered her greatly with attentions." [15]

Hallam Tennyson, in three thick, stuffy volumes about his father, never mentioned the Oxford photographer who came to Farringford to pay his respects to the Great Poet. Mr. Hudson has put together, with the aid of some letters in the Yale collection, a painful story of Dodgson's relations with Tennyson. Dodgson had made his approach via photographs of Agnes Grace Weld, Tennyson's niece, which the poet admired, and there had been visits and pleasant relationships, beginning at Coniston in the Lake District in the summer of 1857 and continuing in 1859 on the Isle of Wight, and including photographs of Tennyson and of his son Hallam.

Dodgson's parody of Tennyson's "Two Voices," ("Three Voices") had appeared in *The Train* in 1856, under the signature of Lewis Carroll, but there is no reason to believe that

Tennyson associated this with Dodgson. The contretemps seems to have occurred as a result of Dodgson's persistence and Tennyson's rough and ready gesture of self-protection.

Somebody was handing around unauthorized copies of some of Tennyson's earlier poems, which he was trying to suppress because they were not up to the standard he set for himself. Two of these had come Dodgson's way, and he went through an elaborate dance with the first, writing to ask Tennyson's permission to keep, and in the second instance even to read, the poems. The first was "The Lover's Tale," the second "The Window."

Tennyson did not even answer Dodgson's letter himself. "Dear Sir,

"It is useless troubling Mr. Tennyson with a request which will only revive the annoyance he has already had on the subject and add to it.

"No doubt the 'Window' is circulated by means of the same unscrupulous person who placed 'The Lover's Tale' in your hands.

"It would be well that whatever may be done by such people a gentleman should understand that when an author does not give his works to the public he has his own reasons for it.

Yours truly,
Emily Tennyson."

Dodgson recognized this as virtually an answer from Tennyson and dealt with it as such, politely but firmly trying to extract an apology for the unjustified accusation. Tennyson's answer(s) has not been preserved, but Dodgson let himself go in what can only be considered a Dodgson-Carroll letter. On one side of the sheet he wrote:

"Sir, you are no gentleman.

"Sir, you do me grievous wrong by such words. Prove them or retract them!

"I reiterate them. Your conduct has been dishonorable.

"It is not so. I offer a full history of my conduct. I charge you with groundless libel: what say you to the charge?

"I once believed even worse of you, but begin to think you may be a gentleman after all.

"These new imputations are as unfounded as the former.

Once more, what say you to the charge of groundless libel?
"*I absolve you.* Say no more."

This is followed by the words "Turn over." On the verso is written:

"My Dear Sir,

"Thus it is, as it seems to me, that you first do a man an injury, and then forgive him—that you first tread on his toes, and then beg him not to cry out!

"Nevertheless I accept what you say, as being in substance, what it certainly is not in form, a retractation [sic] (though without a shadow of apology or expression of regret) of all dishonorable charges against me, & an admission that you had made them on insufficient grounds.

Sincerely yours,

C. L. Dodgson."

This is in line with Dodgson's explanation of the portmanteau words in *Through the Looking-Glass.* He gives as an example "frumious"—if you wanted to say "fuming" and "furious" and did not know which to say first, you might end up with "frumious." This sounds very like the stammerer's predicament, and that of a man who could not decide whether to let the left hemisphere or the right take over. Surely only a person with these disabilities would write a twin letter on such a serious occasion.

Two years later he offered Tennyson the name of one of the practitioners who worked with stammerers, for Lionel Tennyson. The poet answered briefly and with a minimum courtesy. The loss, it seems today, was mainly Tennyson's.

Greville Macdonald had more gratitude. He wrote: "How happily could my father [George Macdonald, author of *At the Back of the North Wind*] laugh over this unfailing humorist's impromptu drawings, full of the absurdities, mock maxims, and erratic logic so dear to the childheart, young or old! While Dodgson, the shy, learned mathematician who hated inaccuracy, loved to question the very multiplication table's veracity, my father the poet, who hated any touch of irreverence, could laugh till tears ran out at his friend's ridicule of smug formalism and copy-book maxims." [16]

In June, 1867, Matthew Arnold again writes: "Dressed for Balliol. It was an immense party, and we dined at the high table in hall." He gives a list of "important" guests, "besides Mrs. Liddell and a great number of Oxford people. . . . There was a great evening party afterwards." The conclusion is that either Jowett never did forgive Mr. Dodgson for calling him "the lowest term" of Greek professor, or that Mr. Dodgson was present merely as "a clergyman." Not only Jowett's *Life,* but Stanley's, Dean Liddell's and even Ruskin's omit all mention of their acquaintance with Dodgson. But of course they all considered themselves persons of more importance than the don with the luminous prose.

Friendship with Ruskin, as Rossetti found out, was at best a prickly state. He was a genius, but a sick one. He hit the target always, the bull's-eye often. By 1868, however, he was already speaking of the successive failures of his life; great as was the influence he wielded on taste and conscience alike, the untouched and untouchable areas of blank ugliness and oppression weighed him down gradually, piling up to the break-down and spells of madness of his closing years. His long bondage to his parents, his unfulfilled love first for Adèle Domecq, later for Rose La Touche; his unfulfillable marriage to Euphemia Gray: all these were parts of his burden that might have been lightened, but his *Weltschmerz* was, not the egotistic projection of a young Werther, but genuine world-pain, and his determination to show the ladies and gentlemen of his era the bloody thorns under their beds of roses no doubt caused that stubborn closing of the doors of the mind against him which destroyed him in the end.

The preface to the first edition of *Ethics of the Dust,* addressed to young girls, and dated Christmas of 1865, the year of *Alice's Adventures,* presents his audience with every social and moral and religious problem, graded for their age to be sure, and encouraging them to feel that their own hearts are right and good, but in no way softening or side-stepping the horrid facts, and reminding them that a "lady" is a bread-giver. In *Sesame and Lilies* he covers the same fields, telling the girls of the ancient and honorable arts of agriculture, weaving, and building, and of the teacher who said: "I was an hungered, and ye gave me no meat: I was thirsty, and ye gave me no drink . . . naked and ye clothed me not." Eventually Ruskin holds ladies responsible even for war.

He taught regularly in a girls' school, and took, like Carroll, great pleasure in the society of little girls. In his fragmentary autobiography, *Praeterita,* he tells the following story
as of *circa* 1854, though he must have been at least ten years
off on the date: "I never went to official dinners in Oxford
if I could help it . . . when the Princess of Wales came, one
winter, to look over the Art Galleries, I had of course to
attend . . . and then came commands to the dinner at the
Deanery . . . The day before, or the day before that, the
Planet Saturn had treated me with his usual adversity in the
carrying out of a plot with Alice in Wonderland. For, that
evening, the Dean and Mrs. Liddell dined by command at
Blenheim: but the girls were not commanded; and as I had
been complaining of never getting a sight of them lately, after
knowing them from the nursery, Alice said that she thought,
perhaps, if I would come round after papa and mamma were
safe off to Blenheim, Edith and she might give us a cup of
tea and a little singing, and Rhoda show me how she was getting on with her drawing and geometry, or the like. And so
it was arranged. The night was wild with snow, and no one
likely to come around to the Deanery after dark. I think
Alice must have sent me a little note, when the eastern coast
of Tom Quad was clear. I slipped round from Corpus through
Peckwater, shook the snow off my gown, and found an armchair ready for me, and a bright fireside and tea coming up.

"Well, I think Edith had got the tea made, and Alice was
just bringing the muffins to perfection—I don't recollect that
Rhoda was there; (I never did, that anybody else was there,
if Edith was; but it is all so like a dream now, I'm not sure)
when there was a sudden sense of some stars having been
blown out by the wind, round the corner; and then a crush-
ing of the snow outside the house, and a drifting of it inside;
and the children all scampered out to see what was wrong,
and I followed slowly;—and there were the Dean and Mrs.
Liddell standing just in the middle of the hall, and the foot-
men in consternation, and a silence, and—

" 'How sorry you must be to see us, Mr. Ruskin!' began
at last Mrs. Liddell.

" 'I never was more so,' I replied. 'But what's the matter?'

" 'Well,' said the Dean, 'we couldn't even get past the Parks;

the snow's a fathom deep in the Woodstock Road. But never mind; we'll be very good and quiet, and keep out of the way. Go back to your tea, and we'll have our dinner downstairs.'

"And so we did, but we couldn't keep papa and mamma out of the drawing-room when they had done dinner, and I went back to Corpus, disconsolate."

Next evening came vengeance. The facts seem plausible enough, though in addition to a ten years' error in the date, he confuses the fourth daughter, Rhoda, who was too small to go on the trip to Godstow, with Lorina, the eldest, who was fourteen in 1864. He was at dinner at the Liddells', with the Princess and others. "The door from the nurseries opened; and enter Rhoda—in full dress!

"Very beautiful! But just a snip too short in the petticoats, a trip too dainty in the ankles, a dip too deep of sweet-briar-red in the ribands. Not the damsel who came to hearken . . . D'Israeli saw his opening in an instant . . . 'This is, I understand, the young lady in whose art education Professor Ruskin is so much interested!'

"I had never given Rhoda a lesson in my life (no such luck!) yet I could not disclaim the interest." [17] And that is as close to a word about Carroll as searching has revealed in any writing or biography of Ruskin. Dr. Liddell's biographer, though almost a classmate of Mr. Dodgson, never mentions him, nor the name of Alice Liddell, throughout the bulky *Life* of the Dean. The author, Mr. Thompson, who thanks the elusive Mr. T. Vere Bayne for assistance in the book, was the same Reverend Henry L. Thompson who wrote Carroll's obituary in the *Oxford Magazine.* Curiouser and curiouser.

Perhaps it was not so very odd after all. Perhaps Dr. Liddell was the father figure against whom Dodgson expressed his aggression, and perhaps Liddell did not enjoy being the butt of so many sharp little arrows. In one of the numerous pamphlets, *The New Examination Statute,* were three lines:

"J is for (Jowett) who lectures in Attic,
      K is for (Kitchin), than attic much warmer.
      L is for (Liddell), relentless reformer."

Whether it was the layout of the grounds, repairs to the buildings, or the academic regime, Liddell was always changing, and Dodgson always resisting change. In *The Vision of the Three T's* he tackled Mrs. Liddell and her supposed desire to capture a titled or royal suitor for one of her daughters: ". . . the Goldfish, which is a species highly thought of, not only by men, but by divers birds, as for instance the Kingfisher." Probably none of this advanced his case with the Dean, or gave him a place in the Dean's biography.

At Oxford the Liddells also lived well and entertained largely. To Alice, with her numerous brothers and sisters—they were ten in all, including two who died young—the Deanery seemed only a "fair-sized house"—to most it would seem spacious. Dr. Liddell remodeled it, put in new paneling and decorations in drawing-room and hall, opened the long gallery on the first floor and built a stately staircase, called the "Lexicon" staircase because the book paid for it. The gallery was ornamented with three carved lions from the Liddell crest; Alice tells how she and Lorina and Edith used to rush down the gallery to their bedrooms at night, in case the lions should leave their pedestals and chase them. The girls were also timid about the swans when they went boating, but, said Alice, "We were too happy to be *really* frightened." [4]

Born next door to Westminster Abbey, where she was christened, and eventually married, Alice was only four when her father became Dean of Christ Church, and her first meeting with Mr. Dodgson was not long after. With parents who, like the Dodgsons, governed by love and charm, and who expected only excellence from their children, it is not surprising that the young ladies were irresistible.

With less need for childish conspiracy than in their visit with Ruskin, the three eldest used to slip out of the back door of the deanery, along Tom Quad, under the arch, to Mr. Dodgson's rooms. Their governess, Miss Prickett—"Pricks" —came along. She was doubtless the source of the copious misinformation Carroll's Alice spouts so freely. But she was supplemented by masters of French, German, and Italian, and by music mistresses. Alice, at least, attended the School of Art, where Ruskin had the mixed pleasure of instructing her. She also studied cookery and dancing, including, of course, the quadrille.[4]

The strangest hiatus between Carroll and his contemporaries reaches to Edward Lear, in whose biography Angus Davidson says: "There occurred during the autumn of that year [1865], in the world of which, until now, Lear had been undisputed king—the world of Nonsense—an event of the utmost importance, the publication of Lewis Carroll's *Alice in Wonderland*. From Lear's complete silence on the matter it might be thought that he never heard either of the book or of . . . its author; yet this is hardly possible. He was in London when it came out." [18] Lear and Dodgson both knew most of the pre-Raphaelites and moved in overlapping circles; if they never met, they could hardly have escaped hearing each other's *bon mots*. But Carroll never mentions Lear either, and Mr. Madan said there seemed to be "no trace" of Lear in his library.[19] Nevertheless it is unthinkable that Carroll had not read the *Book of Nonsense*, which came out when he was fourteen. Carroll at least eventually appreciated Lear, for Miss Dodgson writes in a letter that he gave her and her sisters one of the Lear books. Perhaps the two lions were mutually carnivorous, like Eugene Field's fierce toy animals, and circled round at a respectful distance to keep from eating each other up.

Chapter 8

Travel with a Porpoise

No wise fish would go anywhere without a porpoise.

MOST OF DODGSON'S TRAVELS, outside of short excursions and vacation trips in England, Scotland, Wales, the Channel Islands, and the Isle of Wight, were travels of the mind and spirit. When he did cross the Channel for a continental tour that included some six weeks in Russia, he traveled less truly than when he sat in the Christ Church library, watching the Liddell chidren play croquet.

His insularity was unimpaired by the continental tour. Except for a few words in later letters, it is vain to seek any references to his Russian trip. *The Russian Journal,* for many years inaccessible in a private collection, was finally published in 1935. The book is interesting only because Carroll's style never leaves him, even in dealing with trivia, and because of the light it thinly sprays on his Anglophilia.

The oddest part of the trip was the choice of a companion —Canon Henry Parry Lidon, a man of a "sweet and gentle melancholy." Dr. Liddon is alleged to have had a "playful manner and a sense of humour," [1] but all the anecdotes illustrate his other side. He was so close a friend of Dr. Pusey that, at the latter's death, Liddon retired to write his life. He was alarmed at the state of Oxford, which "seemed to him to be on the point of becoming a place of purely secular instruction, which might have been founded last week by a company of shareholders. He wished the church might retain two or three colleges altogether and surrender the rest." [1]

Later, as Canon of St. Paul's, "Liddon took us straight up to heaven and kept us there an hour." [1] To be exact, his sermons lasted from forty-five minutes to an hour and a half, and heaven was not the only place visited. "His appeals to emotions were very thrilling, not to say terrible. His sermon on the first five minutes after death made a serious impression that would not easily wear out." [1]

Personally, he practiced meditation and prayer, and "kept a careful rule of life." Regretfully he admitted that not all clergymen could maintain celibacy, and while "recognizing the grave disaster that may follow any attempt to impose" that rule, he still yearned for more men voluntarily to adopt it. Miss Elizabeth Wordsworth, grandniece of the poet, and first principal of Lady Margaret Hall, one of Oxford's earliest concessions to the female desire for learning, thought Canon Liddon objected to women's colleges because he was "afraid of seeing the story of Ruth re-enacted in Christ Church quad." [2]

The former Dean of Christ Church, later Bishop of Oxford, Dr. Thomas Banks Strong, wrote in a letter: "I saw a great deal of Liddon. He was very fond of going into the Christ Church meadow late at night. We had keys and could get out that way. One night we were going round and the corn crake was croaking in the grass. Liddon said 'I like that bird.' I said I thought I had heard birds that sang better. 'Oh, it is not that,' said Liddon, 'to me it represents moral earnestness, it goes on saying what it knows to be unpalatable.' " But he did have a lighter side. The tradition is that he designed the improved form of the New Belfry, which must have endeared him to Dodgson, and that he suggested the title *Through the Looking-Glass, and What Alice Found There.*

What may have appealed to Carroll, apart from the piety common to both men, was Liddon's interest in the arts—especially, of course, the religious arts. After his appointment to St. Paul's, he adorned the church and elevated the services. He loved Bach's *Passions,* Dante's poetry, and painting and architecture that led to heaven; certainly the travelers saw as many museums as churches; but Carroll attended the theater alone. Excerpts from a letter Liddon wrote in 1879 to the Reverend J. Oakley leave no possible doubt as to his position on the theater:

"ON THE PROPOSED CHURCH AND STAGE GUILD
"C. L. Dodgson told me some days ago of the substance of

the Paper which you are so good as to send me, and for which I am very much obliged to you.

"Certainly we must all agree that if the Stage could be enlisted in the cause of Religion and Morality, or even so influenced as not to oppose that cause, it would be an immense gain to the Church of Christ and to mankind at large. . . . Speaking for myself, there is no form of entertainment which I should so entirely enjoy, as good acting. But I have never been inside a theatre since I took Orders in 1852, and I do not mean to go into one, please God, while I live. . . . There would be a great deal to be said for a Guild, composed of theatrical people, having for its object the promotion of a high aim in their profession and of purity of life. But it would be no part of the business of such a Guild to 'assert the right of Churchmen to take part in theatrical amusements'; human nature is quite strong enough to assert 'rights' of this sort without being aided by Guilds." [3]

Since Liddon was one of the authorities Dodgson consulted before his ordination, on the possibility of his continuing to attend the theater, it is interesting to guess why the Canon stretched a point for his young friend. Perhaps he feared the Church might lose Dodgson altogether if the issue were too sharply drawn.

The Russian tour, while unofficial, seems not to have been unimportant. Greville, in his diary, quotes Lord Malmesbury as authority for the statement that the Emperor of Russia, on his visit to England in 1844, had made, without first consulting France, a secret treaty providing for British support of the Greek Church. This was not known till later, says Greville. Collingwood says: "Dr. Liddon's fame as a preacher had reached the Russian clergy . . . he and Mr. Dodgson found many doors open to them which are usually closed to travellers in Russia." [4] Liddon carried messages of good will from the Bishops of Oxford and Salisbury, he met and talked at some length with one of the two Suffragan Bishops of Moscow and with Philaret, the Metropolitan, and the whole visit may have had something to do with restoring the entente of 1844 after the Crimean War. More than a hundred years after the treaty it is interesting to note the continuing thread, through the Anglican-Orthodox amity fostered among Russian émigré groups by the Y.M.C.A. in Paris in the twenties,[5] the Anglican-Eastern-Orthodox Society in the forties, and the visits of high Anglican clergy to the Soviet Union in the 1940's.

Liddon wrote in a letter: "We have seen a great deal of the Russian Church for passing travellers. Of course, the outward forms of Russian religion are even more unlike English ways than those of Roman Catholic countries. But the sense of God's presence—of the supernatural—seems to me to penetrate Russian life more completely than that of any of the Western nations which I have seen, except perhaps the Tyrolese and the Styrians." [3]

Liddon, whether he traveled of his own motion, or whether he was gently shoved by a higher authority, was quite conscious of the political aspects of his trip. Dodgson, like Mary's little lamb, just went along—he had an opportunity to see pictures and plays and attend church to the limit of his capacity, and asked no more. What he thought of Liddon is not recorded.

Derek Hudson[6] quotes Liddon's report on the trip: "The Metropolitan entered warmly into English Church matters, and into the circumstances of Roman Catholicism in England." He could not, says Hudson, " 'understand Newman acknowledging anything so baseless in ecclesiastical history as the Pope's claim of Supremacy.' Liddon reported the interview to Bishop Wilberforce and to Bishop Hamilton of Salisbury, urging them to write letters congratulating Philaret on the fiftieth anniversary of his consecration as bishop. Altogether the envoys from Oxford played a useful part in improving Anglo-Russian relations, though in this respect Liddon was the main agent. Dodgson remained the conventional tourist."

Dodgson of course was a meticulous traveler. He packed each article separately, well wrapped in paper to twice its bulk, and all his luggage except the little black bag was sent ahead—at least on his English tours. On the continent, exposed to the wiles of foreigners, he may well have stayed close to his trunks and bags. He had two pocketbooks, each made up of labeled compartments. Every detail of the journey was planned, and in England the exact change for every contingency placed in one of the compartments. The folds of the brown pigskin pocketbook are labeled, in his beautiful manuscript writing:

"1 Stamps, visiting cards, etc.
2 Envelopes
3 Note paper
4 Stamped envelopes
5 Scrap-book
6 Letters needing answers
7 do not so
8 Letter-cards
9
10 Telegraph forms and *6d.* stamps"

and, on the inside, with the same lettering,

"Rev. C. L. Dodgson, *Ch. Ch., Oxford*"

The immediate impact of the trip seems to have been tremendous. On July 15, Liddon wrote in his diary: "Dodgson was overcome by the beauty of Cologne Cathedral. I found him leaning against the rails of the Choir, and sobbing like a child. When the verger came to show us over the chapels, he got out of the way. He said that he could not bear the harsh voice of the man in the presence of so much beauty." [3]

But Dodgson's own diary, while it notes the devotional, stresses the artistic and humorous aspects. On July 16, he wrote: "We made a round of several of the churches, the effect of which was that I have no very definite idea of any one of them. . . . Liddon went to the table d'hôte at 1½ & I took the opportunity to return to the Apostles' Church to witness a wedding. There were a good many people there, and many children, who ran about the church as they liked, but quietly, and very unlike English children. . . . In going the round of the churches, I was much struck by the numbers of the people we found in them, engaged in private devotions. In one of them there were three women confessing at the same time in three different confessionals: they hid their faces in their hands, and the priest held a handkerchief in front of his face, but there were no curtains. The number of children, who seemed to have come by themselves to pray,

was very remarkable: some of them had books, but not all
—most of them, I think, looked at us as we walked about,
but they soon went back to their devotions, and one by one
they got up and went out again, evidently coming and going
just when they liked. I noticed no men or boys engaged in
these devotions. . . . We had agreed to try the journey to
Berlin by night . . . the seats in the carriage were made to
draw out till they met and formed a very fair bed, and there
was a green silk shade to draw over the lamp when we wanted
the carriage dark, and we managed to pass a very comfortable night, though I am sorry to say Liddon did not sleep. . . .

"July 17(W) . . . They gave us a ticket with a number on
it, and we were obliged to take a cab, which had that number, on the stand—a regulation that would not be long endured in England. . . . We dined at 3, at the table d'hôte
(mem. that *potage à la Flamande* means mutton-broth, that
duck is eaten with cherries, and that it is *not* the thing to
wish a clean knife and fork during the repast), and in the
evening we strolled about, and finding services going on at
St. Peter's (Evangelical), we went in and heard about 20
minutes of a very fluent extempore sermon. . . .

"July 18 (Th.) We paid a second long visit to the great
picture-gallery (containing 1243 pictures) arranged by the
great art-critic, Waagen . . . in some [pictures], Mary has
placed the child on the ground, and is kneeling before Him in
prayer—and in one, a very fine piece of colouring, Joseph is
represented asleep, with the angel whispering in his ear. . . .
One of the most wonderful pieces of *the finish* I ever saw is
a triptych by Van [der] Weyden, representing scenes after
the death of our Lord—in one where Mary is weeping, each
tear is a carefully painted hemisphere (or rather more) with
its own point of light and its own shadow—and there is a
book lying on the floor with the leaves a little fluttered open,
where one of the clasps hangs so that its shadow crosses
the edge of the leaves, and tho the shadow is perhaps not an
inch long altogether, wherever there is the least opening between the leaves, the artist has carefully carried the shadow
in along the surface of the inner leaf. In taking a general
view of the pictures one did not get much impression of
beauty, but one could hardly pick out any pictures where a

little examination did not reveal marvels of execution . . .
the chapel where the Princess von Liegnitz lies buried. Her
tomb consists of an exquisitely carved marble figure lying on
a couch—a most marvellous effect is produced by filling some
of the windows in the roof with violet-coloured glass, which
gives an indescribable softness and dreaminess to the marble."[7]

Liddon's entry for July 20 follows: "Saturday.—After
breakfast went with Dodgson to the Jews' Synagogue. The
music was equal to some of the very best I have ever heard
in Christian churches. It was easy to detect the germ of the
Gregorian tunes. The ceremonial at the unveiling and replacing of the Torah was very impressive." Liddon's editor
says: "At Königsberg he fell ill, and Dodgson compelled him
to see a doctor, who, he says, is 'like a very intelligent
Chinese.' "[3]

Dodgson's diary resumes on July 21, Sunday: ". . . Once
they found a large dog lying down, and at once arranged
their dance round it, and sang their song to it, facing inward
for that purpose: the dog looked thoroughly puzzled at this
novel form of entertainment, but soon made up his mind that
it was not to be endured, and must be escaped from at all
costs . . . The German I talk is about as good as the English
I hear—at breakfast this morning, for which I had ordered
some cold ham, the waiter, when he had brought the other
things, leant across the table, and said to me in a confiden-
tial undertone, 'I brings in minutes ze cold ham.' . . .

"July 28 (Sun.) . . . The only share the congregation had
in the service was to bow and cross themselves, and sometimes to kneel down and touch the ground with their fore-
heads. One would hope that this was accompanied by some
private prayer, but it could not have been so in all cases: I
saw quite young children doing it, with no expression on their
faces which even hinted that they attached any meaning to
it, and one little boy (whom I noticed in the Kazan Cathedral) whose mother made him kneel down and put his forehead to the ground, could not have been more than 3 years
old. They were doing all the bowing and crossing before the
Eikons as well, and not only that, but when I was waiting
outside for Liddon (I went out when the sermon began) I
noticed great numbers do it while passing the church door,

even when they were at the opposite side of an enormously broad street. A narrow piece of pavement ran from the entrance right across, so that everyone driving or walking by could tell the exact moment when they were opposite. . . .

"The more one sees of these gorgeous services, with their many appeals to the senses, the more, I think, one learns to love the plain, simple (but to my mind far more real) service of the English church.

"I found out too late that the only English service here is in the morning, so in the afternoon we walked here and there about the marvellous city. . . . I saw one poor woman go up to the picture of St. Peter, with her sick baby in her arms . . . one could almost read in her worn, anxious face, that she believed what she was doing would in some way propitiate St. Peter to help her child." [7]

On July 28, Sunday, Liddon records: "After church a long argument with Dodgson." Unfortunately his editor deleted the subject matter. The entry continues: "Today I feel that for the first time in my life I stand face to face with the Eastern Church. To the outward eye she is at least as imposing as the Roman. To call her a petrifaction here in Russia would be a simple folly. That, on the other hand, she reinforces Rome in the cultus of the B.V.M. and other matters is too plain to be disputed." In a letter he writes: "I cannot understand anybody coming here and saying that the Eastern Church is a petrifaction. Right or wrong, it is a vast, energetic, and most powerful body, with an evident hold upon the heart of the largest of European empires; indeed, a force within the limits of Russia to which I believe there is no more parallel in the west." [3]

He writes in a letter, after meeting one of the Suffragan Bishops of Moscow:

"Bishop Leonide is most cordial in his dispositions towards the English Church. He had no doubt, I think, at all about the validity of our Orders, and he rejoices to make the most of all points of *rapprochement*.

"He very earnestly advised me, for instance, to get the English Church catechism translated into Russ, with notes, in order to point out its fundamental agreement with the orthodox doctrine. And the English Ordinal in like manner. He 'would endeavour to circulate these documents among his clergy, so that we might be better understood.' He entirely admitted our claim to approach the Eastern Church on a distinct ground from that of the Lutherans and the Protestant communities in general. . . . On Monday, Bishop Leonide allowed me to accompany him to Troitska, about forty miles from Moscow. There I had an interview with Philaret, the Metropolitan. . . . We discussed the 'defects' (as the Metropolitan considered them) of the English Communion Service, *several* of which (as I insisted) are common to it, with the Roman and other forms of the Petrine Liturgy, which the East had recognized before the Separation. . . . The Metropolitan entered warmly into English Church matters, and into the circumstances of Roman Catholicism in England. He thought the principle of Development was fatal to the old Church principle of an unvarying tradition of the Faith of the Apostles; he 'could not understand Newman's accepting it, or acknowledging anything so baseless in ecclesiastical history as the Pope's claim of Supremacy.' . . ." [3]

Dodgson's journal for August 4, Sunday: "In the morning we had a long, and unsuccessful search for the English Chapel. Afterwards I went alone, and luckily fell in with a Russian gentleman who could speak English, and who kindly went with me to the place.

"Aug. 11 (Sun.) We attended the English church in the morning, as Liddon had undertaken to preach. . . ." [7]

On August 15, Liddon remarks: "Up at six . . . we saw a Russian College inside as well as out. Dodgson drew it; but in this way we lost three-quarters of an hour and only arrived at Virschchusk at two. Dodgson found one of the monks, F. Nicolas, who could speak French, and he was accompanied by F. Benedict. We saw the Church of the Holy Sepulchre thoroughly; it is an 'exact' copy of that at Jerusalem.

"August 17 . . . On reaching Troitska, we went to the Church of the Assumption, where the liturgy was being celebrated by the Archbishop of Jaroslaf, assisted by eight other Bishops . . . Dodgson made his way round to the other side of the church, and so into the very sanctuary itself; but I was drifted about in the nave, and saw and heard little or nothing, except the choir. . . . After this there was a long delay, during which Dodgson made several efforts to get hold of the Bishop, but to no purpose. . . ." [3]

Dodgson's entry for August 23, Friday: "We gave the day to miscellaneous occupations. Called on the secretary of Count Tolstoy (the Count is away).

"In our wanderings, I noticed a beautiful photograph of a child, and bought a copy, small size, at the same time ordering a full length to be printed, as they had none unmounted. Afterwards I called to ask for the original, and found that they had already printed the full length but were in great doubt what to do, as they had asked the father of the child about it, and found he disapproved of the sale. Of course there was nothing to do but return the *carte* I had bought. At the same time I left a written statement that I had done so, expressing a hope that I might still be allowed to purchase it. . . .

"Aug. 25 (Sun.) . . . as the service was in Greek, we were able to follow it with the help of books, in spite of the pronunciation—and to join in it throughout, excepting one or two passages referring to the Virgin Mary.

"Aug 26 (M.) We had little time for anything but to prepare for our departure. The photographer called (at No. 4 Great Morskoi) to bring the pictures, as the father Prince Golican had given them leave to sell them to me.

"Aug. 29 (Th.) . . . Breslau, which we reached at 8½ P.M. It was pleasant to see the country growing more and more inhabited and cultivated as we got further into Prussia —the fierce, coarse-looking Russian soldier replaced by the more gentle and intelligent Prussian—the very peasants seemed to be of a higher order, more individuality and independence: the Russian peasant, with his gentle, fine, often noble-looking face, always suggests to me a stubborn animal, long used to bearing in silence, harshness and injustice, rather than a man able and ready to defend himself . . . the courtyard behind [the church] which was evidently the playground for the girls' school, and a very tempting field for the photographic camera: after the Russian children, whose type of face is ugly as a rule, and plain as an exception, it is quite a relief to get back among the Germans with their large eyes and delicate features.

"Sept. 2. (M.) We visited the great picture gallery in the morning. Two hours of gazing was enough for me: and it might all have been well given to the great 'Sistine' Madonna. . . . I went to the theatre in the Royal Garden, from which I had to walk home about a mile (some of it country) in the dark, and, it is needless to say, lost my way.

"Sept. 9 (M.) Thorley and I visited 'Théatre Vaudeville' in the evening to see *La Famille Benviton,* a capitally acted play—every part without exception being well and carefully played. 'Fantan' was played by one of the cleverest children I ever saw (Mdlle. Camille' as the bills called her) who could not have been more than 6 years old.

"Sept. 12 (Th.) . . . A pavilion where Chinese music was going on. . . . It was just the kind of music, which, once heard, one desires never to hear again. . . . We made up for it in the evening by going to the 'Opéra Comique' to hear *Mignon*—a very pretty spectacle, with charming music and singing—the heroine, Mdme. Galli-Marie, contributing a very large share of both departments of beauty. . . .

"Sept. 13 (F.) . . . At 7 P.M. I quitted the 'Hôtel des Deux Mondes,' on my way to Calais, which I reached after a peaceful and slumbrous journey, at about 2 A.M. . . . I remained in the bow most of the time of our passage, sometimes chatting with the sailor on the lookout, and sometimes watching, thru the last hour of my first foreign tour, the lights at Dover, as they slowly broadened on the horizon, as if the old land were opening its arms to receive its homeward bound children— till they finally stood out clear and bold as the two light houses on the cliff—till that which had long been merely a glimmering line on the dark water, like a reflection of the Milky Way, took form and substance as the lights of the shoreward houses—till the faint white light behind them, that looked at first like a mist creeping along the horizon, was visible at last in the grey twilight as the cliffs of old England." [7]

Old England, that, like most traveling Englishmen, Dodgson had never really left. Though he saw pictures and plays, heard music, attended churches, and ate food in three languages, in the inner sense he had never left Oxford. His later writings show no coloring or modification of his point of view from traveling for three months among people whose preconceptions and habits differed from his. The tall stories of the Professor in *Sylvie and Bruno* about his native Utopia have much more flavor of strangeness and travel than do Carroll's gently ironic descriptions of the "un-English" habits of the Germans and Russians. With his usual paradoxical behavior, then, he was most English when traveling, and most foreign at home.

The only sign of his trip appears in a letter to Maud Standen, written in 1890, when she was evidently traveling in Russia, asking her to write him girls' names "in Russ—(in printed capitals, please: the *written* Russ bothers me) with the pronunciation. I used to know the alphabet pretty well, but that was when I went to Russia in 1867, and I'm beginning to forget now. . . . As a whole, I think Moscow is the most wonderful sight I have ever seen."[8]

His outer life was simple, in fact monotonous. He preferred it so, because simplicity and a dependable routine gave him more freedom to explore and cultivate his inner world. His few other experiences and his limited circle of acquaintances and friends he used and transmuted for his own purposes, as any artist, more especially a poet, must. His surface was that of a not too unusual professor, but his inner world of fabulous monsters was refined, polished, and articulate to a degree we can expect only from a poet or a painter. That he was both, one actually and the other potentially, seems clear enough.

Chapter 9

An Oxford Chiel

Leave the young Tutors uncontrolled and free,
And Oxford then shall see—what it shall see.

FOR THREE HUNDRED YEARS, all incoming Fellows, Heads, Vice-Chancellors, and other responsible persons chosen to govern Oxford University swore to abide by the statutes *as they stood*. This meant simply that the University could not legally be reformed from within. Early in the nineteenth century the old forms were pinching and scratching so unbearably that Parliament and the Crown finally took a hand in pulling off the badly stuck haircloth garments.

In 1832, a bill was proposed in Parliament to abolish the religious tests which excluded about one-half the nation—all dissenters and "absenters"—(non-church-members) from receiving Oxford degrees. Henceforward numerous voices, including Jowett's and Gladstone's, thundered that Oxford was a national institution. In thirty years the bill was passed, by inches, as the kind-hearted Irishman cut off the puppy's tail. "Gladstone's rude draft [1854] carried the kernel of the plan"[1] which was so long maturing.

In 1856 the "Religious tests" bill took this form: "From and after the first day of Michaelmas, 1856, no person shall be required upon matriculating, or upon taking, or to enable him to take, any Degree in Arts, Law, Medicine, or Music, in the said University, to take any oath or to make any declaration or subscription whatever; but such Degree shall not, untill the person taking the same shall, in such manner as the University may from time to time prescribe, have subscribed a Declaration, stating that he is *bona-fide* a member of the Church of England, entitle him to be or to become a Member of the Senate, or constitute a Qualification for the holding of any office, whether in the University or elsewhere, which was heretofore always held by a Member of the United Church of

185

England and Ireland and for which a Degree has heretofore constituted one of the Qualifications."[1]

Not only dissenters were excluded from Oxford. Although the Fellowships, Scholarships, and Exhibitions were supposed to aid various degrees of poverty and of academic standing, in effect the cost pretty well excluded poor boys. In the forties, if they did manage to stick it out, humiliation was the sauce for every dish, as *Tom Brown at Oxford* graphically shows. Merely the larger half of the nation—the women—were discriminated against, until finally, in 1908, the B.A. examination was opened to them. In the eighties they began slowly trickling in to lectures, one by one—plus chaperon, and sometimes even plus watch-dog—until the establishment of Somerville College (1879), Lady Margaret Hall (1879), and St. Hugh's College (1886) gradually gave them seats of learning of their own. During these decades, the bars were let down to other suppressed majorities, with the founding of Mansfield College for the dissenting clergy and Ruskin College for workingmen in the 1890's.

At last, in 1882, the Senate Statutes abolished the clerical fellowships and the requirement of celibacy. Speaking of some of the intracollegiate restrictions, Mark Pattison, one of the most active of the reformers, said: "The abolition of the close fellowships has not only done more for us than all the other enactments of the measure together, but it is the only one that has completely answered the expectations formed from it." [1] Perhaps he would have been willing to extend this remark to cover the removal of the restrictions that kept the dons, as a later commentator said, "cryptogamous." No celibate himself, married to an exceptionally attractive platinum blonde, or as Mrs. Humphry Ward described her in the language of the time, *blonde cendrée*,[2] he was appreciative of the taste and charm with which she dressed, and anxiously critical of the women students and teachers who neglected their appearance, as many of them did at first. A certain Head Mistress is alleged to have held her skirt and blouse together with a large visible safety pin. The proper costume of the time was the "neat coat, small hat, and fur boa of Du Maurier's pictures," [3] but the ladies who strove for academic freedom sometimes went to odd lengths in their sartorial freedoms. They tended to short skirts and short hair before anyone had learned how to make abbreviations attractive, and worst of all, they tended toward slovenliness. Mark Pattison's pretty blonde wife, with her white dress, always with "a spot of black and a spot of blue," kept herself charming. No wonder her husband seemed pagan to his neighbors, with their dowdy wives or none at all, and no wonder that, when he died, the pretty blonde widow (of fourteen months) married the hero—or villain—of the Dilke divorce scandal.

Too late for Dodgson, for Bayne, for many of their generation, the medieval ban was lifted. Dodgson's diary for May 17, 1878, simply says, "Meeting of Governing Body to discuss suggestions for Commissioners. The abolishing celibacy was carried by 15 to 12, and the reducing clerical students from two thirds to one third by 14 to 13."

When the fellows were at last permitted to marry, the privilege was extended gradually, to only four at a time. There was a mad scramble to be first. Mrs. Humphry Ward said: "Nobody under the rank of a head of a college except a few privileged professors, possessed as much as a thousand a year. The average income of the new race of married tutors was not more than half that sum. Yet we all gave dinner parties and furnished our houses with Morris papers, old chests, and cabinets and blue pots. The dinner parties were simple and short. The ladies dressed in Liberty stuffs—very plain in line, but elaborately smocked, and evening dresses cut square or with Watteau pleats, and amber beads." [2] This was the period when Mrs. Liddell's carriage drove in slow stately fashion up and down St. Aldate's, and when her handsome daughters had reached an age to wear smart bonnets to church.

Dr. Liddell's reforms were beginning to show results, and Oxford was beginning to overtake the rest of the world. Modernism and tradition, however, still struggled in the university reorganization. The two main conflicts were, first, that between jurisdiction and prerogatives—University versus constituent colleges—and, second, that between the tutorial and the professorial methods of teaching. "Each college is a little polity by itself," says Goldwin Smith. "Oxford is a federation of colleges." [4] An American has only to think of states' rights versus the federal government. The colleges had gradually usurped the functions of the University, and it took a great deal of legislative upheaval to restore the balance. Mark Pattison's portrait of the teaching methods is most succinct: "There is but one possible pattern on which a University, as an establishment for science, can be constructed, and that is the graduated professoriate. This is sometimes called the German type. . . . The German University is an association of men of learning and science under the title of Professors. The Professor of a modern University ought to regard himself primarily as a learner, and a teacher only secondarily. His first obligation is to the faculty he represents; he must consider he is there on his own account, and not for the sake of his pupils. He must hold himself up to a higher standard of attainment than the possession of so much as has to be communicated to the pupil. We can not communicate that which we have not got. To make others anything, we must first be it ourselves . . . the aim should be the conversion or restoration of college endowments to the maintenance of a professional class of learned and scientific men." [1]

From this it is possible to see what Oxford was not, and to adumbrate what it was. Bishop Gore's statement in the House of Lords called Oxford a "playground for the sons of the wealthier classes, and not in any serious sense a place of study at all." Gentleman Commoner John Ruskin, in the 1840's, wrote: "I gave a chess party last night . . . Liddell appeared too . . . Liddell was soliloquizing to this effect on the figure that he should cut at collections: 'I've had three lectures a week from Mr. Brown, and have attended five in the term; I've had ditto from Mr. Kynaston, and have attended two in the term; and three a week from Mr. Hill, and I've attended three; and I'll be dashed if I don't come off as well as the whole set of you." [5] And in fact, the examinations were so graded that "nothing but extreme incapacity, extraordinary want of school-education, or gross idleness at the University will absolutely exclude a student from his degree." The subject matter, of course, was chiefly linguistic and ecclesiastical.

It is hard now to realize how recently the books and

methods of our own time originated, and how many of them
had their origins in this same maligned Oxford in this same
Victorian era, when these very men who were lashing their
tails in titanic struggles over large and small issues, were also
laboriously producing the fruits of scholarship.

Immense crevasses were gradually filled with monumental
works. There was no serviceable Greek lexicon before Liddell's (a labor of nearly sixty-seven years). There was no
good translation of Plato before Jowett's—a mere forty years'
job. There was no unified, comprehensive science of linguis-
tics before Max Müller, whose enormous translations of
Oriental literature were also brought out at Oxford, after he
had nearly given up hope and carried them back to Germany.
Aristotle's works, combed over, shredded, and mangled since
the Middle Ages, had never been presented in a coherent and
unified fashion until Mark Pattison's lectures. Three different
editions of the Greek Testament appeared between 1859 and
1861, including one by Charles Wordsworth of Christ
Church. And this was the gestation period of the great Murray Dictionary, which took seventy-six years and a great
corps of assistants. Sir James himself moved to Oxford in
1885 with—literally—tons of material he had been collecting
since 1857. The last volume published in his lifetime came
out in 1926, and the final supplement, still containing much
of his work, in 1933.

Dodgson, too, put in his penn'orth. None of his works
reached, or pretended to reach, monumental proportions,
but as teacher, as educator, as clergyman, he had ideas on
every issue that touched Oxford. According to one Oxford
historian, he, who lamented the time wasted on "impositions"
in public school, had to set "lines" as penalties to compel
students to attend his rather dull lectures.[6] But he wished to
see as many students as possible pass in their examinations
and go on to more creative work. He wrote one pamphlet to
show how a change in the method of marking would enable
more students to pass (Hilary Responsions). Elsewhere he
speaks of "This Upas-tree of competitive examinations! Beneath whose deadly shade all the original genius, all the
exhaustive research, all the untiring, lifelong diligence by
which our forefathers have so advanced human knowledge,

must slowly wither away, and give place to a system of cookery, in which the mind is a sausage, and all we ask is, how much indigestible food can be crammed into it!"

A young graduate in correspondence with his former tutor, Warde Fowler, wrote: "Is it the examination system, or the charms of outdoor Oxford, or national feebleness, or overwork at school (including games), dullness of lectures, or over-conscientiousness on the part of tutors, who do so much for their pupils that they extinguish the desire, natural (I should imagine), to human beings as to cats and dogs, to find out things for themselves?" [7] Mark Pattison thought he knew what was behind it all. He suspected that the examination system that developed in the universities was Jesuit in origin —he claimed they "got boys learning tricks by examining them often."

Eventually something had to be done. In November, 1888, *The Nineteenth Century* published "a strong protest against the dangerous mental pressure and misdirection of energies and aims, which are to be found in nearly all parts of our educational system," signed not only by Dodgson, but also by Max Müller, George Baden-Powell, J. A. Froude, Sir Arthur Sullivan, George Frederick Watts, Annie Besant, and many others. The old guard retaliated, and the controversy went on in *The Nineteenth Century* for months. The following February, an anecdote appeared, vouched for by Dr. Priestly, of a mother of a large family who had "taken chloroform at the birth of another child, and inquired, as soon as she was conscious, whether the newcomer was a boy or a girl. On being informed it was a boy, she burst into tears, exclaiming, 'Oh dear! Those dreadful competitive examintions!' " [8]

Dodgson's idea, however, was by no means to reduce the amount of learning the undergraduates were to absorb. As early as 1864, in a letter to the Vice-Chancellor (published as *The New Examination Statute*), he resigned from the office of Public Examiner in Mathematics, because he considered that both classics and mathematics were "degraded" by the statute of February 2, 1864, permitting "candidates for a degree to forsake Classics after Moderations (the preliminary examinations), except so far as was needed for a Fourth Class in the Final School of *Litterae Humaniores,* if they wished to graduate in Science." After all, with his "First" in mathematics, he managed to take a second class in classics and a third in history and philosophy, without undue strain.

There was no school, or chair, or professor of English Literature at Oxford till 1896, and when the "English Honours School" was finally established, no one was admitted to it unless he had "obtained honours in some other final honours school or has satisfied or obtained honours from the moderators in Greek and Latin literature." [9] There is something to be said, from the evolutionary or global point of view, for treating English literature as a branch of the classics—but neither of these approaches was in question. Carroll lived his days out in the milieu where English literature was considered rather as a contemptible appendage to the classics—a paradox which may have helped him to retain his natural modesty.

Needless to say, he was a dreadfully conscientious teacher. He had printed formulae and notes, and a system for working all sorts of problems. His extreme precision as a lecturer was said to make him rather dull. In 1932 Sir Herbert Maxwell wrote *The Times* about the "lean, dark-haired person of Charles Dodgson, before whom, as mathematical lecturer, we undergraduates of Christ Church used to assemble. Very few, if any, of my contemporaries survive to confirm my impression of the singularly dry and perfunctory manner in which he imparted instruction to us, never betraying the slightest personal interest in matters that were of deep concern to us. Yet this must have been the very time when he was framing the immortal fantasia of *Alice*." He did wish his students to do well, but otherwise seems not to have reached out to them at all. Until the nineties, when he had a chance to teach logic to girls at Lady Margaret Hall and the Oxford High School, teaching never was a real pleasure to him.

D. B. Eperson in *The Mathematical Gazette* says of his *Fifth Book of Euclid Treated Algebraically* (1868): "It is a method of ratios, for the Pass Schools at Oxford [the examinations which the men who did not try for honors had to take]. It is as clear as possible, but beyond the comprehen-

sion of most pass-men. The bearing of such a piece on Lewis
Carroll is that it shows how he never evaded difficulties, but
made sure of his ground step by step, and sympathized with
the faltering progress of his pupils."

He made a lasting mark neither as a mathematician nor as
a teacher, but his obituary in *The Oxford Magazine* said that
his *Euclid and his Modern Rivals* was believed to have
ousted "from public school teaching one at least of unsound
modern manuals."

Three years after the publication of *Alice* he moved into
the suite he occupied for the remainder of his life—the best
suite, said Miss Arnold, in all of Oxford. The exact number
of rooms is still disputed. Collingwood said four bedrooms
and four sitting rooms. Mr. S. G. Owen, who knew the suite
in Carroll's time, wrote Professor Harry Morgan Ayres that
since the arrangement is complicated and has been altered, it
can no longer be settled.[10] Now, as then, the large and sumptuous apartment is a unit, with a big oak door, formerly
marked in white letters, "the Rev. C. L. Dodgson," opening
onto the slippery, tortuous oak stairway, which may have
given Carroll the idea of Father William kicking his son
downstairs, for it raises powerful thoughts of safety and its
opposite.

The windows of the large room, with a sort of balcony below them, overlook St. Aldate's (pronounced St. Olds). The
two little turret rooms are part of the main room, still much
as it was in Carroll's day except for the fireplace, which after
World War I was stripped to uncover the underlying Tudor
structure. The pity is that to give Henry VIII his place in
the sun, the red and white tiles which De Morgan made to
Carroll's order were removed and mounted on a screen that
greatly reduces their effect.

The fireplace tiles in Dodgson's room were no accident,
no sudden impulse. On December 27, 1882, he notes in his
diary, "Called on Mr. De Morgan about tiles." On the 31 of
May following he writes, "Went to Mr. De Morgan before
breakfast, and had a talk about tiles, etc. Back to Oxford."
Over a year after the first talk, on January 24, 1884 he
writes, "Had new grate, with tiles, put into small room." But
we have to wait three years for the famous ones that concern us

Tiles from the De Morgan Potteries, formerly on Lewis Carroll's fireplace at Oxford. Permission to reproduce these tiles has been granted by Christ Church, Oxford.

here. March 4, 1887 we find, "Called on Mr. William De Morgan and chose a set of red tiles for the large fire-place."

The large boat may have some relation to *The Hunting of the Snark,* and it can be no accident that the animals include a Gryphon, a Dodo, a Beaver, a Fawn, and an Eagle. There are also a number of little birds, and a crane impaling a fish. While he may have chosen the tiles from stock, it seems more likely that De Morgan, an artist and literary man, designed them to order. There have been disputes as to whether the tiles inspired the poems, or vice versa. The tiles were ordered in 1887, eleven years after *Snark* was published, but well before *Sylvie and Bruno,* so that the "Little Birds" poem which weaves in and out of that book as the little birds tile did on the fireplace, may have been a result of his gazing first into the fire and then on the tiles. Indeed, he speaks of his practice of staring into the fire and seeing faces.

Enid Stevens, his favorite of the nineties, says: "As I sat on Mr. Dodgson's knee before the fire, he used to make the creatures have long and very amusing conversations between themselves. The little creatures on the intervening tiles used to 'squirm' in at intervals. I think they suggested the 'Little Birds are Feeding' &c, in *Sylvie and Bruno.*" [11]

The rest of the room, in 1930, had not been changed since his time, except that the then incumbent, the late Professor R. H. Dundas, had a larger library and consequently more bookshelves. Mr. Madan said of Carroll's books: "It is a miscellaneous library of about 5,000 volumes—not that of a collector *at all,* and really *ordinary.* They are such as Ruskin, Shakespeare, Scott, Coleridge, Keats, Browning, Christina Rossetti, Wordsworth, Dickens, Kipling, Stevenson, and so on, some medical, scientific, and theological works, and nursery tales, fairy stories, and children's books of all kinds." [12] It appears that his mathematical library too was far from exceptional.

He did avail himself of the great men around him, perhaps because he made friends by preference with writers and artists, especially those whose works he owned or admired. But one friend, who was also an expert, and with whom he carried on an instructive correspondence, was the physician, Sir James Paget. Once Dodgson saw a man in the street having an epileptic fit, and saved him from falling.

Then he realized he had no idea what to do next. To forestall future embarrassments, he bought a set of bones and a considerable library of anatomical works, and with the stimulus of correspondence with Sir James, put himself *au courant*.[13]

The paintings he owned were also principally by or of personal friends. Over the fireplace hung three paintings of little girls, one of them Miss Gertrude Thomson's portrait of Enid Stevens, and another a portrait of a child in a blue coat, carrying a pair of ice skates. Other painters represented were Arthur Hughes, an early pre-Raphaelite, to whose daughter Carroll wrote a pixy letter about three flat cats; a Mrs. Anderson; and Heaphy, the "ghost painter," whose daughter visited Carroll at Eastbourne after her father died. Although he owned none of the ectoplasmic paintings, Carroll seemed inclined to believe in their genuineness.[13]

The small bedchamber opened out of a slightly larger north dining-and-living-room. A windowless closet with red glass in the door was clearly the photographic dark room; across from it was probably the studio. Another small room was probably used for storage—costumes perhaps, of which he kept a great number; and then there were the two little turrets he promised to Isa when she married, so that she and her husband could separate instead of quarreling! [14]

Sometimes he viewed an Oxford spectacle, or photographed it, from the flat roof, to which there once was easy access. Outside the gate, just across St. Aldate's, is the original of the Wool and Water shop, looking much as it did when the Sheep sat behind the counter, except that the street has been widened, making the shop lighter and less dreamy. In late 1961 word came from Mrs. K. Fogaty in London that the Wool and Water Shop is doomed.

Mr. Christopher Hussey, who lived in the rooms, writes:

"In my time the room was probably much as it was in his —a typical late Georgian apartment with a plain green paper on canvas covering the original timber and plaster walls. For the sake of revealing these very ordinary Tudor walls and a fireplace, this *historic* décor, including the Carroll fireplace, has been swept away.

"But of course Lewis Carroll must have made the rooms

very different in his time. Mr. Strong, now Bishop of Oxford
but in my time Dean of Christ Church, told me various tales
about the old man: his horror of draughts, for instance. The
room is a draughty one, as it has four doors—one in each
corner, one of them a projecting oriel. His theory was that
there could be no draughts if the temperature was equalized
all over the room. Accordingly he had a number of thermometers about the room, and near each one an oil stove.
Periodically he made a round of the thermometers, adjusting
the adjacent stove according to the reading. All cracks under
doors were boarded up with coats, rugs, etc. Dr. Strong said
Lewis Carroll was exactly like the White Knight, full of his
'own inventions'—usually singularly unpractical. He had a
very elaborate gazolier hanging from the ceiling, and elaborate instructions for lighting it pasted on the door of his
room, though I gather he allowed no one to light it but himself." [15]

Shades of Uncle Skeffington!

One of the Misses Dodgson wrote: "To get rid of mice in
his rooms, a square live trap was used, and he had a wood
and wire compartment made which fitted on to the trap
whose door could then be opened for the mice to run into
the compartment, a sliding door shutting them in, and the
compartment could then be taken from the trap and put
under water; thus all chance of the mice having an agonized
struggle on the surface of the water was removed." [11]

Having so many rooms gave rein to his ingenuity. On
March 12, 1874, Dodgson records: "We dined a party of
eight. . . . The evening went off successfully, I think. We
met in the small room, dined in the large rooms, went back
again for dessert, during which the large room was converted into a drawing-room. This seems to be the best way
of using my rooms for a party."

In the dark room and studio he became one of the best
amateur photographers of his time, as well as one of the
first to take photography seriously. It also seems probable
that he was the inventor of the first self-photographing device. His portraits, many of which have been often reproduced, are at least equal in composition to anything of our
own time. Hundreds, perhaps thousands, of these portraits

still exist; for naturalness, ease, grace, lighting, line, and composition, they are remarkable for their time and still creditable today. His greatest successes were with child subjects. He photographed the Liddell children, the Bowman sisters, the Arnold girls, and dozens of others—singly, in pairs, in groups—in a variety of costumes: Chinese, Cinderella, parlor maids, beggar maids, Dolly Varden—whatever struck his fancy and fell within the range of his materials and ingenuity. Many of the costumes, which he kept in a trunk and closet, were from the Drury Lane pantomimes.

Helmut Gernsheim has done the definitive book, *Lewis Carroll, Photographer*. Text and photographs complement each other to give the whole story. Dodgson's diary for April 13, 1858, says, "I had hardly time to see much of the Photographic Exhibition, and must go again to look it over thoroughly. There are many very beautiful things here, but very little done in grouping—my favorite subject."

Mr. Green comments: "This, the fifth exhibition of the Photographic Exhibition in London, was the only occasion on which Dodgson exhibited his own photographs publicly. Item No. 174 lists four photographs by 'C. L. Dodgson': (1) Portrait; (2) Group of Children from Life; (3) Little Red Riding-Hood; (4) Portrait of a Child." [16]

Gernsheim says Dodgson did not join the Oxford Union Photographic Club or the Oxford Literary and Photography Club, both founded in the seventies. He knew many of the other prominent photographers, and in fact had himself photographed by Rejlander. With Julia Margaret Cameron, about whom Mr. Gernsheim published another fabulous book, he had an uneasy relationship.

Gernsheim described Dodgson's visit to Mrs. Cameron on the Isle of Wight. "They spent a happy evening at Mrs. Cameron's home looking at each other's photographs. She had then been photographing for only a few months, but characteristically spoke of her pictures 'as if they were triumphs of art,' as Lewis Carroll records with a touch of mockery, adding more critically, 'some are very picturesque, some merely hideous. She wished she could have some of my figures to do *out* of focus—and I expressed an analagous

Lewis Carroll holding his camera lens, photographed by
Rejlander.

wish with regard to some of her subjects (i.e., to do them *in focus!*)."

He knew and used techniques that are still good, says Gernsheim. He had an eye for background, and for grouping as well as character. "Parents, unless famous, he dispensed with, even then they were secondary to their daughters."

He never would retouch a photograph, and even persuaded Isa, vain little actress that she was, to have a professional photographer take an unretouched portrait. She was no more charmed with the result than with the broad-toed shoes Uncle Dodgson had made especially for her, because he hated high-heeled shoes with pointed toes.

In 1932 Alice Liddell still vividly remembered her experiences with Dodgson's photography. First he would tell the sisters stories to get them into a happy mood. Then he would bring out his camera. "Being photographed was a sobering and frightening experience. The reward was to be invited into his awesome and mysterious dark room. . . . Alice kept the photographs. Some of them even today [wrote her son] bring back to her the excitement of those moments spent in the dark room watching the negatives gradually take shape as he rocked them gently in the acid bath." [17]

Photography began to be important in the fifties. The first chairman of the Photographic Society, founded in 1853, was an artist—a good augury. Brussels held an Anglo-French Exhibition, the emperors of Austria and of Russia presented snuff boxes to eminent photographers, and the Royal Artillery and the Royal Arsenal found uses for the new process. Since the first practical daguerreotypes were made in 1839, this was nineteenth century railroad tempo. Ruskin was in the very first car. He wrote (in *Praeterita*): "It must have been during my last days at Oxford that Mr. Liddell . . . told me of the original experiments of Daguerre. My Parisian friends obtained for me the best examples of his results; and the plates sent to me in Oxford were certainly the first examples of the sun's drawing that were ever seen in Oxford, and, I believe, the first sent to England." [18] Carroll, a few years younger, bought his first camera in 1856. If not "first," he was certainly one of the best.

The dispute was already raging whether photography was or was not an art. "Artistic" pictures were those that were out of focus, and the props were horrendous—cliffs, rocks, terraces of papier mâché. To his credit, Carroll always worked cleanly, free from nonsensical trappings. Mr. H. P. Robinson, to whom he sent his negatives after he gave up printing them himself (about 1875), wrote: "The technique was much in advance of the photography of the day, and although all of them were portraits, there was evidently great effort made, often successful, to obtain pictorial effect."

The portable dark room he carried on vacations was shown at the Centenary Exhibit in London. It was a cupboard and stand, 21½ x 17½ x 4 inches. Also exhibited was a folding case containing portraits of members of Common Room. His photographs of adults were mostly of men: figures of literature, the stage, the university, and especially the church. They included Ruskin, Tennyson, the Rossettis, George Macdonald, Ellen and Kate Terry, Faraday, Dean Stanley, Archbishop Longley, and assorted prelates. He angled for the Prince of Wales' photograph, but had to content himself with an autograph. The Duke of Albany stood for him, however. All the portraits are excellent, freely posed, natural studies, good compositions that testify he took photography seriously as an art.

Being Lewis Carroll, he also took it humorously. His verses, "Hiawatha's Photographing," blend Longfellow's famous meter with his own famous impishness. Hiawatha photographs a family, one by one, in characteristic poses—each picture proving worse than the last. Then he takes the group; the result is lifelike but horrible. Everyone rebels; Hiawatha folds up his camera with a few choice remarks, and "Thus departed Hiawatha." Perhaps this was a Carrollian version of something that had really happened. Knowing what a tempest brewed in that silent teapot, we cannot tell whether he was reporting his true feelings while exaggerating the facts.

"A Photographer's Day Out," which appeared in the *South Shields Amateur Magazine* in 1860, is a faintly amusing overstrained story about a young man who burned to photograph his Amelia. Taking her picture despite terrific obstacles, he is beaten up by the ruffians and wakens to find his plates destroyed. This would have made an early Chaplin film, but is now of interest only to collectors.

The main charm of photography for his artist soul was its difficulty. Miss Arnold says: "Photographing or being photographed in those days was a very different thing than it is now. For a nervous child, dressed up as a heathen Chinese, a beggar girl, or a fisher maiden, to keep still forty-five seconds at a time was no mean ordeal. . . . With the whimsical contrariness which was characteristic of him, as soon as the wet plate with all its attendant difficulties and messiness went out, and the clean, convenient dry plate came in, he abandoned photography, and not one photograph did he ever take by the new and infinitely simplified process." [19]

His letter to Miss Thomson of July 9, 1893, says:

". . . *all* 'dry plate' photography is inferior, in artistic effect, to the now-abandoned 'wet-plate,' but as a means of making *memoranda* of attitudes, etc., it is invaluable. Every figure-artist ought to practice it. If I had a dry-plate camera, and time to work it, and could secure a child of a really good figure, either a professional model, or (much better) a child of the upper classes, I would put her into every pretty attitude I could think of, and could get, in a single morning, 50 or 100 such memoranda. Do try this, with the next pretty child you get as a model, and let me have some of the photos." [20]

Like so many of Carroll's inventions, this adumbrates something actually adopted later, for instance by Carl Akeley in revolutionizing museum practice, replacing "stuffed" animals by habitat groups in which every detail of form, proportion, position, and movement is worked out with the help of photography and slow motion pictures. How Carroll would have enjoyed the Roosevelt Hall in the American Museum of Natural History!

His photography was a regular part of his life and must have been some consolation for his inability to draw as he wished. Collingwood says: "In his first letter to Miss Thomson he speaks of himself as one who for twenty years had found his one amusement in photographing from life—especially photographing children; he also said that he had made attempts ('most unsuccessfully') at drawing them . . . he might often have been seen in her studio, lying flat on his face, and drawing some child-model who had been engaged for his especial benefit. 'I *love* the effort to draw,' he wrote in one of his letters to her, 'but I utterly fail to please even my own eye—tho' now and then I seem to get somewhere *near* a right line or two, when I have a live child to draw from. But I have no time left now for such things. In the next life, I do *hope* we shall not only *see* lovely forms, such as this world does not contain, but also be able to draw them.' But . . . he had great faith in his own critical judgment; and with good reason, for his perception of the beautiful in contour and attitude and grouping was almost unerring." [13] Later letters to Miss Thomson show him still drawing little girls from life, to within three months before his death.

How is it, that with all his interest, diligence, and taste, he could not draw? From childhood, when he illustrated his own magazines, through the *Alice Underground* period and the Russian tour, when he sketched incessantly, to the last year of his life, he was drawing. He even took sketchbooks along on his vacations and filled them with portraits of little girls by the seaside. He took lessons from Miss Thomson, who corrected his notebooks carefully, and from another friend. His eye was good, and what the eye sees the hand can reproduce. He said somewhere that his hand was "untrained." Which hand? The left? Many of his drawings are so nearly good, so interesting in themselves, that if he had switched over to his left hand they might have been really good.

A commentator on the illustrations of *Alice* remarks that Carroll's original drawing "made Alice left-handed"—the very words—in the picture where her hand stretches out fanwise from the White Rabbit's window; whereas Tenniel changed the picture over to show Alice's right hand. A small straw indeed, but the same commentator adds: "Twenty of the Tenniel illustrations are finely executed duplicates of Carroll's originals and adhere to his composition and detail with accuracy and fidelity." [21] Does not this augur that Tenniel unconsciously chose her right hand as Carroll chose her left?

Harry Furniss claims that he was a dull man, and amusing only because of a "peculiar twist in his brain that gave his mathematical mind a bent towards some humorous side line of thought"—again, perhaps, a left-side-line!

How did his handwriting turn out so beautifully in the *Alice* manuscript if he was writing with his wrong hand? As Demosthenes the stammerer became Demosthenes the orator —by doubly overcoming a double obstacle. His ordinary handwriting was just fairly legible, and varied a good deal. He told Isa he took extra pains with anything that was to go to the printers because it was not right to give others trouble on account of one's own shortcomings. As in everything else he tackled, he never stopped trying to improve himself.

After Harry Furniss started to work on *Sylvie and Bruno*, "Carroll wrote to me, when I acknowledged his first sketch —an idea for an illustration—as follows, 'I fear your words ("I had no idea you were an artist") were, to a certain extent, rote sarkastic, which is a shame! I never made any profession of being able to draw, and have only had, as yet, four hours' teaching from a young friend who is herself an artist, and who insisted on making me try, in black chalk, a foot of a Laocoön! The result was truly ghastly, but I have just sufficient of a correct eye to see that every drawing I make, even from life, is altogether wrong anatomically, so that nearly all my attempts go into the fire as soon as they are finished.' " [22]

Nonsense art presumably started with Edward Lear, who painted birds for a living, gave lessons to young Queen Victoria, and considered joining the pre-Raphaelites; he could certainly have put bones into his figures if he had wished. Carroll struggled hopelessly to find the bone, and Ruskin, whose interest lay in organic form, ruthlessly discouraged him. In our own day Thurber leaped joyfully from amoeba to man, woman, and dog, ignoring the lowly amphioxus and intermediate vertebrates, and our contemporary Ruskins would have been happy to suppress him likewise. In each case, fortunately, the pictures have survived; while thousands of Carroll's perished in the waste basket, perhaps enough remain.

Alice Liddell remembered "an inexhaustible flow of the most delightful fairy tales, illustrated as he went along by quaint pencil and ink drawings done on any handy bit of paper . . . all of which found their way into the waste basket." The three sisters would storm his rooms, pull him over to the sofa, crowd around, and clamor for stories and drawings. Alice particularly regretted the loss of one caricature he made for her as a result of an unusually festive evening. At the time of the marriage of the Prince of Wales to Alexandra, in 1863, little Alice, then eleven, went out into the High Street at night, hand in hand between Charles and his brother, to see the illuminations. One, especially large and imposing, said in letters of fire, "May they be happy!" "Afterwards Mr. Dodgson drew a caricature of it for her, adding to it two large hands holding very formidable birches with the words 'Certainly not' beneath them." [17]

Captain Hargreaves relates that on the one occasion during her childhood when she was cut off from Mr. Dodgson—the six weeks during which she lay in bed recuperating from a broken thigh bone, incurred when her pony fell with her— Carroll did not visit her once. Alice was recalling her childhood to her son, after nearly seventy years. We must grant her some small misremembering. Dodgson's diary for April 21, 1863, says, "I went to see Alice, who is laid up with a sprained leg, and stayed about an hour with her and Rhoda." Whether the wrong diagnosis came from Dodgson, from the doctor, or from Alice, there seems little doubt that this is the same incident, and that the charge of neglect should be removed. "He came to the Deanery only rarely, usually when there was a half holiday. He must have written the sisters hundreds of letters"—all of which, like the drawings, ended in the waste basket. No doubt his own poor estimate of the drawings caused the girls to treat both sketches and letters as ephemera. "After the Alice books began to make him famous Alice realized she should keep [the letters]. . . . She has less than a dozen now—all written after the *Alice* period." [16] Mrs. Liddell had made her burn the earlier ones! [23]

In his study he had "scores of green cardboxes, all neatly labelled," containing all manner of lists, "one of them, that of unanswered correspondents, generally held seventy or eighty at a time, exclusive of autograph hunters, whom he did not answer on principle." [13]

Miss Dodgson has a marked catalogue of the sale of her uncle's effects in the Holywell Music Room, Oxford, May 10 and 11, 1898. It includes "watches, clocks, opera glasses, telescopes, 1 aneroid, 1 microscope, pair of combination Field, Marine, and Theatre glasses in case, pocket sun dial, rules, mathematical instruments and geometrical solids, 2 artist's lay figures 'and sundries,' model of hand and foot, skull, skeleton of head and foot, dumb bells, clothes brushes, 6 travelling ink pots, Trytograph printing case (for making notes at night.)"

There exists a paper with measurements and positions for the pictures in *Through the Looking-Glass,* and another, a long and minute list of typographical errors and minor changes for *Wonderland.* In 1890 he published an odd little pamphlet, called *Eight or Nine Wise Words about Letter-Writing,* in the same envelope with the *Wonderland Stamp Case,* containing pockets for every denomination of stamp from a halfpenny to a shilling. He combined precision with whimsicality in this little packet, in true *Wonderland* style. The stamp case fits into an inner envelope so that when it is pulled out there is a metamorphosis of the Duchess' baby into a pig, and on the reverse side, of the visible Cheshire Cat into the vanishing ditto.

The pamphlet contains a rule "Write Legibly," and the minutest details of writing, addressing, stamping, and posting a letter, as well as explaining his method of "registering," or recording, letters sent and received—a cumbrous filing system. "You will find it perfectly simple, when you have had a little practice, and will come to regard the 'making-up' as a pleasant occupation for a rainy day, or at any time that you feel disinclined for more severe mental work." There is the gist. His life was a game, even his logic, his mathematics, and his singular ordering of his household and other affairs. His logic was a game, and his games were logical, and that is the Tangled Tale.

One function of his extreme tidiness and meticulousness was to ward off the unexpected. He did not like, for instance, to be come upon suddenly, but it was his elfin pleasure to come on others in that way. One of his well-known formulas, of which all his friends complained, was, "because you have asked me, therefore I cannot come." He much preferred to drop in informally at tea time.

The former Miss Maud Standen, later Mrs. Archbold Ffooks, one of the most persistent collectors of Carrolliana, wrote that when her family, vacationing on the Isle of Jersey, gave a large "At Home" for Carroll, he did not appear, but came quietly and unexpectedly to tea. The advantage, Mrs. Ffooks writes, was theirs, since they were able to enjoy his conversation without distraction. "He disliked being lionized," she concluded.

A Miss Manners described how, when he was asked to stay to dinner, he cited his usual glass of wine and biscuit as a reason for not sharing their meal, but offered to carve for them. The joint was a small neck of mutton, with which he seemed unfamiliar and ill-at-ease. He finally dismembered it, "relating meanwhile the story of a shy young man who had been asked to carve a fowl, the joints of which had been wired together. . . . The task and the story both finished, our visitor gazed on the mangled remains and remarked quaintly, 'I think it is just as well I don't want anything, for I don't know where I should find it.' " Mutton—Alice, Alice —Mutton.

Another time, Miss Vera Beringer, who played "Little Lord Fauntleroy," told Mr. Reed that when he came to dinner once, she heard a crash of metal in the hall and found that in pulling out his handkerchief, he had also spilled a pound's worth of copper and silver.[23] Perhaps such an incident inspired his compartmented pocketbook.

His nephew, Major Dodgson, told this bit of his uncle's repartee to Mr. Reed: leaving the University Church after a dull sermon, they met the preacher, Mr. Stubbs. It was raining, and Carroll offered to lend Mr. Stubbs his umbrella. "The loan was refused, with the remark, 'No thanks, I don't mind getting wet; in fact I like getting wet!' To which Mr. Dodgson replied, 'You were dry enough in the pulpit this morning!' "[23]

The only recorded instance of Dodgson's making friends with an undergraduate after he became a don, occurred early in the seventies. The liaison officers were little girls—the

Hatch girls. Young George Baden-Powell, then tutoring with their father, one day heard formidable growls under their parlor table. He got down on hands and knees and growled back. The three little Hatch girls were under the table—and so was Mr. Dodgson.

This introduction initiated a real friendship. Mr. Baden-Powell entered Balliol in 1871, in 1876 took the chancellor's prize for an English essay on *The Political and Social Results of the Absorption of Small Races by Large,* and then naturally went into politics. From 1885 till his death in 1898 he was Conservative Member of Parliament for the Kirkdale Division of Liverpool. During his tenure he was knighted for service to the empire. His main interest was always in the colonies, and in 1886 he was able to be of service to the Dodgson family and to the population of Tristan de Cunha, a tiny island in the South Atlantic.

An undergraduate with less skill in handling the little golden key was a Mr. Arthur Girdlestone, of New College, who visited Mr. Dodgson one evening on business. His host was sitting at a writing table, surrounded by piles of MSS arranged with mathematical neatness, many of them tied with tape. After the business was disposed of, the caller was invited to sit down and have a glass of wine. Dodgson talked quietly and seemed tired, until the conversation turned on children, when he instantly seemed refreshed. Girdlestone asked if children never bored him. He said, "They are three-fourths of my life," and became the taciturn, weary mathematician again.[14]

His "dinner parties"—usually a twosome with a little girl as guest—blended method and charm. After each party he entered a diagram in his diary, showing who the guests were and where they sat. To prevent repetitions, he also kept a menu book. He considered table linen a waste of money, so set his table with cardboard mats, but the entertainment was lavish, on the child scale. Any little gadget will amuse and interest a child, if the host can, as Carroll could, enter into the child's mind. He might show her some new system of filing papers, of boiling a kettle, of lighting the gas; or he would show her his vast collection of stylo pens and pencil sharpeners, or would do tricks with a little convex mirror, with clockwork bears, mice and frogs, or Isa's favorite toy, "Bob the Bat," which could be wound up to fly about the room. The ceilings were high, usually giving "Bob" plenty of room, but once "he" flew out of the window and landed squarely on a tray that a scout was carrying. The tray crashed loudly.

Isa tells, too, how he invariably made tea by swinging the teapot for exactly ten minutes, meanwhile walking up and down the room, telling anecdotes. He claimed the tea was better so.

Music boxes were among the *pièces de résistance*. He had a number of these, and when they had played themselves out, he might vary the entertainment by running them backwards. He also had an "orguinette" which played paper rolls of music. Once he ordered twelve dozen of these rolls on approval, and called in a musical don to help him select appropriate numbers. He was suitably modest about his own musical understanding, and wrote Arthur Sullivan: "What I know of your music is so delicious (they tell me I have not a musical ear, so my criticism is valueless, I fear)." But in his own way he loved music, and hung over the box, raising and lowering the lid to improve the effect. A favorite, with which he opened every concert, was "Santa Lucia." . . . A musical performance, noted by a little girl, took place when "Mr. Dodgson, father, and I went to pay a visit to Mr. Saul (a fellow of Magdalen College), whose rooms were full of musical instruments. He was practicing the big drum. Father undertook the cello, and Mr. Dodgson hunted up a comb and some paper."

If the music was below standard, the food was excellent, though served on cardboard mats, and his conversation entranced his visitors, though it must have taken all his charm to make some of the subjects interesting. He might take up the time before dinner by telling his visitor about the interviewers and autograph hunters who plagued him. Or he might give her a moral talk, such as telling a child who was afraid of riding a train, "But surely you trust God? Do you think he would let you come to harm? To be afraid is to *distrust*." Or he would take her on his lap in a big chair before the fire, and tell her stories about the animals on the tiles. He claimed they represented his various methods of receiving visitors!

He might meet the child on her own ground, and show her drawings of fairies, that "You can't be sure don't really exist." Perhaps best of all was when he drew pictures himself —not as pretty as the fairy pictures, but "full of expression in a few dramatic strokes—hair on end with fright, hands raised in horror, or faces broad with smiles." One story ended with the words, "My dear, you are a Perfect Goose!" and, by reversing a picture of a little man and woman and their house beside the lake, there *was* the Perfect Goose! [14]

His economy in table linen was part of his plan to live simply and have money on hand to help his friends. When someone wrote asking for a loan, he replied, "I will not lend, but will *give* you the £100 you asked for." And no price was too high for lessons for his child friends.

Isa, who was one of his chief beneficiaries, also describes his methodical habits—the large number of trunks he traveled with, the clipper he used on his nails instead of scissors, and his five sizes of note paper, which he stocked to make sure of exactly the right size for any letter he planned. "Let me see," he would say, "for this letter I will use number three size; that should meet the case exactly." And, said Isa, "It always did."

The character he created while his natural juices flowed freely was Alice, fresh as early morning. As he gradually desiccated and petrified into bachelorhood, he was gestating quite another character, the hero of the next chapter—the White Knight.

Chapter 10

Escape Through the Looking-Glass

> *Then it really has happened after all! And now, who am I? I will remember, if I can! I'm determined to do it!*

AFTER ANOTHER SEVEN YEARS under the dread hierarchy, the Reverend Mr. Dodgson had lost his key to the Garden of Eden. So, as he says himself, he deliberately set out to recapture the mood that produced *Alice's Adventures*—with a curious kind of success. *Looking-Glass* is a masterpiece—only a shade less than *Wonderland*—but it already exudes the ripe flavor of approaching decay and disintegration into the cruel (on paper) and unusual Mr. Dodgson and the sentimental-religious Louisa Caroline, as one of the Oxford parodists signed "The Vulture and the Husbandman."

A certain grimness and harshness of *Through the Looking-Glass* derive from the Red Queen and her consort. The plot is Berkeleyan and horrible—"Who dreamed it?" If Alice dreamed it, then the Red Queen was really one of Dinah's kittens, and the Red King merely a chess piece—but suppose it was the Red King's dream?

The chess game, instead of Reds and Whites, might be divided into Lefts and Rights, with Carroll on the Left side. The Red King, Queen, and Knight, are all strong and disagreeable characters; the White royalty, weak and ridiculous, but amiable. Was Archdeacon Dodgson—as the righteous representative of established order—strong, unreasonable perhaps, though hardly disagreeable? The Red Queen's rules of behavior are the rules of a right-handed world interpreted by a left-handed child, who feels he is asked to do everything backwards. Hence the idea of going the other way to reach the top of the hill, and of running hard without getting anywhere. If the dream is the Red King's, the world belongs to father—if it is Alice's dream, little Charles has a place in the world. Every child has such fantasies—the wonder is to have remembered them in the twilight state before sleep, and to have been able to write them down before they faded.

This chess game, so much—perhaps so consciously—like Life (as Carroll would write it), is played on several planes, has several interpretations, and no definitive triumph. Although Carroll claims it is a complete game, Mr. Madan says "it is not up to chess standard, and had no normal checkmate." The White Knight does win permission to escort Alice to the last brook. Does this mean "Carroll's Alice-self finds that the left way is the right way"? Professor Harry Morgan Ayres, who recognizes the White Knight as Carroll's spokesman, finds it significant that he is the only one with the courtesy and wit to help a lost child—"the one 'creature' in all the two books that shows a touch of human affection for the little girl." [1]

Dr. A. L. Taylor, in his ingenious book *The White Knight*, has a good deal to say about Carrollian games. He thinks of the chess game as seen from the standpoint of the pawn, who does not grasp the whole picture. None of the pieces do; even the Queens, who can see more of the board, don't know. "To understand one's part in a game of chess, one would have to be aware of the room and the unseen intelligence which is combining the pieces.

"The moves of the two Queens are inexplicable to Alice because of a limitation in her powers. . . . But if the length of the board is time, the breadth of the board must be time also, a kind of time known only to mathematicians and mystics: the kind of time we call eternity.

"When she became a Queen she could see both ways. At the end she comes to the door with Visitors Bell on one side and Servants Bell on the other—she had gone full circle in time, which unknown to her was a little planet like that in *Sylvie and Bruno Concluded,* in which 'the vanquished army ran away at full speed, and in a very few minutes found themselves face to face with the victorious army, who were marching home again, and who were so frightened at finding themselves between two armies that they surrendered at once.' "

The book has one grim defeat in the trappings of victory.

Humpty Dumpty demonstrates *Looking-Glass* methods by analyzing "Jabberwocky." The youth slays the Jabberwock— is the author trying to tell himself, by writing the poem backwards, that this is a disastrous victory? What drove Charles back into himself and his childish memories? Was it not his acceptance of ordination without resolving his doubts? For him, taking orders was, implicitly, giving in to his father. No one, reading the elder Dodgson's letter, would say he exercised no tyranny over his son.

The letter shows how stern the Archdeacon was under his gentleness. His grandniece, who recalled little else about him, said that he had "decided ideas" about his children's character development.[2] A mere lifted eyebrow, in a home keyed to sensitive response, is more urgent than infinite beatings in a more happy-go-lucky environment. How could anyone revolt against the Canon, with his charm, his faultless altruism, his perfect fatherhood?

Even less could Charles revolt against his mother, the vague, the gentle, the good, with the soft voice that was never raised. Charles was the eldest son, probably the favorite. He had the energy to attempt revolt, but loyalty blocked him. His loved ones and the whole social system were against him. He has left brave and heartening documents of his struggle against distortion, locked in the velvet-lined iron maiden of his period, and his caricatures of that iron maiden helped later generations to master her. Nobody knows how many middle and late Victorians found life more bearable because of the *Alice* books, or how often Carroll's gallows humor helped other sensitives to bear the cross, or even to wriggle out from under it in a good-natured way. Yet the timeless quality of *Looking-Glass*, as of *Wonderland*, rests not on the neurosis of a man or of an age, but on the genius that illuminates our essential nature.

An admirer gushed, "Mr. Dodgson is broad—as broad as Christ." [3] He shared other characteristics with Christ too; at least the Christ of the nineteenth century stained-glass attitudes. One interpretation of the Christ story is that he crucified his infantile jealousy of his father and love of his mother by renunciation (Hamlet, Oedipus). Carrying the renunciation to its logical end, he gave up everything, including life.

Whether that was the historic Christ is not the question here. But for millions of persons, for two thousand years, the cross has symbolized this very renunciation of jealousy and power, and the crucifixion of the animal natural man, beginning with his infant desire to supplant his father.

Dr. Greenacre[4] sees the same problem. She says ". . . the search is for a love which will avoid or control all aggressiveness and hostility, and with it all sexuality; a love in which natural human instinctual pressures will be converted into duty, obligation, denial, and sanctity, in which conscience will take the place of instinct, and will sacrifice freedom of thought as well as of action."

Charles left his father enthroned. In *Sylvie and Bruno* it was as true king of Elfland. In *Through the Looking-Glass* the Red King's dream may be considered as requiring abject submission to the father, the potent king who could annihilate the other characters simply by awakening. Charles surrenders everything—except his sense of humor. The unpleasantness of the Red King in no way represents the charming Canon Dodgson, but may show how Charles felt in his early childhood about his father's power. The conflict in his nature comes out all through the chess games, with the characters split into Reds and Whites. The Reds are fierce and irritable, the Whites gentle and sheepish—literally sheepish in the White Queen's metamorphosis. In the attempt to separate out pure forms, the opposites always encroach. An artist who travels too far toward "purity" always produces horrors too, and whoever, dissatisfied with the rainbow scheme of nature, tries to achieve whiteness, is startled to see black shadows at his heels.

The attempt to curb his youthful revolt also did strange things to Charles. The younger generation, knocking at the door, is not usually too disturbed at the older generation's shudders (or bluster). But Charles, who describes the proper feeling for God (perhaps for his earthly father too) as a sort of dread—not fear, but respect and love tempered with reverence—lacked the courage to make the final thrust and dethrone his father. "Jabberwocky" * is not so much a parodied epic as an epic in reverse. The hero does slay the monster,

* See Appendix C.

but not with the ring of the true victor—and he is welcomed by his parent, instead of by a beautiful maiden. To such a pass is Beowulf-Siegfried fallen. In *The Hunting of the Snark*, the hero is eaten by the monster.

The hero is supposed to attain to the maiden and to the throne of the old king. But the most Charles was able to become, in *Through the Looking-Glass*, was—a queen. He was no more capable of kingship than Edward the Eighth. Despite the reinstatement of Bruno's father as King of Elfland, Bruno will never make a king either.

In a sense, *Jabberwocky* and *The Hunting of the Snark* are the same poem. Carroll says so himself, indirectly—he says *The Hunting of the Snark* "is laid in an island frequented by the Jubjub and Bandersnatch—no doubt the very island in which the Jabberwock was slain." His stifled impulses toward self-assertion and toward the normal sex life kept sending him weird messages, of which these two poems are about the clearest. Since *Jabberwocky* was written several years before the book, he had time to perfect the intricately camouflaged sex symbolism—but then he proceeded to give himself away, first in Humpty Dumpty's explanations, and later in the introduction to *Snark*, where he explains "and the bowsprit got mixed with the rudder sometimes." Originally he planned to use the Jabberwock for the frontispiece of *Looking-Glass*, but finally substituted the White Knight, after sending a questionnaire to thirty mothers of little girls.

It has been hinted that his sex symbolism, and therefore presumably his sex life (in the mind—for no one claims he had any other sort), remained on an immature level. But it seems that he made at least one attempt to escape from celibacy into matrimony. If there was such an attempt, it was frustrated, and must have left him permanently discouraged; there is no intimation of a second. That the attempt, or the falling in love, occurred between the telling of the first *Alice* story in 1862 and the printing of the second late in 1871, is suggested by the increased sentimentality and the increased shadow in the latter. His first defeat was his acceptance of ordination; his second, less certainly documented as to names, dates, and reasons, was surely his failure to achieve a satisfactory adult love-relationship. The second defeat shows in a

certain asperity of the *Looking-Glass* creatures—those that
are not on the "sweet" side.

Several signposts point to disintegration; moments when
the author steps out of character and reminds the reader that
it is a dream, as in the boat ride, when the rushes fade so
quickly, and he announces that, being dream-rushes, they
must fade even faster than real ones. In transcribing *Alice's
Adventures Underground* into the published version, he carefully deleted all such passages. In fact, therein lies his invention
of a whole new genus of literature, in which "psychological facts" are treated as objective fact—in which coexistence
in the mind implies ability to coexist objectively. The dead,
the unborn, the non-existent, talking animals, humans in impossible situations—all are taken for granted, and the dream
is not disturbed.

To *Alice* and its calm transference of the preposterous and
magical into the everyday, can be traced such books as David
Garnett's *Lady into Fox,* Christopher Morley's *Thunder on
the Left,* James Hilton's *Lost Horizon,* the works of Robert
Nathan, A. A. Milne, and many others. Gertrude Stein and
James Joyce were Carrollian adepts. Works of imagination
had existed before, but the special technique of the dream
was Dodgson's own invention. Swift, for instance, takes pains
to explain everything in *Gulliver.* Even *A Midsummer
Night's Dream,* which has been called the first nonsense book
in English, carefully prepares the groundlings for miracles to
come. But the utter simplicity of the opening of *Alice* is dis-
arming, and no explanations are required.

"Alice was beginning to get very tired of sitting by her
sister on the bank and of having nothing to do: once or twice
she had peeped into the book her sister was reading, but it
had no pictures or conversations in it, 'and what is the use
of a book,' thought Alice, 'without pictures or conversations?' "

There, in one paragraph, is the protagonist, her age and
temperament, the setting, and the mood. The next paragraph
mentions parenthetically that the hot day "made her feel very
sleepy and stupid," and introduces the White Rabbit. By
paragraph three the Rabbit has taken the watch out of its
waistcoat pocket and started down the rabbit hole, and in

paragraph four Alice is down after it. Just in that easy, insinuating way our dreams bring us truths from *l'autre monde.* The method, once learned, became a part of our literary technique, and we forgot where we learned it, just as we forgot that the King's Messenger was the first to say, "As large as life and twice as natural."

Dodgson knew his technique, but he slipped a second time in *Through the Looking-Glass,* where Alice listens to the White Knight's parting song, while the sunset falling on his hair makes a picture that she remembers in after years. This is more definite and more sentimental than the few transitions of the sort he permitted himself in *Wonderland,* which remains a flawless work of art because of the balanced tensions between the many threads of his nature. By 1871 the webbing had begun to give and sag a bit.

Through the Looking-Glass, like *Wonderland,* is an infinite onion, with many other leaves. After all, Carroll was a philosopher, which means he transmuted his experiences into something beyond life. It is not for nothing that Eddington referred five times to *Through the Looking-Glass* in his *Nature of the Physical World,* or that writers on relativity, semantics, and other modern paths up the mountain, frequently use Carrollian quotations for signposts. As a mathematician he was a great poet. Under the guise of nonsense he shows the ephemerality and unimportance of our most cherished categories, including time and space, and his social criticism is present by implication. The pacifists of 1914 might have described the soldiers fraternizing in the trenches in terms of the wood where things have no names. The stern categories called them back to the logical-nonsensical business of murdering one another as the fawn that trustfully allowed Alice to put her arms around its neck inside the wood, emerged suddenly exclaiming, "Why—I'm a fawn—and you're a human child!"

Space is annihilated in the garden of talking flowers. Alice and the Red Queen were "running hand in hand, and the Queen went so fast that it was all she could do to keep up with her: and still the Queen kept crying 'Faster! Faster!' but Alice felt she *could not* go faster, though she had no breath left to say so.

"The most curious part of the thing was, that the trees and other things round them never changed their places at all: however fast they went, they never seemed to pass anything. 'I wonder if all the things move along with us?' thought poor puzzled Alice. And the Queen seemed to guess her thought, for she cried 'Faster! Don't try to talk!' "

The Queen continues to hurry her along. " 'Are we nearly there?' Alice managed to pant out at last.

" 'Nearly there!' the Queen repeated. 'Why, we passed it ten minutes ago! Faster!' "

When they stop, Alice leans against a tree, which to her surprise is the tree they had stood under before they started running.

" 'Well, in *our* country,' said Alice, still panting a little, 'you'd generally get to somewhere else—if you ran very fast for a long time as we've been doing.'

" 'A slow sort of country!' said the Queen. 'Now, *here*, you see, it takes all the running *you* can do, to keep in the same place. If you want to get somewhere else, you must run twice as fast as that!' "

Carroll seems to have been anticipating twentieth century New York. This is a wholly original sort of thinking, now made familiar by Einstein, but in the nineteenth century just coming slowly to birth, here and there, in the minds of scattered philosophers. Carroll upsets everything, tests everything, and does not hesitate to change the frames of reference.

A later chapter subjects time to the same procedure. " 'Living backwards!' Alice repeated in great astonishment. 'I never heard of such a thing!'

" '—but there's one great advantage in it, that one's memory works both ways.' . . .

" 'What sort of things do *you* remember best?' Alice ventured to ask.

" 'Oh, things that happened the week after next,' the Queen replied in a careless tone. 'For instance, now,' she went on, sticking a large piece of plaster on her finger as she spoke, 'there's the King's Messenger. He's in prison now, being punished: and the trial doesn't even begin until next Wednesday: and of course the crime comes last of all.'

" 'Suppose he never commits the crime?' said Alice.

" 'That would be all the better, wouldn't it?' the Queen said, as she bound the plaster round her finger with a bit of ribbon."

Next the Queen shouts that her finger is bleeding. Then her brooch flies open, and finally she pricks herself. She is now perfectly calm, having bound up her finger, bled, and screamed.

Carroll started playing around with time when he wrote his early essay, later given as a lecture before the Ashmolean Society, *Where Does the Day Begin?* Then in *Wonderland,* the unfortunate Hatter has insulted Time, so that it is always five o'clock, with no time to wash the tea-things. The idea develops in *Sylvie and Bruno,* in the Professor's native planet where everything is different, and whence he brings the Outlandish watch with the reversal peg. Does the extreme regimentation of Charles's own life suggest a repressed desire to be temperamental and unpunctual? He just missed the complete absurdity of Kant, whose neighbors in Königsberg set their watches by his regular afternoon walk; but he succumbed to the tyranny of time in fact, while trying to escape it in theory. A true Carrollian solution.

How often he lets off steam by permitting some horror *almost* to happen, then diverting it to something commonplace! Suggesting that the Red King might have dreamed the whole world, he permits Alice to waken and find the Red Queen reduced to a kitten, implying the same of the King. But the choicest and subtlest shock to be found anywhere, even in Carroll, is Humpty Dumpty's remark to Alice. " 'Seven years and six months!' Humpty Dumpty repeated thoughtfully. 'An uncomfortable sort of age. Now if you'd asked *my* advice, I'd have said, "Leave off at seven"—but it's too late now.'

" 'I never ask advice about growing,' Alice said indignantly.

" 'Too proud?' the other enquired.

"Alice felt even more indignant at this suggestion. 'I mean,' she said, 'that one can't help growing older.'

" '*One* can't, perhaps,' said Humpty Dumpty; 'but *two* can. With proper assistance, you might have left off at seven.'

" 'What a beautiful belt you've got on!' Alice suddenly remarked."

It is so subtly done that many readers fail to realize just what is implied by "proper assistance." Perhaps Greville Macdonald did not think through Carroll's argument that he, Greville, would be better off with a marble head, because then he would not have to have his hair combed. There was the letter, too, that Charles wrote his sister, "If I had shot the Dean I could not have had more said about it!"

Is some childhood reminiscence behind his speaking of seven and a half as an "uncomfortable age"? His own transition from thinking of himself as Bruno, to thinking of himself as Alice, seems to have occurred between five and seven. As the Gentleman in White Paper said to Alice, "So young a child ought to know where she's going, even if she doesn't know her own name." Charles himself must have been in the wood where things have no name. Or did a Caterpillar or a Wood Pigeon ever ask him who he was?

And who was Alice in the second book? In part, of course, she was still Charles Dodgson. And in part she was a new Alice, Alice Raikes, whose father, a distant connection of the Dodgsons, was Postmaster General, and whom Carroll met quite by chance.

He was visiting an uncle who lived in Onslow Square, South Kensington. One day, strolling in the gardens and watching some children at play, he heard one addressed as "Alice." He introduced himself to her, saying, "So you are another Alice. I am very fond of Alices." Then he asked all the children into his uncle's house, to show them "something rather puzzling." He gave Alice an orange, and asked her which hand she was holding it in.

"My right hand," said Alice.

There was a long mirror across one corner of the room. He said, "Go and look at the little girl in the glass over there and tell me which hand she is holding the orange in."

Alice stood before the glass and slowly said, "She is holding it in her left hand." He asked her how she could explain that. She thought a moment and then said, "Supposing I was on the *other* side of the glass, wouldn't the orange still be in my right hand?"

This was perfect. Dodgson laughed and said, "Well done, little Alice, it's the best answer I've had yet." He told friends that this episode gave him the idea of a " 'Looking-Glass Country' where everything would be reversed," and to that extent Alice Raikes entered the *Looking-Glass*. But Alice Liddell was there too. The period between the two Alices may correspond with the period mentioned by Mrs. Skene, when Charles interrupted his visits to the Liddell family, because, she said, of a difference arising from his extreme sensitiveness. The nostalgic poem seems to date the breach:

> *I have not seen thy sunny face,*
> *Nor heard thy silver laughter:*

it begins. It ends:

> *It shall not touch, with breath of bale,*
> *The pleasance of our fairy-tale.*

Pleasance is an unusual word. It is also Alice Liddell's middle name; further, he closes *Through the Looking-Glass* with an acrostic on her full name.

Other threads bind the two books. The King's Messengers, Hatta and Haigha, are our old friends Hatter and Hare, from the Mad Tea Party. Tenniel lets us in on the secret, showing Hatta still with his cup of tea and sandwich, and hat that was neither his nor stolen—a high hat such as Dodgson commonly wore. Hatta is just out of gaol, where he has been living on oyster shells since the trial. Professor Ayres presents some ideas about secondary sources for the names "Hatta" and "Haigha." [1] He also reproduces some drawings from the Junian codex in the Bodleian, to which both Carroll and Tenniel must have had access, giving plausible sources for the "Anglo-Saxon attitudes."

Following Shane Leslie, Taylor[6] thinks the Tweedles are High and Low Church, and their struggle is the Oxford Movement. "Strife is the pattern throughout; strife in and about the church; the spirit of Guy Fawkes' Day is symbolized in the first chapter and the nursery rhymes were chosen to fit into the strife-pattern. . . .

" 'Rattle' and 'ritual' are almost the same word. . . . But it was Low Church which spoiled High Church's rattle or ritual. . . . The monstrous crow which ended their mock-heroics is the threat of disestablishment which certainly did cause the English Church to sink its differences." All these topical interpretations are of interest, and lend depth to the weaving. Perhaps they are all true. But somehow the pearl of every one of Lewis Carroll's books is the poem at its heart.

Carroll's philosophy became steadily more conscious and more concentrated, from *Wonderland* to *Looking-Glass,* from *Looking-Glass* to *Sylvie and Bruno,* with its moralistic detours. But, as his philosophy became more conscious, it also grew more concentrated, drier, and less nutritious. Still in his best vein, but unlike anything in *Wonderland,* is this half-dreamy, half-waking episode from *Looking-Glass:*

" 'Things flow about so here!' she said at last in a plaintive tone, after she had spent a minute or so in vainly pursuing a large bright thing that looked sometimes like a doll and sometimes like a work-box, and was always on the shelf next above the one she was looking at," like J. W. Dunne's receding rainbow.[7]

Comparing this with Alice's soliloquy when she was falling down the rabbit hole reveals a more mature, less naïve mind —but Dodgson's emotions did not mature to correspond; he aged without mellowing. The Tweedle brothers are a special university type—querulous, meticulous, infantile, quarrelsome. Alice asks for guidance out of the wood and is answered with irrelevant and trifling animosities, boasting, cowardice—all the vices of the desk soldier. Oxford was biting into his bone and Dodgson was biting back.

Both Martin Gardner[8] and Dr. Taylor have modern scientific explanations for Alice's remark to the kitten that Looking-Glass milk might not be good to drink. Gardner refers it to the left-handed stereoisomers, and suggests Looking-Glass milk might be anti-matter, and both it and Alice might explode on contact. "For after all, except in size, Alice does not change at all in her strange journey."

Taylor refers to Pasteur's discovery in 1846 of polarized crystal, left-handed and right-handed tartaric and paratartaric acid. "Pasteur also noted the universe was dissymmetric."

Gardner refers Alice's difficulties with the vanishing goods on the shop shelves to the vanishing electron. His *Annotated Alice* is a useful and beautiful book, with only one flaw—

he has made it a book for adults because he believes the *Alice* books have lost their audience of children!

Dinah, whose ectoplasm, the Cheshire Cat, escorted Alice through *Wonderland*, is still behind the scenes. She is the mother of the two kittens that metamorphose into the two queens, and at the very end Alice suggests that Dinah was Humpty Dumpty, "however, you'd better not mention it to your friends just yet, for I'm not sure." Humpty Dumpty is a long way from the humorous, graceful, evanescent Cheshire Puss. In fact he is the essence of materialism—his fall shakes the woods from end to end. And contentious—was there ever the like? His explanation of the portmanteau words is too well known to quote, but it is commonplace that they have enriched the language and penetrated the dictionary and the law courts.

Tenniel took the trouble to make the Lion and the Unicorn likenesses of Gladstone and Disraeli, as his cartoons of the two alternating Prime Ministers in *Punch* demonstrate. This lends point to Alice's passage with the King:

" 'Does—the one—that wins—get the crown?' she asked, as well as she could, for the run was putting her quite out of breath.

" 'Dear me, no!' said the King. 'What an idea!' "

So much for politics—and much more in two paragraphs than the many labored pages in *Sylvie and Bruno*.

Carroll covers "civilized warfare" in the tournament between the Red and White Knight:

" 'I wonder, now, what the Rules of Battle are,' she said to herself, as she watched the fight, timidly peeping out from her hiding-place. 'One Rule seems to be, that if one Knight hits the other, he knocks him off his horse; and if he misses he tumbles off himself. . . .' "

The White Knight is the gem of *Through the Looking-Glass*. He is the only character in the book with any sweetness of temper; although he falls off his horse and makes the ridiculous upside-down inventions of a left-handed person trying to live right-handed, he shows Alice-Charles the way out of the wood, which none of the others had the sense or the courtesy to do.

Taylor[6] seems to have been the first to notice that "The

principle which eluded the White Knight was of course gravity. The word gravity is carefully avoided during the whole of this chapter, but he looked a little grave, and more than once he remarked gravely. The pun has no existence for him or Alice. . . . As a planesman or inhabitant of the surface, 'balance' was an idea he had failed to grasp."

His theory is that the Knight is like an animal trying to understand the human world from his flatland basis, who believes he has no chance, as we have no chance, of reasoning about the universe. . . . Dr. Taylor believes the White Knight stands for pure science and the Aged, Aged Man for applied science.

Looking-Glass ends with the coronation and banquet. The awakenings in the dream books grow more nightmarish each time, from the first Alice mildly brushing the leaves off her face, through *Looking-Glass* Alice shaking the Red Queen into a kitten after the dreadful banquet, to a still more dreadful one in *Sylvie and Bruno Concluded,* where everything shakes and changes, ending with Prince Uggug's transmogrification into a porcupine.

The dream did not belong to the Red King, because the Red Queen becomes a kitten; the kindly old bumble-headed Don Quixote, the White Knight, shows Alice out of the wood —she is crowned and becomes a Queen herself. The story has a happy ending, but it is hardly a happy story. The black shadow of Jabberwock hangs over it from the earliest pages; Jabberwock, standing for failure, in the sense of burying and betraying some at least of the ten talents. Escape is no longer so complete or so satisfying as in *Wonderland,* though the moment when Alice steps through the gauzy looking-glass never loses its thrill.

Perhaps it was part of Carroll's plan for his books to end weakly. The alternative is "came the dawn," or the wind-up of *Sylvie and Bruno. Through the Looking-Glass* could have finished with the characteristic remark of the White Queen, that Hatta is in gaol, being punished; the trial will come next Wednesday, " 'and of course the crime comes last of all.'

" 'Suppose he never commits the crime?' said Alice.

" 'That would be all the better, wouldn't it?' the White Queen said."

There sits Hatta, looking for all the world like Charles Dodgson in one of his doleful moments, meditating on the uncommitted crime for which he is incarcerated in Oxford, in his reverend collar and high hat, puzzling over Bruno's problem of spelling LIVE backwards. . . .

Chapter 11

Matilda Jane

Lover of children! Fellow-heir with those
Of whom the imperishable kingdom is!
Beyond all dreaming now your spirit knows
The unimagined mysteries.

The heart you wore beneath your pedant's cloak
Only to children's hearts you gave away;
Yet unaware in half the world you woke
The slumbering charm of childhood's day.

THESE STANZAS from a poem *Punch* published two weeks after his death, express something that Carroll's personality conveyed in life. He had tapped the fountain of youth, and kept the gateway open to the other world. But what *was* his *autre monde?*

Many Carrollians consider this question sacrilege. He was the last saint of this irreverent world; those who have surrendered the myths of Santa Claus, of the stork, of Jehovah, hang their last remnants of mysticism on Lewis Carroll and will not allow themselves to examine him dispassionately. Alexander Woollcott, whose last rites, conducted in a theater, were uncompromisingly secular, rejoiced that no one had yet tried to uncover Carroll's sources, or in Collingwood's phrase, to "lift the veil from those dead sanctities." [1] But as the March Hare said to Alice, "Why not?"

Though much of Carroll's insomnia was due to theological conflicts, some of it arose from the complete negation of his sexual needs. He had an odd, and of course frustrated, love for little girls—in part identifying himself with them, in part substituting "child-friends" for more difficult and responsible adult relationships.

In the happy home of the Dodgson family there was sunshine on the surface, but there were shadows as well. Dr. Greenacre [1] has studied some of them. It was she who remarked that of the three out of eleven children who married, none did so until both parents were dead. There is not much about weddings in Charles's diary. On April 13, 1869, he says, "Mary's wedding-day. I had come over the day before to be present, and 'give her away.' The day was exceptionally lovely."

On June 30, 1883, he records, "Skeffington and Isa left. We have done a good deal of sight-seeing and it has given me the opportunity of really getting to know my sister-in-law, whom I had hitherto only seen once for a few minutes." It is interesting to compare this with the first such entry, for August 9, 1871: "Wilfred's wedding-day. May it be the beginning of many, many happy years for him and Alice!" This may be partly because Wilfred had married an old family friend, Alice Jane Donkin, of whom Charles made numerous photographs, including "The Elopement." He refers to her often in the diaries, and wrote a letter of warm approval to his brother about her child-training methods.

Dr. Greenacre says of his childhood, "There seems little doubt that Charles was loved dearly by his mother and was her favorite, but he was forced to relinquish his infancy unusually early, for the sister Caroline was born the following year, with Mary born when he was three, Skeffington when he was four, and Wilfred when he was six. . . . Neither Charles Dodgson nor Lewis Carroll had many good words to say for babies. 'Throw them away.' 'Tie them in knots and send them into the wilderness.' 'Roast them well and serve them as appetizers for the main meal.' "

Isa Bowman speaks of his kissing her "passionately" when she was no more than ten or eleven years old, and after he had just decided to forgive her for drawing a caricature of him. She also speaks of his holding her close while telling her the part of the story where "the children came to a deep dark wood," on the beach near Eastbourne.[3] It is just as well to divide Isa's statements by half—she shows the precocious emotional developments of a stage child, and her book gains little by being called *The Story of Lewis Carroll, by the Real Alice in Wonderland*. Isa played Alice on the stage, but she knew that could not make her the "real Alice"! Dividing by half, there are still plenty of kisses in her book, and in published letters of Carroll to many other little girls.

One lady, who was taken out by Dodgson when she was a child, told Derek Hudson she was rather surprised to be kissed by him in the middle of a performance in a theater. "As their daughters approached the 'dangerous age,' some mothers grew understandably cautious, and Dodgson's diary for 1880 records that he kissed a girl in that year whom he thought to be fourteen but who turned out to be seventeen; when he wrote a 'mock apology,' the mother replied sternly, 'we shall see that it does not recur.' " [4]

The following letter is not one that Ethel Rowell included in her charming article on Dodgson in Harper's Magazine:

Ch. Ch. Oxford June 25 /98

"Dear Mrs. Rowell,

"The being entrusted with Ethel for a day is such a great advance on mere acquaintanceship, that I venture to ask if I may regard myself on 'kissing' terms with her, as I am with many a girl-friend a great deal older than *she* is. Considering that—she being 17 and I 63—I am old enough to be her *grandfather,* I hope you won't think it a very out-of-the-way suggestion. Nevertheless, if I find you think it wiser that we only shake hands, I shall not be *in the least* hurt. Of course I shall, unless I hear to the contrary, continue to shake hands only.

Very truly yours,
C. L. Dodgson"

The title of Ethel Rowell's article is "To Me He Was Mr. Dodgson," and she tells with what affectionate awe she regarded him. It seems strange that none of the girls, except the one who spoke to Mr. Hudson, seems at all shaken by the incongruity of his two rôles when he tried to play them simultaneously.

Mrs. Skene remarked that he was unique among young men, especially in university circles, in paying attention to girl children. [5] Mr. Madan said he was unpopular at Oxford because he lampooned his colleagues and mystified them with a procession of child visitors. Since celibacy was required of the Students and surreptitiously encouraged throughout the University, children must have been fabulous monsters indeed, to be gaped at and dreaded, but hardly cultivated. Carroll's own fondness for them, while natural enough, was rather complex. He had no adult love life at all; there is no evidence of any love, frustrated or otherwise, in his diaries, and nothing in his published writings shows an adult understanding of love. His closest approach to a love story, *Sylvie and Bruno,* is diluted with noble talk and suppressed emotion. The hero, first supposed dead, feebly revives in the last few pages—the whole book is far from robust.

Mr. Reed says Carroll greatly admired Ellen Terry, which is axiomatic, adding, however, that while he admired her as an actress and a person, he was "one of the very few men— possibly the only man—who had known Ellen Terry in her prime without falling in love with her!" The most extreme comment in the diaries was about a hair-brusher: "I can imagine no more delightful occupation than brushing Ellen Terry's hair!" [6]

He admitted preferring women friends to men, but his very ease in remaining strictly friendly implies that some switch must have been thrown. Gertrude Thomson tells the odd story of their first meeting. After seeing some of her fairy designs, he wished to know her, and he arranged by letter to meet her in South Kensington Museum. She arrived a little early, wondering how they would know each other.

"At that moment a gentleman entered, two little girls clinging to his hands, and as I caught sight of the tall slim figure, with the clean-shaven, delicate, refined face, I said to myself, *'That's* Lewis Carroll.' He stood for a moment, head erect, glancing swiftly over the room, then, bending down, whispered something to one of the children; she, after a moment's pause, pointed straight at me." Miss Thomson asked how he had found her so soon; he replied, "My little friend found you. I told her I had come to meet a young lady who knew fairies, and she fixed on you at once. But *I* knew you before she spoke." [1] Did he bring the children along as chaperons?

In 1879 he dreamed: "I was staying, with my sisters, in some suburb of London, and had heard that the Terrys were staying near us, so went to call, and found Mrs. Terry at home, who told us that Marion [Polly] and Florence were at the theatre, the 'Walter House,' where they had a good engagement. 'In that case,' I said, 'I'll go on there at once and see the performance—and may I take Polly with me?' 'Certainly,' said Mrs. Terry. And there was Polly, the child, seated in the room, and looking about nine or ten years old: and I was distinctly conscious of the fact, yet without any feeling of surprise at its incongruity, that I was going to take the *child Polly* with me to the theatre, to see the *grown-up* Polly act!" [1] Like Alice, he had found the magic key and could slip in and out of the garden of childhood.

He must have developed that device years before, to keep from growing up. In *Through the Looking-Glass,* Alice's age, seven and a half "exactually," draws from Humpty Dumpty the remark that she might profitably have left off at seven. Carroll protested audibly when his child friends matured—he refused to go walking with a young lady who had just put her hair up, unless she would take it down again, and he claimed that he "lost" his friends when they grew up and became "uninteresting."

He seems even to have had a moment of infidelity to Alice Liddell. On May 11, 1865, when Alice had just passed her thirteenth birthday, he wrote, "Met Alice and Miss Prickett in the quadrangle: Alice seems changed a good deal, and hardly for the better—probably going through the usual awkward stage of transition."

His love life was confined to these spiritualized relationships with little girls—plus insomnia. An affectionate soul, he should not have been the ascetic he undoubtedly was. Certain families seem to tend that way; out of eleven Dodgson children, only one girl and two boys married. Carroll's suffering, fastidious expression is that of one crucified from principle; but the effect of his sentimental poems and letters yearning for the innocence of childhood—especially girlhood—implies that his impish Bruno-self never ceased to plague him.

The closest hint of even a frustrated love affair with a grown woman is the justly famous quotation from Collingwood: "One can not read this little volume [*Three Sunsets*] without feeling that the shadow of some disappointment lay over Lewis Carroll's life. Such I believe to have been the case, and it was this that gave him his wonderful sympathy with all who suffered. But those who loved him would not wish to lift the veil from these dead sanctities, nor would any purpose be served by so doing. The proper use of sympathy is not to weep over sorrows that are over, and whose very memory is perhaps obliterated for him in the first joy of possessing new and higher faculties." [1] No wonder broken hearts so rarely healed then—for some sort of broken heart is implied.

Was it, as in Carroll's poem "Stolen Waters," dated 1862, that

> *I kissed her on the false, false lips*

or was it, as in "Faces in the Fire," dated the same year?

> *Those locks of jet are turned to gray*
> *And she is strange and far away*
> *That might have been mine own today*

These poems were both written when he was thirty, in the same year as the telling of the *Alice* story. Their badness implies the absence of any actual background experience, but their attitude keeps recurring in later works. Throughout *Sylvie and Bruno,* the narrator, the "I" of the story, repeatedly hints that he is barred by age from competing for the heroine. Did Carroll ever actually fall in love with one of his little girl friends? It is fantastic, but not impossible.

His close association with children was both cause and effect of his prolonged youth. He told Isa that children had a refreshing effect on him that was "almost physical," and that his mind was most in tune with their minds when he was tired. Here is a letter he wrote to a child friend who seems to have weathered the critical period and retained his regard: "I always feel specially grateful to friends who, like you, have given me a child-friendship and a woman-friendship. About nine out of ten, I think, of my child-friendships get shipwrecked at the critical point 'where the stream and river meet,' [sic!] and the child-friends, once so affectionate, become uninteresting acquaintances, whom I have no wish to set eyes on again." [7]

After his own family, his closest relationships were with the Liddells, in spite of all formalities, protocol, and esthetic distance—even in spite of his guerrilla war with the Dean, and Mrs. Liddell's with him. It was a war in which the wounds were not fatal, and in which love outweighed the negative feelings. In a letter written in 1945, Wing Commander Caryl Hargreaves, speaking of his grandmother's (Mrs. Liddell's) feeling for Dodgson, said, "She seems to have mingled approval with disapproval in a strange way—but when Lorina came out—or became of a marriageable age, disapproval of Mr. Dodgson seeing much of the girls seems to have got the upper hand."

On June 25, 1870, Dodgson's diary records: ". . . (photographed Salisbury children.) This morning an almost equally wonderful thing happened. Mrs. Liddell brought Ina and Edith to be photographed, first visiting my rooms, and then the studio."

And on November 16, 1871, he wrote: ". . . party given by Owen in the new Common Room, where I met the Deanery party. I took in Edith Liddell, and found her, (when once the ice was broken,) a very pleasant neighbor."

The next entry is brief. February 7, 1874, he wrote only: "Wedding day of my old friend, Ina Liddell." Lorina Liddell, long after she married Mr. Skene, was still remembered. Her copies of *Sylvie and Bruno* and *Sylvie and Bruno Concluded*, dated Dec. 12, 1889 and Dec. 27, 1893 respectively, are both inscribed: "Mrs. Skene, with sincere regards from the author." He visited her and made friends with her daughters, who still remembered him affectionately in 1930.

On June 26, 1876, the entry is: "To Oxford with Willie Wilcox, etc. On arriving, I was deeply grieved to hear of the death (this afternoon, of peritonitis following measles), of my old friend, Edith Liddell."

In another letter, Wing Commander Hargreaves says, "Edith died of acute appendicitis—a disease not at that time recognized—in great pain. She was the member of the family to whom my mother was especially devoted—& to the day of her death nearly sixty years later she could hardly bear to speak of Edith's death. The bare facts that I have told you above were all that I could extract out of my mother—the subject was still too painful. After Edith's death Sir William Richmond painted a picture of her with her bright red hair which he gave to my mother."

Whatever ups and downs Dodgson may have had with Mrs. Liddell, they were both big enough to surmount their differences at such a time. On December 11, 1876, Dodgson writes, "Mrs. Liddell came in to see the photographs which I had taken in '58, '59, and '60 of Edith; and accepted several of them. In the evening she sent me two recent cartes of her." A few days before her death Edith's engagement to Mr. Aubrey Harcourt of Nuneham had been announced. She was twenty-two. Alice's marriage Dodgson did not record, possibly because he was in Eastbourne at the time and may not have learned of it immediately—or perhaps for some other reason. Alice married Reginald Gervis Hargreaves, J. P., of "Cuffnells," Lyndhurst, Hants, on September 15, 1880. Wing Commander Hargreaves wrote, "I think it may justly be said that of all his girl friends, my mother was the only one with whom he showed any real anxiety to remain in contact after they had reached the twenties & he had grown older."

Another girl who weathered the crisis without losing or being lost was Gertrude Chataway. She wrote:

"To *me* it was of course all perfect, but it is astonishing that *he* never seemed either tired or to want other society. I spoke to him once of this since I have been grown up, and he told me it was the greatest pleasure he could have to converse freely with a child, and feel the depths of her mind. . . .

"I don't think that he ever really understood that we, whom he had known as childlren, could not always remain such. I stayed with him only a few years ago, at Eastbourne, and felt for the time that I was once more a child. He never appeared to realize that I had grown up, except when I reminded him of the fact, and then he only said, 'Never mind, you will always be a child to me, even when your hair is grey.' " [1]

He favored the girls who retained qualities that enabled him to imagine them still as children. This may have been the quality that attracted him to Miss Thomson—some

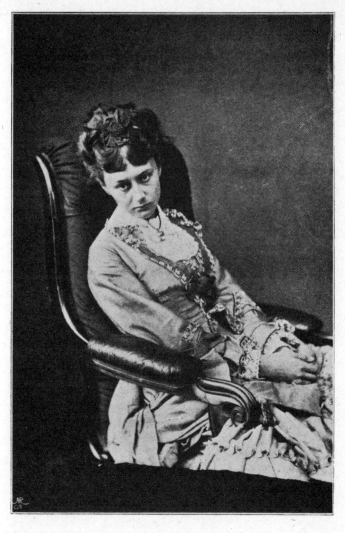

Carroll's last photograph of Alice (1870), from *The Lewis Carroll Picture Book*.

starry-eyed wonder, some freshness of imagination, perhaps. But did he "lose" his child friends, or did he desert them? The hyper-acid Mr. Tuckwell says that at adolescence (without using that word) "the petted loving child friend was dropped, abruptly, remorselessly, finally . . . the little maids put away childish things, he did not; to their maturer interest and day-dreams he could have made no response . . . his pedantry cloaking a responsiveness which shrank from coarser, more conventional adult contact," and so forth.[8]

In his crude academic way Mr. Tuckwell was right, which in no sense excuses his venom and inaccuracy, or his misplaced tone of patronage—he seems never to have realized that his colleague was a major poet! The gingerly explanation of Carroll's preference for children rather than adults is fair enough, nor are the strictures on his faithlessness too strong.

What Mr. Tuckwell wants to say and cannot, for the same reason that the Gian di Bologna "Mercury" in the center court of Christ Church lacks an important masculine attribute, is that Carroll preferred little girls because his emotional clock had been jammed. People have wondered what he did with his love life. Now it can be told. He loved little girls, but, like Peter Pan, he had no intention of marrying them, or, as Mr. Tuckwell prefers to say, "responding to their maturer interests and grown-up day-dreams." [8] Carroll drops them at the onset of the dangerous age, after kissing and embracing them profusely in childhood. Besides Isa's testimony, innumerable letters to little girls revolve about kissing, like the famous "tired in the face" letter, quoted in Collingwood and elsewhere, in which the doctor prescribes rest from kissing and Carroll answers mournfully, "But what am I to do? because, you see, I owe her a hundred and eighty-two more!" The "her" was again Gertrude Chataway, who received another fantastic letter on the weight of kisses she had sent him and the excess postage he had paid on them. To Maggie Bowman, Isa's youngest sister, who sent him "a sack full of love and a basket of kisses," he returned a long and especially pixy letter about a sack full of gloves and a basket of kittens. His ability to convert danger into play was unique.

Children's play prepares for adult activity, but adult play may be either temporary recoil for another spring, or an index of permanent arrest at a childish level. No one contends that Carroll ever attained the stage of adult love. It seems likely that he once made an effort to grow up and marry, but perhaps he was psychologically doomed to fail. A number of straws pointing one way indicate that a breeze has passed. Max Trell has suggested that Carroll was actually in love with the real Alice, Alice Liddell, and proposed honorable marriage to her directly or through her parents. What straws point that way?

First, is it possible? Poe married a thirteen-year-old girl, and Ruskin fell in love with Rose la Touche when she was twelve, though he waited till she was eighteen before proposing to her. Mrs. Skene mentioned a rupture between Carroll and her family while Alice was growing up. Major Hargreaves, Alice's son, told Professor Zanetti that Mrs. Liddell made Alice burn all his letters. Collingwood said: "His first child-friend, so far as I know, was Miss Alice Liddell, the little companion whose innocent talk was one of the pleasures of his early life at Oxford." [1] The surviving letters to Alice begin, "My dear Mrs. Hargreaves"; two of them refer to the manuscript, and one invites her and her husband to tea. One says: "My mental picture is as clear as ever of one who was, through so many years, my ideal child-friend. I have had scores of child-friends since your time, but they have been quite a different thing."[1, 7]

With the reservations that we do not know for certain that he ever contemplated matrimony, or that if he did, his queen was Alice, we do know his emotional tone dried and stiffened between the writing of the two *Alices*.

A presentation copy of *Alice's Adventures Underground,* first edition, reads: "To Her, whose children's smiles fed the narrator's fancy and were his rich reward, from the Author, Xmas, 1886."

Wing Commander Hargreaves has something further to say about his grandmother and Dodgson. "She must have approved strongly in some ways to let the children go round to his rooms so often & unaccompanied when they got there —I have always understood that that was a particular favor in those days. But she cannot have liked him as he was not a frequent visitor to the Deanery—& she made Alice destroy the drawings illustrating the stories. She may have thought those were merely nonsense—&, being possessed of that ruthless spirit of tidying up so common to so many wives & mothers, destroyed them so that they should not 'litter up the place.' But later she seems to have grown rather to disapprove—which may only have been, as her daughters approached marriageable age, she thought it would be a mistake for various reasons, to have a parson 20 years older hanging about, particularly as she may have felt that there was a danger of his falling in love, & she had not the slightest intention of letting one of her daughters marry him (though I'm sure they never wanted to). C. L. D. & Mrs. L. remained on friendly but distant terms."

There is one more remark from Alice's son on this question: ". . . personally I agree with you that he very likely was in love with her—if he was ever in love with anybody. I have always felt in my bones that that probably was the case." What are the possibilities? She was twenty years younger than Carroll, a disparity great but not decisive—successful marriages have leaped greater barriers, and Alice seems really to have had the qualities he attributed to her. Her child pictures are uniformly adorable; the one of her as a young lady is sad but lovely; as an old lady she was still beautiful, still gracious, still charming. Whether Carroll would have made a good husband is a guess. Humorists and fantasts make even worse husbands than the general run of artists. Their devastating charm arises from that very persistence of the eternal boy that may wreck a marriage. Peter Pan was abominable to Wendy. Carroll might have been a ghost-husband, and might have gently, considerately, but relentlessly reproached Alice for not being a ghost herself.

A letter he wrote to a Miss Manners hints how: "Permit me to offer you my sincere thanks for the very sweet verses you have written about my dream-child. . . . Next to what conversing with an angel *might* be—for it is hard to imagine it—comes, I think, the privilege of having a real child's thoughts uttered to one. I have known some few real children (you have too, I am sure), and their friendship is a blessing and a help in life." [1] Now his last letter to Mrs. Hargreaves mentions his inability to realize that she is more than seven years old. A man who wants an angel child does not want a wife, and perhaps Mrs. Liddell was right. But marriage, if he had been able to compass it, might have released him and ripened his powers. In the eighteen-sixties he was still on the frontier of incurable bachelorhood; his complete petrifaction and dissociation set in much later, when he made Sylvie too sweet, Bruno too, too elfin, and Uggug too horrible, to endure. His mournful poems, such as "Faces in the Fire," exude the sickly sentimentality that serves to cover an absence of real feeling. He might have been in love with his own idea of Alice, or some memory of his mother or sisters, or some projection of himself (which the Alice of the story surely was, and not Alice Liddell at all), and daily association with the human being on whom he had hung his ideal might have produced one of those dreadful, intangible domestic tragedies. Who can successfully incorporate another person's ideal, especially when the idealist is as exigent as Dodgson? (If indeed these were the grounds of Mrs. Liddell's fears.)

Contradicting the remark about Alice having been a dream-child, closer to the theory that he was actually in love with the real Alice, is this letter written to her when he borrowed her copy of the manuscript to photograph for the facsimile edition:

> 7, Lushington Road
> Eastbourne,
> August 14, 1885.

"Dear Mrs. Hargreaves,

"I adopt your recommendation most gladly: it is very pleasant to think that you are thus connected with the facsimile edition; of the existence of the original you were of course the chief if not the only cause. You shall have the original back again in (I hope) exactly the state in which I received it, and (of course) one of the earliest copies of the facsimile. May I also have the pleasure of presenting one to your eldest daughter (even if she be not an 'Alice,' which I think unlikely)?" [10]

Even she went back on him, for instead of a daughter she had three sons, which, said Mrs. Skene, was a great disappointment to him. But he seems to have retained a possessive feeling for her, for another letter says apropos of the charming little photograph of his Egeria which he appended to the manuscript: "My own wishes would be distinctly *against* reproducing the photograph" (in the facsimile edition).[10] His wishes were followed—it was not published till after the sale of the manuscript made it familiar. With the last page of the manuscript is a piece of paper with the words "happy summer days. THE END," in Carroll's writing. He probably fastened this over the portrait when the last page was photographed. His own invention, no doubt.

Wing Commander Caryl Hargreaves gives a brief note Carroll wrote his mother on December 1, 1881: "For auld lang syne I want to send a copy of my new book to one without whose infant patronage I might never have written at all." [9]

Once Alice moved to Lyndhurst, the meetings were rare, but as long as her father remained Dean, she visited Oxford. On November 1, 1888, Dodgson notes, "Skene brought, as his guest, Mr. Hargreaves, the husband of 'Alice,' who was a stranger to me, though we had met, years ago, as pupil and lecturer. It was not easy to link in one's mind the new face with the once-so-intimately known and loved 'Alice,' whom I shall always remember best as an entirely fascinating little seven-year-old maiden."

Then, the beginning of the end. On October 27, 1891, he writes: "Heard the important news that the Dean means to resign at Christmas. My hope is that Paget will be the new Dean."

A month later: "Rhoda and Violet Liddell came to tea (first time of entering my rooms). They insisted on waiting on me, as I was laid up with a 'synovitic' knee, and we had a very pleasant two hours."

Ten days after that: "A yet more wonderful experience. Mrs. Liddell and Mrs. Skene came to tea, and proved very pleasant guests."

The following week, December 9: "As Mrs. Hargreaves, the original 'Alice,' is at the Deanery, I invited her also over to tea. She could not do this, but very kindly came over, with Rhoda, for a short time in the afternoon."

This letter, given by Wing Commander Hargreaves, is undoubtedly the invitation:

"My dear Mrs. Hargreaves,

"I should be so glad if you could, quite conveniently to yourself, look in for tea any day. You would probably prefer to bring a companion; but I must leave the choice to you, only remarking that if your husband is here he would be (most) very welcome. (I crossed out most because it's ambiguous—most words are, I fear.) I met him in our Common Room not long ago. It was hard to realize that he was the husband of one I can scarcely picture to myself as more than seven years old.

Always sincerely yours,
C. L. Dodgson

"Your adventures have had a marvellous success. I have now sold well over 100,000 copies." [9]

It is quite possible that when speaking to her son over forty years later Mrs. Hargreaves forgot she had not actually taken tea with Dodgson that day. But for him there was still an anticlimax. The following March 1 he enters this note: "Went to the library, to aid in presentation, to Mrs. Liddell, of a replica Herkomer has made of the ex-Dean. The new Dean presented it, in a graceful speech, and she made a very feeling reply."

In 1942, some interesting items were offered for sale at an auction in New York: A photograph by Carroll of the Richmond painting, "inscribed on the back by Carroll, 'Liddell,' and with his album reference, No. 2463 'J,' also in his hand." A tinted photographic transparency of Alice, taken in 1874, "Inscribed on the reverse, 'A. Liddell, March 18, 1874,' and with instructions for framing."

In 1932 The Times, reporting the sale of the manuscript, mentioned items then owned by Mrs. Hargreaves, including six letters dated 1885, children's books with inscribed poems, two facsimiles of the manuscript, a second edition of Alice* —though he gave her the true first edition, she had surrendered it when he recalled it for imperfect printing. Her

* See Appendix E.

copy was especially bound in blue morocco with a medallion on the front cover of Alice holding the pig. She also had a first edition of *Through the Looking-Glass* and numerous foreign first editions of *Wonderland, The Nursery "Alice,"* and about fifty photographs of her own family and friends, taken by Carroll.

All this adds up, certainly not to prove, but to indicate that Alice Liddell held a very special place in his affections. She was the first and most favored of his girl friends—beyond that a novelist may go, but not a biographer.

So he consoled himself with a procession of Wendies, and lived happily ever after, except for his insomnia. Ellen Terry says:

"I can't remember when I didn't know him. I think he must have seen Kate act as a child [actually it was Ellen herself, whom he saw in her first rôle when she was eight years old], and having given her *Alice*—he always gave his young friends *Alice* at once by way of establishing pleasant relations—he made a progress as the years went by through the whole family. Finally he gave *Alice* to my children . . . Mr. Dodgson's kindness to children was wonderful. He *really* loved them and put himself out for them. The children he knew who wanted to go on the stage were those who came under my observation and nothing could have been more touching than his ceaseless industry on their behalf." [11]

It seems that Ellen Terry was also an old lady subject to forgetting when she wrote, "I can't remember when I didn't know him." He saw her in *A Winter's Tale* on June 16, 1856, and wrote "I especially admired the acting of the little Mamillius, Ellen Terry, a beautiful little creature, who played with remarkable ease and spirit." But he had not yet started introducing himself to child actresses; in fact, it was eight years before he met her.

On December 21, 1864, he writes, "Once more to Stanhope Street. Polly and Benjamin met me in the hall, and in the drawing-room I found Kate Terry, Florence, and to my delight, the one I have always most hoped to meet of the family, Mrs. Watts. . . . I was very pleased with what I saw of Mrs. Watts—lively and pleasant, almost childish in her fun, but perfectly ladylike. Her sister seemed ill and out of spirits, I fancy her gaiety yesterday, and Mrs. Watts' today, were both partly assumed. However, both sisters are charming and I think it a rare piece of good fortune to have made two such acquaintances in one day. I mark this day also with a white stone."

Derek Hudson quotes a letter from Mr. Collingwood to his cousin, Miss F. Menella Dodgson, dated February 3, 1932, in answer to the question she had asked him:

"Nothing I have read in C. L. D.'s diaries or letters suggested—to the best of my memory—that he ever had any affaires du coeur.

"I *think* that Aunt Fanny once told me that it was the family's opinion that Uncle Charles had had a disappointment in love, and that they thought (or she also thought) that the lady in question was Ellen Terry.

"I don't think I ever had the *complete* diary, though possibly Uncle Wilfred had it. (Mr. Hudson has a footnote: "Here Collingwood was mistaken, for his biography includes quotations from all the volumes of the diaries which have since disappeared.")

"The 'shadow' I hinted at had no other basis than what I had heard from Aunt Fanny. When Ellen Terry was just growing up—about 17—she was lovely beyond description . . . and it is highly probable that he fell in love with her. He may even have proposed to her."

This of course was impossible, since when he met her she was already married to Watts, the painter. On July 24, 1863, he had wished to get her to sit for a photograph. But Watts got there first, painted her picture, and married her—he was 45 and she 15. They were not divorced till 1877, though they soon separated.

He saw Ellen in all her plays and took all his little girls to meet her, but nothing about their relationship or the way he wrote about her compares to his relationship with Alice. Even Collingwood finishes the letter about Ellen Terry as follows: "Whereas in regard to the Liddells it was *Alice* who was his pet, and it was his intense love for her, (though she was only a child) which pulled the trigger and released his genius. Indeed it is quite likely that Alice's marriage to Hargreaves may have seemed to him the greatest tragedy in his life."

Ellen Terry was not the only one who understood that he "really" loved little girls. Mr. Collingwood speaks of his attitude toward children, and the strong attraction they had for him—". . . if I were asked for one comprehensive word wide enough to explain this tendency of his nature, I would answer unhesitatingly—Love." [1] But in those days love was rigidly divided into two kinds, and it was clear that Dodgson's love was "pure." To the remains of this dualism in our own time must be attributed the reluctance of even young and healthy Carrollians to admit that he too shared in our common heritage.

He did carry his special method of rechanneling the love impulse to extremes, and his portraits are those of one crucified. Collingwood remarks that "it is not too strong" to say that his face kept its boyishness to the end. On the contrary, it is too weak. What his face actually developed was a girlishness. Since there is no reason to suppose his life was ever perverse in that sense, the best explanation is that he was so much in love with his dream Alice—not necessarily the real Alice at all—that he cultivated her attributes more and more, and partially *became* the real Alice in Wonderland. This gives a clue to his plural personality. He had all the normal attributes of a man, but he outlawed them from his favored or "Alice" self, relegating them, at the beginning and end of his life, to Uggug, the *revenant* of his *Rectory Umbrella* fantasies. During the period of his greatest flowering, his art and probably his life maintained a balance. The all bad Uggug and the too good Sylvie herald disintegration. At the moment of the Mad Tea Party, all his selves met harmoniously. Had he married not too long after that favorable episode, he might have retained enough unity to ward off the dreadful disruption of *Sylvie and Bruno,* and his genius might have gone on flowering to the end. Even *Through the Looking-Glass,* the favorite of mathematicians and logicians, is a trifle overblown.

Dr. Greenacre says, "He seemed to carry always a longing to continue in the idyllic charms of childhood, especially of the period between six and twelve, which is least beset with

sexual pressures. . . . This compulsion to repeat endlessly
the prettiness of childhood bespeaks loudly the horrors of the
jealous conflicts within, portrayed in his crude sketches and
in his early verses. The florid cruelty of the scenes in the
Alice books is masked and softened by the mild and puzzled
characteristics of the little heroine." [2]

He renewed his youth on every vacation. Apart from the
Russian tour and the "reading-party" at Whitby, he always
managed to enjoy the company of little girls; with his not-
very-good drawings in a black and green leather sketchbook,
he memorialized all his friendships. In the sixties he usually
visited the Isle of Wight. In 1864 he made the following notes
at Freshwater:

"Every morning four little children dressed in yellow go by
from the front down to the beach; they go by in a state of
great excitement, brandishing wooden spades, and making
strange noises; from that moment they disappear entirely—
they are never to be seen *on* the beach. The only theory I
can form is, that they all tumble into a hole somewhere, and
continue excavating therein during the day: however that
may be, I have once or twice come across them returning at
night, in exactly the same state of excitement, and seemingly
in quite as great a hurry to get home as they were before to
get out. The evening noises they make sound to me very much
like the morning noises, but I suppose they are different to
them, and contain an account of the day's achievements." [1]

He spent several summers at Sandown, a little fishing
village that gradually grew into a family resort. Because of
the enterprise of the inhabitants and the natural advantages
of the place, the population doubled between 1861 and 1881.
About a semi-circular sweep of bay lie broad firm sands,
excellent for bathing, for wading, and for sketching little girls
at those occupations. To the east rise the chalk cliffs of
Culvers; to the west projects the dark sandstone headland of
Dunnose Point; between, a range of clay and sand cliffs,
broken by a depression in which the town nestles. The air is
bland, and the surrounding country full of charm and variety.
In the sixties there were pleasure boats and carriages, bathing
machines and croquet grounds, and finally a reading room.

The pier was 350 feet long, and the esplanade pleasant for

driving. Originally a link in the chain of forts built by Henry VIII, by 1864 it was anachronistic and useless, so a new fort was erected, first faced with concrete, then armor-plated.

Since Carroll never missed a chance to visit a historic monument, it is likely he must have made at least one trip from Sandown to Brading to see the Roman villa excavated near there in the early eighties. It was in a fine state of preservation, with mosaic flowers, murals, and a tessellated pinacotheca.

In 1875 he met Gertrude Chataway at Sandown. She was a child then, but later she wrote how: "He would come on to his balcony, which joined ours, sniffing the sea-air with his head thrown back, and would walk right down the steps on to the beach with his chin in air, drinking in the fresh breezes as if he could never have enough." [1] The following year *The Hunting of the Snark* appeared, dedicated to Gertrude with a double acrostic on her name in the opening verses.

Beginning in 1876, he seems to have shifted to Eastbourne, for in 1893 Mrs. Dyer, his landlady at No. 7, Lushington Road, said he had spent the last seventeen summers there, and he continued to return every year while he lived. Eastbourne is on the Sussex coast, within Mr. Dodgson's walking distance of historic spots such as Hastings and Pevensey, where the Conqueror landed and where British troops massed in 1803 and 1804 against a similar venture by Bonaparte. Eastbourne, which had first come into fashionable notice in 1780, when some of the children of George III spent the summer there, had a second access of population when visitors came to see the troops, but its greatest growth was in the sixties when the watering places were developed.

The Huxley family too summered there; Mr. Huxley enjoyed the rich deposits of flints and fossils, and Dodgson may have visited them, for Julia Arnold, one of his little girls, married Leonard Huxley. The Gernsheim collection includes a fine photo of Huxley by Dodgson.

The railroad from London made the trip to Eastbourne in 1¾ hours, frustrating the country squires who had intentionally left the roads bad to keep out the city cutthroats and pickpockets, compared to whom Sussex mud seemed trifling. The sea was building shore at that point—the old town was now a mile and a half inland, with a new town between the station and the sea. The long carriage drive wound along the cliff and esplanade; the high road to Beachy Head ran through the hamlet of Mead, and there was a shorter footpath by the Cliff. Beachy Head, a magnificent chalk headland, 575 feet high, juts out into the English Channel.

Though Isa Bowman and her sisters often visited Carroll at Oxford, they much preferred Eastbourne. Isa describes a typical day, saying the routine never varied. Her bedroom door faced his at the head of the staircase; they used to get up "very early indeed," but if Isa was up first, she waited in the hall till a newspaper under his door signaled that she might come in. Breakfast was followed by a chapter from the Bible, which Isa had to repeat in her own words to make sure she would remember it.

" 'Now then, Isa dearest,' he would say, 'tell me a story, and mind you begin with "once upon a time." A story which doesn't begin with "once upon a time" can't possibly be a good story. It's *most* important.' " [3]

After the story they went to swim. Isa was learning to swim at the Devonshire Park baths, but her daily lesson depended on her willingness to endure the daily visit to the dentist. "He had great ideas upon the importance of a regular and almost daily visit to the dentist. He himself went to a dentist as he would have gone to a hairdresser's, and he insisted that all the little girls he knew should go too." He does seem to have retained his teeth to the end.

From the dentist's they returned for lunch, Carroll never having more than a glass of sherry and a biscuit. Lunch was followed by backgammon, "a game of which he was passionately fond, and of which he could never have enough." They then took the long walk to Beachy Head. Even in his last days a walk of eighteen miles was not uncommon, and he records one of twenty-seven miles in inclement weather. Isa was bored and perhaps tired with the long walk, so he invented games and stories to amuse her. "One very curious trait in his character was shown in these walks. I used to be very fond of flowers and animals also. A pretty dog or a hedge of honeysuckle were always pleasant events upon a walk to me. And yet he himself cared for neither flowers nor animals."

Isa was mistaken about animals. During his nine years as Curator of the Common Room, he was also responsible for the cat. When its old age was overripe, Mr. Dodgson "consulted two specialists, one of whom was Sir James Paget." One of his sisters told Mr. Collingwood: "He saw a kitten in the street with a fishhook in its mouth. . . . He carried the kitten to the house of a medical man for relief. . . . Happily the removal of the hook was no difficult matter. Lewis Carroll held the kitten, and I think the doctor was able to snip off the barbed end, so that the hook came easily out. . . . Payment having been declined, Lewis Carroll took the kitten back to where he found it." [12]

He also argued with drivers to take the check-reins off work horses, and urged a painless death for animals used for food. Then there was that kindhearted mousetrap in his rooms.

"Tender and kind as he was, simple and unassuming in all his tastes, yet he did not like flowers! . . . Once, and once only, I remember him to have taken an interest in a flower, and that was because of the folklore that was attached to it, and not because of the beauty of the flower itself . . . he took a foxglove from the heap that lay in my lap and told me the story of how they came by their name . . . how the 'little folk' used to wander at night in the glades, like Titania, and Oberon, and Puck, and because they took great pride in their hands, they made themselves gloves out of the flowers. So the particular flower that the 'little folk' used came to be called 'folk's gloves.' " [3]

In 1890 this same bit of etymology crept into *The Nursery "Alice"*;

"Do you see that Fox-Glove growing close to the tree? And do you know why it's called a *Fox-Glove?* Perhaps you think it's got something to do with a Fox? No indeed! *Foxes* never wear gloves!

"The right word is Folks'-Gloves. Did you ever hear that Fairies used to be called the good Folk?"

On the road to Beachy Head, they would rest at a halfway

point, sitting on the grass. Uncle Charles would make a jumping mouse out of his handkerchief, or do other handkerchief tricks, "better than anyone I ever saw," said Isa. He must have developed those tricks at Croft, where his conjuring so greatly impressed his sisters.

Tea was at the coast guard's house, Uncle Charles carefully limiting Isa's healthy appetite to one cup of tea and one rock cake. Either inside the guard's house, or out on the grass, or a couple of hundred yards down where the view was clearest, there would be stories. In every fairy tale there was a moment when "the children came to a deep, dark wood," and Isa huddled closer to hear the climax. Her companion's insensibility to flowers was balanced by his love of a good sunset. "Just as the sun was setting, and a cool breeze played round us, he would take off his hat and let the wind play with his hair, and he would look out to sea. Once I saw tears in his eyes, and when we turned to go, he gripped my hand much tighter than usual."

Isa and Uncle Charles spent many hours in the concert hall, listening to the concerts, but the young lady said, "Sometimes they were so 'classical' that I must confess I was very bored." So she copied the old ladies, and knitted or embroidered at the concerts. "Uncle" upbraided her for this; Isa felt she was merely mimicking her elders, and should not be reproved.

" 'Do you not realize, my child,' he said severely, 'that the artistes who are entertaining us this afternoon have probably spent a lifetime perfecting themselves at their art? To show such public indifference for their efforts is to insult them. Never let me see you do this again!' " [3]

Of course it is dubious just how "classical" the concerts were. Considering that neither London nor Oxford had come very far musically in the eighties, it is doubtful that Eastbourne was subjected to anything more strenuous than Rossini and Handel. From the concert, whatever it was, Isa and Uncle Charles returned to Mrs. Dyer's house by seven. He never changed his clothes for dinner, at least at Eastbourne. At Christ Church it was often necessary. He had, says Isa, "A curious notion that a child should not change her clothes twice in one day!" [3] For himself, he was by now hopelessly

committed to his black clericals. Even in winter he rarely
wore an overcoat (Isa says "never"); and even in summer,
he never abandoned his top hat. In all seasons he wore the
black and grey cotton gloves (for economy), and he always
looked as if he had just stepped out of a bandbox and a hot
bath. Perhaps this explains his belief that it was not necessary to change clothing during the day.

Even on vacation he remembered the little girl's souls. Isa
said they always went to church twice on Sunday, but without
coercion, lest he antagonize the child and produce a distaste
for church and Sunday such as he had felt in his own childhood. He had ways of inducing his little guests to forsake the
shining sands and sit on a hard bench in a stuffy church. If
the sermon was long and the child young, a little book would
be slipped into the fidgety hand. "It was better far, he maintained, to read, than to stare idly about the church." [3] But he
kept no special books for Sunday reading; and rather than
flatly forbid Isa to sew on the Sabbath, he merely asked her
not to "unless absolutely necessary."

In 1889 he wrote: "I go down every summer to Eastbourne
& I still make friends with children on the beach—& sometimes even (being now an old man who can venture on things
that 'Mrs. Grundy' would never permit to a younger man)
have some little friend to stay with me as a guest. That will
give you some idea of what an 'aged, aged man' I have become! My last guest was the charming child, who lately acted
'Alice' in Mr. Savile Clarke's play of *Alice in Wonderland*." [13]
When the Bowman children stayed with him at Oxford, they
spent only the days in his rooms. At night he took them across
St. Aldate's to a rooming house kept by a woman of reliable
character. But the idea of Mrs. Grundy always intrigued him.

Once Mr. Dodgson spent an afternoon at Brighton with
Isa and her sisters Maggie and Emsie, when they were all
playing in "a drama by Mr. Savile Clarke (it is called *Alice
in Wonderland*)," as he wrote in an article about stage children for the *St. James Gazette*. The sisters were twelve, seven,
and ten years old, full of vitality and animation, which their
friend adduced to show that acting was not harmful to them:
"the intensity with which they enjoyed everything, great or
small, that came in their way—[anyone] who could have

watched the two younger running on the Pier, or have heard the fervent exclamation of the eldest at the end of the afternoon, 'We *have* enjoyed ourselves!' would have agreed with me that here, at least, there was no excessive 'physical strain.' . . . They had been acting every night this week, and *twice* on the day before I met them, the second performance lasting till half-past ten at night, after which they got up at seven next morning to bathe! . . . When you really love the subject you are working at, the 'physical strain' is absolutely nil . . . A taste for *acting* is one of the strongest passions of human nature . . . stage children show it almost from infancy . . . they simply rejoiced in their work 'even as a giant to run his course.' " [1]

The child actresses enjoyed their work, and he enjoyed them. If their work or personalities appealed to him, they would receive a note and a copy of one of his books at the stage door. Such girls were fortunate, for he took a personal interest in their careers and often paid for various sorts of lessons for them. The theater was not yet a respectable profession for women and girls, and any admirer who gave as much and asked as little as Carroll must have been a godsend. He even constituted himself their guardian—especially with the Bowman girls, concerning whose mother he wrote to a Miss Jackson in 1896: "I fancy Mrs. B. is not well-pleased with me, for having sent her an earnest remonstrance about her allowing Nellie and Maggie to go on tour with a company playing *The Water Babes* [not to be confused with Kingsley's *Water Babies*]. It came here on tour, & is a most disreputable play—indecent and profane—I complained about it to the Lord Chancellor." [14]

He engaged the best available teachers for his child friends —a "professor" from the Aquarium to teach Isa swimming, a Swedish singer, a Dutch language-teacher. He himself taught her geography by jig-saw puzzles, and sent her lessons in arithmetic, Euclid, and the Bible. "These lessons continued for years, and when my mother took me to America . . . he sent them by post. For every day in the week, except Sunday, he arranged a schedule of lessons, supposed to last for about three hours, and these were faithfully adhered to." [3]

A letter to Miss Terry thanked her for personally giving Isa

elocution lessons, when he had asked her merely to recommend a teacher. He hints that if she were visiting Oxford he
would like to ask her to one of his famous tête-à-tête dinners,
to which he invited ladies "of every age varying from 12 to
67 (the maximum I have yet had)." He mentions a young
friend "who with a little more experience and a little more
courage to throw herself into a part and let it carry her away,
should be useful in any part where a *lady* is needed."(!) [11]

He wrote an examination paper, said Isa, for a child who
was learning a recitation called "The Demon of the Pit." She
says: "Though his stuttering prevented him from being anything of a reciter, he loved correct elocution, and would take
any pains to make a child proficient in a piece."

When Isa played the Duke of York in *Richard III*, he
wrote her,

"My Lord Duke—
"The photographs which Your Grace did me the honour of
sending arrived safely. . . . I do not wonder that your excellent Uncle Richard would say 'Off with his head!' as a hint
to the photographer to print it off. Would your Highness like
me to go on calling you the Duke of York, or shall I say 'My
own darling Isa'? . . .

"Now I'm going to find fault with my pet about her acting.
What's the good of an old uncle like me except to find fault?

"You do the meeting with the Prince of Wales *very* nicely
and lovingly; and in teasing your uncle for his dagger and
sword, you are very sweet and playful; and—'but *that's* not
finding fault!' Isa says to herself. Isn't it? Well, I'll try again.
Didn't I hear you say 'In weightier things you'll say a *beggar*
nay,' leaning on the word 'beggar?' If so, it was a mistake.
My rule for knowing which word to lean on is the word that
tells you something *new,* something that is *different* from
what you expected. . . .

"One more thing. (What an impertinent old uncle! Always
finding fault) You're not so *natural,* when acting the Duke,
as you were when you acted Alice. You seemed to me not to
forget *yourself* enough. It was not so much a real *prince* talking to his elder brother and uncle; it was *Isa Bowman* talking
to people she didn't care much about, for an audience to

listen to—I don't mean it was that all through, but sometimes you were *artificial*. Now *don't* be jealous of Miss Hatton, when I say she was *sweetly* natural. . . .

"My sweet pet, I *hope* you won't be offended with me for saying what I fancy might make your acting better!

x for Nellie	Your loving Uncle
x for Maggie	Charles
x for Emsie	x for Isa"

Isa says: "In some ways 'Uncle' was curiously narrow. He hated me playing the wicked girl in *The Wicked Squire,* and for the time it ran was never quite so nice to me; he loved Emsie in the same play." [3]

Dodgson seems to have had an order of importance among his girl friends. One mark of favor was to have a book dedicated to her with an acrostic. Two of these girls were friends —Climene Holiday and Marie van der Gucht. He dedicated *The Game of Logic* to Climene, daughter of Henry Holiday, and the *Nursery Alice* to Marie, whose name appears by reading the second letter in each line of the dedication.

He used the same device in dedicating *A Tangled Tale* to his Beloved Pupil, who proves to be Edith Rix. She must have given him more satisfaction than many of the other girls, for he taught her mathematics and she became a computer at Greenwich Observatory.

Nobody knows how many girl friends he had, but at any one time there was a reigning favorite who was superannuated at about fifteen. There seem to have been only four leading ladies*—of course Alice in the sixties, Gertrude Chataway in the seventies, Isa in the eighties, and finally, in the nineties, Enid Stevens, a beautiful child "with dark curls and large, dreamy eyes, like one of Sir Joshua Reynolds' angels." [15] Gertrude Thomson made a pastel of Enid which hung over his fireplace; as the child sat on his knee, listening to stories of the "creatures" on the tiles, she could look up at her own portrait. In 1893 he wrote her a letter inviting her to dinner, and referring to a clock he had sent and some books he wanted her to choose from:

"Please look through this list of books, & cross out the

* See Appendix F.

names of any stories that you either have read, or wouldn't read, even if I gave you 6d. to do it . . . if ever we had to make a Railway journey together (of course that is not the most likely thing in the world—still, it might happen), I should like to be able to bring some book, which *perhaps* might keep you in a *tolerably* good temper for *part* of the time." [Speaking of the clock] "I'm afraid it wasn't worth your acceptance. It was one of two that had been on my chimney piece for ever so long, out of order. I got them put right again, at Rowell's, and brought you one. Tell me what sort of time it keeps ." [13]

He had another bout with Mrs. Grundy at Eastbourne. "Just now she—Mrs. G.—is no doubt busy talking about me and another young friend of mine—a mere child, only 4 or 5 and 20—whom I have brought from town to visit my sisters. [This was Miss Heaphy, daughter of the artist, who had recently died, leaving his daughter rather hard up.] Possibly I mentioned her to you, as one who wants to give lessons in drawing, to children, at their own homes. . . . The doctor had recommended rest, and sea-air, so I have taken her on my hands for a fortnight, we are first having a few days here [Guilford] and shall then have 2 or 3 days with some more of my sisters at Eastbourne: and then I must leave her in their care and return to Oxford. Is it not an *outré* proceeding well worthy of Mrs. G.'s attention?" If Mrs. G. had known him as we do, she would not have worried about Miss Heaphy!

In the nineties he felt toward grown girls as in youth he had felt toward children, to judge from this letter to Miss Thomson, who had made a portrait of May Wilson for him: "To be quite candid, I *don't* like the London picture of May. It looks hard, haughty, & *slightly* offended, & has missed all 3 of the charms I read in her face, viz. sweetness, peacefulness, & sympathy (her eyes look to me as if just ready to fill with tears)." [16]

In the summer of 1961 a tape recording was made with Helmut Gernsheim and Miss Ethel Hatch, the last survivor of the child friends whom Lewis Carroll photographed. Miss Hatch was interviewed in her home, formerly that of George MacDonald, where Dodgson had made many photographs.

The room was lined with Miss Hatch's paintings, many flowers and still lifes, with great warmth and charm. She had tried studying with Sir Hubert Herkomer, who discouraged her. It was Lewis Carroll who helped her find another teacher with whom she was able to find herself professionally.

Miss Arnold reports: "He always used to say that when the time came for him to take off his hat when he met one of his quondam child friends in the street, it was time for the friendship to cease." But by the nineties, as in the case of May, he had extended his age group a little. When he was teaching logic at the Oxford High School, at Lady Margaret Hall, and at St. Hugh's College, he gradually chose his friends from among somewhat older girls. Sometimes, in his earlier years, the cooling of a friendship may have resulted from the parents' refusal to let the girls go to his rooms unchaperoned, "a point on which he was very sensitive." He was his own best chaperon, and while he did a good deal of kissing, he seems to have known, with his usual delicacy and respect for others, when to stop. His little girl friends would not have remembered him with such unanimous glee if he had not always been a good and trustworthy friend to them. There is a total lack of embarrassment in all these dozens of memoirs, which, even after all these years, rings true.

His favorite of the '80's, Isa Bowman, was almost adopted by him. She was the only one of his child friends who was allowed to call him "Uncle Charles," though "Uncle Dodgson" was the name used by the MacDonald children. Wing Commander Hargreaves said his mother brought him up very strictly always to say "Mr. Dodgson," as she did herself.

In the diary for October 3, 1888, he says, "Took Isa back to her family . . . [she] has been with me [presumably at Eastbourne] for five weeks—longer than all last year's guests put together—a very happy time for both of us."

According to Mr. Green in the new *Handbook,* Isa Bowman and her sisters Nellie and Emsie were still appearing on the London stage in 1950. On May 28, 1895, Dodgson wrote in his diary, "Isa Bowman came to see me. She is a 'principal lady' in Miss Cissy Graham's company, who have come to Oxford with *All Abroad.*" At this point Green says, "Isa had also come to tell Dodgson of her engagement, and she recalls that for a moment he seemed quite upset, and showed his annoyance by snatching a little bouquet of roses from her belt and flinging them out of the window, exclaiming, "You know I can't stand flowers." But by next day he was quite reconciled to the loss of one of his favorite child-friends."

In the *Diaries* Mr. Green included an article by the last child friend, Enid Stevens, then Mrs. Shawyer. Here are Dodgson's first notations about her:

On February 27, 1891, he writes: "Took Winnie Stevens for a walk and tea: and, on taking her home, I met, for the first time, her beautiful little sister Enid, who seems a sweet lovable child."

On April 17 he says: "I went as arranged to fetch Enid Stevens for walk and tea—first experiment at having her alone. She was with me from 3 to 6, a charming companion, and, what many children are not, able to *talk*."

June 26 he writes: "Took Enid Stevens to be photographed, and to my rooms for tea." There are many entries about her, and several times he calls her, as he does no one else, "my darling Enid."

Mrs. Shawyer tells how he told her stories from the tiles, and says there were many more stanzas of "He thought he saw—" from the Mad Gardener's Song in *Sylvie and Bruno*. She says the Mad Gardener and the Spherical Proctor from the same book originated on some of their walks, of which they had two or three a week. She speaks of their being curled up together in a big arm chair playing word games, ciphers, mathematical problems, chess, and other games, for which he was always making new rules.

He never hesitated to correct a fault, she said, but it was done as if "from within, not like adult fault-finding." He spoke her own language. She begged her mother to let him take her away, to the seaside or to London. But, she says, "The Victorian mind saw possible evil even in the association of a child of twelve with an old man of sixty-three. He must have had wonderful patience, for he tried again and again, but I was never allowed to go and shall never to the end of my days cease to regret it. Days of close intercourse with one who, however whimsical his mind, was one of the few genuine scholar-saints were denied me because the saint was male and I was a little girl. . . . Our happy companionship was more like that of a grandchild with a much-loved grandfather. . . . I know now that my friendship with him was probably the most valuable experience in a long life, and that it influenced my outlook more than anything that has happened since— and wholly for good."

It would be naïve to say "Lolita," except insofar as diamonds and coal are both made of carbon.

He took infinite pains to entertain children, and when they were not introduced by their parents he introduced himself to them, on the seashore, in railway trains, in the gardens at Oxford. He never went to the beach without safety pins for any little girl who wished to wade (no sun-suits then!), and for casual meetings he was always provided with games, toys, puzzles, and tiny scissors, produced from his pocketbook or from the ubiquitous black bag. Several little girls mention his taking a lock of their hair with the tiny scissors, no bigger than his thumb nail.

He met the three Miss Drurys in a train, when their nurse was telling them a story. At first the eldest sister resented the interruption, but the story was soon forgotten when they clustered around him and he pulled small marvels out of various receptacles. Just before his station, he asked them whether they had read *Alice,* told them he was the author, and promised them a copy. He included a dedication "To Three Puzzled Little Girls," and some substandard verses. These little girls were never dropped from grace, but received presentation copies of all his books, besides visiting him at Guildford and Christ Church.

When a Mrs. MacFarlan was a little girl, she walked along a breakwater at Eastbourne, fell in, and soaked her clothing. She stopped beside her sister, whom a strange elderly gentleman was sketching. "He tore a corner of blotting paper from his notebook and said, 'May I offer you this to blot yourself with?' "

Another ex-little girl described his manner of taking his cue from her remarks, giving her a feeling of personal possession in the story. "It was the most lovely nonsense imaginable."

Miss Ella Monier Williams, later Mrs. Bickersteth, told Mr. Collingwood, "A visit to Mr. Dodgson's rooms to be photographed was always full of surprises." He liked costumes, but not a "dressed-up child"; he preferred a "natural child," often with ruffled hair, in some natural pose. When he wanted a picture of Ella "sitting up in bed in a fright, with her hair standing on end as if she had just seen a ghost," he tried shocking her with her father's electrical machine, but "it failed." [1]

Little May Forshall came to his rooms for lunch and to be photographed in a beach costume like the one worn by Gertrude Chataway at Sandown. From Dodgson's sketch of Gertrude, the costume was a big hat, a long jersey, knee-length striped bathing trunks, and bare feet. When May had trouble putting on her street clothes, tying her hair and buttoning her boots, Mr. Dodgson finally tapped at the door. She confessed her difficulties and permitted him to help her. It was remarkable how easily he buttoned her boots and how fast he made a big bow on top of her head—if May did not know he had seven sisters, five of them younger than he.[15]

The most graphic tale is told by Miss Ethel Arnold, of the five little girls coming down an Oxford path on a foggy autumn day—how they made a barrier to stop a "tall, clerical figure" coming toward them. He stopped, but the ones who held his interest and found their hands clasped in his were the two shy ones, who hung back from the play of the others. They were soon put at their ease, and for Ethel Arnold began a lifelong friendship, qualified only by the fact that after her dachshund bit him, he refused to come to her house, so they met just outside the gate of the Parks.

Mrs. Archbold Ffooks, formerly Miss Maud Standen, wrote in the *Dorset Year Book:* "In spite of the fact that our friendship covered the space of about twenty years, during that long period I saw him only about five times." The first encounter was in the public gardens at Reading, where Dodgson was waiting for a train. He used the time to make the acquaintance of two sisters, using puzzles and the tiny scissors for bait. A few days later first one girl, and then the other received the *Alice* books—there was no mass production about this author. Eventually they paid two visits to his rooms at Christ Church, where they were photographed, and once they had lunch at the Chestnuts in Guildford. They last met him in the Isle of Jersey.

For making acquaintances on the train, his black bag contained credentials from *Wonderland*. On one trip the bag held photographs of the Bowman children, and on another a "small collection of pencils, notebooks, and puzzles, with which he amused a little girl named Nellie Knight and her brother on a train on August 20, 1888." [15]

If he took the child traveling he was equally careful to secure her from boredom. Beatrice Hatch said: "If he took you up to London to see a theatre, you were no sooner seated in the railway carriage than a game was produced and all occupants were invited to play a kind of 'halma' or 'draughts,' of his own invention, on the little board that had been specially made at his design for railway use, with 'men' warranted not to tumble down, because they fitted into little holes in the board!" [17] This invention, like the self-photographing device, is a commonplace today. If his genius had been commercial, he might have piled up a fortune sufficient to please even the banker-collectors of his works.

Another child sat under a tree with him in the Botanical Gardens at Oxford, while he told her the story of the Ugly Duckling—a graceful gesture, since she was of that breed herself. Like all his listeners, she testifies to his magical creation—or recreation—of character. She also attributes her lifelong love of animals to his teachings, pointed with stories of the lives of birds and butterflies, and visits to the Zoölogical Gardens, when they fed the monkeys and "he seemed to enjoy the fun as much as I did." This once more refutes Isa's remarks about his indifference to animals.

Speaking of animals, it is time to see what more is known of Carroll's dislike of boy-children. We have supposed that he was panic-stricken at reminders of aspects of his own nature that he had—nearly—succeeded in refining out of existence. "I *do* sympathize so heartily with what you say about feeling shy with children when you have to entertain them! Sometimes they are a real terror to me—especially boys: little girls I can now and then get on with, when they're few enough. They easily become *de trop*. But with little boys I'm

out of my element altogether . . . An Oxford friend wrote,
'I must bring my little boy to see you.' So I wrote to say
'don't' or words to that effect; and he wrote again that he
could hardly believe his eyes when he got my note. He
thought I doted on *all* children. But I'm *not* omnivorous!
Like a pig! I pick and choose." [1] To Ethel Arnold he wrote:
"There is a baby boy there—about two years old, I think,—
and in this matter you will be of incalculable service to me,
and relieve me of all responsibility as to saying the proper
thing when animals of that kind are offered for inspection." [7]

Many years earlier, when his brother Skeffington was six
years old, he had added this to a letter to his sisters:

"Dear Skeff,
"Roar not, lest thou be abolished."

Occasionally he made a good contact with boys—for instance with the Tennyson boys, Hallam and Lionel, and with
Greville Macdonald, the boy he tried to persuade to exchange
his own head for a marble one. Young Greville was also the
six-year-old literary critic who said "there ought to be sixty
thousand volumes" of *Alice*. He grew up to be a physician
and to write his memoirs, telling how "Uncle Dodgson" took
the Macdonald children to the "Polytechnic for the entrancing 'dissolving views' of the fairy tales, or to go down in the
diving bell, or watch the mechanical athlete Leotard," and
numerous other treats.[18]

He also describes how Uncle Dodgson drew in his copy-
book while the little boy leaned against him. "In the far distance was a train steaming away from its station to negotiate
a bumpy railroad bridge. In the foreground, a very stout
perspiring gentleman was mopping his head with one hand,
while his wife, scraggy and grim, dragged him along by the
other, and shouted at him: " 'It's puffing away fit to burst
itself, John, we shall lose it if you don't run faster.' But out of
his mouth soared a balloon of words: 'I can't run no faster
and I won't go no furder!' " Carroll also drew, in the frame
of a broken mirror, a picture of the Macdonald children
themselves, the drawing of "my sister Mary, not a bit like
her." [18]

Another former boy, the actor Bert Coote, told Mr. Reed
of similar trips, which included his sister, to the Tower of

London, and of the tall tales Mr. Dodgson told the young-sters about that historic spot. The Coote children were gigglers, and seized on any adult eccentricity to exercise their art, but they saw no eccentricity in their friend.[6]

Collingwood also mentions having seen his uncle at ease with boys, showing them puzzles and telling them stories. And that is the sum total—neither statistically nor emotion-ally comparable to the almost infinite stories about girls.

He told the head of a boys' school, whose daughter was one of his little girls, "As a salmon would be on a gravel path, so should I be in a boys' school." Elsewhere he wrote: "I wish you all success with your little boys—to me they are not an attractive race of beings (as a boy, I was simply detestable), and if you wanted to induce me, by money, to come and teach them, I can only say you would have to offer more than £10,000 a year!" [15]

Sometimes the educator in him overcame his distaste for the noisy little animals. He applied a primitive I.Q. test to a little boy, to whose sister he wrote: "I'm rather puzzled which book to send to Sydney. He looks so young for *Through the Looking-Glass*. However, he found out one puzzle (I forget which one it was now: I think the '4 poor men') that I don't remember anyone of his age ever guessing before: So I don't think it will be too old a book for him." [15]

He had a remarkable grasp of the different age levels in childhood and what could be fairly expected of them. He graded his conversation, as he graded his books, "From Nought to Five"; from five to ten; and children over ten he expected to understand all his jokes and not be hurt by his teasing. He preferred children who were easy-mannered and chattered freely—if they were spoiled he had no use for them. He shows in a letter to his brother Wilfred, written in 1887, what kind of children he liked best. The Alice in this letter was his brother's wife.

"Now that I have known scores (almost hundreds) of children, I am perhaps abnormally critical of them: but I must in candour say I *never* met with children of more per-fect behaviour, or more sweetly fascinating, than your Nella and Violet. . . . Nearly all children *I* have known, with such high animal spirits, are apt to be mischievous and troublesome, teasing one another and making themselves a nuisance generally. Alice has somehow managed to make these children combine the high spirits of children with the good manners of grownup people.[16]

Did children really satisfy him completely? Collingwood quotes a letter ending as follows: "Of course there isn't *much* companionship possible, after all, between an old man's mind and a little child's—but what there is, is sweet—and wholesome, I think." [1]

"I think." Is that merely British understatement, or had he a lurking doubt? Did he ever long for female companionship of his own age and development? Mr. Philip Blackburn suggested that perhaps the poem "Matilda Jane," instead of being merely a tribute to his cousin's doll, might be an unconscious protest against the infantile company to which he restricted himself—that Matilda Jane might be his beloved but not always intellectually adequate little girls! The last stanza follows:

> *Matilda Jane, you needn't mind:*
> *For, though you're deaf, and dumb, and blind,*
> *There's someone loves you, it is plain—*
> *And that is me, Matilda Jane!*

The quality that made Oxford habitable without love, as Miss Arnold says, may have helped him to live largely unto himself, and to pick and choose as carefully as he liked. As he aged and disintegrated into his elements, he lived even more alone. The failure of his one (supposed) attempt to live the ordinary life of mankind drove him back into himself— one failure would discourage him permanently. The really jolly bachelors, of course, are not usually complete ascetics, whereas Mr. Dodgson was one to please even the redoubtable Dr. Pusey.

Mr. Hudson, who usually denies any dualism in Dodgson, takes a different stand for once: ". . . he regretted not only the 'might have been' of these relationships but the inherent dichotomy of his character that made it impossible for him to resolve the dilemma of sexual love. Several books in his library with titles like *The Ways of Women* and *Physical*

Life of Women show that he had a deep curiosity about the opposite sex."

A professional graphologist, Dr. M. J. Mannheim, whom Mr. Hudson consulted, came to this conclusion, after studying specimens of Dodgson's handwriting of different periods: "He could not love except in a protective way. He would not have been able to combine love with sexual desire. That preoccupied him, but he remained frightened of his unconscious. He had a strong need to be loved, but marriage except with a very inferior woman appears improbable, though one cannot be dogmatic about such a problem. His past-fixation was too great for him to come to terms with reality or the reality of a woman." [4]

Men cut off from the influence of women seem nearly always to develop eccentricities. Carroll suffered vagaries of memory and confusion of place and person worthy of the Other Professor in *Sylvie and Bruno*. Since his memory ranged from the phenomenal to the abominable, he invented a system of mnemonics for recalling the dates of the Oxford colleges, so that when he showed visitors around, dates dropped from his mouth like pearls.

Muriel Hine relates that when he invited her parents to lunch in his rooms, they arrived to find him standing at his high desk, writing. He greeted them warmly, brought chairs, and sat with them. There was no sign of lunch, but presently in came a "gyp" [scout] with a tray containing one glass of ale and one chop. Carroll waved it aside and kept on talking. The visitors, sensing the situation, suggested his lunch would be spoiled, and left, asking their host to dinner. He accepted. . . .[19]

He cultivated the large and small oddities which to a chronic bachelor are more than meat and drink—which perhaps take the place of wife and child. A paper that appeared shortly after his death said: "In later life he saw very little of children and greatly developed the eccentricities which had always to some extent characterized him. He practiced the abominable affectation of refusing to be known as the author of his great book, acted with studied discourtesy towards journalists, and we fancy was very troublesome in his way of publishing. From many of his old friends he became entirely alienated, yet for the good he did for children he will long be remembered and honored."

His reasons for refusing to admit authorship of his Carroll books in the Dodgson surroundings of Oxford are quite valid. After all, none of his colleagues wrote children's books, and they already gazed on him with suspicion. But he never hesitated to use the books—especially *Alice*—as calling cards to introduce himself to children, as if he said, "Perhaps I look like Mr. Dodgson, but if you look again, you will see Lewis Carroll, and if you look once more and twiddle your eyes, you will see Alice." Or perhaps he popped his various personalities out of the little black bag, like the conjuror he was. With it closed, he was the Reverend Mr. Dodgson— Carroll and all his pixy folk emerged when he opened the bag to take out games, toys, and pictures to show his child friends.

Two contradictory aspects crop out in what Miss Arnold calls his "curious mixture of harmless vanity and an almost morbid shrinking from publicity." He described to her how a detective sat in the room while he turned the pages of the manuscript (Mrs. Hargreaves' property), which he was "determined no hand but [his] should touch." [20] Was he wrong? After her husband died, Mrs. Hargreaves had to sell the manuscript she had kept for sixty-six years; it fetched more than any other manuscript ever sold in England. Or was he wrong when he said he preferred to "have them [his books] ignored"? "Perhaps I am too fanciful, but I have somehow taken a dislike to being talked to about them; and consequently have some trials to bear in society."

He sent a photograph of himself to a little girl, adding a note to her mother, begging her not to spread the word that this was Lewis Carroll. He gently scolds another child who has addressed an envelope to "Lewis Carroll, Christ Church," complaining that if it escapes the dead-letter office it will tell all the letter carriers who he is! He even sent a printed circular to strangers who bothered him, saying that Mr. Dodgson did not claim authorship of any books not signed with his name. On the other hand, he wrote a little girl that he had met two friends who wished to sign the letter with him, and they were Lewis Carroll and Charles L. Dodgson.

The man was a tangled mass of polychromatic threads, forming one of the most complex human patterns that have enriched literature, articulate to an unusual depth of his unconscious and the common unconscious of mankind, controlled and ordered by mathematics and good sense, yet stuttering over the letter P, awkward and bashful with strangers, haunted by thoughts of sins he would never commit—and lonely.

The side-tracking of his affectionate nature permanently distorted him. The problem of sex and the problem of cruelty never left him alone till he died, and in his thinking the two were somehow related. The drawings and poems of his adolescence, the character of Uggug in *Sylvie and Bruno*, plus the recurrent pig-child, indicate that he saw something ugly and even cruel in masculinity, which after all is half of sex. As the third of eleven, it is possible that he heard his beloved mother give a few moans or even some healthy ouches every thirteen or eighteen months. To be sure, every other child with younger sisters and brothers had the same experience before the day of maternity hospitals; some boys were affected to the point of fearing their own powers and others were not. A hundred years later the injury cannot be explained or documented, but injury there clearly was.

Mr. Empson implies that a stanza of the poem at the beginning of *Through the Looking-Glass* meant more than that children dislike to go to bed:[21]

> *Come, hearken then, ere voice of dread,*
> *With bitter tidings laden,*
> *Shall summon to unwelcome bed*
> *A melancholy maiden!*

The poem was dedicated to Alice, and presents a peculiar constellation.

To his curiosity he also set definite limits. By making his world smaller and tighter he made his writings more intense. This produced, however, not the clean suffering of normal grief at loss, or anger at frustration, that can nourish and strengthen a healthy soul, but the sick suffering of a man who believes himself and nature to be VILE—like EVIL, another anagram for LIVE. This idea gradually splits the personality into a pair of opposites, for in his heart each man knows he is divine.

The essence of Carroll is the extreme refinement—one might almost say Christianization—to which he brought the humor of cruelty. A lifelong process of refinement in himself produced the perfection of the *Alice* books. It is possible to trace the crude beginnings and shameless primitive forms of the motifs in his youthful writings, the fusion of opposites in his middle years, and the desiccated sweetness of *Sylvie and Bruno,* no longer blended, but alternated with a cruelty and ugliness that almost return to his early forms.

While his powers were at their apogee, he maintained the proper tension between sadism and sentimentality, giving his writings a subtlety, a delicacy, an extra twist of perversity, an incomparable flavor. His contemporaries differed about his personal charm. Some of his fellow dons were, like William Rossetti, temperate in their enthusiasm. The glowing biography by Isa Bowman reveals an ecstatic admirer; more sober but equally warm appreciations are those of Ethel Arnold and E. M. Rowell. Perhaps the best Carrollian blend is that of Harry Furniss:

"To meet him and to work for him was to me a great treat. I put up with his eccentricities. . . . I put up with a great deal of boredom, for he was a bore at times, and I worked over seven years with his illustrations, in which the working hours would not have occupied me more than seven weeks, purely out of respect for his genius. I treated him as a problem, and I solved him, and had he lived I would probably have still worked with him. He remunerated me liberally for my work; still, he actually proposed that in addition I should partake of the profits; his gratitude was overwhelming." [22]

While not everyone who met him was alive to his genius, his writings cannot be denied universal validity. It may well be a comment on some sort of dullness in them for any of his acquaintances to have missed his fire, or perhaps he carried a dark lantern, and hid his light on occasion. But why was he forever fretting about the "child of the pure unclouded brow," implying that his own brow was in some way shadowed? How does a man of blameless life get the horrors? His very blamelessness may produce them. Creative (other than procreative) impulses, or altruistic or other respectable and elevated desires may also suffer repression. All was not so quiet as it seemed that afternoon when Mr. Dodgson and Mr. Duckworth took the three enchanting daughters of Dean Liddell rowing on the placid Isis.

Chapter 12

Nothing But Love

*He thought he saw a Garden-
Door
That opened with a key*

IN *Silvie and Bruno* the escape is fragmentary. In fact the whole book is fragmentary. It started with "Bruno's Revenge," published in *Aunt Judy's Magazine,* in 1867, continued for years as stories to children, and ended with the publication of *Sylvie and Bruno* in 1889 and *Sylvie and Bruno Concluded* in 1893. Like Bruno's soup, it is made up of "bits of things," but the medium holds it together.

While Carroll worked on it spasmodically, by inspiration (such as it was), it is hardly "padded." In one of his almost Shavian introductions, he points out three lines of "padding" he inserted to bring a picture in at the right place! The weaving is careful, but far too conscious to excite the reader. For instance, he carefully lists the parallels between the "Little Birds" song near the end of Volume II, and incidents in Volume I. He promises to tell which of the parallels were intentional in his projected volume, *Original Games and Puzzles.* This was the book for the illustrations to which Miss Thomson kept him waiting twelve years. It was never published, and the drawings (which illustrated nothing anyhow) were used in his posthumous volume of verse, *Three Sunsets.*

Once he actually did pose a riddle in one book and answer it in a later one: the March Hare's riddle, "Why is a raven like a writing desk?"—propounded in *Wonderland* in 1865 and answered in a note to the eighty-sixth thousand, dated 1896; and in the introduction to *Snark* he explains some of the words in *Jabberwocky,* with fifteen years between books.

Like the *Alice* books, the two volumes of *Sylvie and Bruno* have unity of form and treatment. Unlike the *Alice* books they also have a unity (*e pluribus*) of story, so they can be treated as one. Nothing more seems to have happened to the author between the two volumes than slow disintegration. His Dodgson side splits more and more from his disembodied fairy-tale self. Two of the most engaging characters in these dreadful books are the Professor, who sums himself up with the words, "All of me that is not Bonhomie is Rumination," and the Other Professor, who is always late, always dusty, always falling over furniture and getting shut up in a book. The two of them seem like a further split of the White Knight into two segments.

Carroll would not accept this analysis. He said that, since the *Alice* books had so many imitators, he determined to do something completely different. He only succeeded in distorting and maiming his brain-child. The volumes are readable only where he did recapture some of the spirit of *Alice,* as in the two professors, the gardener, and a few of Bruno's exploits. Only a few. Charm can be overdone, especially fairy charm, though the sanctified little girl Victoria, who could be queen of a great nation and empress of a greater one, based her character on that very quality of which we now find it easy to have enough.

Lewis Carroll's idea was to show what *might* happen *if* fairies existed and had some mingling with human lives. There are two parallel interwoven stories—one, the human love story of Dr. Arthur Forester and Lady Muriel, with her father the Earl and the narrator as secondary characters; and the other story, the antiphonal rise and fall of the Warden and Sub-Warden of Outland, elder and younger brothers, and the children of the former, Sylvie and Bruno themselves. The narrator and some of the other characters weave back and forth between the two stories. At the end of the fairy part, the Sub-Warden remains Emperor because his brother, from whom he filched the title, becomes King of Elfland instead. The regulation fairy-tale appearances and disappearances, and the amulet, are balanced by wholly Carrollian and left-handed inventions like the Outlandish watch with the reversal peg. In fact the whole book is flecked with pre-Einsteinian adumbrations,* one quite astonishing:

" 'One can easily imagine a situation,' said Arthur, 'where things would *necessarily* have no weight, relatively to each

* See Appendix G.

other, though each would have its usual weight, looked at by itself . . . suppose this house, just as it is, placed a few billion miles above a planet, and with nothing else near enough to disturb it: of course it falls *to* the planet? . . . But now as to the relative weight of things. Nothing can be *heavy*, you know, except by *trying* to fall, and being prevented from doing so. . . . Well, now, if I take this book, and hold it out at arm's length, of course I feel its *weight*. It is trying to fall, and I prevent it. And, if I let it go, it falls to the floor. But, if we were all falling together, it couldn't be *trying* to fall any quicker, you know: for, if I let go, what more could it do than fall? And, as my hand would be falling too—at the same rate—it would never leave it, for that would be to get ahead of it in the race. And it could never overtake the falling floor!' . . .

" 'There is a more curious idea yet,' I ventured to say. 'Suppose a cord fastened to the house, from below, and pulled down by some one on the planet. Then of course the *house* goes faster than its natural rate of falling: but the furniture—with our noble selves—would go on falling at their old pace, and would therefore be left behind.' . . .

" 'To avoid that,' said Arthur, 'let us have the furniture fixed to the floor, and ourselves tied down to the furniture. Then the five-o'clock-tea could go on in peace.'

" 'With one little drawback!' Lady Muriel gaily interrupted. 'We should take the *cups* down with us: but what about the *tea?*'

" 'I had forgotten the *tea*,' Arthur confessed. '*That*, no doubt, would rise to the ceiling—unless you chose to drink it on the way!' "

Did anybody but Lewis Carroll anticipate the weightlessness of the space travelers?

The two volumes and their prefaces are an omnium-gatherum of Carroll's and Dodgson's major interests, which changed not at all, and developed by deepening rather than broadening. Arthur pontificates on politics, religion, art, love, science, immortality, and ruined castles; the Professor brings reports from a country close to Erewhon, and instructs his hearers in the use of black light and various types of glass, a megaloscope, a minifying glass, and the old-fashioned looking glass with backward arrangement of everything from time to logic. The book crawls with lessons and morals—the Duchess and the dear Queen would be very much at home.

Yet the "bits of things" are set in a mosaic that does make a whole. While Carroll could make a ghost of himself or his reader with equal ease, and visit back and forth freely between the Here and Now, and the *autre monde,* the unity of the book is achieved by the complex unity of the author. The surface coherence of the parts is merely the odd coherence of the centrifugal Dodgson. The book could easily fly into fragments again; in fact it has twice been edited and published with the fairy part only, once by Edwin Dodgson, home on leave from Tristan da Cunha, and once by Blackburn and White in their omnibus volume, *Logical Nonsense.* This is the more palatable form to read, but to study Carroll's mind the lush lianas are as useful as the fruit trees.

Sylvie and Bruno casts more light on the author than do his masterpieces. To the reader it presents a labyrinth of neurosis, whereas to him it may have represented a health exercise in which he reknitted his disintegrating elements. Whatever the reason, he had a great affection for the book, especially for the nothing-but-love poem. Variations on the theme of love, and the question "What is Love?" are basic to the story, as is that same preposterous poem.

The rift in Carroll's love life shows up clearly here. He overstresses the mother element; the filial attitude toward his God is sickly, and reminiscent of unresolved feelings for his father; his affection for little girls sounds as maudlin as his hatred for little boys is laughable. Prince Uggug in this book is the hideous result of splitting a little boy in two, reserving all the endearing qualities for Bruno and all the snaps and snails and puppy-dogs' tails for "His Imperial Fatness." Eventually Uggug swells up into a porcupine, while his good uncle murmurs, "Loveless, loveless," and Bruno is saved from this fate because he loves—his sister Sylvie, with whom he exchanges nearly as many kisses as Isa did with Uncle Charles.

The approximate ages of the characters are indicated: Lady Muriel, about twenty; Sylvie, about ten; Bruno, surely no more than five, or how could he have retained his garbled grammar? It is hard to imagine him ever bridging the chasm between his private language and the elegant diction of Alice, who is seven in *Wonderland*.

The children's father, who resembles Archdeacon Dodgson, leaves the children in the care of their careless uncle, first giving Sylvie the choice between a red locket inscribed, "Sylvie will love all," and a blue one marked, "All will love Sylvie." The noble girl chooses the first; the book ends with her discovery that they are identical. "And when you look *at* it, it's red and fierce like the sun—and when you look *through* it, it's gentle and blue like the sky!"

Carroll seems to have fallen in love with his new Galatea, who has many attributes of his mother. He wrote Harry Furniss: "As to your Sylvie, I am charmed with your idea of dressing her in *white;* it exactly fits my own idea of her; I want her to be a sort of embodiment of purity." [1] The dedication in the second volume reads:

> *. . . Thou delicious Fay—*
> *The guardian of a Sprite that lives to tease thee—*
> *Loving in earnest, chiding but in play*
> *The merry mocking Bruno! Who, that sees thee,*
> *Can fail to love thee, Darling, even as I?—*
> *My sweetest Sylvie, we must say "Good-bye!"*

Collingwood seems to have guessed that Sylvie might be drawn from Mrs. Dodgson:

"Readers of *Sylvie and Bruno* will remember the way in which the invisible fairy-children save the drunkard from his evil life, and I have always felt that Mr. Dodgson meant Sylvie to be something more than a fairy—a sort of guardian angel. That such an idea would not have been inconsistent with his way of looking at things, is shown by the following letter:—

'My dear Ethel,

'. . . you don't see "how they can be guided aright by their dead mother, or how light can come from her." Many people do believe that our friends in the other world can and do influence us in some way, and perhaps even "guide" us and give us light. . . . My own feeling is, it *may* be so: but nothing has been revealed about it . . . "a mother who has died leaving a child behind her in this world, is allowed to be a sort of guardian angel to that child." Perhaps Mrs. N— believes that.' " [2]

Perhaps Mr. D— believed that too. The first lines of the dedication hint as much:

> *Dreams, that elude the Waker's frenzied grasp—*
> *Hands, stark and still on a dead Mother's breast,*
> *Which nevermore shall render clasp for clasp,*
> *Or deftly soothe a weeping Child to rest—*
> *In suchlike form me listeth to portray*
> *My Tale, here ended.*

Then he continues with "Thou delicious Fay," and so on.

One of his most pixy letters, written on note paper about five inches by three, in minute handwriting, purports to be from Sylvie herself:

Dec. 2, 1867

"Dear Miss Dymphna,

"As Mr. Dodgson has asked me to write for him, I send you a few lines to say that he sent you a copy of *Aunt Judy's Magazine,* that you may read a little story he has written about Bruno and me. Dear Miss Dymphna, if you will come into our wood, I shall be very glad to see you, and I will show you the beautiful garden Bruno made for me.

"Your affectionate little fairy friend,

'Sylvie' " [3]

Why could he not sign the letter "Bruno"? Was he identifying himself with Sylvie, as he had done earlier with Alice?

Even Mr. Langford Reed, who defends Carroll's manliness by citing his fistic prowess at Rugby, and the strength of his handclasp, could not forbear to say: "Bruno is not like a boy—not even one from fairyland—he is more like a roguish little girl pretending to be a boy, and speaking a language no boy would speak, and at times, he becomes very irritating to the reader." [4] For by this time Carroll's well-preserved purity had distilled out any manliness, any heartiness, he may have started with. Sylvie is even too sissy for a real girl. She is the type of little Eva that died in a little white bed all through Victorian literature. Elizabethan fairies and little folk were not shadows of human beings—they had the vitality of their creators. Titania differs from a real woman only in size and magical powers.

The characters in the fairy part of the book are sometimes simple and sometimes multiple transmogrifications of the human characters. Sylvie is surely the fairy form of Lady Muriel. They have similar dispositions and great sympathy for each other, and the narrator hints at a connection. Harry Furniss says: "Then for months we corresponded about the face of the heroine alone. My difficulty was increased by the fact that the fairy-child Sylvie and the Society grown-up Lady Muriel were one and the same person!" [1]

If Sylvie is Carroll's memory of his mother, Lady Muriel may well be another aspect of Mrs. Dodgson, and he switches the girl and the woman back and forth as he did in the dream about Polly Terry. Is Lady Muriel also his lamented Incognita? Her variation of age makes that possible too. Her last link with Carroll's mother is her voice—probably the wife of the Archdeacon would be shy, and it is said she always spoke softly. The descriptions of Sylvie's voice, the sweetness and tininess of it, seem like a voice in memory—and all the more a mother's, fixed forever in the inner ear. Sylvie is about to sing all through the books, but actually does so only at the end—the refrain of the think-it-is-love song.

She speaks to Bruno much as a Victorian mother would speak to her son—as Mrs. Clemens spoke to Sam, which, says Mr. Brooks, kept him a "good boy" and an unfulfilled artist all his life.[5] She tells him to be good, to restrain his impulses, all so sweetly and gently that the loving arms are shackled around him forever, keeping him eternally nostalgic for the lost heaven of infancy. Bruno may be Carroll's idealization of himself as a boy—that is, before he began thinking of himself as a girl—but not too much before! Bruno has the same preoccupations as Charles—bugs and snails and frogs, argument, ineffectual rebellion, "bits from Shakespeare."

In his middle and later years Carroll almost granted life to the remarkably vivid images that visited him. He speaks of sitting in his study, peopling the air around him with faces of absent friends. His niece mentioned that Guildford was supposed to have a fairy ring—that on a walk he asked her quite seriously whether she believed in fairies, and reminded her that at any rate they had not been disproved. She says he was perfectly grave about it and may very well have been in earnest. Why not, since some of our most honored physicists still make pilgrimages to Fairyland, Outland, and other places on the Carrollian map?

He makes himself, the narrator, an elderly invalid, the best friend of Lady Muriel's fiancé, quite out of the running, and a trifle arch about it, like a chronic bachelor trying to prove that his bachelorhood is not of his own making. Supposing Incognita *was* a real woman—Alice, perhaps—and supposing there was a real barrier, such as age, between them—perhaps he chose a *Princesse Lointaine* through a need to fail. However that may be, the "I" in the story is his least glamorous, most Dodgson self.

There may be several sources for one episode in *Sylvie and Bruno*. In the diary for March 17, 1857, we read: "Breakfast with Girdlestone to meet his uncle." Mr. Green's note is: "Robert, undergraduate at Christ Church. His Uncle Charles was a parish priest who twice went through a cholera epidemic without deserting his post."

The hero, Arthur, may also be drawn from Charles Kingsley, who did actually risk his life among the parishioners during a cholera epidemic, and whose character somewhat resembled Dr. Forester's. Carroll knew Henry Kingsley well, and must have known Charles's good deeds. In fact, *Alton Locke* first wakened him to social consciousness, and caused him to pray that God might make him such a worker. Arthur Forester is no doubt a Tory's-eye view of a Christian Socialist. But the plague story may have other elements. Mr. Reed asserts that once Dodgson was missing for two days from his rooms; it leaked out that he had been nursing a poor and friendless college servant, down with typhoid fever in his dingy lodgings in the poorer part of town. This episode may also have enriched the Girdlestone story, and also there may have been a reminiscence of 1833, when the Asiatic cholera that had swept London in 1832 took 169 lives in

Warrington near Daresbury. The rector and curate stayed
on, ministered to the living, and buried the dead; and the
Baynes may have told the story to the Dodgsons.

The setting of *Sylvie and Bruno* is generally understood to
be Hatfield, the home of Lord Salisbury, where Dodgson was
a frequent visitor, and where he actually began telling the
story to Lord Salisbury's children.

On New Year's day, 1884, he writes: "Began the year with
one of those visits I have always enjoyed so much—to
Hatfield. . . . I went so early in the hope of getting a walk,
and had a very pleasant one with Lady E. Cecil. Sat up till
about 1 with the gentlemen in the smoking-room, as usual in
former visits."

Mr. Green says the "Elveston" of *Sylvie and Bruno* is
probably modeled on Hatfield, "the Earl" on Lord Salisbury,
and "Lady Muriel" on one of his daughters. "Hatfield to him
was the ideal aristocratic home. . . . The local setting of
'Elveston,' however, is more like Whitburn."

Carroll furiously disliked the type of woman then known
as a bluestocking—a woman educated past her power to
understand. In poems and drawings he lampooned her
viciously; the prize portrait is that of the female in the picnic
scene who insists on audibly admiring the view and jabber-
ing endless silly questions. She is the aunt of Rupert Brooke's
woman who "came and quacked beside me in the wood."

Miss Arnold found the Dodgson ladies learned but not
silly. As a child, visiting in Guildford, she was somewhat
dismayed by "those rather alarming, austere, devoutly evangelical ladies (one of them, Miss Henrietta if I remember
rightly, an advanced mathematician)." [6] But it was not Miss
Henrietta. Miss Menella Dodgson said that Miss Louisa, the
last survivor, was the mathematical one. Lewis Carroll's
photographs show a pleasant and sympathetic family.

Carroll's best portraits are aspects of himself. In *Sylvie
and Bruno* too the most pleasing characters are chips of his
own block; only among the persons of his inner world was
he perfectly authoritative. When, like the Other Professor,
he bumbled around outside, attending banquets and tripping
over furniture with his nose in a book, he never quite made
connections, nor could he make an objective portrait.

But his internal chain remained unbroken. His thrift in picking up bits of poetry and prose dropped along the way was remarkable. The poem "Matilda Jane," in *Sylvie and Bruno,* was written for his cousin's doll—years later he wrote his cousin to send him a copy. The first stanza of *Jabberwocky* appeared in his youthful magazine *Mischmasch* in 1855; the rest was written at a party years later—the whole appeared in *Through the Looking-Glass* in 1871. The episode of "Black Light," near the end of *Sylvie and Bruno,* called "Bruno's Revenge," was printed in *Aunt Judy's Magazine* in 1867; the next fragment, the story of Uggug, was told to the children of the Marquis of Salisbury, then Chancellor of the University, on one of Carroll's visits to Hatfield House in 1874. It was not for nothing that the farmer's wife taught Bruno:

For wilful waste makes woeful want, and I may live to say How much I wish I had the crust that then I threw away!

The final thread in this complex fabric is that of religious love. Arthur's rival for Lady Muriel, Captain Eric Lindon, is represented as a religious doubter, but on the most elevated grounds. After the doctor gives up hope for Arthur, Eric nurses him day and night, bringing him back to health—then, with an un-Carrollian failure of logic, is converted because Arthur's miraculous recovery was due to Lady Muriel's prayers. Carroll considered this a happy ending, perhaps. It is relieved only by one refreshing moment of sincere pessimism. He says: "Human life seems, on the whole, to contain more of sorrow than of joy. And yet the world goes on. Who knows why?" This resembles some of the passages in the Book of Ecclesiastes that slipped by the censors, and in that simple form of unmistakable sincerity, it is unique in Carroll's works.

He seems to have dabbled in theosophy, which he calls "esoteric Buddhism." This was Mme. Blavatsky's new religion. Max Müller was one of the first to expose her ignorance of Indian cults. Surely Carroll was warned? Nevertheless he says that the fairy episodes were based on what he had read of "esoteric Buddhism." At the end of the first volume, when his suit looks hopeless, Dr. Forester plans to go to India. The flowers that Bruno makes by magic (called a "phlizz"), and that also vanish magically, are native to central India. Before Arthur's projected trip, the narrator quotes:

> *Oh, never star*
> *Was lost here, but it rose afar!*
> *Look East, where whole new thousands are!*
> *In Vishnu-land what Avatar?*

His interest in theosophy probably went no deeper than his passing interest in the "ghost-painter." He was still worrying about jests on "sacred subjects": "And to the speaker himself it must surely bring the danger of loss of faith . . . and he . . . is but too likely to find that, for him, God has become a myth, and heaven a poetic fancy—that for him, the light of life is gone, and that he is at heart an atheist, lost in 'a darkness that may be felt.' "

While the first *Alice* book is a pure lark-song, and the second a lively and pleasurable chess game, *Sylvie and Bruno* is more like an act of self-purgation, or of amalgamation of centrifugal forces. It is some sort of health gymnastic, but in no sense a true art form. It is to art as Indian club exercises are to the dance. Yet some of the "bits" are utterly delightful—gaily sadistic parts, charming moments before the charm begins to cloy. "The Gardener's Song" is equal to anything in *Alice*. There is no need to quote it here, since it is available in several recent books. "The Kingfisher Song" is amusing, with its refrain,

> *Sing beans, sing bones, sing butterflies,*

and the one about the "Little Birds," undoubtedly inspired by the fireplace tiles, is subtle and intricate. Bruno's entertainment of the frogs is a rare parody of amateur theatricals, with his "bits from Shakespeare" that always culminate in a back somersault.

Carroll assured his readers that child audiences of all ages loved "Bruno's Picnic"—no doubt, since it is mostly about eating, and especially about being eaten up. The crocodile that walked on his own forehead is worthy of a place in the *Alice* books, or beside Christina's crocodile, and the boots for horizontal weather would have fitted the White Knight. The Professor springs from the same golden vein, that does indeed run through the book, but mostly underground. What dreary going it is even when the reader is hunting the elusive snark of a Carroll; for the casual reader with no particular motivation, the book is merely a desert with occasional oases.

Carroll's basic assumptions invalidated his self-criticism—else how could he have fancied *Sylvie and Bruno* his life work? The Duchess on the loose dragged in every sort of political, religious, and aesthetic moral. *Sylvie and Bruno* is a protracted fugue of which the themes are the Duchess and the White Knight. All the tiresome, though sometimes illuminating, little tracts and pamphlets imbedded in the two volumes, may be listed under Duchess; the charming, whimsical fancies and left-handed inventions, under White Knight.

Numerous threads tie in with the *Alice* books; for instance, the Professor's boots for horizontal weather—little umbrellas to wear about his knees, just in case it should rain horizontally. (Analogy: the anklets on the White Knight's horse "to guard against the bites of sharks.") The gardener waters flowers with an empty can because it's "lighter to hold," as the White Knight's box for clothing and sandwiches hung upside down "to keep the rain from getting in." The professor's Outlandish watch is related to the Mad Hatter's mad timepiece. The *Wonderland* notion that one befriended by Time could turn the clock hands and skip from breakfast to dinner, develops into the Outlandish watch. The Professor listens to a conversation, then wipes it out by setting the hands back. The narrator borrows the watch and tries to efface an accident with it, but when the time comes round again, the victim lies bandaged and suffering as before. This resembles the incident where Alice vainly tried to undo the knot in the Mouse's tail, merely offending him instead. "The good I fancied I could do is vanished like a dream: the evil of this troublesome world is the only abiding reality," says Carroll. Mary Frances Cleugh, in *Time and Its Importance in Modern Thought,* says: "The success of the

plain man in repairing a blunder, so that it is, to common
sense at least, as if it had never been, makes it seem that
some actions can be reversed, and that 'what's done cannot
be undone' is false."

Sylvie and Bruno contains at least one lesson for our
time: "Said Arthur, 'The number of lunatic *books* is as finite
as the number of lunatics . . . when ninety per cent of us are
lunatics, the asylums will be put to their proper use . . . *To
shelter the sane!* . . . We shall bar ourselves in. The lunatics
will have it all their own way, *outside*. They'll do it a little
queerly, no doubt. Railway collisions will be always happen-
ing: steamers always blowing up: most of the towns will be
burned down: most of the ships sunk—

" 'And most of the men *killed!*' murmured the pompous
man.

" 'Certainly," Arthur assented. 'Till at last there will be
fewer lunatics than sane men. Then *we* come out: *they* go in:
and things return to their normal condition.' "

An echo of Oxford, or perhaps of Professor Teufels-
dröckh's university of Weissnichtwo, reverberates through
Mein Herr's question:

"Am I right in thinking that in *your* Universities, though
a man may reside some thirty or forty years, you examine
him, once for all, at the end of the first three or four? . . .
And what guarantee have you that he *retains* the knowledge
for which you have rewarded him—beforehand, as we should
say?"

The ending is comparable to those of the *Alice* books, but
less movement leads up to the coda. *Sylvie and Bruno* takes
most of the first volume to get under way, and most of the
second to taper off. There are positive nodes in Volume I with
corresponding negative nodes in Volume II—perhaps assembling and resolving nodes would be clearer. The logical
pattern, of course, is complete to the last detail. Structurally,
the book is a musical or mathematical study.

It is true that he claims to have lacked a musical ear, and
certainly his training was of the sketchiest. But he had a fine
sense of rhythm and pattern and weaving, and he certainly
did a great deal of listening to music. There are some indica-
tions that he may even have performed. He was elected to

the Oxford Choral Society, which surely implies participation as well as listening. On December 31, 1856, he gave a magic lantern exhibition for "about eighty children, and a large miscellaneous party besides of friends, servants, etc. . . . I introduced thirteen songs in the course of the performance, six for myself and seven for the children."

He also did a little composing. On October 28, 1862, he mentions *"Miss Jones . . .* a medley-song, which I composed when last at Croft, with the help of Margaret, Henrietta, etc. . . . the tunes running into each other." On January 13, 1876, he says, "The children went to help in acting *Puss in Boots* at Mrs. Head's, for which I wrote them a song, and got fifty copies to distribute among the audience." Mr. Green says no copy is recorded anywhere.

On March 12, 1857, he records an attempt at something really difficult. "I tried the other night to compose a piece of verse imitating the 'effects' of music, but had not much success. Some of what I intended as an explanatory note to it I have today set down, to form a portion of an essay which I think of calling 'Word-Music.'" Mr. Green says "Neither poem nor essay survive."

There was a certain intrusion of theology here, as in all his pleasures. He considered the Cathedral an inappropriate place to hear Bach's St. Matthew Passion—what, one wonders, would have been a more appropriate place? On September 3, 1863, he let loose one of those weird conversations for two voices that took place in his head. "There is a peculiar pleasure in listening to what I call 'unsatisfactory music,' which arises, I think, from the fact that we do not feel called upon to enjoy it to the utmost; we may take things as they come.

"In listening to first-rate music there is a sense of anxiety and labor, labor to enjoy it to the utmost, anxiety not to waste our opportunities; there is, I verily believe, a sensation of pain in the *realization* of our highest pleasures, knowing that now they soon must be over; we had rather prolong anticipation by postponing them. In truth we are not intended to rest content in any pleasure of earth, however intense." Poets as well as saints have noticed this condition before, though sometimes they have drawn different conclusions:

But at my back I always hear
Time's winged chariot hurrying near. . . .

He attended many concerts, and seems often to have gone to London especially for the purpose. He went alone, with friends, with children, and records his preferences freely. His strongest word of praise was "delicious," whether for the music or the rendition. This he used for Jenny Lind in *The Messiah*, for his friend Miss Alice Shute in "Dirge Over Dundee," for *Norma*. Beethoven's *Septum* was "a great treat," "The Mermaid's Song" from *Oberon* on the same program was "heavy." *Barber of Seville* was "all the more tedious to me as I knew hardly any of the music." *Trovatore* he enjoyed, "though the music was rather beyond me at a first hearing." Unlike Liddon, he detested Gregorian chants. But on his Russian tour, he noticed their similarity to synagogue music.

It has been said that none of Dodgson's sisters ever attended a theatrical performance, but Miss Henrietta must have considered it. On January 23, 1873, he says, "The play of 'Patience,' will do well for the first experiment which Henrietta wishes to make in play-going, and Edith Denman is ready to go with us."

He seems to have attended all the Gilbert and Sullivan operettas. *Pinafore* of course horrified him, with the little girls singing "Damme!" The others he called "pretty"— *Mikado, Patience,* and *Iolanthe,* which he liked the least. Did he not recognize his own Arcadia?

On August 13, 1890, he "went to the exhibition of 'Edison's Phonograph.' It is indeed a marvellous invention. As heard through the funnel, the *music* (particularly trumpet-music) was flat: the singing and speaking are better, though a little inarticulate.

"August 13 went to the 'Phonograph' again, at the end of the lecture, to hear the 'private audience' part. Listening through tubes, with the nozzle in one's ear, is far better and more articulate than with the funnel; also the music is much sweeter. It is a pity that we are not fifty years further on in the world's history, so as to get this wonderful invention in its *perfect form*. It is now in its infancy—the new wonder of the day, just as I remember Photography was about 1850."

He seems always to have enjoyed Beethoven, but these tributes have a suspiciously literary aroma. For instance, he mentions the "wonderful" picture of a rapt audience listening to Beethoven play. Those who are old enough to have seen Victorian engravings remember that "wonderful" picture; and some of that deadly reverence creeps into Carroll's mentions of Beethoven. His true loves undoubtedly were ballads and folk songs, for the most convincing picture of Carroll enjoying music is that given by Beatrice Hatch, describing how he hung over the music-box, raising and lowering the lid, for the high point of the evening—"Santa Lucia." [7]

As the first *Alice* book approaches the coda, in the court scene, Alice grows bolder and bolder, till with a crash of the tympani she announces: "You're nothing but a pack of cards!" *Sylvie and Bruno* has a similar scene, where the Warden returns to Outland to forgive the false brother who pre-empted the throne, and Prince Bruno, even before his father's return, grows bolder and contradicts oftener, till the Sub-Warden, who has lied prodigiously, receives a shock (perhaps electrical). The scene darkens, everything rocks; the Warden and his wife drop their foolish expressions. They start telling the truth, all masks fall, and their game is up. This surrealist portrait of liars who have decided to come clean, suggests that Carroll too may have tasted of the fruit of knowledge of truth and falsehood—or how could he have made the picture so exact?

The Mad Gardener is not a pure figure of fun; nor is his song without macabre and sinister overtones. Dr. Greenacre believes that a definite event has here left its footprints on the page, as on Lewis Carroll's life—a childhood observation of the antics of a senile gardener. This figure appears also in the Aged, Aged Man. "The figure appearing sometimes in one guise and sometimes in another, but with its acrobatic, swaying, jigging, snorting rhythm is a typical dream representation of sexual excitement. It is interesting, therefore, to realize that in the very structure of Carroll's stories, these figures all appear as memories which are repeated in dreams. . . . The repetitiveness of this excited figure and his constant association with a secret garden, the concern about whether the memory is good in the onlooker and the reciprocal question whether the silly old fellow's brain has been injured . . . would lead to the conclusion that there was some actual but repressed memory of the author's which was insistently recurring in hidden forms; that probably in his childhood Charles had been stirred at the sight of an older man, perhaps a gardener, in a state of sexual excitement."

The garden door and the key, of course, resume the *Alice* motif—with the odd difference that here the key lets the children *out* of the garden where their uncle has confined them. The magic garden of childhood no longer suffices. The fairyland to which Sylvie and Bruno are always returning may be infancy itself, where the gentle voice of Mother Sylvie murmurs in little Bruno's ears.

The scene in Dogland again belies Isa Bowman's contention that Dodgson was indifferent toward animals. Before the evolutionary concept of man's place on the tree of life flowered, there were two approaches to the lower limbs of the tree—the Aesopian and the Franciscan. Animals were dramatized as caricatures of man, or they were—less commonly—considered in their own right, with distinctive personalities. The Franciscan writers before Darwin were usually naturalists, like Audubon. Carroll's ordinary approach to animals was Aesopian, as in the *Alice* books, where members of Common Room solemnly play Bottom the Weaver—but the dogs in *Sylvie and Bruno* are honest dogs. Bruno astounds the court by treating the king dog, Nero, as an old friend; later Nero confidentially begs the children to throw a stick for him to fetch. This grasp of the doggishness of dogs—royal or not—parallels Carroll's understanding of the humanity of queens—including the poor White Queen.

Finally—"Has he [she] ever been lost before?" "Yes, once,—in a wood." Not Alice—the Other Professor. The two Professors are splits of Mr. Dodgson—the moony one and the genial one—plus caricatures of some of his more moony and less genial colleagues. Not that his Dodgson self erred on the side of geniality. Edward Bok's *The Making of an American* ruefully recounts an entire afternoon spent with Mr. Dodgson, vainly trying to elicit Lewis Carroll, or even an acknowledgment of his existence.

The only other American visitors we find seem to have fared no better. Dodgson's diary, on July 26, 1879 says, "Called on the MacDonalds. . . . Met Mr. Clemens (Mark Twain), in whom I was much pleased and interested." In his *Autobiography* Clemens says, "We met a great many other interesting people, among them Lewis Carroll, author of the immortal *Alice*—but he was only interesting to look at, for he was the stillest and shyest full-grown man I have ever met except 'Uncle Remus.' Doctor MacDonald and several other lively talkers were present, and the talk went on briskly for a couple of hours, but Carroll sat still all the while except that now and then he asked a question. His answers were brief. I do not remember that he elaborated any of them."

On April 30, 1873, Dodgson "Dined with the Max Müllers, and met Mr. and Miss Emerson." We do no better with Emerson's diary. He says, "At Oxford April 30, guest of Max Müller. Introduced to Mr. Dodgson author of *Alice in Wonderland,* Jowett and Ruskin."

Then there were two encounters with unknown Americans. On April 5, 1863, he met ". . . a Mrs. McFarland from Richmond (America), secretary to Mr. Mason, the Confederate Commissioner. I was very glad of getting an opportunity of discussing the question of slavery, for the first time, with an actual slave-holder." And how glad we would be to know what came of it! At least we know that he knew there was a Civil War.

On September 3, 1880, he wrote: "I promised a *Snark* to a quite new little friend, Lily Alice Godfrey, from New York: aged eight, but she talked like a girl of fifteen or sixteen, and declined to be kissed on being wished good-bye, on the ground that she 'never kissed gentlemen.' It is rather painful to see the lovely simplicity of childhood so soon rub off: but I fear it is true that there are no children in America."

Carroll's nonsensical habits sprouted partly from genuine shyness. Shy persons, however, may conceal a high opinion of themselves, and the shyness may arise from a fear of not being able to make their own valuation current. This state of mind, familiar as the "Cinderella complex," crops out all through *Sylvie and Bruno*. Despite a modicum of the normal boy's boastfulness, even Bruno is loaded with good deeds that shrink from the light, and the book is filled with left hands that know not what the right hands do. This is British, Victorian, Christian—but carried to this extreme it is only Carrollian.

And who but Carroll would let Bruno say: "Then I's very glad I *is* a singular boy! It would be horrid to be two or three boys! P'raps they wouldn't play with me!" Alice had no trouble getting herself to play croquet with herself. Was life getting harder for the Dodgson-Carroll symbiosis?

He elaborates his invention, and deepens the channel of his thoughts, but his invention is single—the discovery of the rich mine of the subconscious and dream world, antedating Dr. Freud, and more richly ornamented by the mathematical mode of thinking and the left-handed or looking-glass technique. Fully awake, he may have been a trifle tiresome at times—but in the twilight zone he has no equals.

He did senesce rather than mature. A person who lacks even the *attitude* of the normal sex life—whether he lives it or not is less important—and who never completes his revolt from his parents, can never fully mature, can only shrivel and split up, as Carroll did, or rot, as he did not. His loss of vital fluid shows most clearly in the evolution of his self-portrait from Alice through the White Knight to the elderly invalid bachelor—with, characteristically, "heart trouble"—who is the "I" in *Sylvie and Bruno*.

Another sign of increasing crabbedness was the growing difficulty with his illustrators. Tenniel, after two books, quit him with the remark (to Harry Furniss) that he was impossible. Arthur Frost found him impossible too, but Furniss "solved" him. While these later illustrators were smaller men, Carroll was shrinking too, and Furniss, although no Tenniel, had fortitude. He says: "The unconscious humor of the author's ideas for pathetic pictures was a great relief to me in my difficult task of satisfying such a captious critic. He subjected every illustration . . . to a minute examination under a magnifying glass. He would take a square inch of the drawing, count the lines I had made in that space, and compare the number with those on a square inch of illustration made by Tenniel for Alice. And in due course, I would receive an essay on the subject from Dodgson the mathematician . . . Over the criticism of one drawing, I pretended I could stand Dodgson the Don no longer, and wrote to Carroll the author declining to complete the work."

Carroll wrote that this gave him an opportunity he had been seeking to publish an article on *Authors' Difficulties with Illustrators.* . . . Furniss continues: "The article was not written. I was a problem solver also, and we worked without further friction to the end of the volume and through a second volume . . . which occupied some years more." [8]

A letter to Furniss from Carroll:

[of a sketch of Bruno] "No, no! Please don't give us the (to my mind) very ugly, quite modern costume, which shows with such cruel distinctness a podgy, pot-bellied (excuse the vulgarism) boy, who couldn't run a mile to save his life. I want Bruno to be *strong,* but at the same time light and active —with the figure of one of the little acrobats one sees at the circus—not 'Master Tommy,' who habitually gorges himself with pudding." [2]

The Christian attitude toward money appears again in a peculiar form. Carroll's nephew, Mr. Collingwood, a clergyman like himself, calls him "generous." Mr. Parrish, a banker who owned many of his relics, calls him "extravagant" because he left "only a few thousand pounds." His will, dated Nov. 4, 1871, with two of his brothers as executors, left everything to be divided equally among his brothers and sisters, all of whom survived him. Financially, "everything" was £4,596/7/7d. But of course his books have been bringing his heirs royalties right up to the present moment. He kept on doing remunerative work after he would have liked to retire, because he was conscious of responsibilities toward those with fewer golden geese to supply them. Whether generous or extravagant, he had a fantastic fear of becoming miserly, or whence the strange remark:

" 'But even in giving away *superfluous* wealth, he may be denying himself the miser's pleasure in hoarding?' 'I grant you that, gladly,' said Arthur. 'Given that he *has* that morbid craving, he is doing a good deed in restraining it.' "

Though Carroll announces he will not be responsible for the remarks of his characters, they are mostly such leaden, or at least wooden, puppets that we cannot but hold the puppeteer responsible for their wooden arguments. Did he fear—and how needlessly—that he might hang on to some of the money he earned? With his usual timidity in the presence of anything so ferocious as an instinct, he leaned over backwards and perhaps gave away more than he should, lest he find himself unable to give at all!

His fear of approval was part of his shyness and religious belief (that only God is good). Bruno insists he is not "bonnie," and that the farmer's wife could not have meant him when she said "bonnie childer." The only instinct Carroll seems not to have feared was thirst; here alone he recommended temperance rather than total abstinence. Children's appetites appalled him—his own lunch was "a glass of sherry and a biscuit," or a "glass of ale and a chop," with sometimes a slice of melon for dessert. In the vineyard, however, he was sure of himself and needed no rules. In the nine years he was Curator of the Common Room, his pamphlets show equal distaste for the teetotaler, the wine-bibber, and the drunkard. He presents one of each in *Sylvie and Bruno,* and flays them all. He recommends that a worker should drink in his own home—have a keg and a daily allowance, handing over to his wife payment for each drink. This would cut down the amount of drinking, pay on consumption, and keep the pocketbook full—though how, he does not say. The solution, while hardly Dionysian, shows he felt at home in Vineland. He must have had plenty of opportunity in his youth to observe the notorious drunkenness then prevalent among the marlers and farmers of Cheshire.

Another invention in these bottomless books is a companionate marriage, Victorian style, with the young lady's great-aunt as chaperon—the young man is to apply for a provisional honeymoon rather than tie himself up before knowing how well he will get on with his sweetheart.

Another modern note is the reasoning about bees, and whether they are moved by instinct or reason. Carroll's was one of the earliest suggestions of a group mind among the bees. But his attitude toward science was predominantly ironic. From the beginning of Volume I till near the end of Volume II, the Professor is preparing a lecture which, when he finally delivers it, sounds like Mr. Benchley's famous talk on the *Sex Life of the Polyp,* or Tchekhov's monologue on *The Evils of Tobacco.* The Professor forgets all his points, all his references. Some of the experiments won't work, some specimens have lost their labels, and one flies away, the Professor asking in despair whether anyone has noted the three blue spots under each wing.

What a book! What a noble ruin! Let us bury it with Arthur's words to the officious old gentleman who is admiring the remains of an old castle near the picnic grounds:

"Oh gifted architect! Foreseeing the exact effect his work would have, when in ruins, centuries after his death!"

Chapter 13

Poeta Fit

> " *'before she had this fit'*—you never had *fits,*
> my dear, I think?" he said to the Queen.
>   "Never," said the Queen, furiously, throw-
> ing an inkstand at the Lizard as she spoke. . . .
>   "Then the words don't *fit* you," said the
> King, looking round the court with a smile.
> There was a dead silence.
>   "It's a pun!" the King added in an angry
> tone, and everybody laughed.

FITS HAD A CERTAIN FASCINATION for Carroll. There are the
eight Fits into which *The Hunting of the Snark* is divided—
and Collingwood says he was subject to fainting fits.[1] Then
there was the man with the epileptic fit, who started Carroll
on an extensive study of health and anatomy. It is strange
that he missed the chance for a bilingual pun in the poem
whose title heads this chapter, for he loved puns even more
than fits.

The poem "Poeta Fit, Non Nascitur," of course reverses
the adage. In it he shows how a poet can(not) be manufactured by learning rules and phrases; he also shows how he
cooked up his own serious poetry, most of which is pretty
bad. It was in his humorous poems that his rich unconscious
wove its tapestries. Surely it is because his serious poetry "fit"
and his humorous poetry "nascitur," that the latter is immortal, and the former, whatever he hoped, isn't.

Between his serious verse and his doggerel, both on the
same subject, the doggerel is far better. In 1881 Dr. H.
Daniel, of the Daniel Press, planned a volume to celebrate
his daughter Rachel's first birthday. Carroll answered his
request:

"Dear Daniel,
    "I am much complimented by your wish to include verses

285

of mine in your little *livre de luxe*—and profoundly puzzled to know what the subject is to be. And as Mrs. Daniel has set you on to puzzle me, I enclose, in revenge, certain puzzles for her—Verses written on a set subject, even when one knows something about it, and [are?] pretty sure to be rubbish: but, when one knows *nothing!*

"Is it the Old Testament Rachel—of whose infancy nothing is known? Or is it the actress—of whose infancy nothing is known either?

"Yours sincerely
C. L. Dodgson" [2]

Nov. 22/80

Under the transparent cover of not knowing what infant he was to celebrate, he perpetrated this:

> *Oh pudgy podgy pup!*
> *Why did they wake you up?*
> *Those crude nocturnal yells*
> *Are not like silver bells:*
> *Nor ever would recall*
> *Sweet music's "dying fall."*
> *They rather bring to mind*
> *The bitter winter wind*
> *Through keyholes shrieking shrilly*
> *When nights are dark and chilly:*
> *Or like some dire duet,*
> *Or quarrelsome quartette,*
> *Of cats who chant their joys*
> *With execrable noise,*
> *And murder Time and Tune*
> *To vex the patient Moon!*

If Mr. Daniel, like the patient Moon, was vexed, he recovered, for on March 7 Carroll again wrote him:

"My dear Daniel,

"Your note was quite a pleasant surprise—I had made up my mind that I was under the displeasure of Mrs. Daniel and yourself for having ventured to write such outrageous stuff on such a theme as your child! And I had thought I had better hold my tongue and let the whole thing pass into oblivion—I am penitent now, and ready to do what I can—give me a week's law, and I will see if any happy thought occurs.

"Sincerely yours
C. L. Dodgson" [2]

Of the seven stanzas printed in "The Garland of Rachel," two suffice:

What hand may wreathe thy natal crown,
O tiny tender Spirit-blossom,
That out of Heaven hast fluttered down
Into this earth's cold bosom?

And how shall mortal bard aspire—
All sin-begrimed and sorrow-laden—
To welcome, with the Seraph-choir,
A pure and perfect Maiden?

Rachel, whether pudgy podgy pup or angel child, seems to have borne no grudge, for at fourteen she took part in a charity performance of *Alice* at Oxford. Poor stuff as the doggerel is, it transcends the "serious" form with its macabre ambiguity. Is Dodgson welcoming the little girl to earth or to Heaven? Perhaps—happy thought—all his serious poems were as insincere as this one, and perhaps that is why they were all so bad.

Two full editions of his verse are published, one by Dutton, edited and with an introduction by John Francis McDermott* who also edited *The Russian Journal*. The introduction is carefully and skillfully done, but repeats Dodgson's own error of emphasizing the split in the Dodgson-Carroll entity, and of refusing to understand the Dodgson part. Mr. McDermot is punished by his consequent inability to understand the Carroll side fully. When he says, "Frankly this is to be the book of Lewis Carroll, and I have no intention here of allowing Charles Lutwidge Dodgson, a dull and uninteresting person, to intrude in it any more than is necessary to explain the writer of verse in this volume," he cuts himself off from the unconscious Carroll, who was an escape from, as well as

* See Appendix H.

a refinement and extension of, the conscious Dodgson. Mr. Madan shows a better grasp of how this complex organism operated: "Dodgson's nonsense is never far from logic and mathematics: its wildest flights are chastened and regulated by criticism." [3] The force of his poetry lay in its unconscious origins; his forms were polished and his unreason made reasonable by his conscious mind.

Mr. McDermott unearthed the originals of many of Carroll's parodies, and he always proves the case, though he omits to mention that Florence Milner had already proved it for eight of the poems in her article in *The Bookman* (New York) for September, 1903. Mr. Madan's book, published two years after the *Collected Verse,* notes all these parodies—and more.

The test piece for interpreting Carroll's poetry is certainly *Jabberwocky,* of which Mr. McDermott says no more than that it is a parody of the ballad form. Of *The Hunting of the Snark* he says a good deal more. His analysis of its satire and character studies is worth reading, but he makes no attempt to unriddle the symbolism. Carroll said the Snark was a portmanteau creature—partly snake and partly shark—and disclaimed any conscious meaning. Most readers agree that there are hidden meanings, but differ as to what they are. Excerpts from two early analyses, printed in the *Academy* shortly after Carroll's death, one by Henry Holiday, illustrator of the poem, and one by "M.T.H.," follow:

Mr. Holiday says: "When the nonsense seems most exuberant, we find an underlying order, a method in the madness. . . . Take Jabberwocky for instance . . . the page looks, when we open it, like the wanderings of one insane: but as we read we find we have a work of creative genius. . . .

"Whether the humor consists chiefly in the conscious defiance of logic by a logical mind, or in the half unconscious control of its lovely and grotesque fancies, in either case the charm arises from the author's well-ordered mind. . . ."

Mr. Holiday sees several meanings in the *Snark,* but misses the nearest—that funny as it is, it is basically a tragedy of frustration and bafflement, like the early Chaplin comedies, which are funny because man is a cosmic joke and all flesh is as grass.

M.T.H. says: "Each reader finds the Snark that he deserves. My own is Fortune, and I am always lost in astonishment at people who think it can be anything else. . . . The taste, 'meagre and hollow, but crisp,' I regard as finally settling the question. . . . On my hypothesis the Bandersnatch would be Scandal. In *Through the Looking-Glass* the creature is more than once referred to as extraordinarily difficult to catch. . . . But what is the Boojum? It is a kind of Snark—that is clear from twenty passages. . . . How could it have so distressing an effect on the man called 'Hi'? Well, I think a Boojum is that sort of sudden unexpected luck which puts a man 'above his boots'—carries him into a sphere in which he is miserable, and makes him cut the greengrocer's lady. It is a very dangerous creature, and the warning of the Baker's uncle is more than justified."

In *The Saturday Review of Literature* for March 18, 1933, Arthur Ruhl has a remarkable article called "The Finding of the Snark." Mr. Ruhl attributes his material to Dean Wallace B. Donham of the Harvard School of Business Administration. The 1929 depression stimulated Dean Donham to thinking deeply about business cycles, and he found himself trapped in Carrollian contradictions, from which he rescued his sanity by quoting the *Snark*. Gradually he evolved a *dramatis personae* for the poem, with the Snark as business, the Jubjub as Disraeli, and the Bandersnatch as the Bank of England. He makes a case as good as Shaw's *Perfect Wagnerite*. Shaw said, no matter what Wagner intended, the *Ring* contained all that he, Shaw, found in it. Dean Donham has made an interesting study; like all the others, it is true, and M.T.H.'s remarks still hold—each reader finds the Snark he deserves.

Carroll wrote: "I'm afraid I didn't mean anything but nonsense! Still, you know, words mean more than we mean to express when we use them: so a whole book ought to mean more than the writer meant. So, whatever good meanings are in the book, I'm very glad to accept as the meaning of the book." [4] Elsewhere he says: "It may be taken as Allegory for the Pursuit of Happiness."

The letter to Gertrude Chataway's mother, asking permission to dedicate the poem to her, says: "It is called *'The*

Hunting of the Snark,' and the scene is laid in an island frequented by the Jubjub and the Bandersnatch—no doubt the very island where the Jabberwock was slain."

In the introduction to *Snark,* he mentions a connection with *Jabberwocky,* and these famous coinages appear in both poems, and hardly anywhere else: Jubjub bird, frumious, Bandersnatch, beamish, uffish, galumphing, outgrabe, and mimsy (in *Snark* only as mimsiest).

Another letter says: "I'm afraid I can't explain 'vorpal blade' for you—nor yet 'tulgey wood'; but I did make an explanation once for 'uffish thought'—it seems to suggest a state of mind when the voice is gruffish, the manner roughish, and the temper huffish. Then again, as to 'burble'; if you take the three words '*b*leat,' 'm*ur*mur,' and 'war*ble*,' and select the bits I have underlined, it certainly *makes* burble: though I'm afraid I can't distinctly remember having made it that way." [4]

Humpty Dumpty explains that "mome rath," in *Jabberwocky,* means "green pig far from home." in *Snark,* the barrister's dream is about a pig that deserted the sty. "The Pig-Tale" is about a pig that could not jump. Some of the images in *The Walking Stick of Destiny* (1875) appear in these poems. There have been hints all along that pig (e.g., the pig baby in *Wonderland*), stood for Charles's little boyself, and the metamorphosis of Uggug into a porcupine (prickly pig), because he was loveless, suggests that little boys are not only pigs, but deficient in affection!

The monster in *The Walking Stick of Destiny* is a toad, but in "The Pig-Tale," a frog goads the pig on to its disastrous jump. There are endless and insurmountable difficulties with monsters—*Jabberwocky* reads like a Siegfried nightmare. We expect youths to be welcomed by lovely maidens, not by their parents. In Snark, the hero, instead of conquering the monster, softly and suddenly vanishes away. These are piquant variations, but they indicate that all is not well in the state of Jabberwock.

Eddington approaches the poem quite differently: "By admitting a few numbers even 'Jabberwocky' may become scientific. . . . It would not be a bad reminder of the essential unknownness of the fundamental entities of physics to translate it into 'Jabberwocky'; provided all numbers—all metrical attributes—are unchanged, it does not suffer in the least." [5]

Another recurrent Carrollian motif is loss of name or identity, a form of confusion common in childhood, but usually resolved by maturity. In *Through the Looking-Glass* and *Sylvie and Bruno*, people get lost and forget their names. In *Snark*, the hero is the Baker who left forty-two boxes on the shore, labeled with his name, which he then forgot. He answered to "Hi," to "Toasted Cheese," or to "Candle-Ends." In telling his story, he skips forty years, evoking the thought of the forty-two boxes and Carroll's age of forty-three when he wrote the poem. (Perhaps he was forty-two—publication may not have been immediate.)

The Baker is an amiable Jonah, in the vein of the White Knight and the Professor.

> *I engage with the Snark—every night after dark—*
> *In a dreamy delirious fight:*
> *I serve it with greens in those shadowy scenes*
> *And use it for striking a light:*
> *But if ever I meet with a Boojum, that day*
> *In a moment (of this I am sure),*
> *I shall softly and suddenly vanish away—*
> *And the notion I cannot endure!*

Another famous confusion: "Then the bowsprit got mixed with the rudder sometimes." No doubt. In the introduction he explains gravely how it happened. Now it would be nonsense itself to say that there is no such thing as nonsense, that every remark has some sensible meaning. But a good deal of what was formerly called nonsense, including the works of Carroll, Lear, and Gilbert, often contains pungent unconscious symbolism that pleases us because it expresses what we dare not say otherwise. Robert Frost speaks of "explaining" poetry in "other and worse English"—this would hold for nonsense too—but we are entitled to ask for meanings. As the Red Queen told Alice, even a joke should have a meaning.

Mr. McDermott is within his rights in saying that the haphazard group on the Snark hunt are a "universal satire." They may also represent some of Carroll's fireplace fantasies, or the Dodgson-Carroll Company. While describing how the bowsprit was fastened on, anyhow, across the rudder, Carroll says: "The helmsman used to stand by with tears in his eyes: *he* knew it was all wrong, but alas! Rule 42 of the Code, *'No one shall speak to the Man at the Helm,'* had been completed by the Bellman himself with the words *'and the Man at the Helm shall speak to no one.'* So remonstrance was impossible, and no steering could be done till the next varnishing day. During these bewildering intervals the ship usually sailed backwards."

This may be pure, or absolute, nonsense. It may also embody a touching confession of Carroll's inability to straighten out what his Helmsman knew to be all wrong, because the Bellman had tinkered with the Code to silence him. If the Helmsman, for instance, is Lewis Carroll, and the Bellman, who conducts the enterprise is the Reverend C. L. Dodgson, two of his main personalities appear in their perpetual argument. The other characters are harder to name. The Beaver, perhaps, is his timid, suppressed animal soul, warily watching for the Butcher. In the poem they were reconciled—would not that have been a happy solution for the author! *Snark* has many layers—perhaps this interpretation too is correct, and in addition to satirizing external phenomena, the poem is a humorous account of Carroll's conflicting inner voices, which often produce the effect, as in the Mad Tea Party, of a number of persons in animated conversation.

Some modern innovations are foreshadowed in the rhyme scheme of *Snark,* but it is hard to see how so meticulous a worker could have failed, in his introduction, to remark on the irregularities! While never a supremely musical poet, nor one who could pare away all banalities, Carroll employs a versification often melodious and usually compact, except when rhyme or reason seduce him into a little padding. In *Snark* he tries some modern variations. Beginning with Fit the Second, he uses inner rhymes in the first and third lines of irregularly distributed stanzas. It is effective enough to have been carried all through. Though he never mastered the higher branches of English verse, any more than of mathematics, his poetry, like his mathematics, was underivative. Carroll was a great poet—not in his verse, for he could not convey strong feeling without waxing maudlin—but in his dream stories. Form and content are one; the intense perception of the eternal lying behind the accidental reaches the core of every reader, whether with laughter, tears, or exaltation. That is poetry—but not necessarily verse.

Whenever he consciously tried for the intense and serious, however, Dodgson came to the fore. Lewis Carroll poked fun at him and spoiled his serious verse. "The Garland of Rachel" shows how it was done.

His parodies demonstrate that he had an ear. "The Song of the Manlet," a parody of Swinburne's "North sea," rings true; but oddly he never mastered so simple a technique as the run-on line, which, since Shakespeare broke up Marlowe's mighty line, has been universal in English poetry. This procedure, which should be the rule, is the exception in Carroll, and this is the flaw that gives even his best verse its tum-te tum-te quality. Perhaps his orderly mind demanded that each line should be a unit, but a good prosodist listens before he reasons.

This same reasoning may have prevented his using the other ancient device by which English poets vary their rhythms—the shifting of the verse accent, either by using spondees or by allowing the verse beat sometimes to fall on an unaccented or lightly accented syllable. Swinburne uses this method—especially the Spondee—in the very poem Carroll's "Manlet" was born to mock. In comparing these two poems, it is immediately apparent that Carroll's verse depends on its meanings, hidden though they be, while Swinburne depends on music alone.

In his fortunately rare attempts at blank verse, the lack of run-on lines becomes a serious flaw. "The Path of Roses" is a good—or rather a bad—example. In the last six lines, where his best effort would have shown up, only one line runs over, instead of four or five:

And she arose, and in that darkening room
Stood lonely as a spirit of the night—
Stood calm and fearless in the gathered night—

> *And raised her eyes to heaven. There were tears*
> *Upon her face, but in her heart was peace,*
> *Peace that the world nor gives nor takes away!*

The rhythmic break at the end of each line destroys any possibility of variety or climax. Yet Carroll daily read aloud a scene of Shakespeare.

A Mr. McMechan compares the incident of Alice and the pig baby with Titania and Bottom, and Langford Reed considers *A Midsummer Night's Dream* as the first of all nonsense writings. But Carroll himself, like Shaw, never hesitated to criticize Shakespeare, or even to rewrite him if necessary (e.g., his wish to delete lines from *The Merchant of Venice*). Ellen Terry says: "He was a splendid theatre-goer, and took the keenest interest in all the Lyceum productions, frequently writing to me to point out slips in the dramatists' logic which only he would have noticed! He did not even spare Shakespeare. I think he wrote these letters for fun, as some people make puzzles, anagrams, or limericks." She quotes a long letter in which he asks: "Why did not Hero prove an alibi? If Hero is distracted why didn't Beatrice remember? Why didn't she reply

> *But good my lord, sweet Hero slept not here,*
> *She had another chamber for the nonce.*
> *'Twas sure some counterfeit that did present*
> *Her person at the window, aped her voice,*
> *Her mien, her manners, and that thus deceived*
> *My good lord Pedro and his company.*[6]

"Splendid theatre-goer" he may have been, but he wrote Carroll a good deal better than he wrote Shakespeare; it is lucky that his plan for a bowdlerized edition of the Bard never matured. He did a little better in the pamphlet, *The New Belfry*—perhaps because he used some of the original words!

> *Five fathom square the Belfry frowns;*
> *All its sides of timber made;*
> *Painted all in grays and browns;*

Nothing of it that will fade.
Christ Church may admire the change—
Oxford thinks it sad and strange.
Beauty's dead! Let's ring her knell.
Hark! now I hear them—ding-dong, bell.

Carroll also admired a contemporary who could have taught him something about versification—namely, Tennyson. But when they met, Tennyson knew Dodgson as a photographer. Dodgson risked his reputation in a guess, not entirely wrong, on the authorship of the *Light Brigade.* On March 8, 1855, he notes: "Elizabeth wrote, forwarding me . . . some lines on the Balaklava charge, supposed to be by Tennyson. My opinion is that they are not his, but fair imitation of his style. I do not believe that Tennyson could ever have written such lines as

> *"For up came an order, which*
> *Someone had blundered—"*

or talked about sabres 'sab'ring.' If genuine, they are very unworthy of him." But just as Carroll's taste in music seems undeveloped, it may be that he had not the final edge to his poetic ear. Even his prose, remarkable for its lucidity and appositeness, for its brevity and compactness, is not remarkable for music. It is neither harsh nor suave—it reads fluently, but without vowel sequence, rhythmic variety, or climax. And *yet* he was a great poet.

The strangest thing is that his best musical effects appear in his broadest and most blatant satires. Perhaps he had a puritanic fear of his own poetic self. For instance, this musical but idiotic poem in *Novelty and Romancement:*

When Desolation snatched her tearful prey
From the lorn empire of despairing day;
When all the light, by gemless fancy thrown,
Served but to animate the putrid stone:
When monarchs, lessening on the 'wildered sight,
Crumblingly vanished into utter night;
When murder stalked with thirstier strides abroad,

And redly flashed the never-sated sword;
In such an hour thy greatness had been seen—
That is, if such an hour had ever been—
In such an hour thy praises shall be sung,
If not by mine, by many a worthier tongue;
And thou be gazed upon by wandering men,
When such an hour arrives, but not till then!

This poem is supposed to be a sonnet to the Mayor of Muggleton-cum-Swillside. It is stretching a point to call it a sonnet, but otherwise Carroll shows mastery of all the devices (except the run-on line) that he ordinarily ignores.

This same *Novelty and Romancement*, built around one of his most excruciating puns, indicates that Carroll had a desire to be a "real"—that is, a "serious" poet. Something stopped him; perhaps his standards matured ahead of his technique, but he never wrote poetry that was at the same time honest, comprehensible, and musical. His serious poetry of the think-it-is-love type is so bad because it is so dishonest. A poet who can never be serious without mawkishness is simply—or complexly—dishonest in his emotions; is concealing something from himself, if not from his readers. Though emotional dishonesty be unconscious, poetry cannot be achieved with counterfeit emotion.

Novelty and Romancement tells the story of a young man who dreams that his life's desire is to be fulfilled. He comes upon a sign in front of a store dealing, apparently, in the commodity he has always yearned for. Next day he returns to find he has misread the sign. Instead of Romancement, it is Roman Cement. This typical Carrollian tragedy may rise from a deep well. His Romancement turned to Roman Cement in his hands. He says, in the story:

"What was the great idea of my life? I will tell you. With shame and sorrow I will tell you.

"My thirst and passion from boyhood (predominating over the love of taws and running neck and neck with my appetite for toffy) has been for poetry—for poetry in its widest and wildest sense—for poetry untrammeled by the laws of sense, rhyme, or rhythm, soaring through the universe, and echoing the music of the spheres! From my youth, nay, from my very cradle, I have yearned for poetry, for beauty, for novelty, for romancement. When I say 'yearned,' I employ a word mildly expressive of what may be considered as an outline of my feelings in my calmer moments."

This again may be pure nonsense, but the chances are it is nothing of the kind. He may have felt that he could not be a supreme poet, so he had better be a comic one. The choice was fortunate, but many tears lurk in his comic poems, and they move us more than his conscious tear-jerkers. Nevertheless this reversal weakens the impact, and some of his poems miss fire through being shot at an invisible mark.

He reaches his maximum intensity in *Jabberwocky*, probably because he felt sufficiently concealed to let himself go. His conscious attempts at "strong," or pathetic, or earnest poetry are, without exception, execrable. His own favorite, "A Song of Love," is not even the worst. At least it is funny. *Three Sunsets,* to which he wrote the preface just before he died, and which was published a month later, contains enough of his worst poems. The only redeeming feature of most of them is the date. Of the truly awful examples, all but one were written before *Alice.*

The exception, "The Valley of the Shadow of Death," written in 1868, is the longest and probably the worst. An old man tells his son how he sank deeper and deeper into sin until one day he saw two children reading the Bible, with sun shining on their hair, and heard, "Come unto me, all ye that are heavy-laden." This changed the course of his life, and on that day he met his future wife, who died while the son was an infant. The treatment is worthy of the subject.

"The Path of Roses," in the same volume, was written to Florence Nightingale in 1856. It will bear a little more quotation:

> *So in the darkest path of man's despair,*
> *Where War and Terror shake the troubled earth,*
> *Lies woman's mission; with unblenching brow*
> *To pass through scenes of horror and affright*
> *Where men grow sick and tremble: unto her*
> *All things are sanctified, for all are good.*

You are old, Father William. But he wasn't—he was twenty-four. Compared with the poems in Wonderland, composed from six to ten years later, this indicates that in his case, perhaps, *Poeta Fit*. But a poet with healthy self-criticism would not have reissued a collection of his worst offenses in the very last year of his life.

It is too bad Mr. McDermott omitted these tidbits, for the sad and morbid pleasure of realizing that Lewis Carroll wrote them, repays the reader for their badness. The love interest smells of ink.

"Solitude," written at twenty-one, ends:

> *I'd give all wealth that years have piled,*
> *The slow result of Life's decay,*
> *To be once more a little child*
> *For one bright summer-day.*

"Stolen Waters," written in the spring of 1862, is even more explicit. It is Carroll's "La Belle Dame Sans Merci," or "Faustine"—a poem of combined love and loathing, where the poet shows fear of woman as such. It is the only one of his poems with a real adult kiss—was it an inky one?

> *I kissed her on the false, false lips—*
> *That burning kiss, I feel it now!*
>
> *"True love gives true love of the best;*
> *Then take," I cried, "my heart to thee!"*
> *The very heart from out my breast*
> *I plucked, I gave it willingly:*
> *Her very heart she gave to me—*
> *Then died the glory from the west.*
>
> *In the gray light I saw her face,*
> *And it was withered, old, and gray;*
> *The flowers were fading in their place,*
> *Were fading with the fading day.*

The least Freudian reader will admit something not quite healthy there, and the most Freudian will cry, "Oedipus!" In case this is not clear, take the stanza near the end, at his redemption:

> Be as a child—
> So shalt thou sing for very joy of breath—
> So shalt thou wait thy dying,
> In holy transport lying—
> So pass rejoicing through the gate of death,
> In garment undefiled.

So he took his own advice, so he wrote *Alice in Wonderland,* so he lived happily ever after, a good child, who never grieved his parents.

Mr. McDermott fails to mention Langford Reed's collection, *Further Nonsense Verse and Prose of Lewis Carroll.* But this is just retribution. Mr. McDermott does not borrow from Mr. Reed, whereas the latter simply reprints most of his material from Collingwood, whom he never mentions once in the volume. This has been done before, notably by an American woman who published a *Life* of Carroll in 1910, lifting whole passages from Collingwood's *Life and Letters of Lewis Carroll* without once mentioning his name. She quotes a few magazine articles, but otherwise her material is from Collingwood, except for one statement which is out of her own head. Langford Reed does Collingwood a little better in his recent *Life of Lewis Carroll.* He mentions a volume "written by a relative of the family some thirty years ago and now out of print," though he hints that he learned very little from it. The only newly discovered poem Reed presents in his collection is "The Lady of the Ladle," one of the two printed in the *Whitby Gazette.*

The two editions of Dodgson's poetry printed in the thirties, one by Dutton and one by Macmillan, are long since out of print. Fortunately, however, Dover Publications has issued a paperback called *The Humorous Verse of Lewis Carroll,* which is actually a reissue of the Macmillan edition.

Mrs. Livingston, of the Widener Library, uncovered some of Carroll's early contributions to *College Rhymes,* the Oxford paper he edited as an undergraduate. One is signed "B.B.," and one "R.W.G." They seem authentic enough, but are of no literary importance. In 1857 he also notes: "Began an essay of 'Nursery Songs' for the Train." But, as Green says, "The essay never materialized."

Collingwood in his *Picture Book* reprints another youthful poem, called "The Two Brothers." Charles wrote it for his younger brother and put it in the *Rectory Umbrella* in 1853. It is a long and affectionate ballad of a boy who used his brother to bait a fishhook; it seems about to end with honest fratricide—but the author already knew how to turn horror into comedy:

> She turned herself right round about,
> And her heart brake into three,
> Said, "One of the two will be wet through and through
> And t'other'll be late for his tea!"

Carroll's works, especially his poetry, contain a number of ghosts. His own several selves must have presented themselves as almost objective realities. Almost. He kept sane by treating these visitors from his *autre monde* with a combination of respect and good-humored tolerance that prevented them from plaguing him too much. *Phantasmagoria* is well enough known and sufficiently accessible, but one stanza will show how his *revenants* addressed him:

> My father was a Brownie, Sir;
> My mother was a fairy.
> The notion had occurred to her,
> The children would be happier,
> If they were taught to vary.

The ghost finds he is haunting the wrong man, and departs in haste. The ex-haunted man is sorry to lose him. The rhyming in this piece (1867) is a little irritating—some of the rhymes are dragged in by the hair, screeching. Nine years later, when he came to write *The Hunting of the Snark,* he had learned to incorporate the rhyme words tactfully into the structure.

William Rose Benét, reviewing the McDermott book in

The Saturday Review of Literature, has only praise for Carroll's versification. He quotes another stanza from *Phantasmagoria:*

> *Oh, when I was a little Ghost,*
> *A merry time had we!*
> *Each seated on his favorite post,*
> *We chumped and chawed the buttered toast*
> *They gave us for our tea.*

On this Mr. Benét remarks, "You will note the perfection of the versification." It is smooth and easy reading, to be sure —it rhymes, it scans—but perfection is a strong word from a poet. Even if Mr. Benét rejects Yeats's stern dictum that a sound, especially a vowel, should never follow itself in poetry (*we, each*), he can hardly justify the same vowel sound in three consecutive syllables (*we, each, seated*), with no sound pattern to account for it. Carroll heard consonantal patterns, which gives his verse movement, but the lack of subtle music comes from his innocence of vowel sequences. What *is* good in that stanza is the sequence of T sounds, including the tchumped and tchawed. Perhaps this caused a poet on a busy day to overpraise Carroll's versification. But Mr. Benét says something completely sound: "To sustain the satiric note of apparent rational discourse, achieving nothing but absurdity, and to keep the rapid account of it smoothly and literately going within strict metrical verse structure, is a task just about as hard as that of writing poetry that seems as though it had always been with us, so perfectly is it organized." Whatever its faults, Carroll's verse does give that sensation of having always been there.

The riddle of the Sphinx haunts his poetry. His women are either the impossibly good or the equally impossible bass-voiced "blue-stockings." He is eternally bound to these dread harpies. "The Three Voices," a parody of Tennyson's "Two Voices," is also more than that. It tells a long tale of such a bondage, muddled and confused till the humor breaks down under the stress. His own drawing for this poem, is among his ugliest and funniest.* Another is "She's All My Fancy Painted Him." (The youthful poem which was the germ of the White Rabbit's testimony contains that line.)

If his ear lacked delicacy, his sentiments did not. When Mr. Savile Clarke made the *Alice* books into an operetta, musical exigencies forced Carroll to complete " 'Tis the Voice of the Lobster." Originally the last two lines read:

> *While the panther received knife and fork with a growl*
> *And concluded the banquet by—*

Manifestly the only possible ending is "eating the owl." Yet what does the puckish author do?

> *But the panther obtained both the fork and the knife*
> *So when* he *lost his temper, the owl lost his life.*

The "Little Birds" poem is a loose thread that helps carry the story of *Sylvie and Bruno*. Stanzas of it keep appearing through the two volumes, like a sort of symbolic shorthand, which he also used as a device for resting from the logical-religious side of the book. The motif of *Sylvie and Bruno* is Love—a variation on all its forms—except the physical. In the "Little Birds" poem is embedded the sad "Pig Tale" about the poor porker who could not jump, and killed himself against the pump. Could this be translated to mean that the core of Carroll's sorrowful problem was the arrest of his love life at the child level?

The themes that recur all through his verse are: woman as angel or witch (as she must appear to a man who has killed the wrong Jabberwock); ineffectuality; a yearning for childhood, "purity," and so forth; sadness, solitude, ghosts, "sin" (unreal), and "redemption" (mawkish); and even a tendency to imitate or identify himself with Christ—one of the commonest and most respectable forms of escape from a youth's natural need to rebel and go forward.

* See photographic insert.

He thought he saw an Argument
That proved he was the Pope:
He looked again and saw it was
A Bar of Mottled Soap.
"A fact so dread," he faintly said,
"Extinguishes all hope!"

Chapter 14

Hatter and Hare

"Visit either you like: they're both mad."

A FEW LEARNED MEN, like Bergson and Freud, have approached the question of wit and humor, but Max Eastman is probably the first to analyze laughter with the aid of a lively sense of humor of his own. Everybody knows that humorists are rather a special type of humanity, and serve themselves and their fellow men in rather special ways. To see what several such men had in common—humorists who also wrote for children—and to hear what learned men, both with and without a sense of humor, think about what makes us laugh, may help to illuminate Charles Dodgson's particular funny bone.

Freud, tunneling consciously, meets Carroll in his rabbit hole, and between them they help to uncover the unconscious. Freud finds that wit and dreams have similar effects—to release tension and to guard sleep. Both are devices for conserving energy: the dream guards sleep by letting us act out our wishes and problems in disguise. Thus the dreamer need not awaken till he is refreshed and ready to meet his daily disappointments in their usual guise. Wit, like dream, lets us express in masquerade ideas not socially acceptable in the nude. Freud invented a term, "tendency wit," which expresses something actual, though less inclusive than he at first supposed. It releases aggressive tendencies—either hostile or sexual aggression. Of the latter Carroll yields fewer examples than of the former; and how gory wit can be, all the way from simple boasting to verbal boiling in oil!

Today it is known that other important suppressions besides the two noted by Dr. Freud may inspire a dream, a joke, a neurosis, or a work of art. Some control of the reproductive and self-assertive impulses is required in any civilization, and in our civilization even the benevolent and co-operative impulses have to be suppressed. Freud has taught us to use conscious control based on conscious understanding of inconvenient desires, but suppression still exists and release through laughter is still delightful. Carroll's genius created a universal art form from his personal and social neurosis, and so did that of some of his compeers.

Freud observed that persons with the talent for creating wit often showed "dissociated [split] personalities and a predisposition to nervous afflictions." [1] Havelock Ellis, in *A Study of British Genius,* finds thirteen eminent persons, including Dodgson, Lamb, and Kingsley, who stammered, and says: "there can be no doubt whatever as to the abnormal prevalence of stammering among British persons of ability."

Max Eastman, who likes to challenge German professors, gives over his *Enjoyment of Laughter* to a critique of Dr. Freud. His book contains one striking contribution—the discovery of the human infant as the source of and authority on the nature of the comic, an idea which would appeal to Carroll's blend of playfulness and academicism.

A baby, tickled by its mother, by a stranger—playfully tossed toward one person, then actually thrown to another—this is the emblem of playfulness, of playful disappointment with substitute reward, which is the essence of jest, *provided* the baby knows it is all in fun. Freud overlooked these forms of the comic, forms without "tendency," hostility, aggression, sexuality, or feelings of superiority.[2] But Carroll and his brethren used all these forms, as well as satire, which is also neglected by the Viennese school, but covered by Van Wyck Brooks in his *Ordeal of Mark Twain:*

"A satirist . . . is one who holds up to the measure of healthy-mindedness the obscurantism of the Middle Ages; it is Molière holding up to the measure of an excellent sociality everything that is eccentric, inelastic, intemperate; it is Voltaire holding up to the measure of intelligence the forces of darkness and superstition; it is a criticism of the spirit of one's age, and of the facts in so far as the spirit is embodied in them, dictated by some powerful, personal, and supremely conscious reaction against that spirit."

The wits and dreamers and writers for children who repay comparison with Carroll were chiefly of his own country and time. We stretch the national group to include Hans Christian Andersen, and the temporal group to include Charles Lamb, who died when Carroll was two years old, since both had much in common with him.

They are, then, Charles Lamb, wit and dreamer; Edward Lear, wit; Charles Stuart Calverley, wit and parodist, some of whose works have been attributed to Carroll; Charles Kingsley, dreamer, reputedly a humorous talker, though his writings are gently satiric, sometimes bitter; Sir William Gilbert, wit and satirist, and once at least, in *Iolanthe,* master of fairy fantasy; Sir James Matthew Barrie, an unawakened dreamer with something that is usually called whimsicality, and a refined ferocious humor: Kenneth Grahame, similar to Barrie but healthier; George Macdonald, closer to Kingsley, though without the bitterness; and Hans Christian Andersen, dreamer, humorist, satirist.

John Ruskin knocks for admission here too, but he lacked something. He wrote for children, after his fashion, but Thalia was absent from his christening. His *King of the Golden River,* written for his young cousin Euphemia Gray, who lived to marry Ruskin and to elope with John Millais, is a moral tale without humor and, save for the word-painting, almost without charm. *Sesame and Lilies* and *Ethics of the Dust* must have produced Christian Socialist stigmata on thousands of upper-class girls, and may have drawn a few into some useful work, but the comic spirit that would have kept the books, and Ruskin's mind, alive, was missing. Of the others, not one really lost his wits, save Lamb, and he briefly. Lear suffered epileptic attacks all his life, but mad he never was. The others toppled wildly on their gyroscopic vehicles, yet never left the track. Perhaps humor is a form of self-medication as well as a social service.

Carroll carried, in addition to the tribal taboos shared with his neighbors, a load of personal taboos on the Freudian patent impulses of sexual and hostile aggression. His wit was a safety valve that helped keep him sane: hence the classic remark when he was congratulated about some prizes, "If I had shot the Dean I could hardly have had more said about it." Another safety valve Carroll used more freely than some of the others was his ability to evoke a dream state at will, to pull out the costumes and set his marionettes to work.

Alice is the critical intelligence and the loving heart passing naïvely through the life of her time, making quiet comments on war, politics, the academic spirit, education, human
relations, the arts and sciences—everything except religion.
Carroll, like Kingsley and Macdonald, withdrew there. All
three were committed to the Church of England; where in
other fields their criticism hews to the line, the Rock of Ages
stands without a chip. Their incurable gentility and belief in
the fatherhood of God kept them from completing the revaluation of all values that Nietzsche advocated, and that the
major satirists, from Aristophanes to Shaw, have dared. How
much of Carroll's and Kingsley's stammering came from their
incomplete revolt against their fathers and their fathers' God?

Every one of these brethren solved some of his problems
by different forms of wit and humor, and Lamb and Lear, as
well as Carroll, resorted to puns, which, says Dr. Freud, "can
be formed with very little effort . . . by a similarity of structure, sound, or initial letters . . . a bad play on words, because it does not play with the word as a word, but merely
as a sound." [1] This cheapness of effort cheapens the jest for
the reader. The pun curled at the heart of Carroll's *Novelty
and Romancement* destroys what is otherwise a sad funny
story—instead it is greeted by those uncouth noises that
herald a pun.

The pure jest is rare anywhere, and seems always to have
a symbolic core, such as the famous one in *The Hunting of
the Snark*, "Then the bowsprit got mixed with the rudder
sometimes." In the insult category Carroll is a master. The
subtlest example is Humpty Dumpty's challenge to Alice to
leave off growing at seven—she says "One can't help growing
older," and Humpty Dumpty answers, "One can't, perhaps,
but two can." The Mad Tea Party is of graceful insult all
compact.

One of Freud's weakest theses, betraying his own lack of
comic sense, attributes the comic to a feeling of superiority.
Carroll's best examples of the comic and naïve appear in
Sylvie and Bruno—for instance, Bruno's "bits from Shakespeare," each "bit" ending with a back somersault off the
stage.

"Humor," says Freud, "is the means of obtaining pleasure

despite existing painful affects. Unfortunate persons can gain humoristic pleasure and give the neighbors pleasure too. Humor can be enjoyed alone. *Galgenhumor* (gallows humor) is produced at the cost of a great expenditure of psychic work. Economy of sympathy is one of the most frequent causes of humoristic pleasure. Mark Twain's humor usually shows this mechanism." [1]

The White Knight is the apotheosis of humor, calmly enduring all his difficulties, philosophizing head down at the bottom of the ditch. Carroll's image of himself was the White Knight. Here is part of a letter to a little girl named Gaynor Simpson:

"As to dancing, my dear, I *never* dance, unless I am allowed to do it in *my own peculiar way*. There is no use trying to describe it: it has to be seen to be believed. The last house I tried it in, the floor broke through. But then it was a poor sort of floor—the beams were only six inches thick, hardly worth calling beams at all: stone arches are much more sensible, when any dancing, *of my peculiar kind*, is to be done. Did you ever see the Rhinoceros and the Hippopotamus, at the Zoölogical Gardens, trying to dance a minuet together? It is a touching sight." [3]

Dr. Freud again rides his favorite horse too far: "Displacement, false logic, absurdity, easy thinking, pleasure in nonsense, survive in the learning of children and in the adult under toxic influences." [1] He says that the child's play and the neologisms of the insane "afford an escape from the critical reason," just as drink does. But Carroll was essentially sane—his neologisms are partly pure play, partly camouflage, and they arose under no toxic influences other than the fears and taboos of his environment. He *did* need rest from the relentless logic of his conscious thought processes, and humor and topsy-turvydom gave him that rest. Nevertheless much of his nonsense cannot be considered "pure" nonsense, because it is apt to be more sensible than that which it supplants. For instance, Carroll's "Father William," nonsensical as it is, has more sense and dignity than Southey's original, with its portrait of a bargaining deity:

In the days of my youth I remembered my God
And he hath not forgotten my age.

Had Carroll used on Holy Writ the critical intelligence with which he pierced the apocryphal piosities of Southey, Wordsworth, and Watts, he would not have needed to drug himself nightly with puzzles, games, and Euclidean figures. Of his fellows, Kingsley and Macdonald were full-fledged Church of England parsons; Lamb, on the other hand, interrupted his schooling when he could go no farther without ordination. Calverley's father, like Carroll's and Kingsley's, was a clergyman, but Calverley seems to have escaped any spiritual conflict.

All these writers had a multiple relationship to the child, of which sympathy is one aspect. Freud missed, and Max Eastman uncovered, the simple childishness and pure fun in the comic. But Mr. Eastman overproves his case and sees "pure" nonsense where symbolism is also present. Carroll did have unusual sympathy with children and grasp of their viewpoint, but the cleverest child in the world could not have written the *Alice* books. Carroll is the last writer who could be cited as an example of "pure" nonsense, simply because his art permits him to meet his readers on numerous planes simultaneously, and to blend meaning with non-meaning in an irreproducible bouquet.

Mr. Eastman speaks of a recent play: "The pleasure derived from it was still a pleasure in pure nonsense—a childish pleasure, exactly of the sort you find so frequently in *Alice in Wonderland*." Later he quotes the passage from *Through the Looking-Glass*, where the Red Queen and the White Queen are explaining to Alice their system of having five nights at once—"five times as warm *and* five times as cold." He continues: "That too is pure nonsense dressed in the perfect appearance of sense." Logically however, it does make sense! Of the first stanza of *Jabberwocky* Mr. Eastman says: "These verses are superior to most rhymes, not only because of their musical perfection, but because they combine a completer nonsense with a more meticulous plausibility. Every meaningless word is designed with inimitable skill to suggest those words most rich in meaning which the poets choose. Compare them with cruder verse from Edward Lear."

But the very Carrollism of Carroll was that even *Jabberwocky* had meaning discoverable without too much of the German professorial method demolished by Mr. Eastman. While children are "purer" than Dr. Freud feared, without being as "pure" as Carroll hoped, neither they nor their play are entirely devoid of meaning. As the Red Queen said to Alice—"What do you suppose is the use of a child without any meaning? Even a joke should have some meaning—and a child's more important than a joke, I hope."

Much of Freud's interpretation of the dream applies to the daydream too, except that the latter, elaborated into an art form, becomes social. The creator of dream stories has an opportunity to communicate in universal symbols, and to utilize the sensations of vastness and freedom that originate in the unconscious. If the dream writer has sufficient scope, humanity, and wit, he may be a universal genius. Not all the other humorists fulfilled these conditions; but Lamb and Andersen, like Carroll, developed this dreamy quality. Andersen's stories too are beloved of children and grown-ups. Lamb's loss of his child audience in the last fifty years may be due to his deliberate archaism—he wrote an eighteenth-century English that repels a modern child more than Elizabethan idiom. How is it that Lewis Carroll felt the need for a "Girls' Shakespeare"? Lamb's *Tales* have all the good Elizabethan bawdiness filtered out.

Barrie struck twelve once—with *Peter Pan*—a subtly unwholesome sweetmeat, like most of his books. In *Sentimental Tommy* alone is the sentimentality absorbed by the character, leaving none for the presentation. Some of his plays, while reasonably harmless, are at best faintly debilitating. A commentator remarked that his extreme sentimentality was the mask and cloak of a basic heartlessness. He is poor daily bread for children—his perversity is too charming, and a child with an elfin tendency would find it too easy to live wholly in the Barrie dream-world—a world enervating for one who has to make his way on earth. Carroll's superiority

over Barrie is that his mawkish writings are his dull ones—
he never succeeds in making sentimentality seductive.

Charles Kingsley and George Macdonald each wrote one
book that is loved by children and adults. In both *The Water
Babies* and *At the Back of the North Wind,* a little boy
suffers poverty and trouble and dies. Kingsley's boy dies near
the beginning of the book, which continues his adventures as
a water baby. The child in *At the Back of the North Wind*
dies at the end, after somnambulistic absences that prepare
for his death. Neither of these books is sentimental—that is,
the authors show genuine tenderness for a genuine human
child. Kingsley and Macdonald were both fathers, and the
children of both were still writing affectionate memoirs about
their happy home lives well into the twentieth century. Calverley too had a family, and Kenneth Grahame wrote *The
Wind in the Willows* for his son, who died in early manhood.
Gilbert was happily married, Barrie unhappily; Lamb, Lear,
and Andersen, like Carroll, were bachelors, and—perhaps
also like Carroll—not by choice. Lamb proposed to Fanny
Kelly, who rejected him because "An early and deep-rooted
attachment has fixed my heart on one from whom no worldly
prospect can well induce me to withdraw it." Andersen yearned
for Jenny Lind; Lear had to consider his epilepsy; and Carroll, like the Cheshire Cat, fades out when we question him.

As to family lives, Lamb and Lear were brought up by
their elder sisters and Grahame by numerous aunts and
uncles (the "Olympians"), while Andersen and Barrie had
close emotional ties with their mothers—in Barrie's case too
close.

The lost child—Peter Pan; the misunderstood child—the
Ugly Duckling; the dream child—Lamb's Alice and John; the
dead child—Tom and Diamond; the changeling—Gilbert's
favorite theme; the cheated orphans in Kenneth Grahame's
stories—something unsatisfied, "something lost behind the
ranges" in every case. In part, at least, the lost, etc., child is
the author's own self, his lost youth, calling for rebirth in
beauty and humor; but of all these men, only Dodgson
identified himself with a girl child.

They have all been to the Never Never Land at the Back

of the North Wind, to the Snow Queen's country—to the edge of insanity; in Macdonald's case by imaginative projection only; in the case of Lamb, over the edge and back again. They all fetch a treasure from the borderland for readers who are too busy or too timid to explore for themselves the cold, dark, lonely places of the spirit.

Both Eric Partridge [4] and Elizabeth Sewell [5] compare Lear and Carroll. Mr. Partridge says, ". . . of Lear's blends (hardly less happy), several antedate Carroll's by at least nineteen years. Nor was he the first to use them, although he may have been the first writer to coin them deliberately.

"Jespersen says these . . . portmanteaus have played a part in word formation, e.g. blot black spot dot, twirl twist whirl.

"In the first *Alice* antipathies is the only malapropism. Looking-Glass, following Lear's second *Nonsense Book,* has more (but *Jabberwock* was partly written before)."

Dr. Sewell goes a great deal further. She is not looking for influences, but evaluating the amount of disturbance present in the two writers. She feels that Lewis Carroll's search for closed systems is a search for security of an intensity that goes almost to the brink, whereas she finds Lear sane although odd. She finds two separate systems, logic and nonsense, used by both writers, and refers all questions to Thomas Aquinas, because she agrees with Harry Morgan Ayres that Carroll especially had the makings of a "great scholastic."

She says, "Nonsense as practised by Lear and Carroll does not, even on a slight acquaintance, give the impression of being something without laws and subject to chance, or something without limits, tending towards infinity. . . . The unfailing mental delight, if one may use such a phrase, afforded by Lear and Carroll does not suggest an endless succession of random events, than which nothing is more boring, nor does it point to a universe out of control, frighteningly akin to lunacy.

". . . I think we are justified in regarding Nursery Rhymes as a useful addition to the Nonsense structure we are studying, and it is interesting that they, like the more literary forms of nonsense, have flourished more in England than anywhere else. . . .

". . . in the *Alices* themselves may be found the principles on which Nonsense is constructed. Lear provides Nonsense in an almost perfect state of simplicity, where the principles are acted on but not stated. With Carroll things seem to be different, for though he too is constructing Nonsense in words he is at the same time thinking and writing about words, and this may provide clues, even if, since this is Nonsense, the clues may seem a little odd."

Lamb, Kingsley, Gilbert, and Barrie, like Carroll, had dual personalities. Each one had a pseudonym for his second self —Elia, Parson Lot, Bab, and—what shall we say for Barrie? He called his second self MacConnachie, but he composed a whole letter to Ellen Terry in the guise of Sentimental Tommy, signing it "T. Sandys." Lamb wrote about "the late Elia" with all the detachment of one literary man writing the obituary of another, and Gilbert signed all his early poems and drawings "Bab." Kingsley was less clearly split from "Parson Lot," but he could slip back and forth between work and play moods with wonderful speed and lability.

Lamb and Kingsley made unsuccessful attempts to write for the theater. Andersen's plays were performed, but are now forgotten. Gilbert, in spite of his phenomenal success, grieved over the failure of his serious dramas. After six such failures, he decided that the public had spoken, and sensibly gave up. Only Barrie had complete success as a dramatist— for Gilbert without Sullivan was more poet than playwright. But it is easy to see how the make-believe world of the theater would appeal to these earnest playboy dualists.

Most of them had more of a quarrel with their destiny than writers usually do. Lamb, Lear, and Andersen had poverty-stricken homes. Lamb's life particularly reads like a nightmare. His aged parents and aunt sat about senescing till Mary stabbed her mother; then followed Mary's recurrent attacks, Charles's lifelong care of her, and his inability to escape the counting-house because she needed his support. He stammered, he drank, he smoked to excess; his quiet heroism, like his lapses, was lightened by his wit.

Lear was weighted with fears and mannerisms. He made his way from poverty to prosperous middle years, and he died in the loneliness he had always dreaded. His *First Book of Nonsense Verse* appeared in 1846, with his own illustrations; it is unthinkable that Carroll did not know it as a child. Mr. Madan found "no trace" of Lear in his library, but the book may have been in his father's home, or the boys may have passed around a copy at Rugby.

Andersen's father was a cobbler. Hans had a minimum of schooling, made unbearable by the teasing of his fellows. He was the original Ugly Duckling—awkward, gangling, countrified. Luckily he made a hit on the stage as a comic shepherd, and his success enabled him to remain in Copenhagen and receive the king's patronage for his education. He still hated school and fitted into no pattern. To the outer eye he can never have become a swan, but when he read his fairy tales aloud, drawing rooms hushed, cigars went out, knitting dropped—all harkened to the despised fairy tales he never would have bothered to write without his friends' insistence, so easily did they rise in his mind. Lewis Carroll's child friends too recall his never-ending stories. With another Alice to persuade him to write them, he might not have wasted so many years on his Dodgson pamphlets. And Andersen too hoped to base his enduring fame on a "serious" work about the Wandering Jew!

One who noted a resemblance between Carroll and Andersen was Harry Furniss, who said: "Lewis Carroll was as unlike any other man as his books were unlike any other author's books. It was a relief to meet the pure innocent, simple dreamer of children, after the selfish commercial mind of most authors. Carroll was a wit, a gentleman, a bore, and an egotist—and, like Hans Andersen, a spoilt child. It is recorded of Andersen that he actually shed tears, even in late life, should the cake at tea be handed to anyone before he chose the largest slice. Carroll was not selfish, but a liberal-minded, liberal-handed egotist, but his egotism was all but second childhood." [6]

Kingsley's hidden conflict with his father was different from Carroll's. The elder Kingsley was a fox-hunting squire, but when his family met with reverses he returned to college and took orders, for which he was unsuited. Charles Kingsley, an idealistic youth, said that his father had all the talents except that of using what he had. In contrast to his father, Charles suffered years of doubt before ordination, but he finally took orders whole-heartedly, as he did everything. Rather than criticize his father, perhaps, he became a crusader against larger evils, which really troubled him objectively too. He was one of the active founders of the Christian Socialists and the co-operative movement, and a Chartist to boot. Some of the abuses he fought were actually abolished or ameliorated in his lifetime, partly because of his efforts, but he never ceased to wrestle with his angel, and he said he had often been in hell. He too stultified his mind to refrain from religious criticism, but he was a vigorous and useful citizen. After being abhorred and attacked in his youth, and without changing his opinions in the least, he was lauded by Dean Stanley in Westminster Abbey after his death. He was the most energetic of the lot, and the only one to see other than literary results from his work.

Gilbert cannot easily be capsuled in a paragraph. He was a complex oddity—partly a typical burly blunt John Bull type Englishman—but he carried within him the pixy that made fun of himself and all traditions. He suffered from the conviction that he was an ugly man, though this was hardly true, except perhaps by contrast with his beauty as a child, when painters begged him to sit for them. Another odd childhood experience may have given him a slant toward melodrama— he was actually kidnaped by Italian brigands at the age of two, and ransomed for £25! The ugliness theme runs through all his works—"the rich attorney's elderly, ugly daughter" sings contralto in every opera, and the changeling child is almost as constant. But Gilbert, like Kingsley, had a social vision that transcended his personal grievance, so a few words will not do him justice.

It is a temptation, however, to polish off Barrie with a very few words, right out of a case book—mother complex plus Scotch Calvinism. Some of the critics are pretty harsh with Barrie, and there seems to be an agreement that there was something seriously wrong even with his art form—that it is closer to a neurosis than is permissible, and that its effects are literally sickening rather than heartening. Still it would be hard to part with Peter Pan, if only because he is such a perfect portrait of the wrong boy for a healthy Wendy to fall in love with.

Kenneth Grahame's trouble is clear and simple. His parents died when he was small, and, along with his brothers and sisters, he was raised by aunts and uncles who took good physical care of him, but were stupid and unimaginative about their promises. The Grahame children seem to have been high-strung and fanciful: the motive for flight is evident, and was later strengthened, perhaps, by fifteen years in the Bank of England.

Macdonald shows no injury to his personality and no hardships in his environment. His life, both artistic and familial, seems to have been uniformly happy and fruitful, and he died at an advanced age, surrounded by an adoring family. But he seems to have had a touch of Scotch mysticism and a distinct intuition for psychological truths that were not officially uncovered till after his death. For instance, his novel, *The Portent,* about a somnambulistic woman and her cure, exactly parallels a cure of a post-traumatic amnesia reported by Boris Sidis many years later. In both the true and the fictional story, there is total dissociation of personalities, and the cure in each case consists in repeatedly evoking the original personality until a crisis is reached, when both personalities clamor for recognition and a fusion finally takes place. Macdonald's story seems to have sprung from purest intuition, without even a personal neurosis as a springboard.

Another bond certain of these brethren had with Carroll is their love of drawing. Lear, Kingsley, Gilbert, and Andersen had distinct talent. Gilbert made not only drawings, but also cardboard figures and floor plans for all his operettas; Lear made his living as a painter of birds and landscapes; Andersen drew well and made fascinating paper silhouettes for children's birthdays—but the adults often begged or stole the little figures.

M. Cammaerts says: "The enormous success of the *Book of Nonsense* was no doubt due to the intense satisfaction and sincere artistic pleasure derived from the perfect harmony existing between the pictures and the text. . . .

"The power of Lewis Carroll was more limited, and it remains an open question whether he would have been able to illustrate adequately the two books on *Alice* if he had followed the impulse which led him to illustrate the first. The quality of his sketches is very unequal, but when he succeeds, as in the four drawings illustrating the ballad of 'Old Father William,' his technique follows Lear's very closely, and he remains faithful to the spirit of grotesque simplicity which distinguishes his master's works and which we might be allowed to call 'the Nonsense Style in Art.' " [7]

Calverley comes last because he had little in common with the rest, except his ability as a parodist. Emotionally he seems to have been the healthiest of them all. He was a fortunate youth who because of jolly escapades transferred himself, in advance of a request from the college authorities, fom Balliol College, Oxford, to Christ's College, Cambridge, and distinguished himself by being the first man in history to receive first prize from both colleges for Latin composition. He was active and physically courageous; had not his health been ruined and his life shortened by a fall on the ice, he might have had a brilliant career in his choice of professions. His "Questions on the Pickwick Papers" have been, quite comprehensibly, attributed to Carroll. His parody on Rossetti is indeed Carrollian:

BALLAD

The auld wife sat at her ivied door
Butter and eggs and a pound of cheese
A thing she had frequently done before
And her spectacles lay on her aproned knees.

The farmer's daughter hath soft brown hair
Butter and eggs and a pound of cheese
And I met with a ballad, I can't say where,
Which wholly consisted of lines like these.

Carroll and Calverley both honored the same poem with a parody; only two stanzas of Calverley's are given here:

DISASTER

I never loved a dear gazelle
But I was given a parroquet—
(How I did nurse him if unwell!
He's imbecile, but lingers yet.)

He's green, with an enchanting tuft;
He melts me with his small black eye:
He'd look inimitable stuffed,
And knows it—but he will not die!

This is Carroll's version:

I never loved a dear gazelle
Nor anything that cost me much:
High prices profit those who sell,
But why should I be fond of such?

To glad me with his soft black eye
My son comes trotting home from school;
He's had a fight but can't tell why—
He always was a little fool!

But, when he came to know me well,
He kicked me out, her testy Sire:
And when I stained my hair, that Belle
Might note the change, and thus admire

And love me, it was sure to dye
A muddy green, or staring blue:
Whilst one might trace, with half an eye,
The still triumphant carrot through.

The original of both versions was from Thomas Moore's "Lallah Rookh":

I never nurs'd a dear gazelle
To glad me with its soft black eye
But when it came to know me well,
And love me, it was sure to die.

Carroll recognized his affinity to Calverley, and planned to collaborate with him, but the plans fell through, except that the identity of the paraphrase in the first line of this poem imples some mutual understanding, for the original reads:

I never raised a young gazelle.

John Macy says: "Calverley was a scholarly amateur: his three hundred pages of translations from Greek and Latin cost him more labor and no doubt seemed to him more important than his hundred pages of original verse. Yet in those few pages he became the father of English parody." [8]

After studying all the other men who were comparable to him, after thoroughly examining the *ambiente* for the not-Carroll, it should be easier to say what *was* Carroll, and Carroll alone. As closely as X can be communicated, then, it was his flavor. It was more than flavor, it was taste—his exquisite taste, his perfect delicacy of feeling, his considerateness, his accurate balance.

What Carroll lacked was what all England lacked—abandon. The Apollonian gospel had triumphed over the Dionysian to such an extent that one had to travel at least to Scotland or Wales to find even a presentable household goblin, such as Chesterton attributed to the Macdonald home. In England there remained only those wishy-washy fairies whose portraits Gertrude Thomson completed in time for *Three Sunsets* to be printed—after Carroll's death. They might as well have been angels and done with it. How would an Englishman have responded to a Scandinavian kobold or any of the witches and goblins Gorki inherited, along with nothing else, from his grandmother? The Englishman would have recited a few stanzas from Watts—at least until Carroll laughed him out of church—or have converted the kobold into a busy bee. Carroll may not have succeeded in his task of spiritualizing the pig-child, but he did make friends in adult life with symbolic crocodiles and fabulous monsters, as in his childhood he played with actual frogs and worms. In Looking-Glass land all this is sensible, nor is there anything odd about a draftsman whose best drawings were made with an old box camera, a dramatist whose only operetta was written by someone else, or an immortal poet whose greatest poetry was in prose form.

Chapter 15

The Bridge

Every idea of mine, that cannot be expressed as a Syllogism, is really ridiculous.

As THE RIVER BROADENED more and more between Lewis Carroll and the Reverend Charles Dodgson, his need grew for an ever stronger and more elastic bridge by which he might slip, unobtrusively, back and forth. Such a bridge, firmly rooted in both sides of his personality, and stretching at need, he wove inextricably from the powerful gossamer threads of his games of logic and mathematics, and his logical and mathematical games.

But the contradictions were not only in his own mind, though he was the suppressed guinea pig who best embodied them. That famous untrue story about Carroll and Queen Victoria points the moral—the story that the Queen, after reading *Alice in Wonderland,* asked for his other works and received a packet of abstruse mathematical pamphlets. The story is doubly untrue; first, Carroll specifically controverts it in the Advertisement to *Symbolic Logic.* Second, no mathematician considers Dodgson's works in the least abstruse, nor did he make such pretensions for them. Specialists consider his writings elementary, not because they are always easy in the layman's sense, but because they do not use the calculus. (Yet his tutor, Professor Bartholomew Price, published several works on the calculus.) Dr. Warren Weaver says, ". . . the more elementary aspects of calculus represented the upper limits of Dodgson's mathematical flights, and . . . even in calculus, he had such vague and inaccurate notions about infinitesimals that one must confess that he lagged behind the best knowledge of his times." [1] In logic Dodgson's place is somewhat higher, but it is still as poet that he functioned best. As Weierstrass said, "It is true that a mathematician who is not also something of a poet will never be a perfect mathematician."

Charles took his B.A. at the end of 1854, just at a favorable moment for a young mathematician. Eric Bell says: "The year 1855, which marks the death of Gauss and the breaking of the last link with the mathematicians of the preceding century, may be taken as a convenient point of reference. In 1855 Weierstrass (1815-1897) was forty; Kronecker (1823-1891), thirty-two; Riemann (1826-66), twenty-nine; Dedekind (1831-1916), twenty-four; and Cantor (1845-1916), a small boy of ten." [2] But Dodgson was, to some extent, carried by the stream; in his own time he cut no channels, though today we may see some of his work on the levee. In a letter, Dr. Bell says: "His range was about that of a freshman today in a good technical school, though the freshman would have clearer ideas about elementary things than C.L.D., and would not be so far behind his own times mathematically as C.L.D. was behind his all through his mathematical life." [3]

Yet in his character, and especially in childhood, Dodgson showed some of the stigmata of the greater mathematicians. Like Newton's, his childish games were creative and inventive, and, like Newton, he beat up the school bully, though, unlike him, he did not rub his adversary's nose on the church wall. Like Leibniz, he invented games based on the theory of probabilities, and like Abel and Jacobi, he had a passion for inverting problems. But he gave little study to his predecessors, except to Euclid: nor did he give much more to his contemporaries. Dr. Bell says again: "British mathematicians have often serenely gone their own way, doing the things that interested them personally as if they were playing cricket for their own amusement only, with a self-satisfied disregard for what others, shouting at the top of their scientific lungs, have assured the world is of supreme importance." [2] This criticism was justly aimed at Dodgson more than once.

But he asked good questions, though he posed some of them in forms that straddle two fields and are, for that reason or others, unanswerable as he presented them. The question seventeen-year-old Charles asks in his *Rectory Umbrella*— "Where Does the Day Begin?"—is still unanswered. In that form it is necessarily unanswerable, and it is little better as he presented it in his lecture before the Ashmolean Society. "If a man could travel round the world so fast that the sun would always be directly above his head, and if he were to start traveling at midday on Tuesday, then in twenty-four hours he would return to his original point of departure, and would find that the day was now called Wednesday—at what point of his journey would the day change its name?" To break this question down and deal with it justly requires the most modern astrophysics, relativity, non-Euclidean geometry, semantics, syntax, and logic. It was typical of the questions he was asking all his life, in his classes, in his rather insignificant mathematical and logical textbooks, and much more cogently in his poetic works, which, nevertheless, would have failed of their prophetic and provocative significance if he had been less conscious of and less curious about mathematical processes and their common sense, everyday relations. When an astronaut has seen three sunsets and three dawns in five hours, is he three days older?

Dodgson hovered all his days tantalizingly close, not so much to solving his problems, many of which still seem insoluble, as to catching the boat that was going his way and making at least part of the journey as co-pilot. For instance, he was close enough to Faraday to take his picture (and to use an electrical machine for making a little girl's hair stand up and produce a photograph of a frightened child without actually frightening her—much). That he never grasped Faraday's discovery of the atomic nature of electricity and its importance for modern science is not so strange, since Faraday himself did not make the proper deduction from his experiment, leaving it for R. A. Millikan to do in our own time.

But he could have known, studied under, and read the works of Henry John Stephen Smith, who preceded him at Rugby by only a few years, whose master, like Dodgson's, was Bonamy (not Bartholomew) Price, and whose father like Dodgson's received a laudatory letter from Dr. Tait. Surely Smith was held up to Dodgson as an example all through Rugby, and, since Smith was made fellow of Balliol in 1849 and was Savilian Professor of Geometry from 1860-83, and gave the only contemporary lectures in any British university on modern geometry, it would seem that Dodgson might have sought him out. Dr. Bell says: "Carroll could have got straightened out on geometry in one hour, if he had consulted Smith," [3] so we must assume he did no such thing.*

While close enough to Todhunter to borrow some of his illustrations for *Euclid and His Modern Rivals,* he seems not to have read Todhunter's *History of the Theory of Probabilities* (published 1865). Like Leibniz, Pascal, and other founders of that method, Dodgson took an interest in games and betting, and wrote numerous papers on aspects of calculation—tournaments, voting, ciphers, the eight-hour law, new games and new rules for old games, all based on attempts at simplification or justice, all mathematically ingenious, and all as practical as the White Knight's plan to dye his whiskers green, and always use so large a fan that they could not be seen.

Willard Gibbs was a Yankee solitaire whose life span closely approximated Dodgson's, and whose ellipse intersected his at two known points, though neither cut shows on Dodgson's life line. Both men contributed to *Mind,* and Gibbs and his friend the astronomer, Hubert Anson Newton, chuckled together over *A Tangled Tale* and the puzzles from *Alice.*[4] Awareness of Gibbs (who said "Mathematics *is* a language"), as of Riemann, Lobatchewsky, Clausius, or Boole, would have altered Dodgson's whole understanding of mathematics, so it cannot be assumed—rather, it may almost be said to be disproved.

Dodgson was close enough to Riemann and Boole to be asking himself their very questions—but not to read them. He owned Boole's book, but it is easier to suppose that he failed to read it, than that he failed to use Boole's methods after reading him. The only reference to Boole in the diaries is dated November 20, 1884: "In these last few days I have been working at a Logical Algebra and seem to be getting to a simpler notation than Boole's [The Mathematical Analysis of Logic. 1847]."

Bishop Strong, who had plenty of opportunity to observe Dodgson and sympathized with his complexities, claimed he preferred to work out problems by himself rather than to read what had been written on his subject. A "gift of eccen-

* See Appendix I.

tric originality," the Bishop calls it. Dr. Bell prefers to say "obstinate and willful ignorance."

As to Riemann, the case is clear. In *Euclid and His Modern Rivals,* which is *not,* despite the title, about non-Euclidean geometry, Dodgson mentions no truly non-Euclidean geometer. The nearest is Legendre, whom he praises, with the one qualification that his book is too difficult for beginners. But Legendre was early, and missed an essential point. Dr. Bell says: "He tried to prove an equivalent of Euclid's parallel postulate; but his proof is vitiated by his tacit assumption (which he overlooked) that 'space' is necessarily infinite." [3] Without Riemann or his equivalent, Dodgson could hardly have made the leap to non-Euclidean geometry. In one of his other little books, however, his *New Theory of Parallels,* he tackles the very problem which was the springboard for non-Euclidean geometry, Euclid's axiom about parallel lines. Dodgson saw the difficulty about treating it as an axiom, thereby lifting himself out of the company of circle-squarers and angle-trisectors with whom those innocents are classed who lack that insight. In fact this very *New Theory of Parallels* includes a hopeful quietus to the circle-squarers themselves, who had descended on Dodgson in their inky hordes after the death of Augustus De Morgan left them without a sympathetic correspondent. His particular pacifier is a series of hexagons inscribed in a circle.

As Cassius J. Keyser says: "Euclid's fifth postulate differs from all the others . . . and there is no better proof of the subtlety and power of the old Greek geometer than his assumption as undemonstrable that which required twenty-two centuries to prove such." [5] In his *New Theory of Parallels* Dodgson takes this approach: "Will the gentle reader be so kind as to join me in contemplating, for a few minutes, the Infinite Space which surrounds our tiny planet? We believe —those of us, at least, who answer fully to that ancient definition of Man, *'animale rationale,'* that it *is* infinite. And that, not because we profess to have grasped the conception of Infinity, but because the contrary hypothesis *contradicts* Reason: and what contradicts Reason we feel ourselves authorized to deny. *Both* conceptions—that Space has a limit, and that it has none—are *beyond* our Reason: but the former is also *against* our Reason, for we may fairly say 'When we have reached the limit, what then? What do we come to? There must be either Something, or Nothing. If Something, it is *full* Space, 'plenum'; if Nothing, it is *empty* Space, 'vacuum.' That there should be neither of these is absurd. Such an hypothesis is most [in]tolerable.' " (For here is one proofreader's error that slid by him—it is printed "tolerable.")

Here he shows himself a jump ahead of Legendre, realizing *what* he is assuming about the nature of space—and Ruskin is a jump ahead of him. The latter's book, *Elements of Perspective* (1860) shows a grasp of the geodesic which hints at the solution: "This line is properly, in each case, called the 'sight-line' of such plane; but it is only properly called the 'horizon' in the case of a horizontal plane, and I have preferred using always the term 'sight-line,' not only because more comprehensive, but more accurate; for though the curvature of the earth's surface is so slight that practically its visible limit always coincides with the sight-line of a horizontal plane, it does not mathematically coincide with it, and the two lines ought not to be considered as theoretically identical, though they are so in practice."

Dr. Bell asks why Dodgson should have ignored the works of William K. Clifford, "probably the most brilliant geometer Britain produced in the 19th century. . . . His translation of Riemann's paper 'On the Hypotheses which lie at the Bases of Geometry,' appeared in *Nature* in 1873. Dodgson, if he ever read this masterpiece—it must have been available in his college library—never gave any evidence of having understood what it was all about." [2] Dr. Bell asks further whether Clifford's professed atheism might have scared Dodgson off. Indeed it might. On the Euclidean question, Clifford has this to say: "He knows, indeed, that the laws assumed by Euclid are true with an accuracy no direct experiment can approach . . . but he knows this as of Here and Now; beyond his range is a There and Then of which he knows nothing at present but may ultimately come to know more." [6] If these two men could have pooled their intimations of relativity . . .

The above problem is handled perhaps most neatly in Coxeter's *Non-Euclidean Geometry*. "For a line to be unbounded and yet of infinite length, it merely has to be reentrant, like a circle. The great circles on a sphere provide a model for the finite lines on a finite plane, and, when so interpreted, satisfy the modified postulate. But if a line and a plane can each be finite and yet unbounded, why not also an n-dimensional manifold, and in particular the three-dimensional manifold of the real world? In Riemann's words of 1854: 'The unboundedness of space possesses a greater empirical certainty than any external experience. But its infinite extent by no means follows from this; on the other hand, if we assume independence of bodies from position, and therefore ascribe to space constant curvature, it must necessarily be finite, provided this curvature has ever so small a positive value.'

"According to the General Theory of Relativity, astronomical space has positive curvature locally (wherever there is matter), but we cannot tell whether the curvature of 'empty' space is exactly zero or has a very small positive or negative value. In other words, we still cannot decide whether the real world is approximately Euclidean or approximately non-Euclidean."

Dodgson's question, as always, was a good one. As usual, he posed it so that it must be restated to answer it. What provokes Bishop Strong, however, and his other academic critics, is the playfulness with which he presents his perfectly valid and fundamental problems. Yet it is that very playfulness which makes him so quotable, and in the good sense provocative.

Today the top men in the physical sciences, philosophy, mathematics, logic, and semantics not only work together as a world society, pooling their results, criticizing one another's works, and trying to deliver a coherent picture of the functioning universe, but they make conscientious and often brilliantly readable attempts to share the advances with the common man (*homo non-mathematicus*). And while textbook writers only occasionally and gingerly evaluate some obscure work by Charles Dodgson, the poetical-mathematical philosophers quote Carroll freely—e.g., Eddington, Russell, Whitehead, Millikan. And Carroll has forged ahead of Dodgson among the professors and textbook writers as well—Clement V. Durell, William Garnett, R. B. Braithwaite, A. S.

Russell, Warren Weaver, D. B. Eperson, and R. M. Eaton all quote him.

A little book which is *sui generis* is Philip E. B. Jourdain's *The Philosophy of Mr. B*rtr*nd R*ss*ll*. This is a satire on Russell's detractors and on illogic wherever found, and quotes extensively not only from Russell but from the *Alice* books, *Snark, Sylvie and Bruno,* and the puzzles and paradoxes. The book is in good standing, for it was incorporated in the first edition of Russell's *Mysticism and Logic.*

One logical question, first proposed by Aristotle, was more fully stated by Dodgson in a form used by Zeno, and was answered by Russell and Whitehead in *Principia Mathematica.* Carroll's essay, "What the Tortoise Said to Achilles," is to be found in *Logical Nonsense,* in *Mind,* Vol. IV, 1895, and, with the caudal pun amputated, in R. M. Eaton's *General Logic.* Aristotle says: "If behind the prior stands no primary, we could not know the posterior through the prior (wherein they are right, for one cannot traverse an infinite series); if on the other hand—they say—the series terminates and there are primary premisses, yet these are unknowable because incapable of demonstration, which according to them is the only form of knowledge. And since thus one cannot know the primary premisses, knowledge of the conclusions which follow from them is not pure scientific knowledge nor properly knowing at all, but rests in the mere supposition that the premisses are true."

Dodgson's form of this is based on Zeno's (evidently he would read predecessors if they wrote in Greek). Dr. Bell says: "A quantity which approaches zero as a limit is called an infinitesimal. An infinitesimal is not necessarily an exceedingly small quantity; the smallness is not the important matter, but the fact that it can be made small. Zeno's paradox of Achilles and the tortoise rested on infinitesimals. Achilles was a certain distance behind the tortoise and attempting to overtake it. Zeno argues that he can never do so, for, says he, while Achilles is traveling half the distance the tortoise has moved forward, etc. If these half distances were traveled in finite intervals of time Zeno's argument would be correct. But the intervals of time are approaching zero as well as the distance." [2]

In the Carrollian essay, Achilles tries Euclid's first Proposition on the Tortoise:

"(A) Things that are equal to the same are equal to each other.

"(B) The two sides of the Triangle are things that are equal to the same.

"(Z) The two sides of the Triangle are equal to each other.

" '. . . Z follows logically from A and B, so that anyone who accepts A and B as true, *must* accept Z as true.' "

Achilles sets himself the task of forcing the tortoise to accept the hypothetical "If A and B are true, Z must be true." In this form it too is insoluble. Professor Harold N. Lee, of Newcomb College, New Orleans, writes: "In Russell and Whitehead's *Principia Mathematica,* the primitive proposition 1.11 (p. 94) is stated in a manner different from that of the other primitive propositions, and it is pointed out that it, as a principle of inference, is not to be confused with a true theorem about implication. It has to stand outside of the system of the true theorem about implication. (In this connection, 1.11 is also a principle of inference, but I consider it to be a corollary of 1.1, and not an independent principle.) Professor H. M. Sheffer thus distinguishes between those primitive propositions he calls 'prescripts' and those he calls 'descripts'; and the 'prescripts' must stand outside of the 'descripts.' Carroll's essay is the first place that points out the necessity of this distinction as far as I know. In *Principia* at 1.1, Russell refers to his discussion in his *Principles of Mathematics,* section 39. Here he has a page-long treatment of Carroll's essay." [7]

Eaton handles it a little differently. He says: "That an act of violence (i.e., judgment, belief) is necessary to break a chain of *implications* and effect the passage to an *inference,* is amusingly illustrated by Lewis Carroll's imaginary discussion between Achilles and the Tortoise. The Tortoise refuses at each step to accept unconditionally the implication, which Achilles proposes, as true, thus generating a new and more complex implication." [8]

Dr. Bell says: "In current terminology, the question he raised is one of metalogic (or of metamathematics.) The 'standing outside' is the important thing; recognition of this state of affairs is comparatively recent; it has become of fundamental importance in the discussion of certain of the classic paradoxes. . . . Evidently Dodgson knew what he was doing; he could not have foreseen how influential remarks like his were to become after 1920." [3]

But in his own day Dodgson was no more regarded than regarding. W. E. Johnson, whose three-volume work on *Logic* long remained a classic, speaks as follows of Carroll's "Logical Paradox," which also appeared in *Mind* (Oct., 1894, the year before "Achilles"), and was reprinted in the *Picture Book:* "The consistent application of this interpretation yields the above solution to the whole problem and reduces to equivalence the four propositions numerated in Mr. Lewis Carroll's note. . . . The solution is however independent of any particular views that I have here brought forward, and would be endorsed by all logicians who have applied the rules of logic to complicated problems, though the answers might assume various apparently different forms." But Bertrand Russell, in his *Principles of Mathematics* gives it a footnote: "The principle that false propositions imply all propositions solves Lewis Carroll's logical paradox in *Mind*. . . . The assertion made in that paradox is that, if p, q, r, be propositions, and q implies r, while p implies that q implies not-r, then p must be false, on the supposed ground that 'q implies r' and 'q implies not-r' are incompatible. But in virtue of our definition of negation, if q be false both these implications will hold the two together, in fact, whatever proposition r may be, are equivalent to not-q. Thus, the only inference warranted by Lewis Carroll's premisses is that if p be true, q must be false, i.e. that p implies not-q; and this is the conclusion, oddly enough, which common sense would have drawn in the particular case which he discusses."

This is in line with what Mr. Russell says in his *Inquiry into Meaning and Truth:* "Outside of pure mathematics the important kinds of inference are not logical; they are analogical and inductive." It is certain that Dodgson guessed that, but he could not prove it to his own satisfaction; the tools were shaping, but he had not access to them, and could not complete the process unaided.

Dr. Strong tells of Dodgson's attempts, of which *Through the*

Looking-Glass was the art form, to solve common sense problems by mathematics or logic, or at least to relate the processes he understood to the life forms which baffled him. Sometimes he would ask his class at Christ Church, "If it takes ten men so many days to build a wall, how long will it take 300,000 men?" Invariably some member of the class would give a very small figure as the answer, and Carroll's hope was never fulfilled of finding an undergraduate who could see what he was driving at. In mild despair he would say, "You don't seem to have observed that that wall would go up like a flash of lightning, and that most of those men could not have got within a mile of it." [9]

This was one of his eternal problems. Dr. Strong says: "Why should a sum worked accurately fail when it comes in contact with mere details of fact? It would be natural to assume that figures if trustworthy at all would lead to infallible results. His system of logic was really an attempt to deal with ordinary sentences and ideas as if they were mathematically defined, so that by processes of a quasi-mathematical character, infallible conclusions could be reached."

Or, as Bertrand Russell says again in his *Inquiry,* "The purpose of words, though philosophers seem to forget this simple fact, is to deal with matters other than words. If I go into a restaurant and order my dinner, I do not want my words to fit into a system with other words, but to bring about the presence of food. I could have managed without words, by taking what I want, but this would have been less convenient." This is one approach. Another is that taken by Von Mises, in his *Probability, Statistics, and Truth.* (Dr. Bell quarrels with the translation and his suggested improvements are in brackets.) ". . . the old disparity between purely mathematical concepts with their 'endless precision' and the realities of the physical world.

"What is the ultimate value of Heisenberg's uncertainty relation [principle]? We must see in it a great step towards the unification of our physical outlook. Until recently, we thought that two different kinds of observations of nature existed, statistical observations on the molecular scale whose results are of an exactly predetermined [previously determinable] character. . . . We now realize that no such distinction exists in nature . . . a certain apparent contrast between the two parts of physics has disappeared with the advent of the new concept of matter."

At times Dodgson seems reaching out for the then unborn techniques of general semantics, some of whose creators and disciples quote him rather freely. For instance, Alfred Korzybski uses three quotations—not from *Through the Looking-Glass* this time, but from *Wonderland*, in his *Science and Sanity*. Dr. Korzybski says: "The need of International Languages, or a *Universal Language* besides mathematics, is becoming increasingly urgent . . . the possibilities of the Basic for a scientific civilization are unlimited, *provided* the Basic is *revised* from a non-Aristotelian, non-identity, point of view." If these concepts had matured in his time, it seems likely Dodgson would have echoed them heartily, and contributed to them. Yet when Dr. Strong tried to lead him in this very direction, he shied away.

The Bishop says: "I tried to raise the question of the relation of words and things, but he always declined to write on this problem." [9] His reason may actually have been diffidence, for in relation to his logical and mathematical works he was consistently—and becomingly—modest. Save in the field of morals, where his standards were angelic and unattainable, his self-evaluations were objective and reliable, and indeed his eminence depends neither on his textbooks nor on his pedagogy.

Considering the abstractness of the problems that interested him, and his total lack of interest in or sympathy for the run of undergraduates, it is not surprising that, careful and conscientious as he was, he was considered a poor teacher. A. S. Russell says: "I asked one of them [his former pupils] if Carroll's lectures were bad. He said they were as dull as ditchwater. I asked another if he was a poor tutor. He said that he and others once signed a round robin to the head of the college, asking to be transferred to other hands. Dodgson himself probably realized his deficiencies here, for though his tutorial duties were slight, he gave them up before he was fifty." [10] Most Oxford writers would not even speak of him as a "tutor," though he tutored undergraduates in mathematics. The distinction is that those called "tutors" were assigned certain students to whom they taught some subjects, rather than, as in Dodgson's case, certain subjects to be taught to all comers. The few who were reading for Honors in Mathematics were the few who fell to Dodgson. Dr. Strong said he was mathematical lecturer but never tutor. "The main part of his teaching must have been concerned with the arithmetic and Euclid necessary for the responsions. . . . Those who went to his lectures probably went in a class and not singly." [9] Dr. Bell says: "The indicated material of C.L.D.'s lectures shows the incredibly low level of mathematics in the Oxford curriculum of his day." [3]

In his diary for November 30, 1881, Dodgson wrote: "I find by my Journal that I gave my *first* Euclid lecture in the Lecture-room on Monday, January 28, 1856. It consisted of twelve men, of whom nine attended. This morning, I have given what is probably my *last:* the lecture is now reduced to nine, of whom all attended on Monday: this morning being a Saint's Day, the attendance was voluntary, and only two appeared—E. H. Morris, and G. Lavie. I was lecturer when the *father* of the latter took his degree, viz., in 1858.

"There is a sadness in coming to the end of anything in life. Man's instincts cling to the Life that will never end." [11]

But as far as teaching went, the best was in store for him. In his last years he taught logic at the Girls' High School in Oxford, and at Lady Margaret Hall and St. Hugh's College. Here the pupils as well as the subject interested him, and all testimony shows that he was an unusually fine teacher!

His books on logic were two—*The Game of Logic* (1886) and *Symbolic Logic, Part I,* 1896. He also wrote nine *Papers on Logic,* 1886. R. B. Braithwaite quotes Jowett's remark that "logic is a dodge," and says "Carroll tried to make it as good a dodge as possible. Carroll's dodge was to interpret all propositions in terms of the existence or non-existence of classes, and then to represent the classes by regions in spatial diagrams and their existence or non-existence by putting counters or marks in the appropriate regions. . . . Carroll's innovation is confined to his using square diagrams which permit of an extension to a greater number of classes than do

Venn's circles and ellipses . . . He was thinking about the nature of hypothetical propositions, consideration of which has largely influenced recent developments in logic . . . necessity in inference for an act of violence to cut the chain of hypothetical propositions . . . for Whitehead and Russell's first elementary proposition—anything implied by a true proposition is true . . . Lewis Carroll was ploughing deeper than he knew. His mind was permeated by an admirable logic which he was unable to bring to full consciousness and explicit criticism. It is this that makes his *Symbolic Logic* so superficial and his casual puzzles so profound. Logic has two closely related tasks—the analysis and criticism of inference and the analysis of the propositions or judgments that are used in the inference. . . . Humpty Dumpty must take an honorable place among those who have attempted to free us from the bondage of symbols that are our own creation." [12]

Jabberwocky has been used for teaching English grammar, by Professor Charles Carpenter Fries, in his book *The Structure of English* (Harcourt Brace, New York, 1952). He quotes the first stanza, following with Alice's remark " 'Somehow it seems to fill my head with ideas—only I don't exactly know what they are.'

"What are the 'ideas' she gets and how are they stimulated? All the words that one expects to have clearly definable meaning content are nonsense, but any speaker of English will recognize at once the frames in which these words appear.

" 'Twas——, and the——y——s
Did——and——in the——;
Al——y were the——s,
And the—— ——s——.'

"The 'ideas' which the verse stimulates are without doubt the structural meanings for which the framework contains the signals. Most of these nonsense words have clearly marked functions in frames that constitute familiar structural patterns. These 'ideas' seem vague to the ordinary speaker because in the practical use of language he is accustomed to dealing only with total meanings to which lexical content contributes the elements of which he is conscious."

Professor Carpenter uses the insights gained from *Jabberwocky* as Xrays to expose some underlying structures of the language. This is one case of proliferation from a Carrollian leaf that would certainly have pleased and fascinated the beamish boy himself.

C. I. Lewis' *Survey of Symbolic Logic* gives him the following footnote: "See Lewis Carroll's *Symbolic Logic* for the particular form of the square diagram which we adopt. Mr. Dodgson is able, by this method, to give diagrams for as many as ten terms, 1024 subdivisions."

Dr. Bell says: "As a mathematical logician, he was far ahead of his British contemporaries. If he had lived in Germany, instead of in England, the story would have been quite different: he had in him the stuff of a great mathematical logician." [3] Yes, or if he had read the German books published in his time, or if he had not loaded the dice against himself in the ultimate proposition . . . He could neither master it nor leave it alone.

In a letter to Miss Thomson, Dodgson wrote: "All my mathematical books are published at a loss; & the new book, although I dare say it will pay *ultimately,* is a heavy outlay to begin with: & my worldly means won't stand much more loss." [13] But his logico-mathematical unimportance was in no way due to a lack of natural ability, nor of hard work. He took a First in Mathematics when Bosanquet, later one of the chief logicians of his time, took a Second, and he showed interest and talent in mathematics from childhood, when he begged his father to explain logarithms to him.

Since his achievements fell short of his abilities, he must be considered relatively to have failed. Instead of dignifying logic and mathematics for themselves, he played with them as escape forms. In literature, that is permissible and even desirable, so that his literary *opera* were works of art, but logic and mathematics, *as such,* demand to be taken seriously. He tried to create two forms—one was a brilliant success, the other a still-birth. But the same blood flowed in both—the same questions he posed unsuccessfully in his textbooks, in the Mad Tea Party and in the colloquies with Humpty Dumpty and the Tweedle brothers, turn into magic crumbs that bring the winged answers to our window sills.

Two straws hint that logic and mathematics were playthings rather than serious avenues to truth: First, he was minutely particular about form, and second, he was less particular about meaning.

The journal, *Nature,* to which he had been a contributor, wrote shortly after his death:

"A characteristic of all his work was the absoluteness of expression at which he aimed, so that his definitions and proofs should be logically perfect. This carried a certain severity into his work, since, as he himself remarked, a semi-colloquial style is apt also to be semi-logical, as nothing is more easy to forget, in an argument which is interwoven with illustrative matter, than what has, and what has not, been proved. It further tended to require the repetition of what might for exactness have to be a somewhat cumbrous periphrasis, to prevent which, therefore, he introduced a number of new terms and symbols; few of these, however, have been adopted into general use, although of the latter some are extremely expressive, and in his hands were of great value." [14]

Now what *was* the meaning about which he wished to be so exact? Dr. Strong says: "It is true that the diagrams and mathematical formulæ are often extraordinarily ingenious, but the assumption which was at the bottom of the whole speculation will not bear investigation. In the *Logic* Mr. Dodgson carried to the most violent excess his habit of developing unexpected results and unnoticed inferences. He tried to give words a sharply defined meaning, as if they were mathematical symbols, but also conveyed negative information in various directions. And all this had to be drawn out and taken into account in his system. Besides his principle of analysis, Mr. Dodgson was ruled by a great belief in formulæ in which letters (as in algebra) took the place of words. This confidence naturally led him to think of sentences as mere forms of which the concrete meaning was insignificant. Thus, if anyone were to attempt to solve the complicated problems which are set at the end of *Symbolic Logic,* he would find that the actual propositions occurring in them are quite irrelevant. Any propositions would do quite as well, whether they had a rational meaning or not, provided they contained the requisite number of symbols." [15]

One difficulty here is that Dr. Strong uses the word "logic" in the modern sense, which, as Professor Lee points out, "insists on the use of variables which do not have concrete meaning, such as Carroll insisted on and Dr. Strong does not seem to like." [7] Dr. Strong is asking of Dodgson something he never postulated or pretended to. And Dr. Bell says that the very absence of "concrete meaning" makes for correct logic. . . . Dr. Strong continues: "Mr. Dodgson's originality of mind was his chief danger. He read comparatively little of the works of other logicians or of mathematicians who had dealt with the same subjects as himself. He preferred to evolve the whole out of his own mind without being influenced by others. There was a gain in this but there was also a loss. . . . If the latter [*Symbolic Logic*] is a failure as a logic, it is surely because a gift like his of eccentric originality lends itself but poorly to rigid analysis and systematic exposition." [15]

Granted, then, his exactness, and even more the poverty and in fact indifference of his content, it is still questionable whether this was wholly because of the *quality* of his mind—that "eccentric originality" which produces better poetry than textbooks—or whether here again his difficulty was not with the artificial *direction* he had imposed on that mind, whose originality expressed itself in meaningless arabesques because he dared not shoot straight at the question—"Is the faith of my fathers logical? Does it fit in with common sense? Is it certain and eternal? Or will it crumble if I examine it too closely?" Dr. Bell calls attention to the introduction to *The New Theory of Parallels*, in which Carroll lauds pure mathematics in these terms: "The charm lies chiefly . . . in the absolute *certainty* of its results: for that is what, beyond all mental treasures, the human intellect craves for." This Dr. Bell relates to the scourge of Puseyism, the search for Absolute Truth, and all that was the reverse of Dodgson's adumbrations of relativity. Poor Jacob, wrestling nightly with his angel, lamed, muffled, courageous, making a jest of his halting gait, forever in agony lest he discover irrevocably that the "Great Architect of the Universe now begins to appear as a pure Mathematician." [16]

Some basic crippling that forced him to grind away at an often empty mill might explain the inefficiency of his marvelous mind machine—the incessant hard work, the little to show for it, except when the little was so perfect, as in the *Alice* books, that it would be ingratitude to ask for more. About *Symbolic Logic* he said: "It has cost me *years* of hard work, but if it should prove, as I hope it may, to be of real service to the young, and to be taken up, in High Schools and private families, as a valuable addition to their stock of healthful mental recreations, such a result would more than repay ten times the labour that I have spent upon it." The mountain labored and brought forth a dancing mouse. Of *The Game of Logic*, it is only necessary to say that it was a kindergarten version of the later book, and in both books the premises are genuine Carrollisms.

Dr. Weaver says, "Lewis Carroll was, in a tantalizingly elusive way, an excellent and unconsciously deep logician. But when he tried to approach logic head on, in a proper professional way, he was only moderately successful. It was when he let logic run loose that he demonstrated his true subtlety and depth. In fact, for a full measure of his stature as a logician we must look into Wonderland." [1]

It is probable that his attempt at sweetening logic for the young (consciously!) was never really successful. Mr. Hudson got his friend Marghanita Laski to try the *Game of Logic* with her children. They enjoyed it at first, "But after page thirteen, there was no use pretending it was a game for children any more. . . .

"I think—I hope—that the other seventy-five pages of the book were meant for post-graduate university students, for I gave them up when my children did.

"We played the game a second time at their insistence, and a third at mine. After that, it went into the book-shelf, and was brought out only for adult guests."

The most pretentious of his mathematical books, *Euclid and His Modern Rivals*, is signed by Dodgson, but contains considerable Carroll material. It was still in use as a textbook in English schools in 1930. In the prologue he says: "I am content to run some risk, thinking it far better that the purchaser of this little book should *read* it, though it be with a smile, than that, with the deepest conviction of its seriousness of purpose, he should leave it unopened on the shelf." Fortunately he reverses here the position he took in the in-

troduction to the *Treatise on Determinants*. The latter made
no ripple, and the former is still read, necessarily with a
chuckle, for it lifts some leaves from *Alice*.

" 'For they can *not* be *not* parallel . . .'

" 'Should I be justified in calling this a somewhat *knotty*
passage?' "

When the Mouse's tale suddenly came to a "not," it will be
recalled, Alice said: "A knot! Oh, do let me help to undo it!"

Or this echo of the White King's conversation with Alice
when she saw Nobody coming down the road, and he complained that his eyesight barely allowed him to see somebody.

"Niemand: The final list, was it? Well, ask your friend
whether since the drawing up of that list, any addition has
been made: he will say, Nobody has been added.

"Minos: 'Quite so.'

"Niemand: 'You do not understand. *Nobody*—see you not?'

"Minos: What—You mean—?

"Niemand: (solemnly) I do, my friend, *I* have been added
to it!

"Minos: (bowing) The committee are highly honored, I am
sure.

"Niemand: So they ought to be, considering that I am a
more distinguished mathematician than Euclid himself, and
that *my* Manual is better known than Euclid's. Excuse my
self-glorification, but any moralist will tell you that I—I alone
among men—ought to praise myself."

The ghostly melting away at the end is reminiscent of his
dream books—in fact the whole is supposed to be the dream
of an over-tired examiner. Yet not all a dream. Once Dodgson really did undertake to correct papers, and did it so
thoroughly that he was up all night.

The book contains "eighteen propositions, of which no one
is an undisputed axiom, but all are real and valid theorems,
which, though not deducible from undisputed axioms, are
such that, if any one be admitted as an axiom, the rest can be
proved." On the contentious "axiom" about parallel lines,
Minos says: "An absolute proof of it, from first principles,
would be received, I assure you, with absolute rapture, being
an *ignis fatuus* that mathematicians have been chasing from
your age down to our own."

"*Euclid:* I know it. But I cannot help you. Some mysterious flaw lies at the root of the subject. Probabilities are all I have to offer you. Now suppose you were assured, with regard to two finite lines, placed before you, that when produced in a certain direction, one of them *approached* the other, that is, contained two points, of which the second was nearer, to the other Line, than the first, would you not think it probable— if not absolutely certain—that they would meet at last?

"*Minos:* Utilizing, as I suppose you will allow me to do, my knowledge of the properties of *asymptotes*, I should say 'No. The mere fact of *approach*, granted as to lines, does not secure a future *meeting*.'

"*Euclid:* But . . . you will find, I believe, an eternal distinction maintained in this respect, between straight and curved Lines: so that Lines of the one kind *must*, if they approach, ultimately meet, whereas those of the other kind need not."

If only to these ghosts could be joined the ghost of poor Dodgson, murmuring, "But if space is curved, thereby insuring the curvature of all lines . . .?" Whether or not he is now in the heaven he foresaw in *Sylvie and Bruno,* where all of mathematics would open to him, he has notably helped to bring that heaven nearer on earth. Clement V. Durell calls the Theory of Relativity the "reply of modern mathematics to the prayer of Roger Bacon." He speaks of the world of Alice behind the looking-glass, which he calls the world of Alicia and Euclid. "A young lady . . . seeing an inverted image of herself in a large concave mirror, naïvely remarked to her companion, 'They have hung that mirror upside down.' Had the lady advanced past the focus of the mirror, she would have seen that the workmen were not to blame. If Nature deceived her, it was at least a deception which further experiment would have unmasked."

And the Presidential Address to the London Branch of the Mathematical Association in 1919, entitled, "Are We Living Behind a Convex Mirror?", was given by Professor William Garnett, who, in the *Mathematical Gazette,* uses *Alice Through the [Convex] Looking-Glass* as an "easy introduction to the conception of variable units of space and mass, and so prepares the mind for the Theory of Relativity."

In *The Nature of the Physical World,* Eddington refers to Carroll five times. One quotation follows: "Mr. Wells in *The Time Machine* and Lewis Carroll in *Sylvie and Bruno* give us a glimpse of the absurdities that occur when time turns backwards. If space is 'looking-glassed' the world continues to make sense, but looking-glass time has an inherent absurdity which turns the world drama into most nonsensical farce."

D. B. Eperson says: "Dodgson certainly showed the superiority of Euclid's geometry as a logical treatise, while the Modern Rivals have succeeded in providing us with less formal and less formidable textbooks which are better suited to the adolescent mind." Perhaps this is damning with faint praise, but the same A. S. Russell who spoke of his poor teaching says: "In the small world of elementary geometry, arithmetic, and algebra he was a supreme master."

Dr. Taylor has called attention to Dodgson's foreshadowing of Abbott's *Flatland* by twenty years. The introduction to *Dynamics of a Parti-cle* begins, "It was a lovely autumn evening, and the glorious effects of chromatic aberration were beginning to show themselves in the atmosphere as the earth revolved away from the great western luminary, when two lines might have been observed, wending their way across a plane superficies.

"The elder of the two had by long practice acquired the art, so painful to young and impulsive loci, of lying evenly between his two extreme points, but the younger, in her girlish impetuosity, was ever longing to diverge and become an hyberbola or some such boundless and romantic curve."

Dr. Taylor thinks this is Lewis Carroll and Alice: "Yes! we shall at length meet, if continually produced!" But ". . . the superficies continued to intervene." [17] It is of course quite possible he was telling his love for Alice in this characteristically cryptic fashion; it is even possible he believed she returned his love, but Wing Commander Hargreaves was very firm about the impossibility of this. Alice Liddell did quite enough in firing his genius—let us ask no more of her.

There is one clear piece of evidence against Alice's ever having felt romantic about her White Knight. One of the Liddell family stated positively that a member of the royal family was in love with Alice, that she reciprocated, and that this was considered an impossible match, which takes care of the fact that she married rather late. Mr. Hargreaves came upon the scene and carried off the prize, but not immediately. He proposed to her on the steps of Covent Garden, after the opera.

Dodgson's last mathematical work appeared in the issue of *Nature* that announced his death. Says Mr. Russell: "It was a new way of doing long division shortly. A case he gave in illustration was the division of 867815921857031527640092 by 9993. This was typical of the things that interested him . . . In his *Pillow Problems* the reader was invited to prove in his head that three times the sum of three squares is necessarily the sum of four squares, to evaluate to a mere matter of a hundred terms the series of products 1x3x5, 2x4x6, 3x5x7 . . . to visualize the points on a plane on which three cylindrical towers of different breadths had been set up, at which all would appear equally broad, or to find new expression for the chance that if an infinite number of rods got broken one of them at least would break exactly in the middle. The fact that the problems were done in Dodgson's head is most informing. It is a pity that he did not write an account of his methods of doing mental work. Light on the difficult problem of how calculating boys do their sums is very badly wanted. He might have made a most valuable contribution there."

He suggests his methods in the introduction to the book of *Pillow Problems* which he wrote to pass the time for other insomniacs. It must have been germinating for many years. He says: "When I first tried this plan, easy geometrical problems were all that I could manage; and even in these, I had to pause from time to time, in order to renew the diagram, which *would* persist in getting 'rubbed-out.' Algebraical problems I avoided at first, owing to the provoking fact that, if one single co-efficient escaped the memory, there was no resource except to begin the calculations all over again. But I soon got over both these difficulties, and found myself able to remember fairly large numerical co-efficients, and also to retain, in the mind's eye, fairly complex diagrams, even to the extent of *finding my way* from one part of the diagram to another. The *lettering* of the diagram proved such a troublesome thing to keep in the memory, that I almost gave up using it, and learned to recognize points by their situation only."

This is the same man who, on returning the greeting of a man on the street, asked politely where they had met before. "I was your host last night," the other responded. Carroll's memory was no weaker than his logic. If both failed him, it was because of preoccupation in the first case, and prejudice in the second. For even when he was working at mathematics, as we have seen, part of his mind was still occupied with his religious difficulties, or perhaps he used the mathematics as a screen against his worries. The lifelong struggle to maintain the repressions set up in his early years drained his energies, side-tracked his mind, and prevented it from functioning freely. To this ever-present tension alone can be attributed the unimportance of so clear and original a mind in its chosen fields.

One more work by the Carroll-Dodgson firm, with Carroll directing and signing it, has now been reprinted in the Everyman edition of *Alice,* and in the later omnibus editions. Dover Editions has come out with a paperback edition of *Pillow Problems* and *A Tangled Tale,* in one volume, and *Symbolic Logic* and *The Game of Logic* in another. This work is amusing enough to read, though only an inveterate gamester would work out the one or more algebraic problems supporting each chapter. The story is *A Tangled Tale,* first published in 1886 uniformly with the facsimile of *Alice's Adventures Underground,* and illustrated by Arthur B. Frost.

Carroll asked another of those extraordinary questions, this time giving his own answer: "If a cat can kill a rat in a minute, how long would it be killing 60,000 rats? Ah, how long indeed! My private opinion is, that the rats would kill the cat." *Do* bats eat cats?

Capt. Raymond Rallier Du Baty's *15,000 Miles in a Ketch* (Thos. Nelson & Sons, London, n.d.) contains evidence that Edwin Dodgson might have enlightened his brother on this question. The captain's book, which seems to have appeared around 1910, says:

"In the time of the last chaplain Mr. Dodgson, the brother, I am told, of Mr. Lewis Carroll who wrote a famous book called *Alice in Wonderland,* there was a plague of rats which threatened to destroy the whole population by eating up all their sustenance.

"They came to Tristan on a schooner called the *Henry B. Paul,* which was run ashore on the far side of the island, four miles away from cultivated ground. The islanders ignored the clergyman's plea that these ship rats should be at once exterminated, believing that they would not give trouble, as they were so far away.

"In the course of a few months, during which they bred tremendously, the vanguard of an army of rats appeared among the potato fields and devoured everything on their march. Then with reinforcements they turned to the wheat-fields and devoured the corn. With relentless ferocity they next attacked the rabbits, which were also prolific in the island and waxed fat on their prey. Now they invaded the settlement itself, and seemed to have no fear of the human inhabitants, who on their side had become panic-stricken.

"It reminds one of the Pied Piper of Hamelin. Grey rats, brown rats, fathers and mothers, uncles and cousins, fat old fellows, and frisky youngsters came in battalions to the houses of the Tristan folk; scrambling over the stone walls, into the tussock-gardens and the cattle-pens, getting into the lumber sheds, and invading the front parlours and the back bedrooms of the stone-built cottages. On one occasion, when Mr. Dodgson was going to bed, he saw what he imagined to be his black kitten on the bed, a comfortable resting-place. Cats were imported into the island to exterminate this plague, but the rats exterminated the cats!"

A Tangled Tale is made up of several interwoven stories, resolving at the end. Nearly half the volume is appendix—the answers to the problems, both those received from readers during serial publication, and Carroll's own. In these magazine ventures, like a modern columnist, he habitually achieved a chatty, intimate relationship with his readers, as in the "Syzygies" he published in *The Lady.* And he introduced this chatty manner into some of his mathematical works. He was one of the early humanizers and popularizers of science. If his mathematical works had been more successful, his influence would have been greater in this direction too. He debunked, so far as he could, the Heap Big Medicine Man complex. Like Alice among the strange creatures of Wonderland, he addresses a hypothesis by a punning name and causes the lion of science to gambol like a lamb. Then, striding from hummock to hummock, he attains the minute eminence of *Symbolic Logic.* . . .

His eternal game of hide-and-seek with himself gave birth to infinite little games—too many to list here, though they do belong on the Bridge. They are listed in the *Bibliography,* the *Handbook,* and the catalogue of the Parrish Collection (available in the New York Public Library). Dover has also republished *The Lewis Carroll Picture Book,* under the title *Diversions and Digressions of Lewis Carroll,* also in paperback. This book contains many of the games, riddles, and so forth. The games are amusing for children on a railway journey, or for adults who are bored because the journey seems less interesting than the destination. Carroll invented his games to kill, not boredom, but fear—the fear that his mind would carry him to unsuitable conclusions.

Some of his games had notable results. The game of falling down the rabbit hole, of stepping through the looking-glass, and some of the elfin games in *Sylvie and Bruno* made a deeper impression on modern readers than his conscious scientific works. It was as poet that he functioned best. Perhaps Alice's remark to the White Knight, when he fell off his horse once too often, best describes his career:

" 'I'm afraid you've not had much practice in riding,' she ventured to say, as she was helping him up from his fifth tumble.

"The Knight looked very much surprised, and a little offended at the remark. 'What makes you say that?' he asked, as he scrambled back into the saddle, keeping hold of Alice's hair with one hand, to keep himself from falling over on the other side.

" 'Because people don't fall off quite so often, when they've had much practice.'

" 'I've had plenty of practice,' the Knight said very gravely: 'plenty of practice!' "

He gives Alice a long dissertation on riding, falling off twice more while elucidating with gestures.

" 'Plenty of practice!' he went on repeating, all the time that Alice was getting him on his feet again. 'Plenty of practice!' "

Chapter 16

The Sword of Tweedledum

"There's only one sword, you know,"
Tweedledum said to his brother; "but you can
have the umbrella—it's quite as sharp."

As a last social gesture, Mr. Dodgson accepted the Curatorship of the Common Room in 1882 following the resignation of T. Vere Bayne, who had held it for twenty-one years. Dodgson resigned in a year, but it took eight more years to make the resignation finally effective; in that time he wrote about eight hundred letters a year on Common Room business. He kept the ledgers himself as well, except for about a pound's worth of clerical help annually, paid for out of his own pocket. He ordered the wines, took charge of the servants and the cat, attended to decoration and repairs, including the electric bell (on the agenda for nine years), took the responsibility for magazines and newspapers, introduced afternoon tea in 1884, and made as many improvements as he could slip or push past a rather obstructive committee.

The Common Room, kept open from 8:00 A.M. to 10:00 P.M., was the club to which Senior Students and their guests retired after dinner in Hall, for wine, dessert, and conversation. In the daytime it was used for reading and writing, tea, and more conversation. Wine and groceries were also sent out to the rooms of Senior Students, the wine cellar containing about 25,000 bottles.

After dinner in the majestic Hall, with centuries of Christ Church men looking down on them from the walls, the members of High Table and their guests made their exit through the huge doors to the great staircase, where the portraits were beginning even then to encroach. (In 1930 a posthumous portrait of Dodgson too, by Herkomer, scowled rather grimly near the beautiful fan-vaulted ceiling he loved and defended in his *New Belfry* pamphlet.) The diners moved on to the

Common Room for wine or dessert, reading or sociability, with smoking, in those days, in a separate room.

The rooms were out of repair, and needed new wall papers, new tiles for the fireplace, better lighting and ventilation, more comfortable chairs, and especially more efficient management. All this was busy work for Dodgson, and effectively kept him from writing anything of importance. During those nine years, apart from mathematical works and numerous pamphlets, he published *A Tangled Tale, The Nursery "Alice,"* and *Sylvie and Bruno* (Volume I). None of these are of prime importance, and the draining off of time and energy into curatorial channels may have destroyed, and certainly hindered, his creativity.

The first of his *Curator* pamphlets begins:

"TWELVE MONTHS IN A CURATORSHIP"
BY ONE WHO HAS TRIED IT.

"This book is NOT a plagiarism—as its name might at first suggest—of *Five Years in Penal Servitude*. Nor, again, is it meant to traverse precisely the same ground as *Six Months on the Tread-Mill*. There is a GENERAL resemblance, no doubt, to both the above works: still, it may be claimed for the present memoir, that it deals with SOME phases of humanity not hitherto analyzed, and narrates SOME woes that are peculiarly its own.

"An apology is needed for its great length: but I have not had time to condense it into smaller compass."

The *Curator* pamphlets, amusingly written, but basically trivia, are hard to read and hard to leave alone, because, though heavily corked, they have a tantalizing aroma of Lewis Carroll. They unfold a drama of the sort that takes place whenever a reformer tries to improve by reason and good sense over traditional slovenly methods. Man loves nothing so much as his habits, and loves no one so little as the innovator who tries to apply common sense to common activities. Add to this the quiet, superior, smiling stubbornness of the Cheshire Cat, and the Cheshire Cat's ability to fade out when demands for his execution grew too strong, and it is easy to see how exasperating Carroll must have been in Oxford, where people had been muddling along since the days of Henry Simeonis.

The *Curator* pamphlets, beginning in 1884, became more and more frequent. In 1886 Carroll issued *Three Years in a Curatorship, by one whom it has tried:*

"And now, within the last few days, the Common Room, ever anxious to oblige their Curator in all things, had devised a new Code of Rules, which fitted him to a T, like a new pair of handcuffs—a Code of Rules which, as they fondly hoped, he would welcome as something really striking and stringent."

"This was the Code":

"RULES FOR THE WISE-COMMITTEE":

"1. There shall be a Wise-Committee consisting of one person, excluding the Curator, whose duty it shall be to assist the Common Room in the management of the Curator.

"2. The member of the Committee shall be self-elected.

"3. No business shall be transacted, unless at least one member of the Committee shall be present. . . .

"5. Nothing shall be done, or left undone, by the Curator without the concurrence of the Committee. And, if the Curator shall complain of cold, it shall be the duty of the Committee to make things warm for him."

Another excerpt: "An old member of Common Room had come to Oxford, who always took pale brandy and soda at dinner, and there was nothing but brown in the cellar. 'What am I to do?' groaned the agonized Curator. 'It will take 3 days to get a Committee meeting to settle from what merchant to get supplies—4 days to get the samples—6 days more to get a meeting to select the brandy and fix the price to put on it—and 4 days to get it. That is over 3 weeks, and the poor old man only stays a fortnight!' So the Curator ordered a bottle of pale brandy on his own initiative, and was accused of 'trampling on the liberties of Common Room!' " This may have been based on fact, for there seems to have been a don, identified only as living at Tunbridge Wells, who was after Carroll's scalp. Could this have been the mathematician Sylvester, who did indeed retire to Tunbridge Wells?

Another section of this pamphlet, "Of the Transactions of the Year," begins:

"Transactions are of two kinds, those done and those not done: we will take the former first."

Carroll describes his activities in connection with the ledgers, the coal cellar, the bookshelves, daily papers, new tiles for the fireplace, the experiment of five o'clock tea. The transactions not done must be quoted:

"(1) The re-organization of the electric bell which was originally presented to C.R., in 1870, by Mr. R.H.M. Bosanquet.

"In the record of Meetings of C.R., under date Nov. 30, 1874, I find the following entry:—

" 'Agreed that the electric bell, with the wires, reaching to the Curator's chair, be put in order after having been destroyed two years ago by Mr. S. Owen. Mr. Baynes, Lee's Reader in Physics, arranged this.'

"Nine years have elapsed since this record was made, but the kind feeling, which prompted the offer of Mr. Baynes, is as strong as ever. There can be no doubt that he will be as good as his word, and that the wires will be put in order.

"There have been many other things not done during the year; but I will not further tax the patience of my readers."

Under "Last Words" he concludes:

"When, more than two years ago, I resigned my Lectureship, I looked forward to having (if life and health were given me) some years, before one's powers should begin to fail, for original work. A year after that I, most reluctantly, took the Curatorship, in which not only have I had very hard work (how much I cannot now estimate, but I know it has often lasted from morning to night), but there has also been, owing to circumstances I need not detail, a certain amount of worry —and it takes a very small amount of that, I fear, to unfit me for all such work of my own as I have referred to.

"The hard work is now done, and the future work of the office will probably be trifling: but I feel now that I really *must*, if possible, free myself from further hindrance in the shape of worry.

"I cannot expect anyone to enter into the intensity of my wish to be free from all risk of further worry, in order to do more of the work I have referred to, but I do hope to be believed when I assure C.R. that I am not simply preferring my own pleasure to theirs. The mere pleasure of doing one kind of work rather than another is but a feather in the balance: and money considerations go for nothing: My motive is, most truly, that what I want to do is work for others, and work for which, somehow, I seem specially meant."

With such deprecating words about his own true work, he also hinted that if he were not re-elected, he would not be offended, any more than "the urchin on the village green," who had just broken a window, would mind not being noticed. But they again elected him, on his own terms, and he remained more or less happy, and more tantalizing than ever, for another three years, now and then emitting a rabbity squeak.

In his first attempt at resignation, in 1889, he says that in his six years as Curator he has tried to act "fairly and handsomely" toward all. Now he finds his hands tied and refuses to change his procedure, preferring to resign. He must have carried his point, for it was more than three years before his resignation was accepted. He must have had *some* fun with his quiet sabotage and passive resistance to the Juggernaut of ancient tradition, but the other old fogies must have gnashed their teeth when he laid about him with his wooden sword.

Under the date of May 17, 1889, Mr. Green quotes a passage from Sir Michael Sadler's diary, a passage which Sir Michael got from Barclay Thompson: "T. Vere Bayne was Curator of Common Room. He had no wine committee. He *would* lay in sherry. Dodgson worked out by Calculus that it would last—if he went on at that rate—for 300 years. Using this Dodgsonian calculation, Barclay moved at a C.R. meeting that there should be a wine committee. This was carried. Bayne resigned. Dodgson came over to Barclay in a corner of C.R. and said that he (Dodgson) would never become stiff and autocratic like Bayne. Dodgson was elected Curator. In a fortnight he had become 'clothed with brief authority' and was angrily irritable at any suggestion of change. He drew up a long list of rules. Quickly he himself broke them. Barclay drew attention to this, in moving for amendment. Dodgson was very angry. . . ."

Gems from the pamphlets will bear rereading:

"I may venture to call attention (though in such guarded language as not to incriminate myself) to Rule I, which states that the 'duty of the Committee, (including the Curator), shall be to assist the Curator.' Hence, logically, it is the bounden duty of the Curator 'to assist himself.' I decline to say whether this clause has ever brightened existence for me— or whether, in the shades of evening, I may ever have been observed leaving the C.R. cellars with a small but suspicious-looking bundle, and murmuring, 'Assist thyself, assist thyself!' "

It is odd to see how relaxed Dodgson was about drinking, taking a moderate amount of wine daily and apparently never thinking of it as a danger or a vice, except in excess. About smoking, however, he seems to have had one of his usual difficulties. Mr. Hudson speaks of this "horror of tobacco," but this must be restricted to his own rooms. He often records sitting with the gentlemen in the smoking room till one or two o'clock, and never with any comments.

Mr. Hudson has one story, however, which bears out his statement at least in the case of Dodgson's own castle. "In 1879," says Hudson," he had staying with him Gibson Bowles, editor of *Vanity Fair*. Bishop C. M. Blagden saw him sitting disconsolately on the stairs. When he asked what he was doing there he found that Bowles, returning to Dodgson's rooms, had said very humbly, 'I suppose that I couldn't have a pipe here, could I?' and was met with the answer, 'You know that I don't allow smoking here. If I'd known that you wanted to smoke, I would have ordered the Common Room Smoking Room to be got ready for you.' " [1]

He dealt with the question of co-operative wine-merchants in his own way. "I hold that even if we could get equally good wine, cheaper, from co-operative stores, we ought not to do it: this may raise a smile among those who hold that some, who fail to see that we have any duties towards our tradesmen, recover their keenness of vision when considering *their* duties to us. Still, as nothing would convince such persons, I need only say that, so long as I have the honor of being Curator, I shall not leave any tradesman who has served us well, without a much better reason than the saving of a few pounds." He quotes a book called *From Vineyard to Decanter,* to the effect that the co-operatives charge more for wine than individual merchants, perhaps to make up for losses in other departments, and that their labels are often unsatisfactory because their men are not experts.

An early reading of *Alton Locke* awakened Carroll to some of the problems of poverty and brought the idea of the co-operatives to his attention. The reasons he gave for not supporting them himself were practical ones, but his temperament was essentially individualistic. He was far from indifferent to suffering, however—if it was called to his attention.

On March 4, 1892, he finally succeeded in breaking away: "A memorable day for me. I have long wished to resign the Curatorship, but no successor seemed ready. Now, however, having heard that Strong was willing to be elected, and Common Room ready to elect him, I most gladly resigned. The sense of relief, at being free from the burdensome office, which has cost me a large amount of time and trouble, is very delightful. I was made Curator Dec. 8, 1882, so I have held the office more than nine years."

Edwin Dodgson, whom his brother in their schooldays had called "vulgar but well-intentioned," retained the second characteristic at least. After his ordination, of his own choice he became Vicar of the island of Tristan da Cunha, a volcanic rock in the mid-Atlantic, visited by terrific gales, and inhabited at that time by no more than seventy or eighty persons. The Society for the Propagation of the Gospel, in 1876, had provided £100 a year to support a clergyman at Tristan, but Edwin Dodgson was the first volunteer to be accepted, in 1881, when he sailed on the "Edward Vittery" from East Africa, arriving in March. No sooner had Mr. Dodgson landed than the schooner was wrecked in the harbor, and most of his books and other belongings were lost.

Tristan was still prosperous at this time, and was still visited about once a month by ships, mostly whalers, that left provisions. Edwin Dodgson was welcomed and found the island a pleasant place, where no crime or even quarrels were to be found, and remarkably little illness. Peter Green, an aged Hollander, ruled the population; in 1883 he and Mr. Dodgson had a dispute. Meanwhile the ships were falling off, and so was Mr. Dodgson's health. By 1884, when H.M.S. "Opal" called at the port, the pastor was ready to leave. He brought back reports to England that, since the whaling grounds were changing, the islanders suffered considerable hardship—they were no longer able to obtain flour, salt, brandy, sugar, tea, rice, coffee, blankets and material for clothing.

Before Edwin Dodgson left Tristan, he must have been corresponding with Charles about the problems of the islanders. On September 27, 1883, Charles enters in his diary: "Heard from Edwin, who strongly approves my idea of getting all the Tristan folk moved to the Cape."

By October 19 of that year, he writes, "Went to town by the 9 A.M., to make a beginning in the business about which I heard from Edwin."

On December 30, 1885, he writes: "Edwin joined me, and we called on Lord Salisbury at the Foreign Office, and had a talk (not very fruitful, I fear), on Tristan da Cunha. However, it may have done good simply to bring Edwin into personal relations with him."

Without including all the diary entries, Mr. Green summarizes what was apparently a protracted and exhaustive siege of several government departments, to move the Tristan people either to the Cape or Australia.

On March 4, Edwin Dodgson wrote to the Admiralty concerning an article he had seen in the Sydney newspaper about an unsuccessful attempt of the inhabitants to induce a passing ship to stop. About the same time a letter arrived from Peter Green, relating that some six months before their one lifeboat and all fifteen of their able-bodied men had been lost in this same attempt to reach the passing ship.

Finally Charles Dodgson approached his Oxford friend, Sir George Baden-Powell, who was Kirkdale representative in the House of Commons, and an expert on the colonies. On May 25, 1886, Baden-Powell introduced the question of Tristan da Cunha into Parliament. It was arranged for H.M.S. "Thalia" to visit the island, carrying £100 worth of provisions and Edwin Dodgson, whose passage and board were to be paid by the Admiralty. He believed that the island should be vacated altogether, but he did not succeed in convincing the inhabitants. As a matter of fact, though the British Government was prepared to transport them to Cape Colony, the

Cape Government answered that there was little chance of their making a living there.

The Admiralty arranged for a ship of war to call annually, and Edwin Dodgson stayed on, teaching the children and carrying on his pastoral duties, until December 12, 1889, when he and nine others left on the steamer "Curaçao." The vicar was quite ill this time, and had been deprived of bread and butter for two months and of tea for ten. This was his last attempt to live on the island.

Charles Dodgson, moved by the plight of a handful of variegated Christians, living on a South Atlantic rock in un- usual circumstances, was less able to understand the English workingman's difficulties in making a living under more fa- miliar conditions. *Alton Locke* moved Charles to wish there was something he could do, but grasp the philosophy behind the co-operatives he could not. So he impenitently continued to buy Common Room supplies from the local tradesmen.

He held on to the Curatorship until the summer of 1892, and the nature of the final argument is easy to surmise. Cramped as he was by the rules of his own private world, pressure from without or conformity to rules not of his own making was exceedingly painful. So he resigned, as he should have done effectively at the end of the first year, for the *Curator* pamphlets, amusing as they are in a bitter way, are a poor substitute for the works of Carrollian fancy they cuckooed out of his brain.

Alas, the poor White Knight—how consistently he allowed himself to be deflected from that which only he could do, to that which could have been done equally well by any con- scientious mediocrity, and in fact need never have been done at all!

Chapter 17

Bill the Lizard

"Never!" said the Queen, furiously, throw-
ing an inkstand at the Lizard as she spoke.
(The unfortunate little Bill had left off writing
on his slate with one finger, as he found it
made no mark; but he now hastily began
again, using the ink, that was trickling down
his face, as long as it lasted.)

CARROLL TOO went on writing, and like Bill and the other
jurors, when he ran out of ideas wrote down dates, ages, and
other figures, and reduced the sum to shillings and pence.
When his writing tools, like Bill's, were out of order, he wrote
anyway, and sometimes he too "made no mark." When he
ran out of masterpieces, he tossed off pamphlets, puzzles,
mathematical works of graduated degrees of unimportance,
and even *Sylvie and Bruno,* probably the most work for the
least reward. He was an incorrigible doodler, and sometimes
even his writing became a doodle.

The medieval university, like Amherst, supported a poet
in residence—but unintentionally. The chair of poetry was
never offered to Carroll, nor the chair of English literature,
established only two years before his death. As Mein Herr
remarked in *Sylvie and Bruno,* he was examined once and for
all on graduation; by taking high honors, accepting ordination, and rejecting matrimony, he was able to live rent free
for the rest of his life, much of it in the most sumptuous suite
in the college. The grant was not for his contributions, such
as they were, to logic and mathematics, any more than for
his literary excellence. He played the game, won the prize,
and the matter was closed. A practical joke by an invisible
joker benefited everybody, and Mr. Dodgson by another name
was considerably sweeter. Had there been anybody to question
the ancient ruling that gave him a Studentship, anyone to
check up on the use he was making of his time and his for-

midable set of rooms, it would have been a scandal. After he resigned his lectureship, his duties were self-imposed only, and when he was not actually creating a masterpiece, he filled most of his time with busy work.

From childhood he had been writing prose and verse, and publishing in a small way, in *The Comic Times,* in *The Train,* in *College Rhymes,* as well as in his little home magazines. But he became a professional writer almost by accident. Without Alice to find the golden key, he might never have been able to enter the enchanted garden. The complex interweaving of his multiple personality throws the light variously. When his "Alice" personality was in the ascendant, he was all poet, and produced masterpieces. The black bag, however, contained perhaps as many as four subordinate personalities. Dodgson, the man who carried the bag, was at least a scholarly writer, if not an inspired one. But sometimes Bill the Lizard took over. . . .

Though each of his long books is confessedly made up of "bits of things," and though his one long poem came feet first, announcing its conception with the last line, "For the Snark *was* a Boojum, you see," each book has the same weird sort of coherence he had himself. His perseverance in squeezing out of himself the last drop of ink inherent in each book is reminiscent of a Renaissance craftsman who was also an artist—Leonardo, for instance, or Van der Weyden, who painted the picture in a Berlin gallery, mentioned by Carroll in his *Russian Journal,* in which each individual teardrop is painted separately, and the shadow is carefully carried through to the inner side of each leaf of a tiny book with its pages fluttered open.

The last line of "The Hunting of the Snark" came to him on July 18, 1875. He first thought it finished on November 6 of that year, but continued to add to it till January, 1876. He first told the story of *Alice* in July, 1862. On November 26, 1864, he presented the MS. of *Alice Underground* to Alice Liddell. Three years after the story was told, *Alice's Adventures* appeared. Seven years later the sequel came out. Twenty-eight years after the first telling, the original was condensed and simplified into *The Nursery "Alice."*

In the preface he mentions the children of all ages who

have enjoyed *Wonderland,* and admits an ambition to have it read by "children from 'Nought to Five,' " for whom he prepares a completely rewritten *Alice.* In 1881 he had written a friend: "Shall I send you a Dutch version of *Alice* with about eight of the pictures done large in colors? It would do well to show to little children. I think of trying a coloured *Alice* myself—a 'Nursery edition.' What do you think of it?" [1]

John Francis McDermott, editor of the verse and of the *Russian Journal,* says Carroll "knew nothing about children." [2] Though he sentimentalizes, and projects onto children thoughts and feelings of which only child prigs are capable, a man who "knew nothing about children" could not have written *The Nursery "Alice"* even with *Wonderland* to start from. Carroll uses modern principles of juvenile literature. The book is larger, there is less print on the page—the chapters are shorter and the material cut to about one-fourth. There are twenty pictures instead of forty-two, and they are colored instead of black and white. All poetry except the verse about the tarts is omitted—this may be questionable, but the poetry in the original version was certainly too long and too subtle for small children. Perhaps some of it could have been left in, but children who had read *The Nursery "Alice"* were sure to go on to *Wonderland* when they could read well. The philosophic digressions and the logical puzzles are omitted, and the only new digression added is about a little dog Dash who did not like the porridge the children prepared for his birthday treat.

The Nursery "Alice" was tried on a child under five who knew the *Wonderland* pictures, and who seemed to understand and enjoy every word of it, besides responding to the numerous "I don't think so, do you's" that the author interspersed in the text. He also makes the story revolve about the pictures. A quotation from the beginning and one from near the end will show the method—for *The Nursery "Alice"* is out of print, despite a recent reprint by Hodder and Stoughton. In its first two editions it had gone through 11,000 copies by 1898, but that is a pailful compared to *Wonderland.* Is it the adult readers, then, who keep *Alice* alive? That is what Martin Gardner believes, and that is why he brought out his *Annotated Alice,* explaining and amplifying the jokes for the adults who might wish historical background. It is a fascinating book, and should be supplemented by a new edition of *Nursery Alice,* for the children who actually find the regular *Alice* too difficult.* But there remains a large audience for just *Alice,* neither annotated nor nursery!

The Nursery "Alice" starts with a sentimental preface and a poem called "A Nursery Darling," which shall remain in limbo. Then it begins:

"Once upon a time there was a little girl called Alice: And she had a very curious dream.

"Would you like to hear what it was that she dreamed about?

"Well, this was the *first* thing that happened. A White Rabbit came running by, in a great hurry; and just as it passed Alice it stopped, and took its watch out of its pocket.

"Wasn't *that* a funny thing? Did you ever see a rabbit that had a watch, and a pocket to put it in? Of course, when a rabbit has a watch, it *must* have a pocket to put it in: it would never do to carry it about in its mouth, and it wants its hands sometimes, to run about with.

"Hasn't it got pretty pink eyes (I think *all* White Rabbits have pink eyes); and pink ears; and a nice brown coat; and you can just see its red pocket-handkerchief peeping out of its coat pocket; and, what with its blue necktie and its yellow waistcoat, it really is *very* nicely dressed."

After Alice has upset the jury-box and we are counting the creatures in the picture:

"But that makes only eleven: we must find one more creature.

"Oh, do you see a little white head, coming out behind the mole, and just under the Duck's beak? That makes up the twelve.

"Mr. Tenniel says the screaming bird is a Storkling (of course you know what *that* is?) and the little white head is a *Mouseling.* Isn't it a little *darling?*

"Alice picked them all up again, very carefully, and I hope they weren't *much* hurt!"

* Dover Publications has re-issued *Nursery Alice* in paperback.

He knew what puzzled children in the story and pictures. *The Nursery "Alice"* settles problems that perplexed a generation of readers—for instance, he explains that what looks like the Caterpillar's face is only two of its legs!

Sylvie and Bruno had a similar growth, from "Bruno's Revenge" in 1867, to *Sylvie and Bruno* in 1889, and *Sylvie and Bruno Concluded* in 1893. *Three Sunsets,* published after his death in 1898, contained poems written in the fifties. The first stanza of *Jabberwocky* appeared in *The Rectory Umbrella* in 1857, and the rest of it was written at his cousins' home on a social evening when everybody was writing poetry. *Through the Looking-Glass,* in which the whole poem first appeared, was published fifteen years after the "stanza of Anglo-Saxon poetry" first saw the light under the *Rectory Umbrella.* "Matilda Jane," which he wrote for his cousin's doll, he salvaged years later for *Sylvie and Bruno*. The *Curator* pamphlets, beginning with "Curiosissima Curatoria," from which readers of this book are spared, covered the eight years from 1884-92.

His threads were long and his weaving was deep-piled. For instance, is it usual for even the most elevated novel to sport an index? Yet both volumes of *Sylvie and Bruno* are so endowed, perhaps to enable the reader to find the author's favorite jokes more easily. Double entries of this nature abound: "Boots for Horizontal Weather," and "Horizontal Weather, Boots for." The eighty-sixth thousand of the six-shilling edition of *Alice,* published in 1897, contained a preface, dated Christmas, 1886, which is occasionally reprinted now. This gives the answer to the March Hare's riddle of 1865—"Why is a raven like a writing-desk?" Carroll says that originally he had no answer, and all that occurred to him later was, "Because it can produce a few notes, though they are *very* flat; and it is never put with the wrong end in front! This, however, is merely an afterthought: the Riddle, as originally invented, had no answer at all."

In the preface to *Sylvie and Bruno* he set his readers a puzzle, but this time solved it in the preface. He asked the readers to guess which lines on certain pages were "padding," put there to give the pictures an advantageous position. There are only two or three such in the book—honest workmanship on the Lizard level.

No book was finished, in his mind, till an impeccable edition reached his readers. He recalled not only the first edition of *Alice in Wonderland,* but also a later edition of *Through the Looking-Glass,* because he considered the illustrations imperfectly reproduced. In the second instance he sent around a notice to Workmen's Clubs, hospitals, and so forth, offering the copies he was unwilling to sell (to the British public at least!). The organizations, however, had to fill out a considerable questionnaire before receiving the books. In his *Books and Bidders,* published by Little, Brown in 1927, the year before his purchase of the *Alice* MS, Dr. Rosenbach mentions an experience he had in a London bookshop, where he saw a forger carefully copying dedications to persons long dead, and signatures, in the flyleaves of Carroll books. When Dr. Rosenbach asked him his purpose, he coyly answered, "For the American trade!"

His relations with Macmillan increased in unusualness. Charles Morgan tells how the publishers were expected to buy his theater tickets, send his watch to be mended, bind his books, and tie his parcels in unprecedented ways. "He supplied a diagram, which long hung in the post-room at Bedford Street, showing how the string on all parcels should be, and how the string on his parcels must be, knotted." [3]

Sometimes, however, he resisted lures to doodling. He wrote this letter to his cousin Lucy Wilcox in 1877:

"My dear Lucy,

"I now regard you as a form of Destiny (let us say, as one of the Fates, or one of the Furies) as you are simply bringing on me a flood of strange young ladies, who ask my assistance with a simple and touching confidence suggestive of young— shall we say 'lambs'?

"As if it was not enough to have to lunch and lionize Miss Kate Terry and then yourself, this morning comes a letter from a strange young lady who, after a few introductory remarks, confides to me that she has left school two years and is in want of mental occupation—that she has joined a club of young [ladies] who are to set each other questions for 're-search' but they want an 'Examiner' to look over and correct the answers! Each young lady is to ask three questions a month, and apparently the other eleven are to answer them. That makes 396 answers a month to correct! I pleaded want of time in answer to her request to be her 'guide, philosopher, & friend.' " [1] The most remarkable thing about this remarkable letter is that he actually refused the young lady. It would have been quite in keeping for him to take on such a job—no worse, surely, than his "work" as Curator.

He was unduly generous with the time he should have kept inviolate for his own work, but there were other considerations. A good deal of the time that he was, nominally, putting into his books, went to his everlasting games of making things fit into things, and, to judge from his attempt to get away from his Alice style, of trying to fit a square peg into a round hole. Heaven only knows what is the name for his new style, since *Sylvie and Bruno* is the only example, and until it was reprinted in some of the omnibus volumes, it rested uncoveted and unimitated on a few dusty shelves. (Always excepting the army of Carroll collectors mustered by the manuscript sale of 1928.) Perhaps the book belongs to the exclusive and extinct species of *Didus ineptus*—the Dodo.

It was well enough for him to complain that his illustrators kept him waiting, but his later books dragged along by the weight of his own slowness. *Bruno's Revenge* appeared in 1867, and it was 1885 before he approached Harry Furniss to do the illustrations for the book, which then hastily appeared four years later, followed in another four by the sequel. Carroll explained, to his own satisfaction, why it had taken him so long. He wrote Harry Furniss: "I have a considerable mass of chaotic material for a story, but have never had the heart to go to work and construct the story as a whole, owing to its seeming so hopeless that I should ever find a suitable artist. Now that *you* are found I shall go back to my *Alice in Wonderland* style of work with every hope of making a success." [4]

But he objected to others saying the same, for two years later he wrote: "Anything which would have the effect of connecting the book with *Alice* would be absolutely disastrous. I wish, above all, to avoid in this new book the giving of any pretexts for critics to say, 'This writer can only play one tune: the book is a *rechauffé* [sic] of *Alice*.' I'm trying my very best to get out of the old groove and have no 'connecting link' whatever." [4]

The Furniss letters present a deep mine of information as to his method of writing *Sylvie and Bruno*. Carroll also tells a great deal in his long introduction, and the very conscious manner in which the book was constructed makes it possible to follow much of his procedure. Although he disclaims such intention, the book is clearly autobiographical, and there are hints that he wished to feel elfin and invisible; for example: "The narrator (the whole book will be autobiographical) will not appear in *any* of the illustrations." [4] Elsewhere he makes it clear that "autobiographical" here was a Freudian slip— he is trying to say only "told in the first person." The identification of the narrator with his Dodgson self may be what makes the book so tedious. His identification with Alice, and with the wild, shy, ineffectual creatures in his first books, gives their delicious, dreamlike quality. Take Mr. Dodgson, with his tall hat, his clerical black, his cotton gloves, his housemaid's knee—add a fictional heart disease—and you have a character suitable neither for a romantic novel nor for a pixy tale, but only for the theological-sociological tract that much of that dreadful book is. The spurious maturity that made him think of himself as an elderly gentleman rather than as Alice, was merely a shrivelling, not a ripening. Nevertheless he poured himself into every character in the book, and, though the two volumes are not much to show, artistically, for the time he spent on them, still, from the craftsman's standpoint of work well finished whatever it may be, they are eminently respectable.

Miss Furniss published some of his letters to her father in a magazine in 1930, with her own comments. Like her father, she recognized the duality of the characters. He mentions only Sylvie and Lady Muriel; but she sees that each character in the "fairy" part had a double in the "human" part. This seems to have been no secret even to the author, though in his earlier use of this device, in the double exposures in *Wonderland*, there is no evidence that he knew what he was doing.

In fact, the doubling of the Cheshire Cat with Dinah, the White Rabbit with the March Hare, and so on, are far subtler than the simple ambivalence of the characters in *Sylvie and Bruno*. Here is a letter to Harry Furniss, showing that if Carroll was innocent in his *Alice* days, the innocence did not last till the end:

"My idea is that the narrator, while talking with 'Mein Herr,' gradually passes into the dream state in which 'Mein Herr' becomes the professor. . . .

"As it might be well to make the Professor a caricature of 'Mein Herr,' or rather, since we have settled what the Professor is to be like, to make 'Mein Herr's' sort of face and figure of what the Professor would be like in caricature. The details can easily be altered to meet the picture." [4]

Here is a thoroughly conscious pixy with a long white beard, like one of Snow White's dwarfs. The overstrained secrecy he enforced also cut off all criticism of his books during their incubation period. Yet some of his correspondence with Harry Furniss is a straight bid for sympathy and response to his elfin games. After all, Furniss was not a little girl—if Carroll wrote to him as he did in some of the "spider" letters, it was not to amuse his illustrator, but to evoke a playmate for himself. The Swinburne parody, the poem about the little man with the little gun, contains the line "and his soul shall be sad for the spider."

Carroll tried to draw this himself. "I have failed utterly to get anything the least like a spider. I wished to have a spider portrayed front view and full-faced, because some writer says that the full face of a spider as seen under a magnifying glass is very striking. Could you find one in some book of entomology, or look at a live one?"

The artist spent a day sketching spiders from life, but Carroll was insatiable. ". . . a creature mostly human, but suggestive of a spider nature, would be quite accurate enough . . . the little man sees that the spider is deeply love-stricken, and is in the midst of a 'declaration,' quite unaware that the young lady is out of hearing! Would that not be a subject for pity? I think that the six legs [sic!] which I have tried to represent by that tangle in front, and a globular outline to

the figure, would be spidery enough—I meant him to be laying his hand on his heart, but his chin got in the way!" [4]

From one adult, however fanciful, to another, this is almost
too much. But the worst is yet to come: "It occurs to me that
the reason 'his soul was sad for the spider' was that he saw
that the strictly honourable attentions of that well-meaning
insect had been misunderstood by Miss Muffet. Don't you
think that would be an original reading of that transaction?" [4]

It would have been useless to show his unfinished writings
to most of the adults in his milieu—he was safer with an
artist, especially one who was close enough to understanding
him to be his illustrator. It was canny of Carroll to write such
letters only to children or artists, showing again his sanity,
taste, and feeling for fitness—but his need to write them at
all shows how real his inner world was to him, and how
hungrily he craved to share it. His irreproachable donnish
surface and isolation, then, were more of his elfin tricks to
keep unsympathetic persons from finding him out. It is unthinkable that he should ever have seen any of Harry Furniss'
fussy, old-maidish caricatures of him. Those he would never
have forgiven, though he could make one of himself. A drawing he made of a man, his hair rumpled, with his mouth
presumably open, but covered by his hand, he labeled, "What
I look like when lecturing," and sent to a little girl. But he
could never have endured the Furniss drawings.

The illustrator had tact, however, and his own way of
working with his odd customer. Carroll wrote:

"Never hurry yourself in the least over my work, I beg.
But for the uncertainty of life I would not ask for any continuity at all. Still, as neither of us is secure that his work
will endure for a thousand long years, it will no doubt be
advisable, when this picture is done and approved, to go on
with the others whenever you have time and inclination.

"For the same reason, I intend to devote my three months
by the sea, this summer, to writing out the whole book, in
consecutive form. Then if I were to die, the work could still
be brought out, and the children could read it: that *I* should
not see it would be quite a minor matter—I shall feel much
more at my ease when this is done." [4]

Again he wrote Furniss: "It is now just a year and six months since you undertook the illustrating of my book, and only four pictures are as yet delivered, at which rate it would take more than thirty years to finish the book." But Furniss knew what he was doing. This spider web was not going to tangle him. He purposely sent only drawings for the interspersed poems, knowing he could do all the illustrations for the main part of the book right off, not one a month or one in six months. . . .

"Lewis Carroll came from Oxford one evening, early in the history of the work, to dine and afterwards see a batch of the work. He ate little, drank little, but enjoyed a few glasses of sherry, his favorite wine. 'Now,' said he, 'for the studio!' I rose and led the way. My wife sat in astonishment. She knew I had nothing to show. Through the drawing-room, down the steps of the conservatory to the door of my studio. My hand is on the handle. Through excitement Lewis Carroll stammers worse than ever. Now to see the work for his great book! I pause, turn my back to the closed door, and thus address the astonished don: 'Mr. Dodgson, I am *very* eccentric—I cannot help it! Let me explain to you clearly, before you enter my studio, that my eccentricity sometimes takes a violent form. If I, in showing my work, discover in your face the slightest sign that you are not *absolutely* satisfied with any particle of this work in progress, the *whole* of it goes into the fire! It is a risk: will you accept it, or will you wait till I have the drawings *quite* finished and send them to Oxford?'

" 'I—I—I ap-appreciate your feelings—I—I—should feel the same myself! I am off to Oxford!' And he went." [5]

This was not true eccentricity on Furniss' part, but an attempt, as he said, to "solve the problem" that Carroll was. The artist's tact in meeting the author in the wood where things have no names kept their association alive for the seven years that Carroll was puttering with the book and that Furniss was supposed to be working at the pictures.

Carroll too had sympathy for the inspirational method— his own: "I quite agree with you as to only doing the pictures when you feel 'in the vein,' and that you are working your best. In Ruskin's *Elements of Drawing,* at p. 63, is a sentence that struck me as very good advice indeed: 'Always remember that a little bit perfected is worth more than many scrawls; whenever you feel inclined to scrawl, give up work resolutely and do not go back to it till next day.'

"In the *writing* of this book I try to follow the same rules. The other evening I got out all the papers, and meant to do some hours of work, but after sitting before them for a few minutes, I said: 'It's no use: I'm too dull for it tonight,' and I put them all away again." [4] Considering the infernal dullness of a good deal that went into this very *Sylvie and Bruno,* it would be interesting to read the delenda that actually bored the author!

For times like these, when it did not "come of itself," and when he could not whip himself into creativity, the pillow problems, games, lists, and much of his so-called mathematical "work," served to keep him out of mischief. The system of "registering" letters, described in gruesome detail in his *Eight or Nine Wise Words about Letter-Writing,* was a godsend. He says one should leave the "making-up" of this index until thirty or forty pages have accumulated: "You will find it perfectly simple, when you have had a little practice, and will come to regard the 'making-up' as a pleasant occupation for a rainy day, or at any time that you feel disinclined for severe mental work." He carried his playfulness even into his acutely singular ordering of household and business affairs.

Dr. Warren Weaver published a pamphlet, *Lewis Carroll's Correspondence Numbers.* The register itself disappeared, but Dr. Weaver worked out from MS sources a system for dating his correspondence fairly accurately with the aid of the numbers. The first entry is January 1, 1861, and the last, not numbered, is January 8, 1898. On December 8 the number was 98,471.

Dr. Weaver says further that Carroll used black ink regularly till about 1871, then switched to violet ink, and returned to black after 1891. Other studies have been made of this, and apparently there were periods of fluctuation between the colors. Mathematicians and collectors are able to make deductions from these facts, which are therefore reported here. Mr. Hudson thinks his "purple period" seems to correspond with his periods of depression.

Dorothy Furniss says that Carroll's first letter to her father was numbered 49,627. Carroll himself said in 1894: "I get about 2000 letters off every year: but it isn't enough!" Miss Furniss says: "Mr. Dodgson numbered every letter; he had also many extraordinary notions on the importance of keeping every scrap of information concerning his books safe from inquisitive eyes. He bound my father down to strict secrecy, but made an exception of my mother, to whom he confided the fact that she was one of the most favored women 'for she knew the contents of his book before it had appeared' (i.e., in print)." [4]

He wrote to Mr. Furniss: "I like to feel secure that you and I are the only two living beings who know anything about the content of the book until it appears.

"For my own part, I have shown *none* of the MS to anybody, and though I have let some special friends see the pictures, I have uniformly declined to explain them. 'May I ask so-and-so?' they inquire. 'Certainly,' I reply. 'You may *ask* as many questions as you like.' That is all they get out of me." [4]

He had several of his "own inventions" for insuring the secrecy he required. Miss Furniss says: "He invented a highly involved system of cutting his finished letters into strips, posting indiscriminately in large envelopes, and reading with the aid of a cipher, a system which my father—a very busy man —entirely refused to countenance.

"Nothing daunted, he next advocated the peculiar expedient of reversing the process of illustrating, and suggested that father should 'draw the last picture first, and work backwards,' as Poe tells us he wrote *The Raven*" (and as Carroll tells us he wrote *The Snark*).[4]

Miss Furniss quotes some of the Carrollian games in detail. "The mathematical cast of his mind is very apparent in the manner in which he suggests the simple reduction of a drawing to scale.

'Dear Mr. Furniss:
'When you learn that I worked from 9 till 8½ yesterday, and from 8 to 9½ p.m. today, principally at arranging texts in pages (I have got to p. 112), you will not wonder at my deferring this letter for a day.

'These two pictures are very beautiful; but some one or two little alterations seem desirable.

' "Baby in Flower" (this will be wanted first). The design is too broad for its height. It is 6¾ x 9¾. A page is in the proportion 9 to 14. Now 9:14 :: 6¾ :10½. So it wants ¾ in. in height. But it is obviously impossible to *heighten* it; you've reached the very foot of the card—the only course is to reduce width 14:9 :: 9¾ :6¼.'

"In spite of the fact that my father abhorred everything in the nature of mathematics, they continued to work together in harmony." [4] And in spite of many other factors, including Carroll's impertinence in counting the lines to a square inch of Tenniel's drawing under a microscope, to compare the count with Furniss'!

The American, Arthur B. Frost, a much better artist than Furniss, was also less amiable. He illustrated *Rhyme? and Reason?* and *A Tangled Tale,* and the correspondence survives in the form of carbon copies, made because Carroll hardly trusted the ocean to deliver his mail. The drawings for the former book were made in 1883: the correspondence started enthusiastically, but during work on the second book the author began to register disappointment; his letters became increasingly upstage, finally climaxing in the suggestion that the artist study Tenniel's work to see what Dodgson wanted. Frost grew cooler, and Dodgson reciprocated. His last communication, in the third person, was a brief note arranging to pay Frost through his bankers.[6]

The cream of the jest is that Carroll was dissatisfied with Tenniel too when he was *locum tenens.* Perhaps the artist did not visit Mary Badcock often enough, for Carroll wrote Miss Thomson: "Mr. Tenniel is the only artist, who has drawn for me, who has resolutely refused to use a model, and declared he no more needed one than I should need a multiplication table to work a mathematical problem! I venture to think that he was mistaken, & that for want of a model, he drew several pictures of 'Alice' entirely out of proportion—head decidedly too large and feet decidedly too small." [7]

Does this mean that Mr. Madan was misinformed about Tenniel having broken his lifelong tradition? Did he perhaps use only the *photograph* of Mary? Yet Mr. Madan, who was in communication with Colonel Probert, Mary's husband, seems quite certain that Tenniel went to Ripin to sketch her.

One of the political cartoons Tenniel was always slipping into his illustrations for the *Alice* books may have made a little trouble for Dodgson. Mr. Green says, "Compare Tenniel's Mad Hatter with one of his cartoons of Gladstone in *Punch*, and it will be obvious why reviewers of *Alice's Adventures in Wonderland* in Liberal papers criticized 'A Mad Tea Party' so harshly." This is rather enigmatic, because it is the Lion who looks like the Gladstone caricatures, and there is no similarity between the Lion and the Mad Hatter.

A pattern emerges dimly from Carroll's relationships with his illustrators. Because they were artists, they were kindred souls—up to a point. Carroll was an artist in grain, but some of his secondary characteristics strengthened with age. While his best hope for understanding and sympathy from adults was among artists, even they could not meet him all the way. And Bruno in Oxford had to grow as fast as Alice after drinking from the famous bottle, and had to dress himself up as the Professor, or as Mein Herr, with false whiskers. But lonely he must always have been.

This man who, loving children, had none, and who, with a little encouragement, might have been able to love a grown woman, but who could not, of himself, clear the barriers raised in his youth, had to console himself by drawing and photographing little girls, when possible and convenient, in the nude. His delicacy of feeling and his perfect taste show up in this situation more brilliantly than anywhere else, and mark the barriers of his solitary confinement. He never loses sight of the artistic motivation which raises his sketches to a higher plane than the drawings themselves merit, but, most important of all, he never loses sight of the personalities of the sitters, or, as he would say, of their "immortal souls," and whenever he finds any sign of modest shrinkings or of a tendency toward boldness or forwardness, he immediately abandons the model, and even requests Miss Thomson to make no more nude drawings or photographs of this particular girl ("for *me*")—for even here he makes no attempt to impose his crotchets on anyone else.

He seems to have started drawing from life at the studio of a former child friend who married, lost her husband, and then took a studio in Chelsea where she gave lessons. She wrote an article, signed "E.L.S.," in the *Cornhill Magazine* about Carroll as an artist. Like everyone else, she was mildly impressed with his drawing, but stressed his great interest and concentration. She went out of her way to find him child models; he used to send her lists of children willing to sit, mostly child actresses. "In one of his letters he set forth his ideas on the subject of models. He confessed to having no interest in boy or grown-up female models, having the 'bad taste' to find more beauty in the undeveloped than in the mature form." [8] He told her: "I think twelve would be my ideal age—children are so thin from seven to ten." [8]

Mr. Green identifies the artist as Mrs. Richard Shute, who noted Carroll's extreme primness in her own childhood. "When a stile crossed our path, he went first, and, with averted eyes, and his back turned as much as possible, would hold out his hand to help me over." [8] Gertrude Nafe suggests that these contradictions might hark back to some services that, in so large a family, the eldest brother might have had to perform for some of the five younger sisters!

In the studio, says Mrs. Shute, she supplied the tea, Carroll brought the cakes, and "laid himself out" to entertain the model during the rests, which were "unduly prolonged," to everybody's satisfaction. A letter to Miss Thomson suggests what he was seeking in his relationships with children and his attempts to draw them: "Your remarks on Art are most interesting, tho' I don't quite understand about fairies 'losing grace' if too like human children. Of course I grant that to be like some *actual* child is to lose grace, because no living child is perfect in form: many causes have lowered the race from what God made it. But the *perfect* human form, free from these faults, is surely applicable to men & fairies, & angels? Perhaps that is what you mean—that the artist can imagine, & design, more perfect forms than are ever found in life?" [7]

Some of his other artist friends helped him, too, however odd they may have thought his hobby.

On January 15, 1874, he writes: "I called on the Holidays and found him, Mrs. Holiday, and Winnie. He showed me the drawings he is doing for me (suggestions for groups of two children—nude studies—for me to try to reproduce in photographs from life), which are quite exquisite."

The same year, on June 27, he notes: "I have begun again drawing from life. I have tried Ethel (Napier) once or twice, and today did Kitty, and the landlady's child, Agnes Griffiths."

Four years later he was still at it. On July 17, 1879, he writes: "Miss Thomson arrived from London about 11, bringing one of Sir F. Leighton's models (aged eleven). I did an ordinary portrait of her, and six "studies" [i.e., in the nude, interposes Mr. Green] in arranging which Miss Thomson was of great use.

July 25: "Brought Annie and Frances (and their mother) in a cab and did some more photos of them in the same dress as before [i.e., their favorite dress of "nothing" says Mr. Green]."

On February 4, 1880: "Xie showed me a photo of three young ladies, friends of hers, dressed as boys in a sort of acrobat dress, the eldest being about 16. I must get such a dress for my 12 year old subjects." Could this have been tights?

That spring, on April 1: "Menella [cousin] showed me some excellent photographs of them [her five children], many in next to no dress, and others in none."

Five years later, on May 23, 1885: "Paget, the artist, seems willing to let me draw from life in his studio."

And on June 5, he "spent two hours with Mr. Paget at his studio, and saw some interesting 'studies,' and his two charming little girls Gladys and Dolly." This revealing dichotomy shows up repeatedly, between the children of his friends, who are inviolable, though sometimes rather scantily clad, and the models, always from another class. Dodgson was not alone in his presumption, (on his own level) that there were two kinds of women, but he was almost alone in the courtesy and consideration he showed the "other kind." He had a basic decency that went even deeper than his neurosis, and it is for this that we still love him, with all his oddities.

Gernsheim thinks Carroll gave up photography because of some problem he encountered in connection with photographing nudes. His last photographs, however, were ordinary portraits of friends. The entry for July 15, 1880, is: "Spent morning in printing [photographs]. Gertrude and Geride Drage came at 3, and I spent two hours in photographing them, then toning, filling in etc. till 7." Gernsheim says that is the last entry relating to photographing, and Gertrude and Geride Drage were the last people to be photographed by Dodgson.

Elsewhere he says, "If Lewis Carroll's photographs of nude girls were as sentimental and devoid of artistry as Miss Thomson's drawings of fairies in Three Sunsets, we must be grateful to him for having stipulated that after his death they should be returned to the sitters or else be destroyed. Naturally none of these were pasted in the albums, and as far as I know, none have survived."

Dodgson wrote to Harry Furniss: "I *wish* I dared dispense with *all* costume: naked children are so perfectly pure and lovely, but Mrs. Grundy would be furious—it would never do. Then the question is, how little dress will content her?" [5] But is this altogether consistent, this letter to Miss Thomson? "I confess I do *not* admire naked boys, in pictures. They always seem to me to need *clothes*—whereas one hardly sees why the lovely forms of girls should *ever* be covered up!" [7]

Letters to Miss Thomson abound in phrases like: "She *is* such a sweet little figure!"—"She has a beautiful figure, I think—And she seems nice and modest: but she is turned 14, and I like drawing a *child,* best." "I confess I don't like the smiling and beckoning to supposed spectators—even in a *draped* figure, such an expression would look a *little* too 'bold': in an undraped one, it is, to me, unpleasantly so."

"I am telling Macmillan to send you a *Nursery "Alice"* to give Edith B—, from the Author. It may pave the way for possible 'sittings.'—But I am not wholly selfish. She is *heartily* welcome to it, even if it leads to no such result." [7]

And in his very last letter to Miss Thomson, written three weeks before his death, the postscript reads:

"I'd nearly omitted to say one thing that occurred to me on reading your account of Edith B—. That is, *please* do not draw her, nude, for my pictures, if she has any scruple *whatever,* on the score of modesty—I'm sure a child's instincts, of that kind, ought to be treated with the *utmost reverence*. And if I had the loveliest child in the world, to draw or photograph, & found she had a modest shrinking (however slight, and however easily overcome) from being taken nude, I should feel it was a solemn duty, owed to God, to drop the request *altogether*." [7]

Somehow this is the saddest part in his history. It shows how close he was to being able to jump the last brook into a normal life, and how, with a slightly different set of circumstances, he could have been a happier man. But these few passages occur in more than ninety letters written to Miss Thomson between 1885 and 1897, and the great bulk of the correspondence is in the nature of detailed criticism of the drawings she was doing for *Original Games and Puzzles*. After the drawings were all finished and approved, he decided that they were the wrong size for the book as he planned it, and after mountains of correspondence he decided to use the pictures for *Three Sunsets*. Since they were "fairy pictures," signifying nothing but a mood, they did as well for one book as for another. Carroll had mentioned to Miss Thomson that the pictures were the wrong size, but had then continued to criticize them in a way leading her to believe he had changed his mind, so it must have been a surprise to her that he finally decided to withhold the book and even tried to get her to buy back the copyright of the pictures. The rights and wrongs of the transaction are not clear, since both parties were slightly eccentric.

In all his letters he continued to say what a shame it would be to publish her "beautiful pictures" in any size or form that would not do them justice. He also continued to invite her to spend some time at Eastbourne in the rooms he had taken, when he was not using them himself, (everything to be at his expense); he took her to the theater, sent her expensive art books, condoled with her on her father's death, got her commissions to draw portraits of his friends' children, and finally sat to her for his own portrait, the miniature. Once or twice he asked her to return a book and some photographs he had lent her five years before, but at last he gave up and told her to keep them.

Miss Thomson emerges, faintly limned, as a not too feminine woman, full of artistic temperament, but not a really good draftsman. Her enlargements of the Tenniel pictures for *The Nursery "Alice"* show her lack of style and anatomical precision. But the miniature suggests she had a real sympathy for Carroll and a real feeling for likenesses, and perhaps if she had taken his forty times reiterated advice to draw from life *only*, she would have done a better job of the fairy pictures. The important thing is, however, that she must have been a receptive audience for his touching letters, many of them in the "spider" vein. She must have had boundless patience, too, to draw and redraw the pictures to suit his— usually correct—strictures on their anatomy. But she used a ruse to escape some of the work: contrary to their agreement, she sometimes sent the pictures only (a) in the rough sketch and (c) in their first form, omitting (b), the partly finished pencil sketch which would give her meticulous employer a chance at another check-up. No wonder the book was twelve years coming out, and, when it did appear, it was quite another book. If it had never come out at all, as the White Queen bleated when she was changing into a sheep, it would have been "Oh, much better! Much be-etter! Be-e-e-etter! Be-e-ehh!"

Had he made a hearty bonfire of his lists, files, pocket-books, black bags, music boxes, gadgets for turning on the light, gadgets for writing in the dark, devices for this and that, and stood up to a bare writing table with pen and paper for two hours a day for ten years—the imagination breaks down. He might have written—it is physically if not psychologically possible—from three to six books of the quality of his best work; or, more probably, half a dozen unreadable theological books. Orderly as his Dodgson self was, doodle-bug as his Lizard self was, the Carroll personality took dictation only from within, and only in its own time.

In the article in *The Theatre,* quoted earlier, he speaks of the growth of *Wonderland* from the manuscript version. ". . . . in writing it out, I added my fresh ideas, which seemed to grow of themselves upon the original stock; and many more added themselves when, years afterwards, I wrote it all over again for publication . . . but whenever or however [an idea] comes, *it comes of itself.* I cannot set invention going like a clock, by any voluntary winding up . . . *Alice* and the *Looking-Glass* are made up almost wholly of bits and scraps, single ideas which came of themselves." [9]

That procedure did not develop as he aged, however. He might have done better with a more unified plan in his later years. In any case, the advantage of a bare-table method is that he would *not* have written *Sylvie and Bruno,* though he might still have written the poems in it. For the prose parts depended on his neat little packets of notes, his numbered letters, his "bits of things" written years before, odds and ends of reading in medicine and sociology, and most of all on his increasing religiosity.

Sylvie and Bruno was his biggest doodle, but he never ceased to make dozens of little doodles. Postage, naturally, fascinated him. Besides the *Wonderland Stamp Case* he tackled postage problems on several other occasions. The Postmaster General was a cousin of his, Mr. Henry Cecil Raikes, father of Alice Raikes. Carroll seems not to have known Alice until he met her by chance, but he writes of an "Aunt Raikes" and a "Cousin Raikes" in undergraduate days. The relationship may explain the fact that one of the documents is an official government report, never sold publicly. Someone seems to have sold Mr. Parrish a copy, however, dated 1890—an official report of the Postmaster General on registration of parcels, containing an extract from a letter by the Rev. C. L. Dodgson of December 20, 1889.

He also tried to improve—mathematically—the rules for commissions chargeable on overdue postal orders, and projected a "plan for simplifying money orders by making the sender fill up two duplicate papers, one of which he hands in to be transmitted by the postmaster—it contains a key number which the receiver has to supply in his copy to get the money."

Again mathematically, he proposed to solve the question of the eight-hour law, merely by saying to the workers: "In future we will pay you so much per hour, and you can make up days as you please." It is not recorded that his idea was ever adopted. . . .

Nor had he any better success with his proposals for what amounts to proportional representation, intended to "make the House of Commons, as far as possible, a true index of the state of opinion in the nation"—an end which some historians claim was accomplished by the Parliamentary Reform Bill in the year of his birth.

It is not recorded that Carroll ever played tennis—even cricket was out of his range, and his one attempt to play was a classic failure—but he did not hesitate to improve—again mathematically—on the rules for tennis tournaments. Mr. Madan says: "As usual with Dodgson's ideals of scoring or voting, the scheme proposed is too ingenious and elaborate for general use, though terribly near perfection. The results would be many fewer competitors, a shorter tournament, and less gate money!" [10]

The captain hates the sea, and the writer hates to write. Carroll's genius did not die with the birth of the *Alice* books. *The Hunting of the Snark* is first-rate, and the "Gardener's Song" in *Sylvie and Bruno* is comparable, if not equal, to anything he wrote. It is possible to charge his *dégringolade* to the loss of his Egeria, but the process that harmed his art was the gradual encroachment of his conscious self on the preserves of dreamland, without compensation in the form of increased maturity. A novel with an appendix—an appendix with cross references to the author's favorite jokes! He chopped up his poetic self and fed the bits to the Professor and the Other Professor. And the moral of *that* is, as the Duchess would say—only the brave deserve the fair.

Chapter 18

The Red King's Dream

> ". . . and what do you think he's dreaming about?"
>
> Alice said, "Nobody can guess that."
>
> "Why, about you!" Tweedledee exclaimed, clapping his hands triumphantly. "And if he left off dreaming about you, where do you suppose you'd be?"
>
> "Where I am now, of course," said Alice.
>
> "Not you!" Tweedledee retorted contemptuously. "You'd be nowhere. Why, you're only a sort of thing in his dream!"

IN 1894 CARROLL WROTE, concerning the deaths of friends: "Such news comes less and less as a shock: and more and more one realizes that it is an experience each of *us* has to face before long. That fact is getting *less* dreamlike to me now, and I sometimes think what a grand thing it will be to be able to say to oneself, 'Death is *over* now, there is not *that* experience to be faced again!' " [1] His dream was wearing thin—he was coming awake, perhaps to find that the Red King had dreamed him after all.

He was more willing to preach now. He opened the last full year of his life, 1897, by preaching at St. Mary's in Guildford, where he had been visiting his sisters since Christmas. On March 7 he preached his only sermon at St. Mary's in Oxford, on two texts, one from the Litany, "Give us an heart to love and dread thee," and the other from Job, "The fear of the Lord, that is wisdom."

He spoke for three-quarters of an hour—no small feat, without using the words that made him stammer. He wrote in the diary: "It has been the most formidable sermon I have ever had to preach." The following January *The Oxford Magazine* referred to it: "Some will remember his sermon at St. Mary's last Lent Term; the erect gray-headed figure, with

378

the rapt look of earnest thought; the slow, almost hesitating speech; the clear and faultless language; the intense solemnity and earnestness which compelled his audience to listen for nearly an hour, as he spoke to them of the duty of reverence, and warned them of the sin of talking carelessly of holy things."

Ten years earlier, on January 2, 1887, he noted: "Preached in the morning at St. Mary's, on Mark X 51. I took the headings, written, in my pocket, but did not refer to them." Mr. Green reports that Miss Gertrude Corrie, who was in the congregation that day, wrote in her diary, "Today Arthur and I went to St. Mary's to hear Mr. Dodgson. . . . We liked him immensely; he has a fine face, especially profile. Arthur thought it was a sweet face, seen full. He began without a text, saying how the service had altered in fifty years, and the danger of our coming for what we got—outside accessories—for people spoke of liking and enjoying, just as if it were a musical act, or the opera. There was a danger in his being new to us and we to him. We were to look on him as a fellow wanderer in the garden—a fellow traveller hoping for light like ourselves."

A former choirboy from St. Mary's told Mr. Hudson in 1952 that the boys were sorry when Dodgson preached because he was so slow. "He remembered Dodgson as 'very frail' and his cassock as 'green with age!' 'The most terribly thin man I ever saw,' said Mr. Chalcraft. 'He looked as if he could do with a good dinner.'"

While he was at Guildford he offered to give a series of lectures on logic at Abbott's Hospital there, if as many as six persons showed interest. Since thirty persons attended the first lecture, the series was completed; undoubtedly he was a better lecturer to a mixed gathering than to the somewhat unpredictable undergraduates who had formed his audience twenty years before.

During the same visit he showed the students at the Girls' High School some mathematical puzzles and his *Memoria Technica*. His sisters had been unusually learned young ladies for their time, but female education had made great strides since then. Fifty years before girls had been left to half-trained governesses, whom Carroll called a "down-trodden race," [2] and among whom he claimed to have many friends.

One of the first girls' schools was founded to train clergymen's daughters as governesses. A hundred girls lived in the school, which overworked them with dull studies, dressed them without teaching them taste or care in dress, and permitted them only one visit home a year. Out of pure sympathy for the boredom and ignorance of girls, Frederick Denison Maurice started giving lectures to sisters of his pupils in 1871, forming the nucleus of Newnham College, which by the nineties was, like Girton and others, on the same academic basis as the men's colleges except for the amount of Latin and Greek required.

In 1896 Dodgson was still dubious about the effect of higher education on women's health, deciding that the safest method would be to establish a women's university. It was only four decades since Thackeray had said: "This is the condition of a young lady's existence: She breakfasts at 8, she does Mangnall's *Questions* till 10; she practises till 1, she walks in the square with bars round her till 3, then she practises again, then she sews or reads French or Hume's *History;* then she comes down to play to papa, because he likes music, while he is asleep after dinner." [3] Even Ruskin, champion of liberty, had said: " A man ought to know any language or science he learns thoroughly; while a woman should know the same language, or science, so far as to enable her to sympathize in her husband's pleasures, and in those of his best friends." [4] And now the young ladies were studying everything their brothers did, though with less emphasis on the classics —they had political and debating societies, played lawn tennis and "fives," and even rode bicycles in "rational dress." In the previous year, a physician writing in *The Nineteenth Century* had opposed the limitation of women to tricycles, on the ground that "a sound woman can cycle, and with benefit to herself. The muscles of the lower extremity need development." Victoria was indeed on her last limbs.

(Dodgson did not declare himself on the subject of bicycles for women, but, after trying a friend's "velociman" in 1882, he said, "In youth ride a bicycle, in age buy a tricycle.")

It was in the nineties that a young lady at Girton College remarked, "All might be well if we could have three generations of single women." But just one of the changes in the Oxford Dodgson returned to in January, 1897, was that there were fewer single women—because fewer single men—in academic society. There were married tutors now, and the married tutors had grown daughters, who gave "Cinderella balls" that lasted till midnight.

There were clubs, too, for men and women interested in art, archaeology, *belles-lettres*, music, and "mere" sociability. Jowett had broken the ice, and since his time men and women of distinction in various fields had acquired the habit of visiting Oxford and introducing their wider interests and more cosmopolitan manners. From the seamy side of society other views and influences were coming in. At Ruskin College and in the University as a whole, many of the newer students were workingmen and artisans and sons of small shopkeepers. They raised the tone rather than lowering it, as the diehards had feared they would. In 1898 the Warden of Merton College wrote that the men were "as a whole more virtuous, better conducted, better informed than under George III," and also that ladies were safer without escorts, all over town, because of the "gentleness and frankness in the new generation." He added that religious talk was now open, and the "grave reticence" formerly thought necessary on religious subjects was giving place to freedom of discussion and even to "Christian agnosticism." [5] The mantle of Newman had fallen on Niemand.

Oxford had finally introduced a chair of English literature in 1896. Some nine years before, this plan had almost carried, but instead the philologists had captured the chair by "transforming it into a chair of language and securing it for themselves." For many Oxford men still considered the study of English literature as a "contemptible excrescence on the academic curriculum." [6]

Perhaps because of his simple, healthful routine, Dodgson had suffered remarkably little illness in his life. In 1870 he almost missed Christmas at Guildford because of a bad cough, which kept him in Oxford till December 24. The next entry on illness comes on July 10, 1883: "I have kept my rooms since the middle of Sunday with a sort of ague, with cystitis: I have had two miserable feverish nights, in a state between waking and sleeping, and worrying over the same idea (something about Common Room ledgers) over and over again."

Three days later he felt better: ". . . dined in Common Room, but have not ventured yet on beer or wine."

July 20: "I have had a relapse since last Friday, and yesterday was the worst day I have had. Tonight I am very thankful to feel really better again."

July 26: "During my illness I have been a great novel-reader and have read—the Bar Sinister by C. K. Collins—decidedly clever; Pride and Prejudice—a charming picture of by-gone manners: Old Kensington by Miss Thackeray—lovely writing; A Fair Saxon by Justin McCarthy—excellent; Lady Aroostook by Howells—capitally written—A Chance Acquaintance by the same—not quite so good."

In September of the following year he suffered "a feverish cold of the ague type."

In 1885 he begins to record the scintillating scotoma, as it is now called, which he described as "moving fortifications," sometimes accompanied by migraine headache. He records altogether six of these experiences.

In 1889 and 1890 he had a series of symptoms—a boil, synovitis in first one knee, then the other, ague cystitis, and lumbago. In 1891 he fainted "just at the end of morning chapel. I found myself, an hour afterwards, lying on the floor of the stalls; and had probably struck my nose against the hassock, as it had been bleeding considerably. It is the first time I fainted quite away. I sent for Dr. Brooks. I had some headache afterwards, but felt very little the worse. In the afternoon Mrs. Hoare brought Mabel . . . she seems a nice child, and more refined and lady-like than ordinary stage-children."

It was six months before he felt able to take a train trip by himself. The following Christmas he spent at Christ Church alone, for the first time in his life, with synovitis. He had been seeing the moving fortifications again, and was carrying on a mathematical polemic with Cook Wilson.

There are no more entries on his health.

In 1894 he wrote: "I'm 62, and, though I'm in good working order now (I can easily work ten hours a day) I can't in reason expect many more years of it. At present I'm hard at work (& have been for months) on my Logic-book. (It has really been on hand for a dozen years: the 'months' refer to preparing for the Press)." [1]

In the same letter he gave the lie to any presumptuous biographer who might suppose his life was unhappy. Whether it reflected a mood, or an aspect, or whether it was the simple truth, he must be allowed to give his evidence. "To say I am quite well 'goes without saying' with me. In fact my life is so strangely free from all trial and trouble, that I cannot doubt my own happiness is one of the talents entrusted to me to 'occupy' with, till the Master shall return, by doing something to make other lives happy." [1]

His big "something to make other lives happy" was already accomplished. His Arcadian spirit was no more. *Sylvie and Bruno* reached a comparatively small audience, but he comforted himself with the thought that the price of 7/6 was prohibitive, and plugged away on his *Symbolic Logic,* Part II. In 1896 he had written Louisa about a book he had planned on religious difficulties: "I have changed my plan. It seems to me that *that* subject is one that hundreds of living men could do, if they would only try, much better than I could, whereas there is no living man who could (or at any rate who would take the trouble to) arrange, and finish, and publish, the 2nd Part of the Logic. Also I have the the Logic book in my head: it will only need three or four months to write out." [7] But those months it never got, and no other man did take the trouble to finish it.

In April, 1897, he recorded his "eighteen-mile round," which took five hours and twenty-seven minutes. This was not quite enough, for two months later he bought a "Whitely Exerciser," which pleased him so much that he also bought several for friends.

In the summer he spent the Long Vacation at Eastbourne as usual, often walking twenty miles to Hastings to visit his mother's sisters. When he took young Collingwood on walks, it was the uncle who tired out the nephew on these excursions over the sands of Surrey on a broiling day, the uncle still fully clad in black clerical coat, top hat, and gloves.

On September 27 and 28, he solved some mathematical

problems which had long been worrying him, and in November he solved some others. On October 28, he received the galley proofs of *Eternal Punishment*. On November 20, he saw Winifred Emery play in Barrie's *Little Minister,* a performance which charmed and delighted him. In December, he was still sitting up nights in a cold room over a "tempting problem" sent him from New York. On the twenty-third, he went to Guildford for Christmas with his sisters at "The Chestnuts," taking *Symbolic Logic* along to work on.

His health and mentality were still perfect on the New Year. On January 5, he received the news of the brief illness and death of his brother-in-law, the Reverend C. S. Collingwood, Rector of Southwick. The telegram asked Charles to come to his sister, which he planned to do next day. Instead, he came down with influenza too badly even to read family prayers. Within a week he had bronchial symptoms. He asked his sisters to read the hymn of which every stanza ends, "Thy will be done." He was in no sense ready to die—his work was unfinished, his mind active, his health, till the influenza struck, excellent. His death fits into no pattern of necessity—it was a stab in the dark.

On January thirteenth, he said, "Take away those pillows— I shall need them no more." By the following afternoon he was past needing anything; the doctor left the death chamber saying to his sisters, "How young your brother looks!" [1] He was buried in the Guildford cemetery under a simple white cross cut with the name of Charles Lutwidge Dodgson, and below it, the name of Lewis Carroll—united in death.

Chapter 19

The Flame of the Candle

> "... for it might end, you know," said
> Alice, "in my going out altogether, like a
> candle. I wonder what I should be like then?"
> And she tried to fancy what the flame of a
> candle is like after it is blown out, for she
> could not remember ever having seen such a
> thing.

COLLINGWOOD HEADS the chapter section about his uncle's death: "*Wonderland* at last!" Perhaps Carroll's last dreams were pleasant ones, but it is reserved for his survivors to see how the flame of the candle looks.

"This is a dream story," wrote a critic in *The Athenaeum* in 1865, "but who can in cold blood manufacture a dream with all its loops and ties, and loose threads and entanglements and inconsistencies, and passages which lead to nothing, at the end of which Sleep's diligent pilgrim never arrives? Mr. Carroll has laboured hard to heap together strange adventures and heterogeneous combinations, and we acknowledge the hard labour. Mr. Tenniel, again, is square and grim and uncouth in all his illustrations, howbeit clever, even to the verge of grandeur, as is the artist's habit. We fancy that any real child might be more puzzled than enchanted by this stiff, overwrought story." [1]

The poor man who wrote that was in the predicament of the critic in *Fanny's First Play* who said, "You don't expect me to know what to say about a play unless I know who the author is, do you?" He must have been mildly astonished in 1868 to note that the book was still selling fast; in 1871, when *Through the Looking-Glass* sold 8,000 copies before the author could get one; in 1898 when the total copies of *Wonderland* sold reached 260,000; or, if he was still living, on April 3, 1928, when the original manuscript sold to Dr. A. S. W. Rosenbach for £15,400, a record price for any manuscript ever sold in England. What should be the final voyage of the manuscript took place in 1948, when Dr. Luther Evans, Librarian of Congress, presented it to the British Museum. In January, 1944, with the war going full blast, an 1865 *Alice* sold at Sotheby's for only £720 because it was rebound and in poor condition.

Fortunately, young Greville Macdonald and Henry Kingsley and the Liddell children had better taste and surer judgment than the critic. They knew a good story, without needing to know "who" the author was, and they saved the story for posterity. A writer in *The Academy* immediately after Carroll's death said: "*The Times* book review of the first issue of *Alice* gave high praise to Mr. Tenniel's drawings, but concerning Lewis Carroll's text remarked only that it was 'an excellent piece of nonsense.' *The Spectator* did not, I think, review the book at all, on its first appearance." [2]

By contrast, Canon Sanday preached a memorial sermon at Christ Church, speaking of the "rill bright and sparkling, health-giving, and purifying . . . the fount and spring from which all these varied activities took their direction . . . a deep background of religion." [3]

The year after Carroll's death C. M. Aikman remarks that the *Alice* books are "not merely classics of the nursery," but are quoted in political speeches and newspaper editorials, and suggest cartoons. [4]

It would be impossible now to trace all the uses the *Alice* books have served in quotation and parody, or as sources for book titles. One parody Carroll himself would have enjoyed is H. H. Munro (Saki)'s *Westminster Alice,* illustrated by F. Carruthers Gould with amusing political cartoons not too far after Tenniel. No one could mistake the book for genuine Carroll, but it shows close study and a sort of fellow-feeling—the rhythm, the use of words, the description of the Ineptitude, are all Carrollian.

In an unsigned article in *The Saturday Review* for January 22, 1898, the following appeared: "Today the child is the grown-up man's fairy book, taking the place of the old fairy-tales of chivalry. . . . Almost the first portent, Carroll's books struck the light." The writer extracts a moral from

Alice having been, he says, "put out of Wonderland and Looking-Glass Land for bad behavior. Is not all this a warning against that spirit of the age which will ask too many meanings and try to import too much reason into the Edens still marvellously left to us?" But the extraordinary thing about that number of *The Saturday Review* is an omission. Shaw, in his dramatic review for the week, or for any other week, makes no mention of Carroll's death, though he dealt with the deaths of literary figures who, like Morris and Henley, had no more relation to the stage than Carroll did. The Shavian article that week was about a passion play, and included a long discussion about the morals of the stage, into which he could have fitted Carroll ideally. There must have been some lack of sympathy between the two playboys—Shaw in his letters to Ellen Terry never mentions Carroll, though he asks her, "Do you think at your age it is right?" and uses other quotations in a way that shows he knew the source well. Ellen Terry, who also knew Carroll well, never mentions him to Shaw either. Perhaps he was not taken seriously by his adult contemporaries, but in the case of Shaw it seems not impossible there might have been a temperamental antipathy. Carroll would have been far too old-maidish and class-bound for Shaw.

Alice's question about the flame of the candle may have an answer after all. After his death the Carrollian flame went on burning ever more brightly, and in 1924 even Oxford recognized him. On June 5 of that year, an exhibit opened in Christ Church Library, to celebrate the publication of Mr. Williams' *Bibliography*. "The exhibits included some unique and rare Carrolliana [of course Mr. Bayne's scrap books?]; an extensive and interesting series of Dodgson's works was also on view at the Bodleian* from May 18 for about three months." [5]

In July, 1898, the *Pall Mall Gazette* took an inventory of the popularity of children's books. *Alice in Wonderland* led them all. *Through the Looking-Glass,* lower down, was in the first twenty. It remains to be seen whether Hilaire Belloc was right in saying (in *The Cruise of the Nona*): "I am perfectly certain that [*Alice in Wonderland*] will not long survive the

* See Appendix L.

easy and unquestioned security of the England of Carroll's day." In the first place, the security was only skin deep. In the second place, what of the officer in *Journey's End* who read *Alice* in the trenches; the bombing scene where Mrs. Miniver reads *Alice* to her children; the persistence of *Alice* titles and chapter headings in current books?

There is room for an extensive study of James Joyce's use of Carroll in *Finnegans Wake*. A quick skirting* of the Joycean quicksands yields this gem: "We grisly old Sykos have done our unsmiling bit on 'alices, when they were yung and easily freudened.' " And Dr. Sewell takes the title of one of her chapters from the same bottomless work: "Dodgfather, Dodgson & Coo."

The centenary years saw an exhibit at Columbia University in New York, opened by Mrs. Hargreaves on her eightieth birthday. A few days later she received the degree of Doctor of Letters for having inspired a great work of English literature. . . . In that same year there was also an exhibit in London, where the marionette theater was shown, as well as the miniature tools Carroll had made for his sister Elizabeth, the Hatch collection, and, most poignant of all, "a square cap or mortarboard, much the worse for wear."

Beginning in his own lifetime, when ivory figures of the Tweedle brothers, Wonderland biscuit tins, stamp cases, and other knicknacks appeared, the *Alice* industry has continued † with playing cards, Christmas cards, birthday books—little figures in silver, glass, pottery, enamel—curtain materials— and of course infinite puppet shows, amateur theatricals, motion pictures, professional stage plays, musical suites, settings for the songs, and phonograph recordings.

Shortly after his death and again in the centenary year, Lewis Carroll cots were established in a London hospital. But a strange phenomenon occurred in the east in 1932: "Lewis Carroll's immortal book has been banned in the province of Hunan. . . . Says the war lord, 'Bears, lions, and other beasts cannot use a human language, and to attribute to them such a power is an insult to the human race.' " [6]

Mr. Reed speaks of having seen a good movie of *Alice*,

* Courtesy of Mr. Martin Gardner.
† See Appendix K.

which unfortunately was used as a ballet in a Hollywood film called *Puttin' on the Ritz*,[7] and which Hollywood will not allow to be presented separately. New York saw an excellent dramatization of *Alice* by Eva le Gallienne and Florida Friebus at the Civic Repertory Theater in 1932, and in 1943 Clemence Dane made a new version, which was put on in London with Carroll Dodgson, grandniece of Lewis Carroll, as the Cook.

In 1951 two Alice films arrived in New York almost simultaneously. The Tenniel drawings were still not in the public domain, so the two perpetrators, Walt Disney and Lou Bunin, did their worst.

Both of these productions aimed at the child audience; both relentlessly stepped up the tempo, stepped down the meaning, and broke up the rhythms with recurrent *ballets mécaniques* of endlessly repeated identical units. Both producers permitted themselves unlimited license with the order of incidents, the allotment of speeches to characters, and even the text. Both considered it necessary to omit or cut Lewis Carroll's verses and write new lyrics, which have been quickly forgotten.

An ideal *Alice* film would be a delicate enterprise. It should, like the Bunin film, use both puppets and live actors but would have no other similarity to the film. It would have to be an adult picture on two levels—inside Lewis Carroll's mind, where the other characters become puppets, and in the outside world around him, which was mostly Oxford. It is easy to hear a conversation in Hall, or in the Common Room, and switch to the Mad Tea Party with almost the same words.

A child's *Alice* picture is something else again, but the intense vulgarity and frightening sequences of these two films made them unsuitable for children as well as exasperating for adults. The loudness and fastness of the Disney film destroyed whatever of the poetry and philosophy had not already been expunged. There were some beautiful bits, especially in the Disney picture, but a worthy *Alice* film is still to do. And— Tenniel *is* in the public domain now.

In 1932, English and American magazines and newspapers were full of articles by literati, professors, and just people who had known Mr. Dodgson. Many of these articles, like one in the *Times Literary Supplement,* were mere word-weavings, of no more value in illuminating Carroll than are stories about Beethoven's landladies in increasing enjoyment of the *Eroica.*

An ambitious critique of Carroll is Walter de la Mare's "Carrollian Nonsense," in *The Eighteen-Eighties* (also reprinted as a separate book, *Lewis Carroll*). He gives a true anecdote of Queen Victoria to replace the one we were deprived of by stern fact and Mr. Dodgson, but it is not relevant to Carroll himself.

A few, like Miss Arnold's and Miss Rowell's articles, were solid fact, and still fewer, like Edmund Wilson's in the *New Republic,* shed real light. Mr. Wilson knows his Carroll, though he attributes to the White Queen an episode that belongs to her Red Sister. With his usual clarity, in less than two pages he evaluates and interprets Carroll as others have failed to do in a whole book. Mr. Wilson says, speaking of "the Ruskins, the Spencers, the George Eliots, the Thackerays, and the Carlyles—Dodgson had the advantage over all of them that he was able to work in the fields of mathematics and dreams." Mr. Wilson also senses the hidden irreverence of Carroll's mind "vowed to an academic discipline but cherishing an intense originality, painfully repressed and incomplete, but in the narrow field of [his] art somehow both sound and good." [8]

In his book, *The Shores of Light,* Mr. Wilson reprints and adds to his previous article. He takes issue with my belief that Dodgson's life was a sad and frustrated one: ". . . Dodgson, in terms of his age and place, was remarkably 'well-adjusted.' His enjoyment of the Oxford 'Studentship,' with its relatively agreeable work and exceptionally comfortable quarters which he won on his graduation, was dependent on his acceptance of celibacy; and there is nothing to show that this irked him much." Mr. Wilson also believes that Dodgson was comfortable as the inheritor of a long tradition of service to the Church, and at ease in his admiration for his father.

This seems like mere leaning over backward on Mr. Wilson's part, in order to make sure he will not project his own preferences onto a man so different from himself. It is true we would not have had these particular works of genius without the high-explosive compression that caused the fusion of these gems. But let us not forget the fission of his personality that was the price.

Mr. de la Mare quotes Walter Besant's dictum that *Alice* is one of the very few books in the world "which can be read with equal pleasure by old and young. . . . It is the only child's book of nonsense that is never childish." Mr. de la Mare continues: "And not only that, it admits us into a state of being which, until it was written, was not only unexplored but undiscovered. Nevertheless, like other rare achievements, it was the fruit of a happy accident. For once in a while the time and the place and the loved one came together. . . ."

So Mr. de la Mare also believes that Carroll's love for Alice was "real" love? Let the last word on the question be Carroll's own, the concluding paragraph of *Alice in Wonderland,* where Alice's sister rehearses the little girl's dream:

"Lastly, she pictures to herself how this same sister of hers would, in the after-time, be a grown woman; and how she would keep, through all her riper years, the simple and loving heart of her childhood, and how she would gather about her other little children, and make *their* eyes bright and eager with many a strange tale, perhaps even with the dream of Wonderland of long ago; and how she would feel with all their simple sorrows, and find a pleasure in all their simple joys, remembering her own child life and the happy summer-days."

Is that a sister's reverie or a lover's?

In his introduction to the one-volume *Works of Lewis Carroll,* Alexander Woollcott paid his respects to the psychoanalysts and hoped they would continue to leave Carroll alone. This omnibus volume appeared in 1937, but the analysts had already started on Carroll. In 1935 Esmé Wingfield-Stratford wrote an anti-Freudian book containing a burlesque psychoanalytic interpretation of *Jabberwocky,* purporting to show that Carroll had an Oedipus complex. It is a clever *reductio ad absurdum* of the early psychoanalytic technique, and in the form in which it is presented is neither convincing nor illuminating. Yet if, as the author chooses to suppose, the one who says, "Come to my arms, my beamish boy" is the *parent* of the hero, and if Tenniel made the Jabberwock look like a Victorian Papa, Mr. Stratford's burlesque is not completely off key—only a quarter-tone off.[9]

In his new edition of the *Handbook,* Mr. Green takes issue with "Mrs. Becker Lennon's [sic] psychological interpretation of 'Jabberwocky' which turns on the fact that the 'beamish boy' is welcomed by his parent instead of by a beautiful maiden."

Can there be any other than a psychological interpretation? What Mr. Green has uncovered about the added sources of the poem is new and interesting. Dodgson's cousin, Miss Menella Smedley, rendered into English a long, rambling German poem by Fouqué. Her version appeared in the March 7 and 21 issues of *Sharpe's Magazine,* and there can be no doubt Dodgson read it and used some of it. But what he chose, and what he did with that, remains a psychological question.

The Fouqué hero is a young shepherd lad who sharpens the iron tip of his shepherd's staff and slays the Griffin that has been devastating the flocks. The Duke, or Prince (he seems to have both titles), salutes him:

"Come to my heart, my true and gallant son," and rewards the shepherd with his daughter (which should make the lad his son-in-law).

Mr. Green believes the presence of the beautiful maiden in the German poem "explains" "Come to my heart, my beamish boy!" and removes any question of whom the Jabberwock-slayer was trying to please. Mr. Green has slung a boomerang, however. Uncovering more sources only makes Jabberwocky curiouser and curiouser. Humpty Dumpty had every opportunity to supply the gloss and inform Alice that the hero was about to be rewarded with a beautiful maiden. It is not the Fouqué poem that is under analysis.

On December 30, 1936, when Mr. Woollcott's preface was no doubt already in print, *The New York Times* quoted Dr. Paul Schilder to the effect that *Alice* was unsuitable for children. Dr. Schilder found that Carroll showed "Oral sadistic traits of cannibalism," "enormous anxiety," "fear of being cut to pieces . . . continuous threat to the integrity of the body." He said that the book portrayed "severe deprivations in the sphere of food and drink—when little girls went to see Dodgson they never got enough tea and usually went away hungry." He "takes liberties with time and language . . . world of cruelty and anxiety . . . destruction and annihilation."

For ten days the *Times* resounded with letters, telegrams, and telephone calls setting Dr. Schilder right, and, in *The Nation* for January 30, 1937, Mr. Joseph Wood Krutch reminded Dr. Schilder that it was Freud who first called our attention to the "polymorphous perverse" tendency of all children, and the presence in the most normal unconscious mind of all sorts of primitive vestigia. The best analyst—and Dr. Schilder was one of the best—is not necessarily an authority on literature. It does take more than neurosis to make a writer, and it is possible to be an excellent analyst without much sense of humor or poetic imagination. Freud himself, as Max Eastman has showed, had not an intuitive sense of humor—especially of British humor, which is surely *Ding an sich*. Mr. Eastman's discovery of the baby joke of being playfully tossed and caught by an unexpected person illumines more of Carroll than does the Other Professor's Black Light. Before the baby can be tossed or tickled, it must be reassured —put into a playful mood with persons it recognizes and trusts. Given this situation, it will take the most potentially dangerous games as they are meant—in fun.

But Carroll knew all this intuitively. Remember how he consulted thirty mothers to find out whether the picture of the Jabberwock was too terrifying to use as a frontispiece. By using the White Knight, as he finally decided to do, he introduced the children gradually, through a mild-mannered oddity, to the world of—not cruelty and anxiety, but security in the presence of the unknown. It is doubtful that any intelligent child ever suffered neurosis or anxiety over the *Alice* books, and the officer in *Journey's End* who reads *Alice* in the trenches for consolation has profound verisimilitude.

Dr. Schilder was right about Carroll's own anxieties and peculiar impulses; cruelty was a serious problem with him. But that is where analysts fall down—they may correctly analyze the artist without thereby understanding or enjoying the art. Carroll, being a consummate artist and, essentially, a kind man, solved his problems in his work. His youthful productions show his conflicts in their crudest form, but his brothers and sisters enjoyed the early magazines and had only love and reverence for him, so we must assume that the raw materials were converted into an art form in his personality also. Actually he drew no blood, and sharpened his pen only on opponents well able to defend themselves. His Oxford pamphlets, directed against his peers—so far as he had any peers—were keen-edged. But his sword-juggling and tight-rope walking—often the rope is only a hair—constitute part of the delight he gives children and adults alike. His delicacy, his skill, his perfect taste, permit him to handle the most dangerous materials with pleasure to all.

The final test of a work of art is—not what was in the artist's mind—but what does it do to the audience? And on that score Carroll well deserves the prayer of thankfulness for his gift of laughter which Mr. Wilfrid Partington says was offered up in an English cathedral in the centenary year.

There is a strange passage in Virginia Woolf's *The Moment and Other Essays:* "But the Reverend C. L. Dodgson had no life. He passed through the world so lightly that he left no print. . . . 'My life,' he said, 'is free from all trial and trouble.' But this untinted jelly contained within it a perfectly hard crystal. It contained childhood. . . . For some reason, we know not what, his childhood was sharply severed. It lodged in him whole and entire. He could not disperse it. And therefore as he grew older this impediment in the center of his being, this hard block of pure childhood, starved the mature man of nourishment. . . . But since childhood remained in him entire, he could do what no one else has ever been able to do—he could return to that world, he could recreate it, so that we too become children again. . . . It is for this reason that the two *Alices* are not books for children; they are the only books in which we become children."

The most exhaustive and perspicacious analysis of Carroll's work to date, exceeding Mr. Wilson's in scope, is that of Mr. William Empson, whose *English Pastoral Poetry* gives over the last chapter to a study of the *Alice* books. Every Carrollian should read this chapter, if only because Mr. Empson's findings agree so well with those in the present book.

Mr. Empson makes proper use of the psychoanalytic approach, of which he says: "Its business here is not to discover a neurosis peculiar to Dodgson. The essential idea behind the books is a shift onto the child, which Dodgson did not invent, of the obscure tradition of pastoral. The formula is now 'child-becomes-judge,' and if Dodgson identifies himself with the child so does the writer of the primary sort of pastoral with his magnified version of the swain. . . . (The child is a microcosm, like Donne's world, and Alice too is a stoic.) This runs through all Victorian and Romantic literature; the world of the adult made it hard to be an artist, and they kept a sort of taproot going down to their experiences as children. . . . . One reason for the moral grandeur of the [White] Knight, then, is that he stands for the Victorian scientist, who was felt to have invented a new kind of Roman virtue; earnestly, patiently, carefully . . . without sensuality, without self-seeking, without claiming any but a fragment of knowledge, he goes on laboring at his absurd but fruitful conceptions." The whole chapter is tempting to quote, showing a warm critical sympathy with Carroll, and placing him well at the top, but with affectionate amusement.

Peter Alexander finds relationships between Lewis Carroll and the Marx brothers. The latter told Professor Alexander that people laugh when they overcome the conventions of their normal life. "We laugh at infringements of decorum." He feels that Lewis Carroll, being so bound, wished to be free; his will to escape was facilitated by his command of logic.

"Alice is in their world physically but not mentally, and she can not afford to laugh at it as we can, being outside. The Marx brothers, though less skillfully, create at the beginnings of their films situations which assert false propositions and lead us to regard anything as possible. . . . Groucho is a horse doctor. He feels Harpo's pulse and says, 'Either he's dead or my watch has stopped.' " [10]

Henri Parisot considers Carroll the ancestor of Kafka, Henri Michaux, Alfred Jarry, and Raymond Roussel, and reminds us of the mirrors in Cocteau's film *Le Sang d'un Poète* and *Orphée*. He also feels the surrealist painters such as Duchamp owe him a great deal. He gives partial translations of the *Alices* (the book is in the series *Poètes d'Aujourd'hui,* published by Seghers), but says the difficulties of a proper translation are almost insurmountable.[11]

Hudson speaks of the "three states of being" in *Sylvie and Bruno* as possible instigators of *The Bluebird* and *Mary Rose,* to which we might add *Berkeley Square* and *Brigadoon,* which brings in a hidden element in Lewis Carroll's *autre monde,* the Elysian Fields of the Odyssey—the world of the dead as spirits. His odd remark about the time when he would be able to say "Death is over now" seems to imply a certain uneasiness in the presence of our common enemy.

Though Carroll's own best writing was his simplest, and though all his critics deplore his arabesques, yet he wrings flowery tributes from the sternest stylists. The *Alice* books are inexhaustible, like the *Fifth Symphony,* or Botticelli's "Primavera"—the pattern, the rhythm, the flow, the color, the relation of parts to each other and to the whole, are at the same time so basic and yet so subtly woven that the eye, the ear, the soul never tire of contemplating them. There is also a fruitful joy in returning to them after absence, for each new contemplation yields new beauties, new infinities, strengths, and subtleties, and—in the single case of *Alice*—new humor.

For instance, in rereading *Wonderland,* we find that scene when Alice vainly tries to make the Frog Footman understand that she wants to get into the house. After pages, she finally says, " 'But what am *I* to do?'

" 'Anything you like,' said the Footman, and began whistling.

" 'Oh, there's no use in talking to him,' said Alice desperately; 'he's perfectly idiotic.' And she opened the door and went in."

This is Socrates meditating on the battlefield, while the impatient general simply wins the battle without regard for rules —the perfect logical sequence from nothing back to nothing. If Carroll's meanings were meaningless, it was because he had his tongue in his cheek.

Or this Chaplinesque comedy from *Through the Looking-Glass:*

" 'Ah well, they may write such things in a *book,*' Humpty Dumpty said in a calmer tone. 'That's what they call a History of England, that is. Now take a good look at me! I'm one that has spoken to a King, *I* am: mayhap you'll never see such another: and, to show you I'm not proud, you may shake hands with me!' And he grinned almost from ear to ear, as he leant forwards (and as nearly as possible fell off the wall in doing so) and offered Alice his hand. She watched him a little anxiously as she took it. 'If he smiled much more the ends of his mouth might meet behind,' she thought, 'and then I don't know *what* would happen to the top of his head! I'm afraid it would come off!' "

The snobbish Humpty Dumpty, still affable though he has spoken to a King—pathetic in his absurdity because his fall is so close—reminds us of the death-sentence that never rings so hollowly as at our heights of grandeur; the motherly little Alice, ignoring all nonsense of caste, merely concerned that he might lose the top of his empty head—the whole scene resembles the recurrent one in the early Chaplin films where the little hero had his moment of strutting before his girl, before the eventual catastrophe.

Carroll's Dodgson self was as precise about minutiae as the Frog Footman, and almost as snobbish as Humpty Dumpty —he never forgot to write his cousins when he had met a princess, and he took a great deal of trouble to get a photograph of the Prince of Wales, finally having to content himself with an autograph—but down in his treacle well, where the creatures of his inner life had their home with Elsie, Lacie, and Tillie, he was beyond all cant, all caste, and, in the derogatory sense, all nonsense.

Behold the poet who was no prosodist, the artist who could not draw, the actor who stuttered, the preacher who could barely believe his own doctrine, the dramatist who could not write plays, the instructor of geometry who bored his students, the inventor of games and gadgets, the champion doodler of Christ Church, the Curator of the Common Room—dull, conscientious, kindly, awkward, and lonely. But stutter as he did, irregular as his gait was, left-handed as his approach to a carving knife may have been, in the presence of a basic issue he was fundamentally sound—not only sound, but accurate as a surgeon who makes no unnecessary scars. He carries the imbecilities of the creatures up to a certain point, and then with a sure stroke puts an end to them.

" 'What's your name, child?'

" 'My name is Alice, so please your Majesty,' said Alice very politely; but she added, to herself, 'Why, they're only a pack of cards, after all. I needn't be afraid of them.'

" 'And who are *these?*' said the Queen, pointing to the three gardeners who were lying round the rose-tree. . . .

" 'How should *I* know?' said Alice, surprised at her own courage. 'It's no business of *mine.*'

"The Queen turned crimson with fury, and, after glaring at her for a moment like a wild beast, began screaming 'Off with her head! Off with—'

" 'Nonsense!' said Alice very loudly and decidedly, and the Queen was silent."

For the master of nonsense knew when fun was fun, and when it was necessary to be loud and decided about it. Without solving all his own life problems, or making full use of the science of his own day, he still broke ground that has proved endlessly fertile for his inheritors.

After retracing all we could of his journey, we still do not fully understand how he came to write *Alice.* Perhaps this riddle, like the March Hare's, has no real answer. But we do know that he made himself at home on both sides of the looking-glass, patched up his quarrel with time, and managed to hold the glass for his readers to see how they look under the gaze of—if not eternity, at least an æon, "a very long time."

APPENDIX

Appendix

APPENDIX A

IN THE *Cornhill Magazine,* "E.L.S." writes of "Lewis Carroll as Artist." She claims to have been the artist in whose studio Carroll drew little girls "from the figure," and her story has perfect verisimilitude, even though she does not give her name. (See has since been identified as Mrs. Shute.) She speaks of Carroll as having "two profiles"—says that his eyes and the corners of his mouth did not match, but that he was handsome nevertheless. She is also authority for his having been deaf in one ear, and is most specific about it, since she suffered from the same affliction, and describes the difficulties she had in her childhood (for she started as a child-friend) dodging to keep him on the side of her good ear, since he "did all the talking." But his good ear was also the right one, and he always circumvented her attempts to get on the side most favorable for herself. She always got a crick in her neck on these walks, but claims it was well worth it.

APPENDIX B

IN *The Nineteenth Century* for October, 1887, a Mr. Edward Salmon wrote an article called "Literature for the Little Ones." He said: "Between Tom Hood and Mr. Lewis Carroll—to call Mr. C. Dodgson Lutwidge [sic] by his famous nom-de-plume—there is more than a suspicion of resemblance in some particulars. *Alice in Wonderland* narrowly escapes challenging a comparison with *From Nowhere to the North Pole.* The idea of both is so similar that Mr. Carroll can hardly have been surprised if some people have believed he was inspired by Hood. Both books deal with the contorted events which figure in a child's dream, and both may be almost equally described by some lines from the initial verse of *Alice's Adventures in Wonderland,* addressed to those who in fancy pursue

> *The dream-child moving through a land*
> *Of wonders wild and new,*
> *In friendly chat with bird or beast—*
> *And half believe it true.*

"Though *Alice's Adventures in Wonderland* and *Through the Looking-Glass* are undeniably clever and possess many charms . . . there is nothing extraordinarily original about them, and certainly the former cannot fairly be called, as it once was, the most

401

remarkable book for children of recent times. Both these records of Alice's adventures would be but half as attractive as they are, without Mr. John Tenniel's illustrations. Of the two books, *Through the Looking-Glass* is the more humorous, chiefly owing to the fact that, after Alice has climbed through the mirror, everything is reverse, and that to reach a certain point it is apparently necessary to walk away from it. Mr. Carroll is an irrepressible punster. *Through the Looking-Glass* contains a pun which is particularly good. Alice is introduced to the Leg of Mutton. She immediately asks the Red Queen if she shall cut her a slice. "Certainly not," answers the Red Queen. "It isn't Etiquette to cut someone you've been introduced to." In *Alice in Wonderland* the funniest idea is the little heroine's telescopic physique. Mr. Carroll's style is as simple as his ideas are extravagant. This probably accounts for the fascination which these stories of a child "moving under skies never seen by human eyes" have had over the minds of so many thousands of children and parents.

"To Mr. George Macdonald belongs the credit due to a really original writer." The author then extols *At the Back of the North Wind.*

Carroll with all dignity ignored the miscalling of his name, and in fact did nothing till 1890, three years later, when at the very end of *The Nursery "Alice,"* in the advertising pages, he printed two "cautions"—one, that a story in *Aunt Judy's Magazine* No. 184, wrongly attributed to him, was by Fräulein Ida Lackowitz, and had been supposed to be his work because he forwarded it to the editor. The other caution follows:

"In October, 1887, the writer of an article on 'Literature for the Little Ones,' in *The Nineteenth Century,* stated that, in 1864, 'Tom Hood was delighting the world with' " etc. (See above.) "The date 1864 is a mistake. *From Nowhere to the North Pole* was first published in 1874." That was all he ever did about it.

Through his own imperfect apprehension of Alice, this Mr. Salmon lets us see how his contemporaries felt about the book. In 1886, Salmon took a census of 1,000 girls. (But did he?) The author read by the highest number, 330, was Dickens. Next came Scott, with 226, Kingsley and Charlotte Yonge, each with 91, Shakespeare with 73. After many others came Ruskin with 6 and Lewis Carroll with 5. This hardly squares with what he said later.

APPENDIX C

Jabberwocky has been translated into German, French, Greek, and Latin. Information about the authors, etc., is to be found in *The Lewis Carroll Picture Book,* with the translations, except the French one that appeared in *The New Yorker* on Jan. 10, 1931, written by Frank L. Warrin:

LE JASEROQUE

Il brilgue: les tôves lubricilleux
Se gyrent en vrillant dans le guave,
Enmîmés sont lest gougebosqueux
Et le mômerade horsgrave.

Garde-toi du Jaseroque, mon fils!
La gueule qui mord; la griffe qui prend!
Garde-toi de l'oiseau Jube, évite
Le frumieux Band-à-prend.

Son glaive vorpal en main il va-
T-à recherche du fauve manscant;
Puis arrivé à l'arbre Té-Té,
Il y reste, réfléchissant.

Pendant qu'il pense, tout uffusé
Le Jaseroque, à l'œil flambant,
Vient siblant par le bois tullegeais,
Et burbule en venant.

Un deux, un deux, par le milieu,
Le glaive vorpal fait pat-à-pan!
La bête défaite, avec sa tête,
Il rentre gallomphant.

As-tu tué le Jaseroque?
Viens à mon cœur, fils rayonnais!
O jour frabbejeais! Calleau! Callai!
Il cortule dans sa joie.

Il brilgue: les tôves lubricilleux
Se gyrent en vrillant dans le guave,
Enmîmés sont les gougebosqueux,
Et le mômerade horsgrave.

In spite of the numerous translations of *Alice's Adventures* and of "Jabberwocky," the rest of *Through the Looking-Glass* has resisted all attempts at translation, perhaps because of the difficult word plays.

The Sisters Jest and Earnest, by Maurice Hutton, contains renditions of "The Walrus and the Carpenter," "The Gardener's Song," and "Father William" into Greek.

F. S. Morgan wrote a letter to *The Times* on Jan. 14, 1932, about a papier mâché Jabberwock he saw in his youth.

APPENDIX D

Sewanee Review, April–June, 1940
"Triple Alice," George Shelton Hubbell

HE FINDS three Alices—the original Alice, the ideal Alice, Tenniel's Alice.

Alice Pleasance Liddell married Reginald Gervis Hargreaves (1852–1926.)

He was a typical country gentleman—Eton & Christ Church. A good shot—a fisherman & cricketer—a great reader, especially of French. At Cuffnells, Lyndhurst, Hants, he had an arboretum, wtih Oriental trees, California redwoods, and Douglas pines.

Alice lived there forty years and raised her three sons there. Two, both captains, were killed in World War I. Captain Caryl Hargreaves served in the Scots Guards, and lived to become the father of another Alice. He became Wing Commander Caryl Hargreaves and died in 1954.

L. C. wrote Alice, supposing her first baby was a girl and would be named Alice. "When she asked him to be godfather to her *son,* he characteristically failed to reply." (Captain Caryl Hargreaves, *The New York Times,* May 1, 1932.)

Clair Price, visiting there in 1932, saw no pictures or mementos of Carroll in the library at Cuffnells. The funeral was held in Lyndhurst Parish Church. She is buried in Lyndhurst near her home. (*The New York Times,* with corrections by Commander Hargreaves, who also described an extensive Carroll collection in the library "locked up.")

APPENDIX E

ALICE LIDDELL'S presentation copy was not, as Collingwood thought, a true first edition. After forty-eight copies had been given away, Carroll decided the printing and the reproduction of the illustrations were not good enough—*i.e.,* not perfect—and recalled the whole edition. He was able to do this because of the unusual nature of his arrangement with the publishers, but some of the copies were not returned, and have since fetched fabulous prices.

The remaining 1952 copies were shipped to New York and sold to Appleton, unbound. Charles Morgan, in *The House of Macmillan,* says that Dodgson's correspondence with the firm shows he felt that copies not good enough for England were quite adequate for America; in fact "This opinion was confirmed in 1888. The coloured pictures in the first printing of the *Nursery Alice* were condemned by him as too gaudy. No copy, he said, was to be sold in England; all were to be offered to America. They were offered, and declined as not being gaudy enough."

Mr. John T. Winterich, in his *Books and the Man,* says: "The Appleton copies show the author was somewhat hypercritical in recalling the 1865 *Alice.*" That seems likely. Mrs. Skene had forgotten, till the sale of the original manuscript in 1928, that her sister's copy was not an authentic first. Commander Hargreaves disputed this, but it is what Mrs. Skene conveyed to me.

APPENDIX F

EACH OF the four leading ladies enjoyed the distinction of having a book dedicated to her with an acrostic poem.

Through the Looking-Glass ends with "A boat, beneath a sunny sky," an acrostic on Alice Pleasance Liddell.

The Hunting of the Snark has a dedicatory poem which is a double acrostic to Gertrude Chataway. The first letters reading down spell her name, and the first words of the stanzas are "Girt," "Rude," "Chat," and "Away."

Sylvie and Bruno has an acrostic to Isa Bowman, also double.

Sylvie and Bruno Concluded has a variation—the third letter of each line of the opening poem, read downward, spells "Enid Stevens."

APPENDIX G

IT WAS the writer's good fortune to pick up in Oxford a little book from Carroll's own library, with his rubber stamp and his monogram initial in violet ink. This little book, of only eighty-eight pages, shows up in some of the speculations on time and space in *Sylvie and Bruno,* and probably elsewhere. It is an odd commingling of religion, of the astronomy of the 1870's, and of Einsteinian premonitions. The book, called *The Stars and the Earth, or Thoughts Upon Time, Space, and Eternity,* is anonymous. It was published in Boston by Noyes, Holmes, and Company, in 1874. This copy is the "Fourth American, from the Third English edition." It contains a laudatory article by the Reverend Thomas Hill, saying the book is along the lines of his own *Geometry and Faith.* In spite of the jumble of religion and science it contains some pregnant ideas that undoubtedly stimulated Carroll.

APPENDIX H

JOHN FRANCIS MCDERMOTT, former Professor in the Department of English, Washington University, St. Louis, Mo., is the editor of the *Collected Verse of Lewis Carroll,* published by E. P. Dutton & Co., in 1929. His introduction is original and interesting, but he perpetuates an un-Carrollian error in spelling, for which he must be challenged—namely, "borogroves" instead of "borogoves." The error also appears in Collingwood and in some American editions of *Looking-Glass* (not in the poem itself, but in

Humpty Dumpty's explanation of it). It has become a common American mistake in reciting *Jabberwocky;* nevertheless, no matter how aged and respectable, it is still an error. The first edition of *Looking-Glass* has "borogoves," and so has the manuscript verse in the *Rectory Umbrella*.

The other typographical errors in the volume, and they are many, may be charged to the printers.

APPENDIX I

Mathematical and Logical Works in Carroll's Library
(Information from Miss F. Menella Dodgson, supplemented by Dr. Eric T. Bell.)

Faraday's *Lectures* (popular).

G. S. Carr's *Synopsis of Pure Mathematics,* Vol. I, Part I, London, 1880.

Dr. Bell says: "This book—or L. C.'s possession of at least a part of it—is of interest. The great Hindoo mathematician, S. Ramanujar, d. 1920 at age of 32, taught himself mathematics from this book. Since Ramanujar's time, Carr's *Synopsis* has acquired an immortality neither its author nor any mathematician of C.L.D.'s time would have believed possible."

Schrön's *Logarithms.*

J. N. Keynes' *Studies and Exercises in Formal Logic.*

George Boole's *Laws of Thought.*

Bosanquet's *Logic.* Dr. Bell says: "Outdated, even when written."

De Morgan's *Formal Logic.*

Mill's *Logic.*

Bradley's *Principles of Logic.* Dr. Bell dismisses the author as a "typical Oxford ass."

Welton's *Manual of Logic.* Dr. Bell says: "Not listed, don't know it—probably an elementary text."

Venn's *Logic of Chance* and *Symbolic Logic.*

Chas. Smith's *Conic Sections.* Dr. Bell says: "A hack writer of mathematical textbooks for English cram purposes."

Roach's *Elementary Trigonometry.*

De Morgan's *On Probabilities.*

Messenger of Mathematics, 6 vols. Dr. Bell says: "Pilloried by H.J.S. Smith as trivial compared to any of the great continental periodicals. Smith tried to raise the level by contributing . . . he scarcely succeeded, except for his own articles."

Legendre's *Géométrie.* Dr. Bell says: "A classic, the French substitute for Euclid, but a bad guide for anything connected with parallels—Dodgson's will-o'-the-wisp."

Mathematical Questions, from the *Educational Times.* Dr. Bell says: "Reprints of the problems and solutions in the monthly issues of the *E.T.* Nothing for a competent college teacher to be fooling away his time over." He goes on to say, however, that Dodgson may have taken them for the puzzles.

Wood's *Algebra*.

Bland's *Algebraical Problems*.

Dr. Bell says that De Morgan, Venn, and Mill are "all classics," and that Roach, Wood, and Bland are "mediocre texts. The choice of Wood, Bland, in preference to the available Peacock, is indicative of C. L. D.'s low mathematical taste and poor aptitude for mathematics."

Since Dr. Bell expressed his willingness to take the onus for these opinions, they must stand as his. The author of this book is not in a position to affirm or deny.

APPENDIX J

CURIOSA CARROLLIANA, refer anywhere.

ONE BOOK that cannot be treated in the body of this work still must not be neglected. It is *The Most Remarkable Echo in the World*, by H. M. and D. C. Partridge, privately printed in 1935 by the authors at Hastings-on-Hudson, New York.

The book purports to prove that Mark Twain wrote all the books usually attributed to Edgar Allan Poe, Nathaniel Hawthorne, and Lewis Carroll, and is well worth reading for its own sake. Its value as a study of Carroll must be decided by the reader.

NOTES TO CHAPTERS

Notes to Chapters

CHAPTER 1

1. *The Creevey Papers.*
2. Greville, *The Greville Diary,* Vol. V.
3. *Sylvie and Bruno.* In the preface Carroll says:
"The descriptions . . . of Sunday as spent by children of the last generation, are quoted *verbatim* from a speech made to me by a child-friend and a letter written to me by a lady-friend." No doubt, but the suspicion is strong that his own childhood is involved, e.g., the "square family pew" referred to by Collingwood in the *Life and Letters.* The tone is such as to justify the assumption that he is, essentially, speaking of himself and his own memories.
4. *The Life and Letters of Lewis Carroll,* by Stuart Dodgson Collingwood.

CHAPTER 2

1. *Swift and Carroll,* by Dr. Phyllis Greenacre.
2. *Lewis Carroll,* by Derek Hudson.
3. *History of the County Palatin & City of Cheshire,* by George Ormerod.
4. *Nineteenth Century.* Jan.–June, 1884, "My Schooldays from 1830–1840," by G. G. Bradley, Dean of Westminster.
5. *Quarterly Review,* Jan.–April, 1866, "Female Education."
6. *A Writer's Recollections,* by Mrs. Humphry Ward.
7. *Life and Letters,* by Collingwood.
8. *The Life of Lewis Carroll,* by Langford Reed.
9. Huntington Collection.

CHAPTER 3

1. *Life and Letters,* by Collingwood.
2. *History & Antiquities of Richmond in the County of York,* by Christopher Clarkson.
3. *Essays on a Liberal Education,* by Rev. F. W. Farrar.
4. Amory Collection.
5. *Recollections of a Town Boy at Westminster,* by F. Markham.
6. *The Great Schools of England,* by Howard Staunton.
7. *Lewis Carroll,* by Derek Hudson.
8. *Nineteenth Century,* Oct., 1892, "Stories of Old Eton," by C. Kegan Paul.
9. "To Me He Was Mr. Dodgson," by Ethel Rowell.
10. *Public Schools and British Opinion,* by Edward Clarence Mack.
11. *Arnold of Rugby; His School Life and Contributions to Education,* by J. J. Findlay.

12. *Life and Correspondence of Thomas Arnold,* by Arthur Penrhyn Stanley.
13. *Nineteenth Century,* Jan.–June, 1884, "My Schooldays from 1830–1840," by G. G. Bradley, Dean of Westminster.
14. *Quarterly Review,* Jan.–April, 1894. *Review of Life and Correspondence of Arthur Penrhyn Stanley, Dean of Westminster.*
15. *Matthew Arnold,* by Lionel Trilling.
16. *Catharine and Crawfurd Tait,* by A. C. Tait.
17. *Quarterly Review,* Oct., 1891. Review of *Life of Archibald Campbell Tait.*

CHAPTER 4

1. *A Writer's Recollections,* by Mrs. Humphry Ward.
2. *Oxford and Her Colleges,* by Goldwin Smith.
3. *Oxford and Its Story,* by Cecil Headlam.
4. *Praeterita,* by John Ruskin.
5. *The Christian Socialist Movement in England,* by Rev. G. C. Binyon.
6. *Quarterly Review,* July, 1894. Review of *Life of Dr. Pusey.*
7. *A History of the University of Oxford,* by C. E. Mallett,Vol. I & Vol. III to p. 58.
NOTE: from Vol. I (all other references to this book are from Vol. III): ". . . it was obstinate custom which for five centuries and a half preserved as a part of that ritual the strange old oath never to consent to the reconciliation of "Henry Simeonis" which originated in an affray of 1242."
8. *Quarterly Review,* April, 1897, Review of *Life of Benjamin Jowett.*
9. *Reminiscences of Oxford,* by Rev. Wm. Tuckwell.
10. *Life and Letters,* by Collingwood.
11. *Students' Handbook to the Universities and Colleges of Oxford.*
12. Amory Collection.
13. *A History of University Reform,* by A. I. Tillyard.
14. *Life and Letters of Henry Parry Liddon,* by J. O. Johnston.
15. *The Lewis Carroll Picture Book,* by Stuart Dodgson Collingwood.
16. *An Oxford Portrait Gallery,* by Janet Courtney.
17. *The Life and Letters of Benjamin Jowett,* by Abbott and Campbell.
18. *The Cornhill Magazine,* March, 1898, "Lewis Carroll," by T. B. Strong.
19. *Tom Brown at Oxford,* by Thomas Hughes.
20. *Nineteenth Century,* April, 1897, "Some Changes in Social Life during the Queen's Reign," by Sir Algernon West.
21. *Life of William Makepeace Thackeray,* by Lewis Melville.
22. *Strand Magazine,* May, 1901, "A Visit to Tennyson," by C. L. Dodgson.
23. *Complete Works,* by C. S. Calverley.
24. *Oxford of Today,* by Crosby and Aydelotte.

25. *Harper's Monthly*, July, 1890, "Social Life in Oxford," by E. M. Arnold.
26. *Collected Mathematical Papers*, by H. J. S. Smith.
27. *A Short Course of History*, by Havilland Chepmell.
28. *The White Knight—A Study of C. L. Dodgson*, by Alexander L. Taylor.
29. *Oxford Magazine*, June 4, 1908. Obituary of T. V. Bayne.
30. Private letter from Bishop Strong.
31. *The New York Times*, May 1, 1932, "Lewis Carroll as Recalled by Alice."
32. *Recollections of a Town Boy at Westminster*, by F. Markham.
33. "Henry George Liddell," by H. L. Thompson, in *Dictionary of National Biography*.
34. *Thomas and Matthew Arnold*, by Sir Joshua Fitch.

CHAPTER 5

1. *The Story of Lewis Carroll*, by Isa Bowman.
2. *Life and Letters*, by Collingwood.
3. *The Cornhill Magazine*, March, 1898, "Lewis Carroll," by T. B. Strong.
4. *Swift and Carroll*, by Dr. Phyllis Greenacre.
5. *The Lewis Carroll Picture Book*, by Stuart Dodgson Collingwood.
6. *Bibliotheca Sacra*, 1878, ed. by Edwards and Park, "Christ's Words on the Duration of Future Punishment."
7. *Life of Frederick Denison Maurice*, by J. F. Maurice.
8. *The Future of an Illusion*, by Sigmund Freud.
9. *Locksley Hall Sixty Years After*, by Alfred, Lord Tennyson.
10. *Harper's Magazine*, Feb., 1943, "To Me He Was Mr. Dodgson," by E. M. Rowell.
11. *The Life of Lewis Carroll*, by Langford Reed.
12. Interview with Mrs. Skene.
13. Maggs Catalogue, 449.
14. *The Story of My Life*, by Ellen Terry.
15. *The Story of Gilbert and Sullivan*, by Isaac Goldberg.
16. *Strand Magazine*, April, 1898, "Lewis Carroll," by Beatrice Hatch.
17. *Atlantic Monthly*, June, 1929, "Reminiscences of Lewis Carroll," by Ethel M. Arnold.
18. *Nineteenth Century*, Sept., 1882, "Merton College before the Reformation," by George C. Brodrick.
19. Huntington Collection.
20. *Lewis Carroll, Photographer*, by Helmut Gernsheim.
21. *Lewis Carroll*, by Derek Hudson.

CHAPTER 6

1. *The Cornhill Magazine*, July, 1932, "Alice's Recollections of Carrollian Days," by Captain Caryl Hargreaves.

2. *The New York Times,* May 1, 1932, "Lewis Carroll As Recalled by Alice," by Captain Caryl Hargreaves.
3. *The Lewis Carroll Picture Book,* by Stuart Dodgson Collingwood.
4. *George Macdonald and His Wife,* by Greville Macdonald.
5. *The House of Macmillan, 1843–1943,* by Charles Morgan.
6. *The Rossettis,* by Elisabeth Luther Cary.
7. *Pearson's Magazine,* Dec., 1930, "Lewis Carroll Letters to his Illustrator," by Dorothy Furniss.
8. Private letter from Mr. Falconer Madan.
9. *Burlington Magazine,* April, 1921, "A Portrait of the Ugliest Princess in History," by W. A. Baillie-Grohman.
10. *Edward Lear,* by Angus Davidson.
11. *The Road to Xanadu,* by John Livingston Lowes.
12. *The Story of Lewis Carroll,* by Isa Bowman.
13. *The White Knight—A Study of C. L. Dodgson,* by Alexander L. Taylor.
14. *Willard Gibbs,* by Muriel Rukeyser.

CHAPTER 7

1. *Letters of Matthew Arnold.*
2. *The Richmond Papers,* edited by Mrs. A. W. M. Stirling.
3. Letters from Mr. E. Norman Jones, Assistant Town Clerk of Llandudno, Wales, including quotations from Mr. James J. Marks, County Court Registrar.
4. *The Cornhill Magazine,* July, 1932, "Alice's Recollections of Carrollian Days," by Captain Caryl Hargreaves.
5. *The Diaries of Lewis Carroll,* edited by Roger Lancelyn Green.
6. *Some Reminiscences of William Michael Rossetti.*
7. *The Rossettis,* by Elisabeth Luther Cary.
8. *Life and Letters,* by Collingwood.
9. *Christina Rossetti,* by Mackenzie Bell.
10. *Christina Rossetti,* by Dorothy M. Stuart.
11. Private letter from Miss Dodgson.
12. *The Life of Christina Rossetti,* by Mary F. Sandars.
13. *Three Rossettis,* by Janet Camp Troxell.
14. "The Wife of Rossetti," by Violet Hunt.
15. *Dante Gabriel Rossetti, His Family Letters with a Memoir,* by Wm. Michael Rossetti.
16. *George Macdonald and His Wife,* by Greville Macdonald.
17. *Praeterita,* by John Ruskin.
18. *Edward Lear,* by Angus Davidson.
19. Private letter from Mr. Falconer Madan.

CHAPTER 8

1. *Five Great Oxford Leaders,* by Rev. Augustus B. Donaldson.
2. *An Oxford Portrait Gallery,* by Janet Courtney.

3. *Life and Letters of Henry Parry Liddon,* by J. O. Johnston.
4. *Life and Letters,* by Collingwood.
5. *International Survey of the Y. Men's and Y. Women's Christian Ass'ns.*
6. *Lewis Carroll,* by Derek Hudson.
7. *Russian Journal,* by Lewis Carroll.
8. *Bookman's Journal,* March, 1924, "Letters to Maud and Isabel Standen from C. L. Dodgson."

CHAPTER 9

1. *A History of University Reform,* by A. I. Tillyard.
2. *A Writer's Recollections,* by Mrs. Humphry Ward.
3. *An Oxford Portrait Gallery,* by Janet Courtney.
4. *Oxford and Her Colleges,* by Goldwin Smith.
5. *The Exquisite Tragedy,* by Amabel Williams-Ellis.
6. *A History of the University of Oxford,* by C. E. Mallett.
7. *An Oxford Correspondence of 1903,* edited by Wm. Warde Fowler.
8. *Nineteenth Century,* Feb., 1889, "The Sacrifice of Education to Examination," by Dr. Priestley.
9. *Students' Handbook of Oxford University.*
10. *Carroll's Alice,* by Harry Morgan Ayres.
11. *The Lewis Carroll Picture Book,* by Stuart Dodgson Collingwood.
12. Private letter from Mr. Falconer Madan.
13. *Life and Letters,* by Collingwood.
14. *The Story of Lewis Carroll,* by Isa Bowman.
15. Private letter from Mr. Christopher Hussey.
16. *The Diaries of Lewis Carroll,* edited by Roger Lancelyn Green.
17. *The New York Times,* May 1, 1932, "Lewis Carroll As Recalled by Alice," by Captain Caryl Hargreaves.
18. *Praeterita,* by John Ruskin.
19. *Atlantic Monthly,* June, 1929, "Reminiscences of Lewis Carroll," by Ethel M. Arnold.
20. Huntington Collection.
21. *The Bookman,* New York, Feb., 1908, "The Sketch Books of Wonderland," by Philip Loring Allen.
22. *Some Victorian Men,* by Harry Furniss.
23. *The Cornhill Magazine,* April, 1924, "Alice's Recollections," by Captain Caryl Hargreaves.
24. *The Life of Lewis Carroll,* by Langford Reed.

CHAPTER 10

1. *Carroll's Alice,* by Harry Morgan Ayres.
2. Letter from Miss Dodgson.
3. *Life and Letters,* by Collingwood.
4. *Swift and Carroll,* by Dr. Phyllis Greenacre.
5. *Some Letters from Lewis Carroll,* edited by Beatrice Hatch.

6. *The White Knight—A Study of C. L. Dodgson*, by Alexander L. Taylor.
7. *Nothing Dies*, by J. W. Dunne.
8. *The Annotated Alice*, by Martin Gardner.

Literature
CHAPTER 11

1. *Life and Letters*, by Collingwood.
2. *Swift and Carroll*, by Dr. Phyllis Greenacre.
3. *The Story of Lewis Carroll*, by Isa Bowman.
4. *Lewis Carroll*, by Derek Hudson.
5. Interview with Mrs. Skene.
6. *The Life of Lewis Carroll*, by Langford Reed.
7. *Atlantic Monthly*, June, 1929, "Reminiscences of Lewis Carroll," by Ethel Arnold.
8. *Reminiscences of Oxford*, by Rev. W. Tuckwell.
9. *The New York Times*, May 1, 1932, "Lewis Carroll As Recalled by Alice," by Captain Caryl Hargreaves.
10. Eldridge Johnson Collection.
11. *The Story of My Life*, by Ellen Terry.
12. *The Lewis Carroll Picture Book*, by Stuart Dodgson Collingwood.
13. Maggs Catalogue.
14. Catalogue of Francis Edwards, #659, item 675.
15. *Letters from Lewis Carroll*, edited by Beatrice Hatch.
16. Huntington Collection.
17. *Strand Magazine*, April, 1898, "Lewis Carroll," by Beatrice Hatch.
18. *Reminiscences of a Specialist*, by Greville Macdonald.
19. *The Bookman*, Sept., 1925, Letter from Muriel Hine.
20. *Atlantic Monthly*, June, 1929, "Some Reminiscences of Lewis Carroll," by E. M. Arnold.
21. *Some Aspects of Pastoral*, by W. Empson.
22. *Confessions of a Caricaturist*, by Harry Furniss.

CHAPTER 12

1. *Confessions of a Caricaturist*, by Harry Furniss.
2. *Life and Letters*, by Collingwood.
3. *Letters from Lewis Carroll*, edited by Beatrice Hatch.
4. *The Life of Lewis Carroll*, by Langford Reed.
5. *The Ordeal of Mark Twain*, by Van Wyck Brooks.
6. *Atlantic Monthly*, June, 1929, "Reminiscences of Lewis Carroll," by Ethel Arnold.
7. *Strand Magazine*, April, 1898, "Lewis Carroll," by Beatrice Hatch.
8. *Strand Magazine*, April, 1908, "Lewis Carroll," by Harry Furniss.

CHAPTER 13

1. *Life and Letters,* by Collingwood.
2. Huntington Collection.
3. *Handbook of the Literature of C. L. Dodgson,* by S. H. Williams and Falconer Madan.
4. *Six Letters from Lewis Carroll,* edited by Beatrice Hatch.
5. *The Nature of the Physical World,* by A. S. Eddington.
6. *The Story of My Life,* by Ellen Terry.

CHAPTER 14

1. *Wit and Its Relation to the Unconscious,* by Sigmund Freud. (In *The Basic Writings of Sigmund Freud.*)
2. *The Enjoyment of Laughter,* by Max Eastman.
3. *Life and Letters,* by Collingwood.
4. *Here, There, and Everywhere,* by Eric Partridge.
5. *The Field of Nonsense,* by Elizabeth Sewell.
6. *Confessions of a Caricaturist,* by Harry Furniss.
7. *The Poetry of Nonsense,* by Émile Cammaerts.
8. *The Bookman,* April, 1931, "Her Majesty's Jesters," by John Macy.

CHAPTER 15

1. *Scientific American,* April, 1956, "Lewis Carroll, Mathematician," by Warren Weaver.
2. *Men of Mathematics,* by Eric T. Bell.
3. Private letters from Dr. Bell.
4. *Willard Gibbs,* by Muriel Rukeyser.
5. *Science-History of the Universe,* Vol. VII.
6. *Mathematical Papers,* by W. K. Clifford.
7. Private letter from Prof. Harold N. Lee.
8. *General Logic,* by R. M. Eaton.
9. *The Times,* Jan. 27, 1932, "Lewis Carroll," by T. B. Strong.
10. *The Listener,* Jan. 13, 1932, "Lewis Carroll, Tutor and Logician," by A. S. Russell.
11. *Life and Letters,* by Collingwood.
12. *Mathematical Gazette,* July, 1932, "Lewis Carroll As Logician," by R. B. Braithwaite.
13. Huntington Collection.
14. *Nature,* Jan. 27, 1898, "C. L. Dodgson" (obituary).
15. *The Cornhill Magazine,* March, 1898, "Lewis Carroll," by T. B. Strong.
16. *The Mysterious Universe,* by Sir Jas. Jeans.
17. *The White Knight,* by A. L. Taylor.

CHAPTER 17

1. *Letters from Lewis Carroll,* edited by Beatrice Hatch.
2. *Collected Verse of Lewis Carroll,* Introduction by J. F. McDermott.

3. *The House of Macmillan,* by Charles Morgan.
4. *Pearson's Magazine,* Dec., 1930, "New Lewis Carroll Letters," by Dorothy Furniss.
5. *Confessions of a Caricaturist,* by Harry Furniss.
6. Swann Auction Galleries Catalogue, April 24, 1942.
7. Huntington Collection.
8. *The Cornhill Magazine,* Nov., 1932, "Lewis Carroll as Artist," by E. L. S.
9. *The Lewis Carroll Picture Book,* by Stuart Dodgson Collingwood.
10. *Handbook of the Literature of C. L. Dodgson,* by S. H. Williams and Falconer Madan.

CHAPTER 18

1. *Life and Letters,* by Collingwood.
2. *Letters from Lewis Carroll,* edited by Beatrice Hatch.
3. *Nineteenth Century,* April, 1888, "The Reign of Pedantry in Girls' Schools," by Elizabeth Sewell.
4. *Sesame and Lilies,* by John Ruskin.
5. *Nineteenth Century,* August, 1898: "The University of Oxford in 1898," by George C. Brodrick.
6. *Nineteenth Century,* Feb., 1895, "Language vs. Literature at Oxford," by J. Churton Collins.
7. Huntington Collection.

CHAPTER 19

1. *The Athenaeum,* Dec. 16, 1865 (quoted in *Handbook of the Literature of C. L. Dodgson,* by Sidney Herbert Williams and Falconer Madan).
2. *Academy,* Jan. 22, 1898, "Lewis Carroll at Oxford," by E. S. Leathes.
3. *Life and Letters,* by Collingwood.
4. *New Century Review,* Jan., 1899, "Lewis Carroll," by C. M. Aikman.
5. *Oxford Bibliographical Proceedings and Papers, 1922–6.*
6. Referred to in *Dodgson Handbook.* The article quoted was in *Thought,* 1932.
7. *The Life of Lewis Carroll,* by Langford Reed.
8. *The New Republic,* May 18, 1932, "Poet-Logician," by Edmund Wilson.
9. *New Minds for Old,* by Esmé Wingfield-Stratford.
10. *Leeds Philosophical and Literary Society Proceedings,* Vol. 6, Part viii, "Logic and the Humor of Lewis Carroll," by Peter Alexander.
11. *Poètes D'Aujourd'hui,* by Henri Parisot.

BIBLIOGRAPHY

Supplementary Bibliography

Carter, George Arthur. *Warrington and the Mid-Mersey Valley.* Manchester, E. J. Morten, 1971.

Cohen, M. and Green, R. L. "Lewis Carroll's Loss of Consciousness." *Bulletin of the New York Public Library,* 73 (January, 1969).

Crutch, Denis. *A Century of Annotations to the Lewis Carroll Handbook.* London, The Yellowhammer Press, 1967.

Ettleson, Abraham, M.D. *Lewis Carroll's Through the Lookinglass Decoded.* New York, Philosophical Library, 1966.

Jabberwocky (Quarterly of the Lewis Carroll Society). The County Hall, London S. E. 1.

Phillips, Robert, ed. *Aspects of Alice: Lewis Carroll's Dreamchild as Seen Through the Critics' Looking-Glasses, 1865-1971.* New York, Vanguard, 1971.

Shaberman, R. B. and Crutch, Denis. *Under the Quizzing-Glass.* London, The Magpie Press, 1971. (Available from Mary Crutch, 10 Ardberg Road, London SE249JL, England.)

Weaver, Dr. Warren. *Alice in Many Tongues: The Translations of Alice in Wonderland.* Madison, Wisconsin, The University of Wisconsin Press, 1964.

Weaver, Dr. Warren. "The First Edition of *Alice's Adventures in Wonderland:* A Census." An Off-Print from *The Papers of the Bibliographical Society of America,* 65 (first quarter, 1971), 1-40.

Wood, James Playsted. *The Snark Was a Boojum: A Life of Lewis Carroll.* New York, Pantheon Books, 1966.

Bibliography

THERE IS no need for another biblography for collectors, since Mr. Williams and Mr. Madan in their two volumes have amply and meticulously covered the ground, and the new edition, by Mr. Roger Lancelyn Green, was published by Oxford Press, London, July 4, 1962. The general reader, or even the student who is not a collector, will not require in this book notices of more than one edition, of small items like leaflets and pamphlets with games, with a single poem, and such like small fry. For all such matters the reader is referred to the *Dodgson Handbook*.

The list deliberately omits such books as lack both originality and the honesty to admit their derivativeness.

I follow Mr. Williams' arrangement to the extent of treating separately books by Lewis Carroll and by Charles Dodgson, but I depart from this method in treating together works *about* him (or them).

WORKS BY LEWIS CARROLL

Novelty and Romancement published in *The Train,* October, 1856
Alice's Adventures in Wonderland. Macmillan, 1865
Translations have appeared in numerous languages, and plays and an operetta have been made from the book. A number of books and songs have also appeared.
Phantasmagoria and other poems. Macmillan, 1869
Through the Looking-Glass, and What Alice Found There. Macmillan, 1872
Notes by an Oxford Chiel (Anonymous). James Parker & Co., 1874. Contains six pamphlets previously issued separately; The New Method of Evaluation as applied to Pi, the Dynamics of a Part-icle, Facts Figures and Fancies, The New Belfry of Christ Church, the Vision of the Three T's, the Blank Cheque, a Fable.
Some Popular Fallacies about Vivisection; printed for private Circulation (reprinted from the *Fortnightly Review*. June 1, 1875)
The Hunting of the Snark. Macmillan, 1876
Rhyme and Reason. Macmillan, 1883
A Tangled Tale. Macmillan, 1885
Alice's Adventures Underground. Macmillan, 1886. Facsimile of the original manuscript with Carroll's own drawings from which Tenniel worked in part.
The Game of Logic. Macmillan, 1886
Children in Theatres. Privately re-printed from a letter to the St. James Gazette, probably July 16, or 17, 1887 or 1889
Sylvie and Bruno. Macmillan, 1889

The Nursery "Alice." Macmillan, 1889

Alice in Wonderland rewritten, and with the Tenniel pictures enlarged and colored, about one-fourth the original content, for "children from Nought to Five."

The Wonderland Postage Stamp Case. Emberlin & Son, 1890

Eight or Nine Wise Words about Letter Writing. Emberlin & Son, 1890

Sylvie and Bruno Concluded. Macmillan, 1893

A Logical Paradox. Mind, 1894

Symbolic Logic. Macmillan, 1896

Three Sunsets and Other Poems. Macmillan, 1898

The Lewis Carroll Picture book, by Stuart Dodgson Collingwood. T. Fisher Unwin, 1899

Feeding the Mind. Chatto & Windus, 1907, with a note by William H. Draper, explaining how the manuscript came into his hands.

Six Letters by Lewis Carroll. Privately printed, 1924

Further Nonsense Verse and Prose. Edited by Langford Reed; T. Fisher Unwin, 1928

The Collected Verse of Lewis Carroll, with an introduction by John Francis McDermott. E. P. Dutton, 1929

"New Lewis Carroll Letters written to his illustrator, Harry Furniss," by the artist's daughter, Dorothy Furniss. Pearson's Magazine, Dec., 1930

The Lewis Carroll Book, by Richard Herrick. Dial Press, 1931

Songs from Alice; Music by Frazer-Simpson. Methuen, 1932

Two Letters to Marion. Cleverdon, 1932

The Rectory Umbrella and Mischmasch, by Florence Milner. Cassell, 1932

Alice in Wonderland and Through the Looking-Glass with an Introduction by Mrs. Franklin D. Roosevelt. Washington. National Home Library Foundation, 1932

Selections from his letters to his child friends, together with Eight or Nine Wise Words about Letter-writing, and notes by Evelyn Hatch. Facsimile illustrations and collotype plates. Macmillan, 1933

The Collected Verse of Lewis Carroll. Macmillian, 1933

Logical Nonsense, the works of Lewis Carroll, by Philip Blackburn & Lionel White. Putnam, 1934

The Russian Journal, and other selections from the work of Lewis Carroll, and with an introduction by John Francis McDermott. Dutton, 1935

Complete works of Lewis Carroll, with an introduction by Alexander Woollcott and illustrations by John Tenniel. Reprinted and available as a Modern Library giant. Random House, 1937

Nonesuch Omnibus. Random House, 1939

Mathematical Recreations of Lewis Carroll, Pillow Problems and A Tangled Tale, Dover Publications, 1958

Mathematical Recreations of Lewis Carroll, Symbolic Logic and the Game of Logic, Dover Publications, 1958

Parodies—An Anthology from Chaucer to Beerbohm and after. Edited by Dwight MacDonald. Random House, 1960

The Annotated Alice, Alice's Adventures in Wonderland, Through the Looking-Glass. Edited by Martin Gardner. Clarkson N. Potter, 1960

The Humorous Verse of Lewis Carroll, Peter Smith, 1960

Diversions and Digressions of Lewis Carroll. Edited by Stuart Dodgson Collingwood. Dover Publications, 1961

The Diaries of Lewis Carroll, edited by Roger Lancelyn Green (2 vols.) Oxford, 1954

WORKS BY CHARLES L. DODGSON

Notes on the First Two Books of Euclid (Anonymous). Parker, 1860

A Syllabus of Plane Algebraical Geometry. Parker, 1860

The Formulae of Plane Trigonometry. Parker, 1861

Notes on the First Part of Algebra. Parker, 1861

An Index to In Memoriam. Edward Moxon & Co., 1862 (This was done by Dodgson and his sisters)

The Enunciations of the Propositions and Corollaries with Questions in Euclid Books I and II. Oxford University Press, 1863

General List of Mathematical Subjects and Cycle for Working Examples. Oxford University Press, 1863

A Guide to the Mathematical Student in Reading, Reviewing, and Working Examples, Part I: Pure Mathematics. Parker, 1864

Condensation of Determinants. Taylor & Francis, 1866

Elementary Treatise on Determinants. Macmillan, 1867

The Fifth Book of Euclid Treated Algebraically. Parker, 1868

Algebraical Formulae for Responsions. Oxford University, 1868

Algebraical Formulae and Rules. Oxford University Press, 1870

Symbols, etc., to be used in Euclid Books I and II. Oxford University Press, 1872

Number of Propositions in Euclid. Oxford University Press, 1872

Enunciations, Euclid I–IV. Oxford University Press, 1873

Euclid, Book V proved Algebraically. Parker, 1874

Preliminary Algebra, and Euclid Book V. Oxford University Press, 1874

Examples in Arithmetic. Oxford University Press, 1874

Suggestions as to the Best Method of Taking Votes where More than Two Issues are to be Voted On. Hall and Stacy, 1874

A Method of Taking Votes on More than Two Issues. Oxford University Press, 1876

Euclid and His Modern Rivals. Macmillan, 1879

Euclid, Book I and II. Macmillan, 1882

Rules for Reckoning Postage. Baxter, 1883

Twelve Months in a Curatorship by One Who Has Tried It. Baxter, 1884

Supplement to Twelve Months in a Curatorship. Baxter, 1884

Supplement to Euclid and His Modern Rivals. Macmillan, 1885

Three Years in a Curatorship by One Whom It Has Tried. Baxter, 1886

First Paper on Logic. Baxter, 1886

There are nine of these papers, the first seven printed by Baxter and the last two by Sheppard, also a Note to the last two, covering the years from 1886 to 1892.

Curiosa Mathematica Part I: A New Theory of Parallels. Macmillan, 1888

Memoria Technica (Cyclostyle production). 1888

A Circular about Resignation of Curatorship. 1892

Curiossisima Curatoria. Sheppard, 1892

A Challenge to Logicians, 1892

Curiosa Mathematica, Part II. Pillow Problems. Macmillan, 1893

A Disputed Point in Logic. 1894

A Logical Puzzle. 1894

Symbolic Logic, Specimens. 1894

Logical Nomenclature (Anonymous). 1895

Quadriliteral Diagrams. 1896

Quinquiliteral Diagrams. 1896 (?)

BOOKS
(Articles in Books)

Ayres, Harry Morgan. Carroll's Alice. New York, Columbia University Press, 1936.

Bell, Eric Temple. The Development of Mathematics. New York, McGraw-Hill, 1940.

Bell, Eric Temple. Men of Mathematics. New York, Simon & Schuster, 1937.

Blagden, Claude Martin. Well Remembered. London, Hodder, 1952, pp. 114–15.

Bowman, Isa. The Story of Lewis Carroll, Told for Young People by the Real Alice in Wonderland. London, J. M. Dent, 1899.

Brinton, P. R., trans. The Hunting of the Snark in Latin. Toronto, Macmillan, 1934.

Cammaerts, Émile. The Poetry of Nonsense. New York, Dutton, 1926.

Collingwood, Stuart Dodgson. The Life and Letters of Lewis Carroll. London, Unwin, 1898.

Courtney, Janet Elizabeth. An Oxford Portrait Gallery. London, Chapman and Hall, 1931.

De la Mare, Walter. "Lewis Carroll," in The Eighteen Eighties, ed. by W. de la Mare, Cambridge University Press, 1930.

Dobson, Austin. Collected Poems, Proem, page 576

Eastman, Max. The Enjoyment of Laughter. New York, Simon and Schuster, 1936.

Empson, William. Some Aspects of Pastoral. London, Chatto & Windus, 1935. Published in the United States, 1938, as English Pastoral Poetry.

Fechner, G. T. Kleine Schriften—Space Has Four Dimensions; Paradoxes #2, ? 1946.

Freud, Sigmund. The Future of an Illusion. New York, Liveright, 1928.

Fries, Charles Carpenter. The Structure of English. New York, Harcourt, Brace, 1952.

Frye and Levi. Rational Belief. Dartmouth

Furniss, Harry. The Confessions of a Caricaturist. London, Bradbury, Agnew & Co., 1902. 2 V.

Furniss, Harry. Some Victorian Men. London, John Lane, 1924. Some pages on Carroll in the chapter entitled "Victorian Stars."

G., S. I. "Alice in Dorsetland," in the Dorset Year Book, 1928.

Gernsheim, Helmut. Lewis Carroll, Photographer. New York, Chanticleer, 1949.

Green, Roger Lancelyn. The Story of Lewis Carroll. London, Methuen, 1949.

Green, Roger Lancelyn. Lewis Carroll: A Bodley Head Monograph. The Bodley Head. London, 1960.

Greenacre, Phyllis, M. D. Swift and Carroll. New York, International Universities Press, 1955.

Harvard University Library. Harcourt Amory Collection of Lewis Carroll in the Harvard College Library, by Flora V. Livingston. Cambridge, Harvard College Library, 1932.

Hudson, Derek. Lewis Carroll. New York, Macmillan, 1954.

Hudson, Derek. Writers and Their Work. XCVI. London, Longmans Green, 1958.

Hyman, Stanley Edgar. The Armed Vision—A Study in the Methods of Modern Literary Criticism. New York, Knopf, 1948.

Jourdain, Philip E. B. The Philosophy of Mr. B*rtr*nd R*ss*ll. London, Allen & Unwin, 1918.

Joyce, James. Finnegans Wake. New York, Viking, 1947.

Le Gallienne, Eva (and Florida Friebus). Alice in Wonderland; adapted for the stage from Lewis Carroll's Alice in Wonderland and Through the Looking-Glass. New York, Samuel French (c.1932).
For criticisms of the production at the Civic Repertory Theatre see Arts and Decoration, December, 1933; Catholic World, February, 1933; Commonweal, January 4, 1932; Literary Digest, December 31, 1932; Nation, December 28, 1932; Saturday Review of Literature, December 31, 1932; Theatre Arts Monthly, February, 1933.

Lewis Carroll Centenary Exhibition in London. Ed. by Falconer Madan. London, Bumpus, 1932.

The Lewis Carroll Handbook—Bibliography of Charles L. Dodgson. Ed. by Roger Lancelyn Green. London, Oxford, 1962.

Lucas, Edward Verrall. "Charles Lutwidge Dodgson," in the Dictionary of National Biography, (first) Supplement, II (1901) 142-144.

Mespoulet, Marguerite. Creators of Wonderland. New York, Arrow editions, 1934.

Morgan, Charles. The House of Macmillan. New York, Macmillan, 1944.

Nagel, Ernest. "Symbolic Notation, Haddocks' Eyes, and the Dog-walking Ordinance," The World of Mathematics. Ed. by James R. Newman; New York, Simon & Schuster, 1956.

"The Parodies of Lewis Carroll." Catalogue of an Exhibition with Notes by John Mackay Shaw. The Florida State University Library, 1960.

Parisot, Henri. Poetes D'Aujourd'hui. Paris, Seghers & Cie, 1952.

Parrish, Morris L. Catalogue of Carrolliana; priv. pr., photostatic copy in NYPL.

Partridge, Eric. Here, There, and Everywhere. London, ? 1950.

Partridge, Henry Morton (and D. C. Partridge). The Most Remarkable Echo in the World. Hastings-on-Hudson, H. M. Partridge, 1933.

Powell, F. York. A Life, by Oliver Elton.

Redesdale, Algernon, 1st Baron. Further Memories. . . . New York, E. P. Dutton, 1917.

Reed, Langford. "Foreword" and "The Beginning of *Alice*" in Caroll, Lewis, *Further Nonsense Verse and Prose,* ed. by Langford Reed; Illustrated by H. M. Bateman. New York, Appleton, 1926.

Reed, Langford. Life of Lewis Carroll. London, Foyle, 1932.

Reed, Langford, comp. Nonsense Verses; an Anthology. London, Jarrold's, 1925.

Rosenbach, Abraham Simon Wolf. Books and Bidders; the Adventures of a Bibliophile. Boston, Little, Brown, 1927.

Rukeyser, Muriel. Willard Gibbs. Doubleday, Doran, 1942.

Ruskin, John. Praeterita. London, George Allen, 1907, 3 V.

Russell, Bertrand. An Inquiry into Meaning and Truth. New York, W. W. Norton, 1940.

Saintsbury, George. "Lesser Poets of the Middle and Later Nineteenth Century," in the *Cambridge History of English Literature*, XIII, 186. A paragraph on Carroll.

Sewell, Elizabeth. The Field of Nonsense. London, Chatto, 1952.

Stirling, Anna M. W., ed., The Richmond Papers. London, Heinemann, 1926.

Taylor, Alexander L. The White Knight—A Study of C. L. Dodgson (Lewis Carroll). Edinburgh and London, Oliver & Boyd, 1952.

Terry, Ellen. The Story of My Life. London, Hutchinson & Co., 1908, pp. 384-388.

Tollemache, Lionel Arthur. "Reminiscences of Lewis Carroll," in his *Among My Books,* London, 1898.

Tuckwell, William. Reminiscences of Oxford. London, Smith, Elder & Co., 1900, pp. 160-163.

Vail, Robert William Glenroie. *Alice in Wonderland;* the Manuscript and Its Story. New York, New York Public Library, 1928. (8 pp., Facsim.)

Venn, John. Symbolic Logic. London, Macmillan, 1894.

Ward, Mary Augusta. (Mrs. Humphry Ward.) A Writer's Recollections. London, Collins, 1918.

Weaver, Warren. Lewis Carroll: Correspondence Numbers. Scarsdale, New York, priv., pr., 1940.

White, Elwyn Brooks. Alice through the Cellophane. New York, The John Day Company, 1933 (The John Day Pamphlets, No. 26).

Whyte, Walter. "Lewis Carroll," in *Poets and Poetry of the Nineteenth Century,* ed. by Alfred H. Miles, London, Routledge, 1905, pp. 443-454.

Wilkinson, Eleanor C. A Bibliography of Lewis Carroll. Unpublished; in the Columbia University Library.

Williams, Sidney Herbert. A Bibliography of Lewis Carroll. London, *The Bookman's Journal,* 1924.

Williams, Sidney Herbert (and Falconer Madan). Handbook of the Literature of C. L. Dodgson. Oxford, 1931; Supplement, corrigenda, addenda, Oxford, 1935.

Wilson, Edmund. The Shores of Light. New York, Random House, 1952.

Winterich, John Tracy. "Lewis Carroll and His Alice's Adventures in Wonderland," in his *Books and the Man.* New York, Greenberg, 1929, pp. 266-290.

(Articles in Magazines)

Academy, 53 (January 22, 1898) 98-99. "Lewis Carroll," compiled by E. S. Leathes.

Academy, 53 (January 22, 1898) 99-100. "Lewis Carroll at Oxford," by E. S. Leathes.

Academy, 53 (January 22, 1898) 95-100. "Notes and News," by Peter Newell.

Academy, 55 (December 17, 1898) 469-470. "Lewis Carroll."

Academy, 56 (January 7, 1899) 19-22. "Lewis Carroll's Suppressed Booklets," by E. S. Leathes.

American Mathematical Monthly, 45 (April, 1938) 234-236. "Lewis Carroll and a Geometrical Paradox," by Warren Weaver.

Antioch Review (Summer, 1959), 183. "Editor's Shop Talk," Anon.

Antioch Review (Summer, 1959), 133-149. "The Philosopher's Alice in Wonderland," by Roger W. Holmes.

Atlantic Monthly, 143 (June, 1929) 782-789. "Reminiscences of Lewis Carroll," by Ethel M. Arnold. (This article was reprinted in the *Windsor Magazine,* London, December, 1929, with illustrations.)

Atlantic Monthly (August, 1957), 75. "Mushrooms, Food of the Gods," by Robert Graves.

The Bellman, March 22, 1913. "The Author of Alice," by Randolph Edgar.

The Bellman, 26 (February 1, 1919) 129-130. "Lewis Carroll Memoranda," by Randolph Edgar. Reported in *Current Opinion,* 68 (March, 1919) 188.

Blackwood's Magazine, 242 (December, 1937) 740-746. "Alice," by Guy Boas.

Book Buyer, 18 (1899) 120-123. "Lewis Carroll's Life and Letters," by Ellen Burns Sherman. (Illus.)

Bookman, New York, 9 (1899) 77-84. "The Man Who Loved Little Children," by J. M. (Illus.) pp. 75-76. Note on and pictures from the London stage production, Prince of Wales Theater, opened December 23, 1886.

Bookman, New York, 18 (September, 1903) 13-16. "The Poems in 'Alice in Wonderland,' " by Florence Milner.

Bookman, New York, 26 (February, 1908) 648-651. "The Sketchbooks of Wonderland," by Philip Loring Allen. (Illus.)

Bookman, New York, 62 (September, 1925). Letter from Muriel Hine.

Bookman, New York, 71 (March, 1930) 16-19. "Lewis Carroll; a Contemporary Portrait by Fr-nk H-rr-s," by Hugh Kingsmill. A parody.

Bookman, New York, 73 (April, 1931) 146-157. "Her Majesty's Jesters," by John Macy.

Bookman, New York, 75 (September-October, 1932) 465-471, 584-589. "Those Nonsensical Victorians," by F. W. Knickerbocker. (Illus., facsims.)

Bookman, London, 81 (January, 1932) 220. "Lewis Carroll Rarity; the Wonderful Postage Stamp Case," by C. H. Lea. (Illus.)

Bookman's Journal, March, 1924. Letters to Maud and Isabel Standen from C. L. Dodgson.

Boston Evening Transcript, April 3, 1926, p. 13. *"Alice in Wonderland* Americanized," by George Henry Sargent.

Catholic World, 135 (May, 1932) 193-201. "Lewis Carroll, Mathematician and Magician," by T. Maynard.

Century, 57, N. S. 35 (April, 1899) 231-240. "Some of Lewis Carroll's Child Friends; with Unpublished Letters by the Author of *Alice in Wonderland,*" by S. D. Collingwood. (Illus.)

The Colophon, Ser. 2, V. 1, No. 3 (Winter, 1936) 422-427. "The 1886 Appleton *Alice,*" by F. W. Heron. (Facsims.)

Commonweal, 15 (March 30, 1932) 593. "Lewis Carroll Memorial." Editorial.

Context, Amherst College (Spring, 1952), "The Poet and the Pedant," by Stephen A. Eckhardt.

Cornhill Magazine, N. S. 56 (April, 1924) 445-468. "The Early Writings of Lewis Carroll," by Edward Abbott Parry. Printed also in *The Living Age*, 322 (September, 1924) 465-472.

Cornhill Magazine, 73 (July, 1932) 1-12. "Alice's Recollections of Carrollian Days, Told to Her Son, Caryl Hargreaves."

Cornhill Magazine, 73 (November, 1932) 559-562. "Lewis Carroll As Artist and Other Oxford Memories," by E. L. S.

Cornhill Magazine, 77 (March, 1898) 303-310. "Lewis Carroll," by Thomas Banks Strong. Reprinted in *Living Age*, 217:17.

Cornhill Magazine, 149 (April, 1934) 478-487. "The Art of Nonsense," by Muriel Kent.

The Critic, 29 (January 22, 1898) 54-55. "Lewis Carroll," by A. I. du Pont Coleman.

The Critic, 34 (February, 1899) 135-140. "The Creator of Wonderland," by J. L. Gilder. (Ports.)

The Dial, Chicago, 24 (February 1, 1898) 65-66. "Lewis Carroll," by E. S. Leathes.

English Journal, 10 (March, 1921) 119-129. "A Book within a Book," by George B. Masslich.

English Review, 54 (March, 1932) 276-283. "Lewis Carroll and His Centenary," by E. H. L. Watson.

Good Housekeeping, 94 (May, 1932) 23. "For Lewis Carroll"; verses by Margaret Elizabeth Sangster.

Harper's Magazine, February, 1943. "To Me He Was Mr. Dodgson," by E. M. Rowell.

Harper's Magazine, 81 (July, 1890) 246-256. "Social Life in Oxford," by Ethel M. Arnold. (Illus.)

Harper's Magazine, 103 (October, 1901) 712-717. "*Alice's Adventures in Wonderland* from an Artist's Standpoint," by Peter Newell. (Illus.) Newell illustrated the edition brought out by Harper in 1902.

The Lantern, San Francisco, 3 (April, 1917) 18-25. "The Father of Alice," by Edward F. O'Day.

Leeds Philosophical and Literary Society Proceedings, 6, Part viii, 551-66. "Logic and the Humor of Lewis Carroll," by Peter Alexander.

The Listener, London (January 13, 1932). "Lewis Carroll, Tutor and Logician," by A. S. Russell.

Literary Digest, 113 (May 21, 1932) 16-17. "Alice Comes to Our Wonderland." (Ports.)

Literary World, 29 (February 19, 1898) 57. "Exchanges from English Papers Following Lewis Carroll's Death," by Randolph Edgar.

The Living Age, 342 (March, 1932) 53-57. "Immortal Alice"; reprinted from *The Times Literary Supplement* on the occasion of Carroll's centenary.

London Mercury, 28 (July, 1933) 233-239. "Lewis Carroll and the Oxford Movement," by Shane Leslie. Reprinted in *Essays of the Year*, 1933-34.

Mathematical Gazette, 9 (May, 1918-January, 1919) 237-241, 249-252, 293-298. "Alice Through the (Convex) Looking Glass," by William Garnett.

Mathematical Gazette, 16 (July, 1932) 174-178. "Lewis Carroll as Logician," by R. B. Braithwaite.

Mathematical Gazette, 17 (May, 1933) 92-100. "Lewis Carroll, Mathematician," by D. B. Eperson.

Mentor, 16 (December, 1928) 19-22. "The Man That Was Two Men," by Mary Siegrist. (Illus.)

The Nation, 70 (March 15, 1900) 210-211. Review of S. D. Collingwood's Biography and Isa Bowman's *The Story of Lewis Carroll.*

The Nation, 90 (May 5, 1910) 455. "Lewis Carroll on Letter-Writing," a letter from William E. A. Axon, Southport, England.

The Nation, 98 (March 19, 1914) 294-295. "Sir John Tenniel," by Edmund Lester Pearson.

The Nation, 99 (August 27, 1914) 250. "Alice in Westchester," by Edmund Lester Pearson.

The Nation, 133 (December 2, 1931) 607-609. "Mr. Dodgson and Lewis Carroll," by Dorothy Van Doren.

The Nation, 138 (April 4, 1934) 394-395. "Method or Madness," by Dorothy Van Doren. Review.

The Nation, 144 (January 30, 1937) 129-130. "Psychoanalyzing Alice," by Joseph Wood Krutch.

Nature, 57 (January 27, 1898) 279-280. "Rev. C. L. Dodgson." Obituary.

New Century Review, 5 (January, 1899) 19-33. "Lewis Carroll," by C. M. Aikman.

The New Republic, 71 (May 18, 1932) 19-21. "The Poet-Logician," by Edmund Wilson.

The New York Times, August 24, 1930, v. 12. "Harry Furniss Letters," by Beatrice and Guy MacKenzie.

The New York Times, January 24, 1932, v. 5. "The Alice of *Alice in Wonderland,*" by Clair Price.

The New York Times, May 1, 1932, v. 7. "Lewis Carroll as Recalled by Alice," by Captain Caryl Hargreaves.

The Princeton University Library Chronicle, 17, No. 2 (Winter, 1956). "The Parrish Collection of Carrolliana," by Warren Weaver.

Nineteenth Century, 22 (October, 1887) 563-580. "Literature for the Little Ones," by Edmund Salmon. Hints that *Alice* was stolen from Thomas Hood's *From Nowhere to the North Pole.* (The latter was published in 1874.)

Nineteenth Century, III (February, 1932) 235-238. "Early Theatricals at Oxford with Prologues by Lewis Carroll," by Fred B. de Sausmarez.

Outlook, 138 (November 5, 1924) 357-358. "Figures, Fancies and a Famous Man," by Lawrence F. Abbott. (Ports.)

Oxford Bibliographical Society. Proceedings and Papers, V. I (1922/26). Notes on the exhibit of Carroll and Carrolliana at the Bodleian.

Oxford Magazine, January 26, 1898. Obituary of C. L. Dodgson, by H(enry) L. T(hompson).

Oxford Magazine, June 4, 1908. Obituary of Thomas Vere Bayne.

Pearson's Magazine, December, 1930. "Lewis Carroll Letters to His Illustrator," by Dorothy Furniss.

Proceedings of the American Philosophical Society, 8, No. 5 (October 15, 1954). "The Mathematical Manuscripts of Lewis Carroll," by Warren Weaver.

The Publishers' Weekly, 121 (January 30, 1932) 517-518. "Lewis Carroll Centennial." Editorial.

Punch, 114 (January 29, 1898) 39. "Lewis Carroll." Verses by E. S. Leathes.

Punch, 114 (March 5, 1898) 106. "Alice in Hospital Land." Mr. Punch's approval of the fund to endow an "Alice in Wonderland" cot at the Great Ormond Street children's hospital.

St. Nicholas, 35 (September, 1908) 1012-1016. "How *Alice in Wonderland* Came to Be Written," by Helen Marshall Pratt. (Illus., ports.)

St. Nicholas, 35 (October, 1908) 1078-1082. "Lewis Carroll: the Friend of Childen," by Helen Marshall Pratt.

St. Nicholas Magazine, 59 (May, 1932) 362-363. "Lewis Carroll, Playfellow," by F. Milner.

The Saturday Review, 85 (January 22, 1898) 102-103. "Lewis Carroll as Story-Teller," by E. S. Leathes.

The Saturday Review, London, March 4, 1928.

Saturday Review of Literature, 6 (October 26, 1929) 316. "Round about Parnassus," by William Rose Benét.

Saturday Review of Literature, 3 (March 18, 1933), 490-491. "Finding of the Snark," by Arthur Ruhl.

Saturday Review of Literature, 11 (December 3, 1934) 359. "The Clearing House: Philosophy of Lewis Carroll," by Amy Loveman (bibliographic).

Saturday Review of Literature, 12 (June 22, 1935) 20. "An 1868 New York *Alice*," by John T. Winterich.

The Scholastic, October 1, 1938. "Feeding the Mind" and "Who Was Lewis Carroll?"

Scientific American, 194, No. 4 (April, 1956). "Lewis Carroll, Mathematician," by Warren Weaver.

Sewanee Review, 35 (October, 1927) 387-398. "The Sanity of Wonderland" by George Shelton Hubbell.

Sewanee Review, 48 (April, 1940) 174-196. "Triple Alice," by George Shelton Hubbell. Bibliography pp. 195-196.

The Spectator, 149 (July 16, 1932) 74-75. "Lewis Carroll and Alice," by David Cecil.

The Spectator, 162 (March 10, 1939) 400-401. "The White Knight's Stamp-Case," by Bernard Darwin.

Strand Magazine, 15 (April, 1898) 412-423. "Lewis Carroll (Charles Lutwidge Dodgson)," by Beatrice Hatch. (Illus.)

Strand Magazine, 16 (December, 1898) 616. "Before Alice; the Boyhood of Lewis Carroll," by Stuart D. Collingwood. Printed also in *The Century Magazine,* 1898.

Strand Magazine, May, 1901. "A Visit to Tennyson," by C. L. Dodgson.

Strand Magazine, April, 1908. "Lewis Carroll," by Harry Furniss.

Time, 43, No. 7 (February 14, 1944) 98. Note on Carroll and Macmillan.

The Times, London, January 14, 1932. A letter for P. S. Morgan concerning the *papier maché Jabberwocky.*

The Times, London, January 27, 1832, pp. 11, 12, 14. "Lewis Carroll," by Thomas Banks Strong.

The Times Education Supplement, December 16, 1939, p. 481.

The Times Literary Supplement, May 19, 1927, p. 355. Correspondence: Lewis Carroll letters.

The Times Literary Supplement, March 29, 1928, p. 248. Notes on sales: *Alice in Wonderland.*

The Times Literary Supplement, April 12, 1928, p. 278. Notes on sales: *Alice* and others.

The Times Literary Supplement, January 28, 1932, pp. 49-50. "Lewis Carroll, January 27, 1832." Reprinted in *The Living Age,* 342 (March, 1932) 53-57.

Yale Review, N.S. 5 (April, 1916) 587-604. "Men Who Have Passed for Fools," by Hugh Walker.

Acknowledgments

THANKS ARE DUE

First, to Mrs. Skene, the former Lorina Liddell, who by a half-hour of her company, in the eighty-second and last year of her life, illuminated for the writer the best of the Victorian era, that was exemplified by the Dodgson and Liddell families, and that Charles Dodgson transmuted into enduring fantasy for Alice Liddell.

Second, to Miss F. Menella Dodgson and her sisters, who carry on the gracious tradition of their line, and who contributed many valuable reminiscences of their uncle; most especially to Miss Menella, whose painstaking researches among her uncle's diaries and whose answers to infinite questions were made with infinite patience and care. Next, to these and to the other heirs and executors of the Dodgson estate, who, without seeing the MS of this book, nevertheless gave permission for the use of copyright material, including *The Life and Letters of Lewis Carroll,* and *The Lewis Carroll Picture Book,* both by Stuart Dodgson Collingwood, and unpublished letters of their uncle.

To the Huntington Library and the Amory Collection of the Harvard University Library, for many of these manuscript letters.

FOR KINDNESS, COOPERATION, AND ASSISTANCE:

To Mr. Van Wyck Brooks, first for writing *The Ordeal of Mark Twain,* the book that turned the tide from debunking to sympathetic biographies; and second for reading an early draft of this book and giving his especially valuable criticism and permission for the dedication.

To the late Mr. Falconer Madan, of the Bodleian Library, Oxford, co-author with Mr. Sidney Herbert Williams of the *Handbook of the Literature of C. L. Dodgson,* and author of the *Supplement* to the Handbook; who knew Mr. Dodgson, faithfully collected his works, and also patiently answered numerous questions, and to Colonel Probert for permission to use the photograph of his wife, the former Mary Hilton Badcock, from the *Handbook.*

To Mr. Sidney Herbert Willams, co-author of the *Handbook,* and author of the *Bibliography of Lewis Carroll,* for permission to quote from these books and for answering questions.

To the late Dr. Eric Temple Bell of the California Institute of Technology, for reading the mathematical chapter and giving invaluable advice; for checking and commenting on the list of mathematical works in Carroll's library, and for permission to quote from *Men of Mathematics* and *The Development of Mathematics.*

To Professor Harold N. Lee of Newcomb College, New Orleans, and to Professor Walter B. Veazie of the University of Colorado, for reading the mathematical chapter and giving further references and suggestions.

To Mr. Nathan Lazar of Brooklyn and to Mr. Henry Schneer of New York for help on the first draft of the mathematical chapter.

To members of the Writers' Conference in the Rocky Mountains for careful reading and helpful criticism of the manuscript: Mr. Harry Shaw, Miss Mari Sandoz, Mr. Richard Aldington.

To Professor Elizabeth Selleck of the University of Colorado Library for a great deal of tedious detail work, to Professor Jas. Sandoe, also of the library, for the same, also for rationalizing the bibliography.

To the late R. H. Dundas, incumbent till his death of Carroll's rooms, who kindly showed them, and secured permission from Christ Church for making and using the photograph of the tiles.

To Mr. Christopher Hussey, an earlier incumbent of the rooms, for a letter of valuable information.

To Miss Florence Hellman, Chief Bibliographer of the Library of Congress, for painstaking research.

To old friends in New York for help and encouragement—to the late Dr. Béla Mittelmann, John Rannells, Horace Gregory, and Gertrude Nafe.

TO COLLECTORS FOR THE USE OF THEIR MATERIAL:

To Mr. Eldridge R. Johnson for a letter to Mrs. Hargreaves and the reproduction of the last page of the MS of *Alice's Adventures Underground*.

To Professor J. Enrique Zanetti and to Mr. Philip Blackburn for use of their collections and varied suggestions.

To Mrs. Skene for the picture of "The Sisters," by Sir William Blake Richmond.

To Oxford University for the picture of the tiles.

TO PUBLISHERS:

To E. P. Dutton and Co. for *The Story of Lewis Carroll*, by Isa Bowman; *The Russian Journal* and *The Collected Verse of Lewis Carroll*, both edited by John Francis McDermott.

To The Macmillan Co. for *Selections from the Letters of Lewis Carroll to His Child Friends*, edited by Evelyn Hatch; *The House of Macmillan*, by Charles Morgan; *Mathematical Papers*, by W. K. Clifford; *Letters of Matthew Arnold*, edited by Russell; and *Christina Rossetti*, by Dorothy Stuart.

To W. and G. Foyle, Ltd. for Langford Reed's *The Life of Lewis Carroll*.

To Bradbury, Agnew and Co., publishers of *Punch*, for text from Harry Furniss' *Confessions of a Caricaturist*.

To the Harvard University Press for *Three Rossettis*, by Janet Camp Troxell.

To G. P. Putnam's Sons for *The Rossettis,* by Elisabeth Luther Carey.

To Jonathan Cape, Ltd. for *The Exquisite Tragedy,* by Amabel Williams-Ellis.

To J. B. Lippincott Co. for *John Ruskin,* by R. H. Wilenski.

To Houghton Mifflin for John Livingston Lowes' *Road to Xanadu.*

To Longmans, Green & Co., Ltd. for *The Life and Letters of Henry Parry Liddon.*

To Mr. Walter De La Mare for his "Lewis Carroll," in *The Eighteen-Eighties.*

To Simon and Schuster for Max Eastman's *Enjoyment of Laughter;* and for Eric T. Bell's *Men of Mathematics.*

To Random House for *The Basic Writings of Sigmund Freud.*

To George Allen & Unwin for quotations from *George Macdonald and his Wife,* by Greville Macdonald, and for *Praeterita,* by John Ruskin.

To W. W. Norton for the American version of W. Empson's *English Pastoral Poetry,* and to Chatto and Windus for the British edition, *Some Aspects of Pastoral.*

To John Murray for *Reminiscences of Oxford,* by the Rev. W. Tuckwell; and for Angus Davidson's *Edward Lear.*

To Hutchinson & Co. for *The Story of My Life,* by Ellen Terry.

To Dodd, Mead & Co. for excerpts from correspondence between Mr. Dodgson and Mr. Furniss, from *Some Victorian Men,* by Harry Furniss.

To Thos. Nelson & Sons for *30,000 Miles in a Ketch,* by Captain Raymond Raillier Du Baty.

To *The Nineteenth Century and After* for nine articles dating from 1884 to 1932, and credited in the footnotes.

To *The Strand Magazine* for "Lewis Carroll," by Beatrice Hatch; and "Lewis Carroll," by Thos. Banks Strong.

To *The New York Times* for the articles about "Dr. Schilder and Alice," and to the Sunday *Times* for Captain Caryl Hargreaves' article.

To *The Colophon* for an article by F. W. Heron on "The 1866 Appleton Alice."

To *The Saturday Review of Literature* for Mr. Arthur Ruhl's article, "The Finding of the Snark."

To *The Nation* for Mr. Joseph Wood Krutch's article, "Psychoanalyzing Alice."

To *The New Republic* for Mr. Edmund Wilson's article, "The Poet-Logician."

To the Rev. Thomas Banks Strong for his articles in *The Cornhill Magazine* and *The Times;* also for letters of reminiscence.

To *The Mathematical Gazette* for R. B. Braithwaite's "Lewis Carroll as Logician" and for D. B. Eperson's Lewis Carroll, Mathematician."

To the *Sewanee Review* for Mr. George Shelton Hubbell's "Sanity of Wonderland" and "Triple Alice."

To the *Burlington Magazine* for the pictures of the Ugly Duchess, in Mr. Baillie-Grohman's article.

To *Harper's Magazine* for "To Me He was Mr. Dodgson," by Miss E. M. Rowell.

To *The New Yorker* and to Mr. Frank L. Warrin for the latter's translation, "Le Jaseroque," reprinted by permission of *The New Yorker,* from the issue of Jan. 10, 1931.

To the *Atlantic Monthly* for Ethel M. Arnold's "Reminiscences of Lewis Carroll."

To A. S. Russell for his article in *The Listener,* "Lewis Carroll: Tutor and Logician."

FINALLY, to Miss Eleanor Wilkinson of Columbia University, thanks for the use of her list of magazine articles on Lewis Carroll, and regrets that, owing to the vicissitudes of transatlantic correspondence, the list was credited to me in the *Handbook of the Literature of C. L. Dodgson.* This error was corrected in the *Supplement.*

Acknowledgments for the Revised Edition

In the seventeen years since this book appeared I have received many kindnesses and much courtesy from other Carrollians.

Thanks to the Oxford Press for permission to use the Dodgson *Diaries* and *The Lewis Carroll Handbook,* both edited by Mr. Roger Lancelyn Green.

Thanks also to Messrs. A. P. Watt, representing the Dodgson family, for the *Diaries.*

To Longmans Green for Derek Hudson's monograph on Lewis Carroll.

To the Bodley Head for Roger Lancelyn Green's monograph.

To Methuen & Co., Ltd. for the same author's *The Story of Lewis Carroll.*

To Max Parrish for Helmut Gernsheim's *Lewis Carroll, Photographer.*

To Oliver and Boyd for A. L. Taylor's *The White Knight.*

To Chatto and Windus for Elizabeth Sewell's *The Field of Nonsense.*

To Hamish Hamilton for Eric Partridge's *Here, There, and Everywhere.*

To International Universities Press for Dr. Phyllis Greenacre's *Swift and Carroll.*

To Simon & Schuster for articles in *The World of Mathematics.*

To the *Atlantic Monthly* for Robert Graves's "Mushrooms, the Food of the Gods."

To Clarkson N. Potter for *The Annotated Alice.*

To Miss F. Menella Dodgson and her sisters Miss Violet and Miss Frances for continued kindness and co-operation (continued over thirty-two years).

To Mr. Helmut Gernsheim for permission to quote from his *Lewis Carroll, Photographer,* also for the use of his copy of the last page of the *Alice Underground* manuscript and the photograph of Lewis Carroll by Rejlander (earlier thought to be a self-portrait), for introducing me to Miss Ethel Hatch, with whom he made a tape recording for my radio program, Enjoyment of Poetry, and also for general friendly and scholarly assistance. This last applies also to most of the following.

To Mr. Derek Hudson for quotations from his books, and in his capacity as editor of the Oxford Press, for airmailing me proofs of *The Lewis Carroll Handbook.*

To Mr. Roger Lancelyn Green for his books. The two latter gentlemen I had the good fortune to meet last summer and to find how large an area of agreement we had about Lewis Carroll and one another's work in the field, in spite of differences.

To Dr. Alexander L. Taylor for kindness and permissions.

To return to the United States, thanks again for kindness and permissions to Dr. Phyllis Greenacre, who gave of her time and expertise to sift out some of the analytic problems of Lewis Carroll and our fellow Carrollians, as well as permission to quote from her book.

To Dr. Warren Weaver for quotations from his articles on Lewis Carroll's mathematical and logical aspects.

To Mr. John Mackay Shaw for his *Parodies* of Lewis Carroll.

To Mr. Martin Gardner for quotations from his *Annotated Alice*, also for his bibliography, which covered the years since this book appeared, and for the loan of hard-to-find items from his own collection, as well as for good advice on mathematics and games.

To Miss Suzanne Henig for typing the new bibliography.

Special thanks to the critics who have defended and appreciated this book critically, which always seems to mean those who accept Freudian interpretation as a legitimate part of literary criticism and biography.

To Mr. Stanley Edgar Hyman in *The Armed Vision*.

To Mr. Edmund Wilson in *The Shores of Light*.

To the anonymous reviewer in *The* (London) *Times Literary Supplement* who carried on a long running battle in the mid-fifties defending Freud and my right to use his insights.

Finally to all those who pointed out genuine errors of fact, enabling me to correct them in the present edition.

After another sojourn in Wonderland, only half emerged, it is tempting to pretend I can still communicate with those who were here and are no more, to thank them again not only for what they did but what they were.

To Mr. R. H. Dundas, long-time incumbent of Lewis Carroll's rooms at Oxford, who not only showed me the rooms and got me the photograph of the tiles, but sent me a detailed errata sheet, which made the difference between the first and second edition of this book.

To the members of the Liddell family who received me so kindly and who wrote me so many painstaking letters.

To Mrs. Skene (Lorina), to her daughter Lady Schuster and her sister Miss Rhoda Liddell, and to the son of Alice herself, who wrote immediately after my book appeared to inform me that the story of his death, like Mark Twain's, had been exaggerated. He read the book and wrote me three more letters, full of information and the Oxford aura. I never met him and he too is gone now.

The frankness and gentleness of these people, also of the Misses Dodgson, breathe an aroma of a world—I hope—not wholly lost, though certainly overlaid with gasoline and strontium 90. Contact with them was precious—may their tribe increase! And if they could hear me—thanks.

INDEX

Index

A CATALOGUE OF SELECTED DOVER BOOKS
IN ALL FIELDS OF INTEREST

A CATALOGUE OF SELECTED DOVER BOOKS
IN ALL FIELDS OF INTEREST

AMERICA'S OLD MASTERS, James T. Flexner. Four men emerged unexpectedly from provincial 18th century America to leadership in European art: Benjamin West, J. S. Copley, C. R. Peale, Gilbert Stuart. Brilliant coverage of lives and contributions. Revised, 1967 edition. 69 plates. 365pp. of text.

21806-6 Paperbound $3.00

FIRST FLOWERS OF OUR WILDERNESS: AMERICAN PAINTING, THE COLONIAL PERIOD, James T. Flexner. Painters, and regional painting traditions from earliest Colonial times up to the emergence of Copley, West and Peale Sr., Foster, Gustavus Hesselius, Feke, John Smibert and many anonymous painters in the primitive manner. Engaging presentation, with 162 illustrations. xxii + 368pp.

22180-6 Paperbound $3.50

THE LIGHT OF DISTANT SKIES: AMERICAN PAINTING, 1760-1835, James T. Flexner. The great generation of early American painters goes to Europe to learn and to teach: West, Copley, Gilbert Stuart and others. Allston, Trumbull, Morse; also contemporary American painters—primitives, derivatives, academics—who remained in America. 102 illustrations. xiii + 306pp.

22179-2 Paperbound $3.00

A HISTORY OF THE RISE AND PROGRESS OF THE ARTS OF DESIGN IN THE UNITED STATES, William Dunlap. Much the richest mine of information on early American painters, sculptors, architects, engravers, miniaturists, etc. The only source of information for scores of artists, the major primary source for many others. Unabridged reprint of rare original 1834 edition, with new introduction by James T. Flexner, and 394 new illustrations. Edited by Rita Weiss. 6⅝ x 9⅝.

21695-0, 21696-9, 21697-7 Three volumes, Paperbound $13.50

EPOCHS OF CHINESE AND JAPANESE ART, Ernest F. Fenollosa. From primitive Chinese art to the 20th century, thorough history, explanation of every important art period and form, including Japanese woodcuts; main stress on China and Japan, but Tibet, Korea also included. Still unexcelled for its detailed, rich coverage of cultural background, aesthetic elements, diffusion studies, particularly of the historical period. 2nd, 1913 edition. 242 illustrations. lii + 439pp. of text.

20364-6, 20365-4 Two volumes, Paperbound $6.00

THE GENTLE ART OF MAKING ENEMIES, James A. M. Whistler. Greatest wit of his day deflates Oscar Wilde, Ruskin, Swinburne; strikes back at inane critics, exhibitions, art journalism; aesthetics of impressionist revolution in most striking form. Highly readable classic by great painter. Reproduction of edition designed by Whistler. Introduction by Alfred Werner. xxxvi + 334pp.

21875-9 Paperbound $2.50

JOHANN SEBASTIAN BACH, Philipp Spitta. One of the great classics of musicology, this definitive analysis of Bach's music (and life) has never been surpassed. Lucid, nontechnical analyses of hundreds of pieces (30 pages devoted to St. Matthew Passion, 26 to B Minor Mass). Also includes major analysis of 18th-century music. 450 musical examples. 40-page musical supplement. Total of xx + 1799pp.
(EUK) 22278-0, 22279-9 Two volumes, Clothbound $15.00

MOZART AND HIS PIANO CONCERTOS, Cuthbert Girdlestone. The only full-length study of an important area of Mozart's creativity. Provides detailed analyses of all 23 concertos, traces inspirational sources. 417 musical examples. Second edition. 509pp.
(USO) 21271-8 Paperbound $3.50

THE PERFECT WAGNERITE: A COMMENTARY ON THE NIBLUNG'S RING, George Bernard Shaw. Brilliant and still relevant criticism in remarkable essays on Wagner's Ring cycle, Shaw's ideas on political and social ideology behind the plots, role of Leitmotifs, vocal requisites, etc. Prefaces. xxi + 136pp.
21707-8 Paperbound $1.50

DON GIOVANNI, W. A. Mozart. Complete libretto, modern English translation; biographies of composer and librettist; accounts of early performances and critical reaction. Lavishly illustrated. All the material you need to understand and appreciate this great work. Dover Opera Guide and Libretto Series; translated and introduced by Ellen Bleiler. 92 illustrations. 209pp.
21134-7 Paperbound $1.50

HIGH FIDELITY SYSTEMS: A LAYMAN'S GUIDE, Roy F. Allison. All the basic information you need for setting up your own audio system: high fidelity and stereo record players, tape records, F.M. Connections, adjusting tone arm, cartridge, checking needle alignment, positioning speakers, phasing speakers, adjusting hums, trouble-shooting, maintenance, and similar topics. Enlarged 1965 edition. More than 50 charts, diagrams, photos. iv + 91pp.
21514-8 Paperbound $1.25

REPRODUCTION OF SOUND, Edgar Villchur. Thorough coverage for laymen of high fidelity systems, reproducing systems in general, needles, amplifiers, preamps, loudspeakers, feedback, explaining physical background. "A rare talent for making technicalities vividly comprehensible," R. Darrell, *High Fidelity*. 69 figures. iv + 92pp.
21515-6 Paperbound $1.00

HEAR ME TALKIN' TO YA: THE STORY OF JAZZ AS TOLD BY THE MEN WHO MADE IT, Nat Shapiro and Nat Hentoff. Louis Armstrong, Fats Waller, Jo Jones, Clarence Williams, Billy Holiday, Duke Ellington, Jelly Roll Morton and dozens of other jazz greats tell how it was in Chicago's South Side, New Orleans, depression Harlem and the modern West Coast as jazz was born and grew. xvi + 429pp.
21726-4 Paperbound $2.50

FABLES OF AESOP, translated by Sir Roger L'Estrange. A reproduction of the very rare 1931 Paris edition; a selection of the most interesting fables, together with 50 imaginative drawings by Alexander Calder. v + 128pp. 6½x9¼.
21780-9 Paperbound $1.25

PLANETS, STARS AND GALAXIES: DESCRIPTIVE ASTRONOMY FOR BEGINNERS, A. E. Fanning. Comprehensive introductory survey of astronomy: the sun, solar system, stars, galaxies, universe, cosmology; up-to-date, including quasars, radio stars, etc. Preface by Prof. Donald Menzel. 24pp. of photographs. 189pp. 5¼ x 8¼.
21680-2 Paperbound $1.50

TEACH YOURSELF CALCULUS, P. Abbott. With a good background in algebra and trig, you can teach yourself calculus with this book. Simple, straightforward introduction to functions of all kinds, integration, differentiation, series, etc. "Students who are beginning to study calculus method will derive great help from this book." Faraday House Journal. 308pp.
20683-1 Clothbound $2.00

TEACH YOURSELF TRIGONOMETRY, P. Abbott. Geometrical foundations, indices and logarithms, ratios, angles, circular measure, etc. are presented in this sound, easy-to-use text. Excellent for the beginner or as a brush up, this text carries the student through the solution of triangles. 204pp.
20682-3 Clothbound $2.00

TEACH YOURSELF ANATOMY, David LeVay. Accurate, inclusive, profusely illustrated account of structure, skeleton, abdomen, muscles, nervous system, glands, brain, reproductive organs, evolution. "Quite the best and most readable account,' Medical Officer. 12 color plates. 164 figures. 311pp. 4¾ x 7.
21651-9 Clothbound $2.50

TEACH YOURSELF PHYSIOLOGY, David LeVay. Anatomical, biochemical bases; digestive, nervous, endocrine systems; metabolism; respiration; muscle; excretion; temperature control; reproduction. "Good elementary exposition," The Lancet. 6 color plates. 44 illustrations. 208pp. 4¼ x 7. 21658-6 Clothbound $2.50

THE FRIENDLY STARS, Martha Evans Martin. Classic has taught naked-eye observation of stars, planets to hundreds of thousands, still not surpassed for charm, lucidity, adequacy. Completely updated by Professor Donald H. Menzel, Harvard Observatory. 25 illustrations. 16 x 30 chart. x + 147pp. 21099-5 Paperbound $1.25

MUSIC OF THE SPHERES: THE MATERIAL UNIVERSE FROM ATOM TO QUASAR, SIMPLY EXPLAINED, Guy Murchie. Extremely broad, brilliantly written popular account begins with the solar system and reaches to dividing line between matter and nonmatter; latest understandings presented with exceptional clarity. Volume One: Planets, stars, galaxies, cosmology, geology, celestial mechanics, latest astronomical discoveries; Volume Two: Matter, atoms, waves, radiation, relativity, chemical action, heat, nuclear energy, quantum theory, music, light, color, probability, antimatter, antigravity, and similar topics. 319 figures. 1967 (second) edition. Total of xx + 644pp. 21809-0, 21810-4 Two volumes, Paperbound $5.00

OLD-TIME SCHOOLS AND SCHOOL BOOKS, Clifton Johnson. Illustrations and rhymes from early primers, abundant quotations from early textbooks, many anecdotes of school life enliven this study of elementary schools from Puritans to middle 19th century. Introduction by Carl Withers. 234 illustrations. xxxiii + 381pp.
21031-6 Paperbound $2.50

MATHEMATICAL PUZZLES FOR BEGINNERS AND ENTHUSIASTS, Geoffrey Mott-Smith. 189 puzzles from easy to difficult—involving arithmetic, logic, algebra, properties of digits, probability, etc.—for enjoyment and mental stimulus. Explanation of mathematical principles behind the puzzles. 135 illustrations. viii + 248pp.
20198-8 Paperbound $1.25

PAPER FOLDING FOR BEGINNERS, William D. Murray and Francis J. Rigney. Easiest book on the market, clearest instructions on making interesting, beautiful origami. Sail boats, cups, roosters, frogs that move legs, bonbon boxes, standing birds, etc. 40 projects; more than 275 diagrams and photographs. 94pp.
20713-7 Paperbound $1.00

TRICKS AND GAMES ON THE POOL TABLE, Fred Herrmann. 79 tricks and games— some solitaires, some for two or more players, some competitive games—to entertain you between formal games. Mystifying shots and throws, unusual caroms, tricks involving such props as cork, coins, a hat, etc. Formerly *Fun on the Pool Table*. 77 figures. 95pp.
21814-7 Paperbound $1.00

HAND SHADOWS TO BE THROWN UPON THE WALL: A SERIES OF NOVEL AND AMUSING FIGURES FORMED BY THE HAND, Henry Bursill. Delightful picturebook from great-grandfather's day shows how to make 18 different hand shadows: a bird that flies, duck that quacks, dog that wags his tail, camel, goose, deer, boy, turtle, etc. Only book of its sort. vi + 33pp. 6½ x 9¼. 21779-5 Paperbound $1.00

WHITTLING AND WOODCARVING, E. J. Tangerman. 18th printing of best book on market. "If you can cut a potato you can carve" toys and puzzles, chains, chessmen, caricatures, masks, frames, woodcut blocks, surface patterns, much more. Information on tools, woods, techniques. Also goes into serious wood sculpture from Middle Ages to present, East and West. 464 photos, figures. x + 293pp.
20965-2 Paperbound $2.00

HISTORY OF PHILOSOPHY, Julián Marías. Possibly the clearest, most easily followed, best planned, most useful one-volume history of philosophy on the market; neither skimpy nor overfull. Full details on system of every major philosopher and dozens of less important thinkers from pre-Socratics up to Existentialism and later. Strong on many European figures usually omitted. Has gone through dozens of editions in Europe. 1966 edition, translated by Stanley Appelbaum and Clarence Strowbridge. xviii + 505pp. 21739-6 Paperbound $3.00

YOGA: A SCIENTIFIC EVALUATION, Kovoor T. Behanan. Scientific but non-technical study of physiological results of yoga exercises; done under auspices of Yale U. Relations to Indian thought, to psychoanalysis, etc. 16 photos. xxiii + 270pp.
20505-3 Paperbound $2.50

Prices subject to change without notice.
Available at your book dealer or write for free catalogue to Dept. GI, Dover Publications, Inc., 180 Varick St., N. Y., N. Y. 10014. Dover publishes more than 150 books each year on science, elementary and advanced mathematics, biology, music, art, literary history, social sciences and other areas.